READING THE DEAD SEA SCROLLS

ESSAYS IN METHOD

Society of Biblical Literature

Early Judaism and Its Literature

Rodney A. Werline, Editor

Number 39
READING THE DEAD SEA SCROLLS

ESSAYS IN METHOD

READING THE DEAD SEA SCROLLS

ESSAYS IN METHOD

George J. Brooke

with the assistance of
Nathalie LaCoste

Society of Biblical Literature
Atlanta

READING THE DEAD SEA SCROLLS

ESSAYS IN METHOD

Library of Congress Cataloging-in-Publication Data

Brooke, George J.
    Reading the Dead Sea scrolls : essays in method / by George J. Brooke.
        pages cm. — (Early Judaism and its literature ; number 39)
        Includes bibliographical references and index.
        ISBN 978-1-58983-901-4 (paper binding : alk. paper) — ISBN
    978-1-58983-902-1 (electronic format) — ISBN 978-1-58983-903-8
    (hardcover binding : alk. paper) 1. Dead Sea scrolls. I. Title.
    BM487.B76   2013
    296.1'55—dc23

                                                                        2013022945

Printed on acid-free, recycled paper conforming to
ANSI /NISO Z39.48–1992 (R1997) and ISO 9706:1994
standards for paper permanence.

For Peter and Sonia,
David and Louise,
Rachel and Leon

CONTENTS

Abbreviations

AB	Anchor Bible
ATDan	Acta theologica danica
BA	*Biblical Archaeologist*
BASOR	*Bulletin of the American Schools of Oriental Research*
BETL	Bibliotheca ephemeridum theologicarum lovaniensium
BHT	Beiträge zur historischen Theologie
BibInt	*Biblical Interpretation*
BibOr	Biblica et orientalia
BJS	Brown Judaic Studies
BSOAS	*Bulletin of the School of Oriental and African Studies*
BZAW	Beihefte zur Zeitschrift für die alttestamentliche Wissenschaft
CBC	Cambridge Bible Commentary
CBET	Contributions to Biblical Exegesis and Theology
CBQ	*Catholic Biblical Quarterly*
CBQMS	Catholic Biblical Quarterly Monograph Series
CQS	Companion to the Qumran Scrolls
DJD	Discoveries in the Judaean Desert
DSD	*Dead Sea Discoveries*
EBib	Etudes biblique
FAT	Forschungen zum Alten Testament
FOTL	Forms of the Old Testament Literature
HeyJ	*Heythrop Journal*
HBT	*Horizons in Biblical Theology*
HSS	Harvard Semitic Studies
HTR	*Harvard Theological Review*
ICC	International Critical Commentary
IOS	*Israel Oriental Studies*
JJS	*Journal of Jewish Studies*
JNSL	*Journal of Northwest Semitic Languages*
JQR	*Jewish Quarterly Review*
JSJ	*Journal for the Study of Judaism*
JSJSup	Supplements to the Journal for the Study of Judaism
JSOT	*Journal for the Study of the Old Testament*
JSOTSup	Journal for the Study of the Old Testament: Supplement Series
JSPSup	Journal for the Study of the Pseudepigrapha: Supplement Series
JSS	*Journal of Semitic Studies*
LHBOTS	Library of Hebrew Bible/Old Testament Studies

LNTS	Library of New Testament Studies
LSTS	Library of Second Temple Studies
MSU	Mitteilungen des Septuaginta-Unternehmens
NIDB	*New Interpreter's Dictionary of the Bible.* Edited by Katharine Doob Sakenfeld et al. 5 vols. Nashville: Abingdon, 2006–9.
OLA	Orientalia lovaniensia analecta
OTL	Old Testament Library
OTP	*The Old Testament Pseudepigrapha.* Edited by James H. Charlesworth. 2 vols. Garden City, N.Y.: Doubleday, 1983–85.
RevQ	*Revue de Qumrân*
SBLMS	Society of Biblical Literature Monograph Series
SBLRBS	Society of Biblical Literature Resources for Biblical Study
SBLSCS	Society of Biblical Literature Septuagint and Cognate Studies
SBLSP	*Society of Biblical Literature Seminar Papers*
SBLSymS	Society of Biblical Literature Symposium Series
SBT	Studies in Biblical Theology
SJLA	Studies in Judaism in Late Antiquity
SOTS	Society for Old Testament Studies
StPB	Studia post-biblica
STDJ	Studies on Texts of the Desert of Judah
TBN	Themes in Biblical Narrative
ThWQ	*Theologisches Wörterbuch zu den Qumranschriften*
TSAJ	Texts und Studien zum antiken Judentum
UTB	Uni-Taschenbücher
VTSup	Supplements to Vetus Testamentum
WUNT	Wissenschaftliche Untersuchungen zum Neuen Testament
ZTK	*Zeitschrift für Theologie und Kirche*

PREVIOUS PUBLICATIONS

Apart from chapter 10, which has not been published before, the essays in this book are reprinted from several different sources where they first appeared as listed below. They are reprinted here with permission as indicated.

Chapter 1: "The Qumran Scrolls and the Demise of the Distinction between Higher and Lower Criticism." Pages 26–42 in *New Directions in Qumran Studies: Proceedings of the Bristol Colloquium on the Dead Sea Scrolls, 8–10 September 2003*. Edited by Jonathan G. Campbell, William John Lyons, and Lloyd K. Pietersen. Library of Second Temple Studies 52. London: T&T Clark International, 2005. Republished with the permission of Bloomsbury Publishing Plc.

Chapter 2: "The Formation and Renewal of Scriptural Tradition." Pages 39–59 in *Biblical Traditions in Transmission: Essays in Honour of Michael A. Knibb*. Edited by Charlotte Hempel and Judith M. Lieu. Journal for the Study of Judaism Supplements 111. Leiden: Brill, 2006. Republished with the permission of Koninklijke Brill NV.

Chapter 3: "Justifying Deviance: The Place of Scripture in Converting to a Qumran Self-Understanding." Pages 73–87 in *Reading the Present in the Qumran Library: The Perception of the Contemporary by Means of Scriptural Interpretation*. Edited by Kristin De Troyer and Armin Lange. SBLSymS 30. Atlanta: Society of Biblical Literature, 2005. Republished with the permission of the Society of Biblical Literature.

Chapter 4: "Memory, Cultural Memory, and Rewriting Scripture." Forthcoming in *"Rewritten Bible" after Fifty Years*. Edited by József Zsengellér. Leiden: Brill. Republished with the permission of Koninklijke Brill NV.

Chapter 5: "Hypertextuality and the 'Parabiblical' Dead Sea Scrolls." Pages 43–64 in *In the Second Degree: Paratextual Literature in Ancient Near Eastern and Ancient Mediterranean Culture and Its Reflections in Medieval Literature*. Edited by Philip S. Alexander, Armin Lange, and Renate J. Pillinger. Leiden: Brill, 2010. Republished with the permission of Koninklijke Brill NV.

Chapter 6: "Controlling Intertexts and Hierarchies of Echo in Two Thematic Eschatological Commentaries from Qumran." Pages 181–95 in *Between Text and Text: The Hermeneutics of Intertextuality in Ancient Cultures and Their Afterlife in Medieval and Modern Times.* Edited by Michaela Bauks, Wayne Horowitz, and Armin Lange. Journal of Ancient Judaism Supplements 6. Göttingen: Vandenhoeck & Ruprecht, 2013. Republished with the permission of Vandenhoeck & Ruprecht.

Chapter 7: "*Pesher* and *Midrash* in Qumran Literature: Issues for Lexicography." *Revue de Qumrân* 24 (2009–10): 79–95. Republished with the permission of Les Editions Gabalda.

Chapter 8: "Genre Theory, Rewritten Bible, and Pesher." *Dead Sea Discoveries* 17 (2010): 332–57. Republished with the permission of Koninklijke Brill NV.

Chapter 9: "Room for Interpretation: An Analysis of Spatial Imagery in the Qumran Pesharim." Pages 309–24 in *The Dead Sea Scrolls: Texts and Context.* Edited by Charlotte Hempel. Studies on the Texts of the Desert of Judah 90. Leiden: Brill, 2010. Republished with the permission of Koninklijke Brill NV.

Chapter 11: "Types of Historiography in the Qumran Scrolls." Pages 211–30 in *Ancient and Modern Scriptural Historiography–L'Historiographie biblique, ancienne et moderne.* Edited by George J. Brooke and Thomas Römer. Bibliotheca Ephemeridum Theologicarum Lovaniensium 207. Leuven: Peeters; University Press, 2007. Republished with the permission of Uitgeverij Peeters.

Chapter 12: "What Makes a Text Historical? Assumptions behind the Classification of Some Dead Sea Scrolls." Pages 207–25 in *The Historian and the Bible: Essays in Honour of Lester L. Grabbe.* Edited by Philip R. Davies and Diana V. Edelman. Library of Hebrew Bible/Old Testament Studies 530. London: T&T Clark International, 2010. Republished with the permission of Bloomsbury Publishing Plc.

Chapter 13: "The Scrolls from Qumran and Old Testament Theology." Pages 59–75 in *Problems in Biblical Theology: Essays in Honor of Rolf Knierim.* Edited by Henry T. C. Sun and Keith L. Eades with James M. Robinson and Garth I. Moller. Grand Rapids: Eerdmans, 1997. Republished with the permission of Wm B. Eerdmans Publishing.

Preface

Several people have helped me over the years to formulate my ideas on how the Dead Sea Scrolls might be read. It is always invidious to name names, lest someone important be forgotten, but I think that any book that attempts to make a contribution to debates about method should in some way name those who have been significant influences or sparring partners, so that the reader can all the more readily see where much of what is written in this book is coming from.

Two Philips deserve a special mention. In a long-standing academic friendship Philip Davies has forced me to stand back from the details that have often interested me most to ask questions about questions; he is a master at posing good questions based in sound method, and many of his methodological insights are all the more enduring as a result. A collegial friendship of almost equal length with Philip Alexander has challenged me from the other end of the spectrum; an expert philologist and reader of texts, as well as a major religious historian, in fact a walking encyclopedia on the Bible and its reception in both Judaism and Christianity, he has challenged methodological superficiality with encouragement to look again at texts in context. Though it is not always apparent in the footnotes in what follows, I owe both of them much as I have tried to make my own way with the study of the Dead Sea Scrolls and related compositions from antiquity.

The list of editors of the books and journals where many of the studies were first published indicates those who have invited me to make contributions of various kinds and to them all I am grateful. Several of the papers in this book were first presented in conferences or symposia, and the numerous conversations that followed often sharpened and improved my thinking; my interlocutors all helped bring focus to what is here. Most of the essays are republished with only minor changes and corrections. Chapter 10 is previously unpublished. Chapter 13 has been extensively revised.

The most important and senior contemporary voice of methodological insight into the study of the Dead Sea Scrolls and many other texts is that of Carol Newsom. Though I have often tried to cover topics other than those that she has so incisively treated, I myself and the whole field owe her much. In recent years I have also learned much from a somewhat less senior group of scholars, whose works I admire greatly, not least for their methodological rigor and insight. Among them are Maxine Grossman, Charlotte Hempel, Hindy Najman, and Judith Newman, to name but the most influential.

Judith Newman has been encouraging in several other ways too, not least as the former editor of the SBL series Early Judaism and Its Literature who commissioned this collection. She has also facilitated its preparation through encouraging some of her own students to refine some of the details of what is written here. I owe a special debt of gratitude to Nathalie LaCoste, who has assisted with the overall consistency of the manuscript and compiled the concluding bibliography that makes a contribution of its own for those who want to think a little about what they are doing when they read texts. To my mind it certainly enhances the value of a collection like this, as do the indexes. I am grateful, too, to Rodney Werline, the current editor of the series, for his gentle prodding and encouragement. My thanks, too, to the SBL staff and HK Scriptorium who have been most helpful, prompt, and meticulous.

Other people have challenged me to articulate my ideas clearly too, especially my colleagues in Biblical Studies at the University of Manchester: Adrian Curtis has consistently demanded common sense, Todd Klutz has insisted on sensitivity to lexical choices and the way words work, and Peter Oakes has provided ways for understanding how social contexts are reflected in texts. In addition to the conference venues where several of the chapters were first heard, the Ehrhardt Seminar at the University of Manchester has been a regular forum where many of my ideas have been discussed by kind colleagues, generous honorary research fellows, and inquisitive postgraduate students. Many audiences have listened to me giving either academic or popular lectures on the scrolls and have then posed questions that have helped me clarify what I was trying to say. My wife, Jane, and the family have encouraged and supported, teased and cajoled, and it is to our three children, Peter, David, and Rachel, and their spouses, Sonia, Louise, and Leon, that I dedicate this book.

Manchester
March 2013

INTRODUCTION

This book contains a collection of my essays on how some of the Dead Sea Scrolls might be read and analyzed. There was a time when the field of biblical studies was in the vanguard of the formation and application of innovative methodology. Over the last two generations or so, it has tended to be the case that the field more broadly has been a follower rather than a leader. Within the discipline of the study of the Dead Sea Scrolls and its many specialist subdisciplines, this has been even more the case, with the study of the scrolls lagging behind in many ways even the study of the books of the Bible and their contexts.

The majority of members of the first generation of scholars interested in the Dead Sea Scrolls focused primarily on the reading and editing of the many fragmentary manuscripts from the Judean wilderness. Somewhat surprisingly, in my view, they barely kept in mind their formal training in various disciplines of biblical studies as they read and studied the scrolls. This was evident, most obviously, in the tendency to read history straight off the pesharim, as if that was an appropriate way to read texts that did not even pretend to be historiography. It was obvious, too, in the way that few compositions were assessed closely in terms of source and redaction criticism. As with many things, there were significant exceptions, even among first-generation scholars, but it is taking some time for students of the Dead Sea Scrolls to catch up with their colleagues in biblical studies, let alone with students in other areas of the humanities and the social sciences.

More recent exceptions are now there to be seen in relation to many texts. Attention to reading strategies is evident in several publications, most notably, in Carol Newsom's work of several kinds,[1] and in both the monograph and the edited collection of essays by Maxine Grossman,[2] as well as the less innovative but persistent collection of studies edited by Michael T. Davis and Brent Strawn.[3] This volume complements those works and attempts to draw attention both to how the scrolls can be illuminated by various features of methodological practice and also to how in turn those practices can be called into question by the evi-

---

1. See especially C. A. Newsom, *The Self as Symbolic Space: Constructing Identity and Community at Qumran* (STDJ 52; Leiden: Brill, 2004).

2. M. L. Grossman, *Reading for History in the Damascus Document: A Methodological Study* (STDJ 45; Leiden: Brill, 2002); eadem, ed., *Rediscovering the Dead Sea Scrolls: An Assessment of Old and New Approaches and Methods* (Grand Rapids: Eerdmans, 2010).

3. M. T. Davis and B. A. Strawn, eds., *Qumran Studies: New Approaches, New Questions* (Grand Rapids: Eerdmans, 2007).

dence of the scrolls. Nobody can be an expert across multiple approaches, and some of the essays in this volume suffer from my own inadequate appreciation of all the implications of the methods being used; nevertheless, I have concluded that it is better to attempt to bring the scrolls into dynamic interaction with questions and methods, both old and new, than to be confined to ever narrower specialist concerns, even though those of course serve a purpose.

The studies collected here are clearly not exhaustive of what could be said on method and the study of the Dead Sea Scrolls, but they cover a range of topics, often with very specific agendas or worked examples. Several of them concern my long-term grappling with issues having to do with midrash and pesher. These studies could have been ordered in several different ways. I hope in the short remarks that follow to indicate briefly why they are now ordered in the way they are as well as to explain one or two of the most significant features of each essay.

There is no better place to start than with the fragmentary manuscripts from the Judean wilderness and the compositions that they contain. All texts go through processes of composition and have afterlives, sometimes short, sometimes long. The first essay is an attempt to refocus the concern of textual criticism, a discipline that has commonly thought of itself as concerned almost exclusively with the afterlives of compositions, not least as errors creep in during the processes of scribal transmission. As a result, the canons of textual criticism have generally been formulated in relation to manuscript evidence that is many years, if not several centuries, distant from the production of the literary composition itself, and so, as a disciplined approach to manuscript data, it has commonly been understood to function best when largely independent from those literary production processes. Such a distinction applies especially to canonical texts, not least those of Jewish and Christian traditions.

The first essay is really concerned to point out the possible overlapping continuities between the processes of composition and the processes of transmission, and so to request a fully respected place for textual criticism among other critical approaches that are often more concerned with the ways texts are formed rather than transmitted. But there is really no clear or sharp dividing line between the processes of formation, production, and transmission. The essay argues that text critics should not shy away from asking larger literary questions.

Just as textual criticism should be repositioned so as to contribute to the manuscript evidence that belongs to the transmission of texts that are of increasing authority, so it is important to present a frame of reference for understanding how literary traditions form, develop, influence other traditions, and sometimes decay. Thus, in the second essay, I have attempted to indicate some of the complex workings of literary traditions, especially those that seem to accrue a greater authority than others. This complexity is illustrated by considering several compositions that themselves seem to have complicated histories. In particular the chapter pays attention to what might be taking place in such compilations as 1 Enoch and 4 Ezra as well as in some of the sectarian and nonsectarian Dead Sea Scrolls. Little has been written on the overarching character of tradition. The second essay seeks to plug that hole, in particular by reference to the coherent picture of the topic that emerges when the writings and perspective of one modern scholar are described, assessed, and analyzed.

Inasmuch as the study of tradition is the study of texts within the webs of social history, so a third essay considers how and why it is that any particular individual might be likely to identify with one set of traditions and interpretations of tradition rather than another set. In this study some aspects of deviance theory, as developed in the social sciences, are used to describe and explain how any individual might make the transition from a more common or general attitude to authoritative scriptural texts within widely accepted social norms toward a particular or deviant reading of those same texts. Although commonly concerned with contemporary social contexts, the application of deviance theory enables one to see how individuals, often but not always members of elite groups, come to locate themselves in a particular way in relation to a variety of traditions. It is suggested that a web of social interactions are as important as any particularly convincing interpretation of an authoritative scriptural tradition.

Three essays then develop the idea that traditions can be molded to appeal to various audiences for a wide range of reasons. Deviance theory might help to describe and explain how and why a particular reader comes to identify with a certain tradition and its interpretation. However, another set of ideas can be used to understand some of the processes that are inherent in the transmission and development of literary traditions that are based on earlier authoritative texts and use that authority for their own purposes. Chapter 4 considers the role of memory in the transferral of tradition. Not much has been done from this perspective on the composition of the Dead Sea Scrolls. The concern of this chapter is to underline how both individual scribal memory and also some sense of collective memory play significant roles in such transmission. Individual scribes use their memories in the transmission process, a factor that sometimes lies behind the emergence of some variant readings, but they also pay attention to wider issues of cultural memory as they contribute to the creative adaptation of those compositions on which they work for their own contemporary purposes. The understanding of collective memory as applied to a range of texts in antiquity can also be used to provide some focus concerning why there are certain developments, even embellishments, in the increasing textualization of tradition, and that sometimes those embellishments deliberately distort the tradition. In addition, observations can be made on how and why various institutions use selected traditions to bolster their authority, and on why some aspects of cultural tradition are sometimes forgotten, often perhaps deliberately.

Many factors come into play as those responsible for their composition develop texts that will pay attention to the traditions to which they belong and yet make them contemporary and relevant for a new audience, so that new readers are encouraged to think that it is those they leave behind who are deviant, not they themselves. So the essay that is chapter 5 grapples with the complicated matter of how authors and editors come to construct new compositions that are closely based on earlier authoritative models. With the notion of literary hyper-textuality it is possible to recognize in several of the "parabiblical" compositions that survive from Second Temple times an intense set of concerns that both respect the integrity and authority of the textual tradition that is being reworked and rely on that integrity and authority to move the tradition into a new phase, sometimes both in time and place.

The use of the notion of hypertextuality moves the methodological discussion of this collection of essays toward consideration of the more explicit ways in which literary compositions are created, assembled, and edited. Much of the consideration of the role of memory and of the notion of hypertextuality is related to the so-called rewritten or reworked compositions in which the use of earlier authoritative tradition is generally implicit. In chapter 6 the explicit and implicit uses of literary echoes from the past are the focus of a study on hierarchies within intertextuality. Intertextuality as literary process has been applied in some areas beyond its own usefulness, but if attention is paid to the specifics of citation and allusion, then a case can be made for its methodological retention and application in two respects. On the one hand, it is often possible in Jewish compositions of the Second Temple period to identify earlier texts that are cited or alluded to by a subsequent author. Simply listing citations and allusions is worthy in itself as an indication of what kinds of tradition an author or editor or scriptural interpreter wishes to identify with. But, on the other hand, it is often possible to say more about how such intertexts are being used, since some will appear to have greater authority than others. Sometimes such greater authority is visible in the way a single intertextual pericope can be used several times by a later author, perhaps with a structural purpose in mind or so as to form a thread upon which the beads of other less significant intertexts can be threaded.

In all this it is always necessary for scholars to consider carefully what labels will best describe not only the literary objects that they are studying but also the processes through which they attempt to identify and control their own subjective readings. Chapter 7 considers the specific terms *pesher* and *midrash*. Both terms evidently have a technical role in at least some of the literary compositions in which they are used. In order to appreciate their specific uses, it is necessary to ensure that the terms are placed both within a suitable trajectory of early Jewish traditions and also within a wider map of Semitic philology. As this is done and the sources for comparison are assembled, so a range of choices have to be made about which comparative materials should be given priority. For example, is it more suitable to prioritize Akkadian or Aramaic evidence for the better appreciation of the term *pesher*, and what might a decision for one or the other say about the likely settings that might inform scriptural interpretation? Or, in relation to the term *midrash*, is it more appropriate to work forward from scriptural materials that might have a range of meanings concerning "explanation" or "interrogation," or to work back from subsequent sources and understand the term as meaning something like "study"? Whatever the case, modern readers need to be sensitive to how they construct meaning.

Chapter 8 follows on elegantly from the semantic discussion of pesher and midrash. It is an essay that considers what advantages might be had from applying to the same categories what some literary theorists have to say about genre, since the terms are often taken in context as describing some kind of interpretative processes but then are used in a more general fashion of the genres of interpretative literature in which they occur. This is problematic, and the chapter attempts to move the discussion forward by analyzing the nature of the problem. For the understanding of genre to be salient, the literary corpus that supposedly defines it needs to be delimited while also being open to the addition of new members that both cause a redefinition and indicate that all genres have porous boundaries; there are few, if any, pure examples of texts, not least because all genres evolve and such evolution introduces instability into generic definition. Perhaps one should begin with a single composition and look for comparable texts or perhaps one should begin with a much larger corpus of compositions that all share an agenda of being concerned with the interpretation of authoritative traditions. If the latter option is the case, which seems reasonable to me, then pesher compositions certainly need to be set in a much larger framework of interpretative texts, such as might include the so-called rewritten scriptures in which the interpretation is largely implicit, so that the significant elements of explicit interpretation become all the clearer. From the broader perspective it then becomes possible to identify aspects of form, content, setting, and function each of which can reflect particular matters of authorial intention, historical or literary contexts, the text as artefact, or the likely assumptions of first readers. In all this, cross-cultural analogies can be of assistance too, just as with lexical definitions.

Two essays then consider features of the functions of texts that have generally been overlooked. One aspect of the function of a text concerns the places where it is or might be used. In chapter 9 I have asked a basic question of the explicit running commentaries from caves 1 and 4 at Qumran, which seem to reflect the views of the group at least part of which lived and worked at Qumran itself. The question concerns whether any of those running commentaries reflect in any way the spaces where they might have been used for various didactic purposes. It seems to me to be worth considering, for those and other compositions, whether the particular places and spaces where the texts were read influenced the content of the interpretation in any way, as preachers might refer to the buildings where they are performing, or influenced the dynamics of the performance and its reception in any discernible way. What size of room was used? How was the seating for teachers and students arranged? Can the texts be linked in any meaningful way to the site where some of them might have been composed, taught, edited, copied, and transmitted? In fact little or no local information of direct influence can be discovered in these compositions. This gives rise to a further set of considerations concerning the absence of such contextual reference, and more importantly it allows the modern reader to speak more clearly about what spatial features are indeed to be found in the texts. In many ways the continuous running commentaries encourage their students to conceptualize place and space as having to do with things other than where they study; the study of the commentaries from the perspective of space enables the modern reader to perceive how those texts point their students beyond their immediate circumstances. All this is important for those who would read such continuous pesharim as chiefly concerned with the historical circumstances of the Teacher of Righteousness and his flight to Qumran.

In chapter 10 I have asked a rather different set of questions about the function of the continuous running pesharim, questions that have implications for the understanding of several other sectarian compositions too. In this previously unpublished chapter I have attempted a psycho-dynamic reading of the exegesis in the pesharim. Building on common agreements about the date, form, structure, genre, and language of the pesharim, I move to consider other aspects of these interpretative compositions. First, I discuss how they overcome the experience of the silence of God, perhaps even a sense of divine abandonment, in their understanding of the ongoing processes of prophecy. Interpretation not only releases the meaning of earlier prophetic texts, but it also has a prophetic character itself, since it claims to be conveying the secrets of the texts being interpreted, secrets that cannot be read off the surface of the earlier prophetic oracles. Second, the ambivalent attitude to Jerusalem and the temple is, on the one hand, a strong description of all that seems to be wrong with other Jews and their handling of the tradition, but it is also, on the other hand, the locus of eschatological hope, of restoration and the reestablishment of security. The melancholic experience of abuse and abandonment is overcome in part at least through the interpretation of the same prophetic texts that describe the destruction of the maternal Jerusalem and its temple. Third, the human participants in the drama, the sectarians themselves, are full of self-justification in order that in the construction of an alternative view of the world there is a self-understanding that is full of strategies for coping with disenfranchisement.

The literary compositions from the eleven caves at and near Qumran constantly cause modern readers to think again about the categories they use to describe and analyze them. While there has been some considerable debate around the notions of apocalypse, wisdom, prophecy, and liturgy, there has been little observation about the place of history in the compositions found in the Qumran scrolls. Chapters 11 and 12 address issues of historiography. In chapter 11 I have attempted to describe something of the variety of historiographies apparent in both the sectarian and the nonsectarian scrolls; it soon becomes apparent that the events of the past are engaged in many ways, but not in any extensive fashion that attempts to fill out a linear political history of the centuries immediately preceding the establishment of the sect at some time in the second century B.C.E. There are alternative ways of constructing time and of appreciating the moment for which the elect have been chosen. Chapter 12 is an attempt to expose and expound the assumptions that lie behind the use of the label "historical" to describe both the contents and the genre of a small group of compositions found in the Qumran caves. It soon becomes clear that modern scholars have used and abused the label, imposing a twin set of assumptions on highly fragmentary textual remains. The first assumption is that the label "history" is particularly suitable for people and events arranged in a linear fashion; the second is that the term can be readily applied to those people and events that are seen as elite or pivotal. Both those assumptions can be challenged when the few fragmentary texts that have been assigned the label are set in a broader historiographical context.

A final essay pays particular attention to the way that the Dead Sea Scrolls contribute to, complicate, and qualify the role of the theological reading of the Bible as a whole, especially the Old Testament as a complete unit, about which more theologies have been constructed than for the Hebrew Bible as such. The discipline exercised by Old Testament theologians commonly works with an assumption that it is finely controlled by historical considerations. Those considerations are grounded in historical exegesis that has been characteristic of the last two hundred and fifty years or more in the West and are all to do with the formation of textual traditions, usually many centuries before certain text forms of those traditions became authoritative or canonical. Upon such considerations an edifice is built that seeks to identify the coherence of the collection of compositions that form a scriptural canon. But the scrolls from the eleven caves at and near Qumran show clearly that what is now contained in the Masoretic Text has had a very long compositional and editorial history. It might be possible to describe the developing theological views of any one biblical book as it is passed on in the Second Temple period, but the construction of a theology for the Old Testament as a whole is really possible only as a canonical exercise for a later time.

These essays thus cover a range of topics from textual criticism to the writing of theologies. On the way, there is considerable attention to how texts come to be composed and to the traditions that they re-present. There is consideration of several different aspects of genre, especially matters to do with generic labels and the place of function in appreciating genres. There is also much attention to the readers and writers of the sectarian commentaries. It is the multiple references to the various forms of scriptural interpretation in the sectarian and quasi-sectarian literature that give some overall coherence to this collection of essays and that also indicate that there are still many methodological questions to be asked of those and other sectarian texts for their better understanding.

ONE

THE QUMRAN SCROLLS AND THE DEMISE OF THE DISTINCTION BETWEEN HIGHER AND LOWER CRITICISM

1. INTRODUCTION

In this essay I wish to argue that the Dead Sea Scrolls provide modern scholarship with a very significant opportunity for the mutual illumination of both artefact and method, so that the manuscripts and their contents provoke the refinement of modern reading strategies, and those strategies, once refined and adjusted, serve all the better to assist in the understanding of the manuscripts themselves. Nowhere else in the Mediterranean basin has there been such a remarkable discovery of turn-of-the-era manuscripts, nearly all of whose provenance is known, together with at least one archaeological site largely undisturbed since antiquity. It should be possible to think not only that now is the time for the application of various modern approaches to the evidence for its better understanding, but also that such distinctive evidence should enable new light to be thrown on the methods themselves, because of the concentration of the evidence in time and place and the many opportunities for analysis that such concentration permits.

On that basis, this contribution is concerned to show that a suitable understanding of the so-called biblical manuscripts found in the eleven caves at and near Qumran does much to dissolve the supposed distinction between higher and lower criticism that has long been maintained in biblical studies: it is no longer suitable for one set of experts to think of themselves as taking the "high road," while others take the "low road."[1] Even as late as 1966 Fortress Press considered it worthwhile to republish the second edition of Dafydd R. Ap-Thomas's small *Primer of Old Testament Text Criticism.*[2] John Reumann provided a preface in which he noted that

---

1. To play on the opening lines of the anonymous refrain of "The Bonnie Banks o' Loch Lomon": "O ye'll tak' the high road, and I'll tak' the low road, And I'll be in Scotland afore ye."

2. D. R. Ap-Thomas, *A Primer of Old Testament Text Criticism* (Facet Books 14; Philadelphia: Fortress, 1966). The first edition was published in 1947 (London: Epworth), before

the recovery of ancient Hebrew manuscripts from caves at Qumran and neigh-
bouring areas of the Judean desert in both Jordan and Israel had changed the
textual landscape so that even for laymen and pastors who know no Hebrew,
the finds from the Dead Sea region have focussed attention on the text and on
the need for possible revisions in our English translations.[3]

However, Ap-Thomas's revised *Primer* contained no references to the Dead Sea
Scrolls, as if they were considered unlikely to alter the life of the text critic other
than by providing many new examples that could be fitted into the well-worn
methodologies already established. The reluctance of critical scholarship to
acknowledge that the so-called biblical scrolls require a fresh consideration of
the canons of text criticism is a further demonstration, if any was needed, that
"Qumran scholarship has reached only the toddler stage," as R. Timothy McLay
has recently noted, though he also hopes that "it will no doubt be influential in
the years to come."[4]

In a caricatured form, lower criticism has been concerned over several generations with attempting to establish the original text ("Ur-Text") of each biblical book. Though this is often acknowledged as a difficult task, nevertheless text
critics have set out on their quest along the low road with various assumptions,
many of which have been firmly based in the Enlightenment and its Reformation
and Renaissance roots, such as that the more ancient reading should be sought
and preferred over against any attempt at understanding a received text in its
own right. Perhaps chief among the assumptions of those involved with lower
criticism has been that the quest has indeed to do precisely with the establishing
of the original text. All evidence is considered with such an end in mind. So Paul
Maas for one has written that "the business of textual criticism is to produce a
text as close as possible to the original"[5] echoing John P. Postgate's earlier comment that "the aim of the 'textual critic' may then be defined as the restoration of
the text, as far as possible, to its original form, if by 'original form' we understand
the form intended by the author."[6] The most recent extensive volume of text criticism for the Hebrew Bible by Emanuel Tov has endorsed this approach though

---

the Dead Sea Scrolls were known; the second edition was first published in Britain in 1965
(Oxford: Basil Blackwell).

3. J. Reumann, "Introduction," in Ap-Thomas, *Primer of Old Testament Text Criticism*,
iii.

4. R. T. McLay, *The Use of the Septuagint in New Testament Research* (Grand Rapids:
Eerdmans, 2003), xi. McLay's book is a plea for New Testament scholars, partly stimulated by
the finds of Greek scriptural manuscripts in the Qumran caves, to take far more interest in the
Septuagint than is generally the case.

5. P. Maas, *Textual Criticism* (trans. B. Flower; Oxford: Clarendon, 1958), 1.

6. J. P. Postgate, "Textual Criticism," in *Encyclopaedia Britannica*, 14:708–15, here 709.
Both Maas and Postgate are cited in E. Tov, *Textual Criticism of the Hebrew Bible* (2nd rev. ed.;
Assen: Van Gorcum; Minneapolis: Fortress, 2001), 288.

with some qualification: "it would seem preferable to aim at the one text or different texts which was (were) accepted as authoritative in (an) earlier period(s)."[7]

The inappropriate differentiation between higher and lower criticism has indeed been recognized, but not widely. Tov, a current leading authority on the textual criticism of the Hebrew Bible and its versions, has himself recognized what is at stake. In his authoritative 1992 article on textual criticism,[8] he has commented both that the designation "lower criticism" is "wrong" and that

> [t]he biblical books each developed to the stage at which they were considered finished literary products, and textual criticism concerns itself with charting developments from that point on. The reconstruction of all developments prior to that point is the concern of literary criticism. However, since some form of written transmission must have occurred during the stage of literary growth, sharp distinctions between the two cannot always be drawn.[9]

Tov provides somewhat more coverage of these points in his major handbook on textual criticism of the same date;[10] importantly, the major difference between that edition and the second revised edition (2001) is the adjustment of several of the pages allocated for the discussion of the interdependence of literary and textual approaches.[11]

The major corollary of the search for the original text has been the assumption that scribes are technical copyists and that the vast majority of variants in the surviving manuscript evidence are somehow the results of errors or misunderstandings.[12] The overall view of text criticism as largely concerned with describing matters mechanically has often resulted in the ignoring or denigration of text critics themselves.[13] If scribes are widely believed to have been passive traditors whose only contribution has been to corrupt the texts in their care, translators have fared even worse in the imagination of the text critic, seldom being thought of as faithfully representing their *Vorlagen*. Furthermore, the well-known canons of text criticism enshrine this approach. For example, the notion that the more

---

7. Tov, *Textual Criticism of the Hebrew Bible*, 288.

8. E. Tov, "Textual Criticism (OT)," *ABD* 6:394–412, here 394.

9. Ibid., 410.

10. Tov, *Textual Criticism of the Hebrew Bible*, 313–49.

11. See G. J. Brooke, review of E. Tov, *Textual Criticism of the Hebrew Bible* (2nd ed.), *JSS* 48 (2003): 421.

12. A view put with vigor and humor by none other than A. E. Housman, "The Application of Thought to Textual Criticism," *Proceedings of the Classical Association* 18 (1922): 67–84: textual criticism "is the science of discovering errors in texts and the art of removing them" (p. 68).

13. For example, the 1938 collection of essays on the Old Testament by SOTS members and others deliberately had no chapter on text criticism: H. W. Robinson, "Introduction," in *Record and Revelation: Essays on the Old Testament by Members of the Society for Old Testament Study* (ed. H. W. Robinson; Oxford: Clarendon, 1938), viii.

difficult reading is likely to be the more original prioritizes the difficult reading over against its supposed corruption in a subsequent clarificatory improvement. Or again, the idea that the shorter reading is to be preferred to a longer one is based on the assumption that glosses and expansions are ill-informed tamperings with a more pristine form of the text.

Those who have taken the critical high road in the past have often subscribed to assumptions similar to those of their low-road counterparts, looking for original meaning and authorial intention where none may ultimately be available, simply because the final form of the text seldom represents what may have been "originally" penned. Those engaged in higher criticism have frequently taken at face value the biblical text as established by the text critic. Few commentaries go beyond briefly discussing some difficult readings in handling the textual evidence; virtually none describes the principal manuscripts in which the text they are commenting on survives and discusses the significance of the way the scribes of those manuscripts have worked and in their work have contributed to the understanding of the text. However, from several points of view the zealous distinction between lower and higher criticism is now challenged by the Dead Sea Scrolls in ways that have considerable ramifications for the best description of how the texts of Scripture were transmitted and understood in the late Second Temple period.

2. THE PROBLEM

A prominent example of the persistence of viewing variants as based on scribal error is to be found in the principal edition of 4QGen^g. In Gen 1:5 we find the reading of *ywmm* for the MT's *ywm*: "And God called the light daytime (*ywmm*)." It so happens that this reading is also found consistently in all the targumic witnesses to the text and in the Peshitta; in fact the reading is found there in Gen 1:5, 14, 16, and 18, all places where the word is used in an abstract sense describing daytime over against the night. Only Gen 1:5 is preserved in 4QGen^g. The editor of the principal edition of the scroll has noted this variant tradition, but he offers the following explanation:

> It is possible that the alteration arose from a dittography of *mêm* in an early
> MS or one written in the Palaeo-Hebrew script. In either case there would have
> been no distinction between medial and final *mêm*. Once the error was present
> it could easily have spread to other passages where it seemed appropriate.[14]

The editor's assumption is that it is most likely that the doubling of the *mem* in 4QGen^g derives from an error by a scribe who made no distinction between medial and final *mem*. Subsequent scribes did not correct the error but exploited

---

14. J. R. Davila, "7. 4QGen^g," in *Qumran Cave 4.VII: Genesis to Numbers* (ed. E. Ulrich et al.; DJD 12; Oxford: Clarendon, 1994), 57–60, here 59.

it for other passages too. Since it is obvious that the word *ywm* is used in two different senses in Gen 1, it seems more plausible to me that, from the outset, the extra *mem* was introduced by a scribe to clarify the confusion in the plain meaning of the text caused by the use of *ywm* in these two different ways.[15] The addition of a single letter enabled the reading of an adverbial form that showed clearly the distinction between "daytime" and the twenty-four hour "day."[16] In my opinion, this is a clear example of an exegetical variant being introduced into the text of Genesis. In this instance I consider that it is appropriate to argue that the earlier form of Gen 1:5 had simply *ywm* and that the addition is a secondary clarification which has either been known to the targumists or was created by them for exactly the same interpretative reason, to distinguish between the two uses of *ywm*.

Two ramifications of this way of describing things emerge. In the first place, it would seem preferable to acknowledge that there are such things as exegetical variants in scriptural manuscripts and thereby to acknowledge that at least in the late Second Temple period until the stabilization of the Hebrew text for each authoritative book in a particular form scribes had a creative role in the way in which the scriptural text was presented for their readers and hearers. To my mind this must mean that in some way, however slight, they share the role of the author or authors of the texts they copy and adjust. As such, their contribution has to be considered by those interested in how the text was received, transmitted, understood, and interpreted at an early period.

In second place and on that basis, as those who handle the manuscript evidence join those who deal with the variegated approaches of higher criticism, it becomes increasingly important for commentators to resist viewing the manuscript evidence from the precanonical period with the same lenses as those manuscripts of a later canonical date. To sharpen the issue: it should be immediately apparent that it is inappropriate to ask of 4QGen[g] whether it is an authoritative version of Genesis or an early form of commentary upon the text: it is both and neither.

---

15. On the place of the understanding and interpretation of the plain meaning of Scripture in the transmission and exegesis of the biblical and other texts in the Dead Sea Scrolls, see G. J. Brooke, "Reading the Plain Meaning of Scripture in the Dead Sea Scrolls," in *Jewish Ways of Reading the Bible* (ed. G. J. Brooke; JSS Supplements 11; Oxford: Oxford University Press, 2000), 67–90.

16. Davila seems to allow for this in his preliminary publication on the variant. The reading "is clearly secondary in all these passages and seems to be a systematic alteration" of ywm wherever it is used in an abstract sense in Gen 1:1–2:4a ("New Qumran Readings for Genesis One," in *Of Scribes and Scrolls: Studies on the Hebrew Bible, Intertestamental Judaism, and Christian Origins Presented to John Strugnell on the Occasion of His Sixtieth Birthday* (ed. H. W. Attridge et al.; College Theology Society Resources in Religion 5; Lanham, Md.: University Press of America, 1990), 3–11, here 5.

3. Seven Theses

3.1. Classify Variants Suitably

The enormous range of manuscript evidence for the Hebrew Scriptures that has come from the eleven Qumran caves has shown that variants need to be classified very carefully. I would argue that in place of the old assumption of the text critics on the low road that all variants should be understood as errors until shown otherwise, the dominant assumption among the new breed of textual scholar should be that scribes have played an active part in their enterprise.[17]

An example of a scholar moving in a suitable direction is provided by Bénédicte Lemmelijn's contribution on Exod 7:14–11:10, entitled "The So-Called 'Major Expansions' in SamP, 4QpaleoExod[m] and 4QExod[j] of Ex 7:14–11:10: On the Edge between Textual Criticism and Literary Criticism."[18] Lemmelijn argues that it is indispensable as a first phase in the study of a biblical pericope to evaluate the textual witnesses that are to be chosen as the basis of its literary study. Working with the so-called major expansions in some textual forms of Exod 7:14–11:10, Lemmelijn argues persuasively that "[t]he study of textual variants can be relevant in a double way. First, the textual differences can be very helpful to the discovery and explanation of literary irregularities in the final text. But second, they also reveal the contextual framework in which the text functions."[19] This approach defies the traditional text-critical assumption that all variants must be classified in some way as based on scribal errors.

The kind of classification system for variants that might be suitable can be seen in handling the Isaiah material from Qumran by Martin Abegg, Peter Flint, and Eugene Ulrich, though they are not always explicit about what critical assumptions lie behind their overall presentation of the so-called biblical manuscripts. They suggest a fourfold classification of the variants found in the Isaiah scrolls. "First, some variant readings are major in that they involve one or more verses present in some texts but absent from others."[20] By way of example they mention,

---

17. This has been well recognized in many studies by A. Rofé; see his summary in "Historico-Literary Aspects of the Qumran Biblical Scrolls," in *The Dead Sea Scrolls Fifty Years after Their Discovery: Proceedings of the Jerusalem Congress, July 20–25, 1997* (ed. L. H. Schiffman et al.; Jerusalem: Israel Exploration Society and Shrine of the Book, 2000), 30–39.

18. B. Lemmelijn, "The So-Called 'Major Expansions' in SamP, 4QpaleoExod[m] and 4QExod[j] of Ex 7:14–11:10: On the Edge between Textual Criticism and Literary Criticism," in *X Congress of the International Organization for Septuagint and Cognate Studies: Oslo, 1998* (ed. B. A. Taylor; SBLSCS 51; Atlanta: Society of Biblical Literature, 2001), 429–39. See also her more general study, "What Are We Looking for in Doing Old Testament Text-Critical Research"? *JNSL* 23 (1997): 69–80.

19. Lemmelijn, "On the Edge between Textual Criticism and Literary Criticism," 433.

20. M. Abegg, P. Flint, and E. Ulrich, eds., *The Dead Sea Scrolls Bible: The Oldest Known Bible Translated for the First Time into English* (San Francisco: HarperSanFrancisco, 1999), 268.

first, that 1QIsa[a] lacks Isa 2:9b–10a; these verses, they suggest, were probably an addition to the text by an unknown scribe, though the addition was done early enough to be recorded in 4QIsa[a], 4QIsa[b], the MT and the LXX. Second, Isa 2:22 was not in the Hebrew text translated by the LXX but was inserted later into the textual tradition now found in 1QIsa[a] and the MT. Those kinds of examples are numerous: "the existence of such variants provides a privileged window—one that was unavailable before the scrolls—on the gradual growth process of the biblical text in general."[21] The second category they identify includes hundreds of differences of a minor nature that, when taken together, "provide rich evidence for the use of Hebrew, different spelling systems, and scribal conventions during the late Second Temple period." A third category includes variants usually involving just one or two words; this category differs from the large-scale variants of the first category and the evidence of scribal practices in the second. A fourth category consists of errors such as the omission through homoioteleuton of Isa 16:8b–9a from 1QIsa[a].

This categorization is helpful, first, because it begins with significant and insignificant variants the vast majority of which cannot be described suitably on any view as errors. The old view of scribes as predominantly responsible for the corruption of an original text is neatly avoided,[22] and within the range of variants it is possible to see room for deliberate exegetical improvements being introduced into the texts.[23] In addition it is helpful to see that at least in this case there is no necessary prioritizing of one manuscript or manuscript tradition over another; too often, even when text critics acknowledge the need for neutrality, the MT becomes the normative base text and all variants are deemed deviations from it. It should be noted that the understanding of the variants in the manuscripts of Isaiah is not as difficult as for some scriptural books for which there are one or more editions or recensions.

3.2. Give Up the Pursuit of the Original Text

A second thesis forced upon us by the first, by the suitable appreciation of the variety of the evidence itself, is that in many cases it is simply no longer appropriate to embark on the quest for the original form of the text,[24] and especially no

---

21. Ibid.

22. This view is perpetuated somewhat by Tov: "If textual corruption in the development from reading a to other readings is assumed, the aim of this comparison is to select the one reading that was presumably contained in the original form of the text" (*Textual Criticism of the Hebrew Bible*, 291).

23. As I have long argued: see G. J. Brooke, "The Biblical Texts in the Qumran Commentaries: Scribal Errors or Exegetical Variants"? in *Early Jewish and Christian Exegesis: Studies in Memory of William Hugh Brownlee* (ed. C. A. Evans and W. F. Stinespring; SBL Homage Series 10; Atlanta: Scholars Press, 1987), 85–100.

24. A. van der Kooij has restated the aim of textual criticism as the quest for the original

longer fitting to consider the MT as representing some form of Ur-text. Attention to the individual manuscripts and their scribes implies that the starting point of the modern discussion of the text should be the artefactual evidence itself. There is certainly a place for historical exegesis, but the evidence of the scriptural manuscripts from Qumran strongly suggests that the best way to an understanding of earlier forms of the text is through paying attention to how each generation of Jewish and Christian traditors of the text has understood and used the text. On the basis of the evidence from the Qumran caves, juxtaposed with the Samaritan Pentateuch and the LXX, that can now be known in part for the generations who lived in the last three centuries before the fall of the temple in 70 c.e.

The strength of this thesis may become apparent by listening to almost the first written evaluation of 1QIsaᵃ, penned in a letter from William H. Brownlee to his fiancée Louise Dunn on February 23, 1948, just four days after the scroll had been brought to the American School in Jerusalem for identification and assessment:

> The largest scroll is about twenty-four feet long and ten and a quarter inches high. It contains the entire text of Isaiah.... The material for dating is scanty, but from the samples we have seen the manuscripts may be safely dated between 200 B.C. and 200 A.D.... I have read twelve verses of Isaiah, sufficient to know that the text is very important for establishing the true text of the book.[25]

It is clear that the subsequent scholarly treatment of 1QIsaᵃ was overwhelmingly disparaging,[26] but, although 1QIsaᵃ should be reinstated as a significant witness, few would wish to think that their reading of it would be solely for establishing the "true text of the book."

The strongest case for abandoning the quest for the original text has been made by Shemaryahu Talmon. This is the result of his attention to the social function of texts and groups of texts, which has meant that primary focus is given to the role a text has in any particular social context:

> The further back the textual tradition of the Old Testament is followed, i.e. the older the biblical manuscripts perused ... the wider is the overall range of textual divergence between them.... The fact indicates that variation as such in the textual transmission cannot be laid exclusively at the door of careless scribes,

---

form of the text, that is, its final redaction, but he has acknowledged that often this is unobtainable ("Textual Criticism of the Hebrew Bible: Its Aim and Method," in *Emanuel: Studies in Hebrew Bible, Septuagint, and Dead Sea Scrolls in Honor of Emanuel Tov* [ed. S. M. Paul et al.; VTSup 94; Leiden: Brill, 2003], 729–39, esp. 729–33).

25. W. H. Brownlee to L. Dunn, February 23, 1948; from the Brownlee Archive held at the John Rylands University Library of Manchester.

26. The variant readings of 1QIsaᵃ were famously declared to be "worthless" by H. M. Orlinsky, "Studies in the St. Mark's Isaiah Scroll IV," *JQR* 43 (1952–53): 329–40, esp. 340.

or of sometimes unscrupulous, and sometimes well-meaning, emendators and revisers.[27]

Faced with textual diversity in the earliest strata of the textual tell, the search for a pristine Ur-text has to be abandoned.

Though not yet willing to follow the lead of his mentor, Tov has concluded that the aims of textual criticism should be formulated as follows:

> The study of the biblical text involves an investigation of its development, its copying and transmission, and of the processes which created readings and texts over the centuries. In the course of this procedure, textual critics collect from Hebrew and translated texts all the details in which these texts differ from one from another. Some of these differences were created in the course of the textual transmission, while others derive from an earlier stage, that of literary growth.[28]

A further effect of recognizing that textual criticism is not about discovering the original form of a text is the ability then to discern that in many instances what has become normative in the MT is actually not the most original form of a text.[29] Naive assumptions about the value of the MT for establishing what was taking place at the earliest stages of the production of any text must be abandoned.

3.3. RECOGNIZE THE ROLE OF THE SAMARITAN PENTATEUCH AND THE VERSIONS

It is evident that there has been a lively renewed interest in the Samaritan Pentateuch and the scriptural versions, especially the LXX, since the discovery of the so-called biblical manuscripts at Qumran and elsewhere. At least part of this interest derives from the stimulus provided by the scrolls themselves.[30]

---

27. S. Talmon, "The Old Testament Text," in *The Cambridge History of the Bible*, vol. 1, *From the Beginnings to Jerome* (ed. P. R. Ackroyd and C. F. Evans; Cambridge: Cambridge University Press, 1970), 159–99; quoted and updated in Talmon, "The Transmission History of the Text of the Hebrew Bible in the Light of Biblical Manuscripts from Qumran and Other Sites in the Judean Desert," in Schiffman et al., *Dead Sea Scrolls Fifty Years after Their Discovery*, 40–50, here 46.

28. Tov, *Textual Criticism of the Hebrew Bible*, 289–90.

29. Many examples of this phenomenon can now be cited, but two discussions by E. Ulrich illustrate the phenomenon well; see his studies "4QJoshua[a] and Joshua's First Altar in the Promised Land," in *New Qumran Texts and Studies: Proceedings of the First Meeting of the International Organization for Qumran Studies, Paris 1992* (ed. G. J. Brooke with F. García Martínez; STDJ 15; Leiden: Brill, 1994), 89–104 (96: 4QJoshua[a] and Josephus preserve an earlier form of the text than MT-LXX); "The Developmental Composition of the Book of Isaiah: Light from 1QIsa[a] on Additions in the MT," *DSD* 8 (2001): 288–305 (305: of "these ten readings, 1QIsa[a] preserves the original text most often").

30. For the Greek versions see, notably, the discussion prompted by HevXIIgr: D.

The scrolls have provided overwhelming evidence that the vast majority of the variant readings in the Samaritan Pentateuch represent a recension of the Torah known in Palestine in the late Second Temple period well beyond the confines of the Samaritan communities.[31] Only a few of the readings in the Samaritan tradition can be clearly designated as sectarian variants. Manuscripts such as 4QpaleoExod[m] and even manuscripts of the Reworked Pentateuch are replete with readings that align them in some way with the Samaritan Pentateuch.[32] There is an increasing need for scholars to recognize that the Samaritan Pentateuch is an authentic witness to the pluralism of the books of the Torah in the latter half of the Second Temple period and that it stands in need of both literary and textual analysis.[33] The creative activity of the scribes responsible for the so-called Reworked Pentateuch can also be labeled as both textual and literary and is in need of the kind of analysis that has only rarely been attempted so far.[34] Such analysis should also include the assessment of the authoritative status of the Reworked Pentateuch.[35]

Barthélemy, *Les devanciers d'Aquila* (VTSup 10; Leiden: Brill, 1963); E. Tov, *The Greek Minor Prophets Scroll from Nahal Hever (8HevXIIgr) (The Seiyâl Collection I)* (DJD 8; Oxford: Clarendon, 1990).

31. For a general description of the Samaritan Pentateuch and its fresh reconsideration since the discovery of the scrolls, see B. K. Waltke, "Samaritan Pentateuch," *ABD* 5:932–40.

32. For the details, see J. E. Sanderson, *An Exodus Scroll from Qumran: 4QpaleoExod[m] and the Samaritan Tradition* (HSS 30; Atlanta: Scholars Press, 1986); and P. W. Skehan, E. Ulrich, and J. E. Sanderson, eds., *Qumran Cave 4.IV: Palaeo-Hebrew and Greek Biblical Manuscripts* (DJD 9; Oxford: Clarendon, 1992), 65–70; E. Tov, "The Textual Status of 4Q364–367 (4QPP)," in *The Madrid Qumran Congress: Proceedings of the International Congress on the Dead Sea Scrolls, Madrid, 18–21 March 1991* (ed. J. Trebolle Barrera and L. Vegas Montaner; STDJ 11; Leiden: Brill, 1992), 43–82; and E. Tov and S. White, "Reworked Pentateuch," in *Qumran Cave 4.VIII: Parabiblical Texts Part I* (ed. H. Attridge et al.; DJD 13; Oxford: Clarendon, 1994), 192–96.

33. A brief but helpful catalogue of the kinds of textual and literary variants in the Samaritan Pentateuch is offered by J. C. VanderKam and P. W. Flint, *The Meaning of the Dead Sea Scrolls: Their Significance for Understanding the Bible, Judaism, Jesus, and Christianity* (San Francisco: HarperSanFrancisco, 2002), 93–95.

34. A start has been made by E. Tov, "Biblical Texts as Reworked in Some Qumran Manuscripts with Special Attention to 4QRP and 4QParaGen-Exod," in *The Community of the Renewed Covenant: The Notre Dame Symposium on the Dead Sea Scrolls* (ed. E. Ulrich and J. C. VanderKam; Christianity and Judaism in Antiquity 10; Notre Dame, Ind.: University of Notre Dame Press, 1994), 111–34.

35. "I have not yet studied 4Q364–367 in detail, but in light of this documented pluriformity of the developing text of the Scriptures, it may turn out that such works are more properly classified as 'biblical' (i.e., scriptural) works rather than 'paraphrases' or 'reworked' biblical texts" (E. Ulrich, "The Bible in the Making: The Scriptures Found at Qumran," in *The Bible at Qumran: Text, Shape, and Interpretation* [ed. P. W. Flint; Studies in the Dead Sea Scrolls and Related Literature; Grand Rapids: Eerdmans, 2001], 51–66, here 65 n. 50).

As is well known, the scrolls have stimulated Septuagintal studies in numerous ways.[36] In particular they have provided ample evidence that several of the major variants between the LXX and the proto-MT have their origin in a pluralism that existed in Hebrew tradition. The most well known instance of this involves the book of Jeremiah, whose formation and transmission history are very difficult to disentangle.[37] This pluralism of both text and form needs a clearer voice in the description of textual realities in the Second Temple period; it is not adequately described when reduced to a set of variants that are the preserve of the classical text critic.

In addition to the evidence of the Samaritan Pentateuch and the versions, especially the LXX, there is a renewed place for taking into account the evidence of the New Testament authors, the Jewish Pseudepigrapha and the writings of Philo and Josephus inasmuch as these can contribute to our understanding of the vitality and variety of authoritative traditions up to the end of the first century C.E. The overall point is that when all the evidence for the textual variety of various authoritative scriptural books in the late Second Temple period is considered in detail, it is increasingly difficult to retain a clear distinction between the roles of the text critics and those involved in literary analysis.

3.4. Reassess the Role of Scribes

The variety that is to be found in the evidence from the Judean Desert together with that of the versions and other witnesses challenges several widely held assumptions. Among them is the assumption of much textual criticism that Jewish scribal practice in the late Second Temple period was largely mechanistic. This is in need of reassessment. Some work has already been undertaken in this direction, and it is not necessary to rehearse it in detail at this point, provided that it is acknowledged that few, if any, copyists were just scribal automata.[38] Social issues, the status of scribes, their education and influence, general rates of literacy and schooling, as well as the whole business of manuscript production and the commerce in the materials required, are all in need of clarification.[39]

---

36. See, e.g., the significant conference volume, *Septuagint, Scrolls and Cognate Writings: Papers Presented to the International Symposium on the Septuagint and Its Relations to the Dead Sea Scrolls and Other Writings (Manchester, 1990)* (ed. G. J. Brooke and B. Lindars; SBLSCS 33; Atlanta: Scholars Press, 1992).

37. On the evidence of the manuscripts of Jeremiah from the Qumran caves, see E. Tov, "Jeremiah," in *Qumran Cave 4.X: The Prophets* (ed. E. Ulrich et al.; DJD 15; Oxford: Clarendon, 1997), 145–207, and the literature cited there.

38. I am grateful to Philip Davies in a response to my presentation for suggesting that in several ways authors and scribes may have similar textual mentalities; this observation deserves further consideration.

39. Among an increasing range of studies, see especially P. S. Alexander, "Literacy among Jews in Second Temple Palestine: Reflections on the Evidence from Qumran," in *Hamlet on a Hill: Semitic and Greek Studies Presented to Professor T. Muraoka on the Occasion of His Sixty-*

One example must suffice to illustrate the point. Most students of Qumran would acknowledge that there is a strong case that some of the manuscripts found in the caves at and near Qumran were in fact actually penned there. Perhaps it is indeed the case that many or all of those written in the so-called Qumran scribal practice are products of those who resided at Qumran.[40] At the least, the presence of a number of inkwells at the site indicates that there was some scribal activity there. However, none of the sectarian compositions found at Qumran distinguishes scribal activity from the other roles that some of the residents might have had. As a result, it is not unlikely that those who copied the scrolls were also among those who were required to study:

> And in the place where there are ten men, there shall never lack a man to interpret the Law, by day and night, continually, a man relieving his companion in turn. And the Many shall watch in community for a third of every night of the year, to read the Book and to study the Law and to bless together." (1QS 6:6–8)

In a community that in many ways considered itself to be the ongoing presence of scriptural Israel, it is not possible to distinguish between members who were diligent students of the authoritative scriptural text and those who were responsible for copying it. The scribe was an actively interested transmitter of the text. It seems reasonable to suggest that that was also the case in earlier generations.

To draw an analogy from Qumran to the way in which scribes in the Second Temple period might have been active and creative participants in the transmission of authoritative texts is not to say that all scribes necessarily worked in the same way or with the same responsibilities. There were several different kinds of scribes in the Second Temple period; Christine Schams, for one, has outlined something of the pluralism of scribal location and role.[41] More general issues relating to the difficulties in determining the role of scribes in how certain texts become authoritative have been outlined by Philip R. Davies.[42] Whatever the case, it seems that the trend in recent studies has been toward acknowledging the creative and influential role of scribes. They were not mere copyists, as later medieval tradition might lead one to suppose. As a result, it is not suitable to treat them within one form of critical investigation as those responsible for errors, but

Fifth Birthday (ed. M. F. J. Baasten and W. Th. van Peursen; OLA 118; Leuven: Peeters, 2003), 3–24; C. Hezser, *Jewish Literacy in Roman Palestine* (TSAJ 81; Tübingen: Mohr Siebeck, 2001); A. R. Millard, *Reading and Writing in the Time of Jesus* (Biblical Seminar 69; Sheffield: Sheffield Academic Press, 2000).

40. See, e.g., E. Tov, "Further Evidence for the Existence of a Qumran Scribal School," in Schiffman et al., *Dead Sea Scrolls Fifty Years after Their Discovery*, 199–216.

41. C. Schams, *Jewish Scribes in the Second-Temple Period* (JSOTSup 291; Sheffield: Sheffield Academic Press, 1998).

42. P. R. Davies, *Scribes and Schools: The Canonization of the Hebrew Scriptures* (Library of Ancient Israel; London: SPCK, 1998).

to acknowledge more explicitly their literary skills, even their contribution as "authors."

3.5. Resist Eclectic Editions

It has often been pointed out that the textual criticism of the New Testament has generally been practiced differently from that of the Hebrew Bible. For the New Testament, the search for the original text has resulted in the production of eclectic editions that, it may be noted, nowhere existed in any manuscript. Such an eclectic edition is a scholarly invention,[43] but as such it is not particularly problematic because the vast majority of variants between the extant witnesses of the various works that constitute the New Testament are relatively minor.

For the Hebrew Bible, the tradition has been to work with a known manuscript and produce from that particular representative of the transmission of the text a diplomatic edition. With the availability of the so-called biblical scrolls from Qumran, there has been an undercurrent of interest, with Ronald S. Hendel as one of its more prominent leaders, which has argued that it is now time for an eclectic edition of the Hebrew Bible.[44] However, Tov's summary of the aims and procedures of textual criticism in his comprehensive introduction still acknowledges the ongoing value of producing diplomatic editions for the books of the Hebrew Bible, basing any edition on a particular manuscript form of the text.[45]

The general reluctance of scholars to proceed down the road of eclecticism for the Hebrew Bible seems correct for a number of reasons. To begin with, it is the unstated aim of many eclectic editions that they are concerned to reconstruct a supposed Ur-text; I have already noted that, for Talmon and others, the scrolls have shown that the search for the Ur-text is in many instances a vain quest. Moreover, it is clear that what has been fixed for each book of the Hebrew Bible is not necessarily its earliest form; thus to search to establish that might well lead to ignoring the authoritative text, which the majority of those using the text experience. Furthermore, it seems to me that eclectic texts should be avoided for the very reason that they minimize the contribution of individual scribes and the specific creative traditions to which they may severally belong. In addition, there

---

43. It is interesting to note that some current NT text-critical projects are attempting through electronic means to enable the individual scholar to establish not only what individual manuscripts may have read but also what they look like. This point was brought home to me in a presentation by D. Parker, K. Wachtel, U. Schmid, R. Mullen, B. Elliott, and J. Balserak, "Digital Editing: A New Generation of Greek New Testaments" (paper presented at the 2003 meeting of the British New Testament Society in Birmingham).

44. R. S. Hendel, "The Text of the Torah after Qumran," in Schiffman et al., *Dead Sea Scrolls Fifty Years after Their Discovery,* 8–11. Hendel has suggested how an eclectic edition might be produced in idem, *The Text of Genesis 1–11: Textual Studies and Critical Edition* (New York: Oxford University Press, 1998).

45. Tov, *Textual Criticism of the Hebrew Bible,* 289.

are multiple features in any manuscript that are often neglected by those concentrating on the text alone; principal among these are the paragraph divisions and spaces between sections, which manuscripts variously represent. Spacing has now been brought into focus by those who work in the field of Delimitation Criticism, whose insights are emerging from the Netherlands in a new series called aptly Pericope.[46] So far the attention of scholars involved in this approach has been largely given over to the divisions presented in the various manuscripts of the MT, but Odil Hannes Steck[47] and Ulrich have made contributions on the analysis of 1QIsaᵃ from this perspective. Ulrich has wisely insisted that the evidence "is the production of the last person who copied the text, not necessarily of earlier copies; if one wishes to see in these final products the intentions or indications of original authors, there is a weighty burden of proof required to establish a continuous link."[48] Overall it is probably particularly important to resist eclectic editions of the Hebrew Bible, because it is becoming increasingly evident that each scriptural book has its own complex story to tell. For example, it can be stated without much qualification that "the Masoretic Text is a chance collection from a wide pool of circulating texts."[49] The point does not need to be belabored further. The production of eclectic editions inevitably reduces the amount of attention that is given to individual scribes and their traditions and so encourages the continuation of the divorce of text criticism from other more literary approaches to the scriptural text.

3.6. ABANDON CANONICAL LENSES

Much in textual criticism of the Hebrew Bible as traditionally practiced has given priority to the MT. Although it is now well recognized that variants should not be described as if the MT or any proto-MT form provides the norm against which all other witnesses to the text are to be measured, nevertheless it is still the case that the MT dominates the discussion. The obvious reason for this is that for each and every biblical book the MT contains what may be understood as a complete form. But the use of the MT in this way has another distorting effect, which

---

46. M. C. A. Korpel and J. M Oesch, eds., *Delimitation Criticism: A New Tool for Biblical Scholarship* (Pericope 1; Assen: Van Gorcum, 2000).

47. O. H. Steck, *Die erste Jesajarolle von Qumran (1QIsa)*, vol. 1, *Schreibweise als Leseanteilung für ein Prophetenbuch* (SBS 173; Stuttgart: Katholisches Bibelwerk, 1998); in his German translation of 1QIsaᵃ Steck indicates precisely where the various spaces and the paragraph markers occur.

48. E. Ulrich, "Impressions and Intuition: Sense Division in Ancient Manuscripts of Isaiah," in *Unit Delimitation in Biblical Hebrew and Northwest Semitic Literature* (ed. M. C. A Korpel and J. M. Oesch; Pericope 4; Assen: Van Gorcum, 2003), 279–307, here 280. Ulrich discusses examples from Isa 19:15–16; 23:1–2; 34:9–10, 17.

49. E. Ulrich, "The Text of the Hebrew Scriptures at the Time of Hillel and Jesus," in *Congress Volume: Basel 2001* (ed. A. Lemaire; VTSup 92; Leiden: Brill, 2002), 85–108, here 98.

might be characterized as the anachronistic prioritizing of the canonical form of the text. This is obvious in many ways, but no more so than in the way in which the so-called biblical manuscripts from Qumran are called biblical, even though scholars are aware of the numerous borderline cases that would suggest that the label does not work well. It is evident that there are compositions in the Qumran library that are authoritative for the community that collected them together, but it is a rare scholar who can declare that the books of Chronicles or Ezra or Nehemiah were not authoritative at Qumran.[50]

Ulrich has put this well:

> The present situation in scholarship is that there is a need for a revised mentality and for a paradigmatic revision in our categories and criteria. The reason that the scriptural scrolls surprise us is not the scroll texts themselves but our categories and criteria for assessing the biblical text in antiquity. The common default mentality of biblical scholars (or, our faulty mentality) is that the Masoretic Text is the standard text and canon of the Hebrew Bible, and that texts (or books) which are not identical to the Masoretic Text are sectarian, or vulgar, or nonbiblical. But the problem is not the scrolls, but rather (a) the presuppositions of scholars and students, and (b) the theories regarding the history of the biblical text.[51]

Abandoning the canonical lenses also has an effect on how one considers scribes and their activity, as has been mentioned above. From a canonical perspective it is tempting to view scribes solely as copyists, as was largely the case in relation to the Hebrew Bible from late antiquity onward. In the Second Temple period, however, scribes were creative participants in the transmission process, and their activity needs analysis in ways that take into account its complete character. The analytical approaches of the so-called higher critics are required for this undertaking.

3.7. END AND TRANSFORM THE DISTINCTION BETWEEN HIGHER AND LOWER CRITICISM

In a programmatic essay, Arie van der Kooij has commented that the Dead Sea Scrolls have changed the landscape of textual criticism:

> In earlier days textual criticism was considered to be "lower criticism." In the light of the developments which have been outlined in this paper, there is good reason to assert that textual criticism in the post-Qumran era can be regarded

---

50. An exception is A. Lange, "The Status of the Biblical Texts in the Qumran Corpus and the Canonical Process," in *The Bible as Book: The Hebrew Bible and the Judaean Desert Discoveries* (ed. E. D. Herbert and E. Tov; London: British Library; New Castle, Del.: Oak Knoll Press, 2002), 21–30, here 24.

51. Ulrich, "Text of the Hebrew Scriptures at the Time of Hillel and Jesus," 92.

as a part of "higher criticism." We may congratulate ourselves on this promotion.[52]

However, whereas van der Kooij argues that the promotion of textual criticism
is the result of the wider range of skills that the text critic must employ given
the greater complexity of the evidence that is now available, I would argue that
the character of the evidence has caused not just a promotion but a significant
change in how all critical approaches to the Bible might pose their questions, so
that textual criticism is seen not as a complex preliminary to the literary analysis
of texts but an indispensable part of such analysis when undertaken so that there
is a holistic account of the evidence.

With the transformation of all critical approaches to the text it may be that
the kind of role occupied by text criticism in the past will increasingly in the
future be occupied by linguistics and its specialty of discourse linguistics. M.
O'Connor has recently made a plea that discourse linguistics should be kept well
apart from all kinds of exegetical methods, including textual criticism, even
though they have something in common.[53] I suspect that O'Connor's plea is not
entirely appropriate, given that even he acknowledges that there is some overlap
between linguistic concerns and the interests of textual critics. All approaches to
the reading of texts need appropriate application and careful integration. None
should think of itself as supremely objective or scientific, or as the exclusive pre-
requisite before other forms of critical reading strategies can be applied to the
texts. The ending of the distinction between categories of criticism frees scholars
to treat each textual variant with questions appropriate to it whether these derive
from comparative Semitic philology, literary analysis, grammatical studies, the
principles of classical textual criticism, or whatever.

4. CONCLUSION

In this contribution I have attempted to argue from several different perspectives
that, in light of the Dead Sea Scrolls, the distinction between higher and lower
criticism needs to be drawn to a close and transformed. To put it another way,
the scrolls show that textual criticism needs to move beyond a quasi-ontological
view of the text, as if the text has some absolute form somewhere that can be
determined before its meaning is then realized through other methodological
approaches; there needs to be a move toward a more functional view of the text.
Such a functional view concentrates far more on the transmission history of texts

---

52. A. van der Kooij, "The Textual Criticism of the Hebrew Bible before and after the
Qumran Discoveries," in Herbert and Tov, *Bible as Book*, 167–77, here 75.

53. M. O'Connor, "Discourse Linguistics and the Study of the Hebrew Bible," in Lemaire,
Congress Volume: Basel 2001, 17–42, here 40.

and asks of them (and their manuscript witnesses) what they were copied for, whether it might have been for legal, political, didactic, liturgical, or some other communal or individual purpose. The diversity of attestation is allowed to stand and is not reduced to a chosen, preferred reading. Though some will undoubtedly continue to sing "You take the high road and I'll take the low road," before too long, in light of the Dead Sea Scrolls, the textual criticism of the Hebrew Scriptures will be set to a different tune.

TWO

THE FORMATION AND RENEWAL
OF SCRIPTURAL TRADITION

1. Introduction[1]

This essay is a consideration of some aspects of the formation and renewal of scriptural tradition. Of what does tradition consist? What are its parameters? Although the term "tradition" is widely used, not least by scholars of the Bible, even in the titles of books[2] or as the label for a critical way of life (*Traditionsgeschichte*), comparatively little has been written that explicitly discusses the constituent parts of tradition or its motivating forces.[3] In one of the few studies directly addressing the topic in relation to the Dead Sea Scrolls, John J. Collins has described how tradition is based on a collection of writings that was acknowledged as authoritative, and he has offered some comments on the ways in which innovation was achieved through rewriting, through the appeal to revelation, and through the role of authoritative interpreters.[4] In this essay, which is a reflection on the overall concerns of one scholar's lifetime contribution to the study of

---

1. This essay is based on a lecture that I delivered at a study day in March 2003 at King's College London in honor of Professor Michael A. Knibb, F.B.A. I first met Michael in 1978 in the Deanery at Salisbury, over a glass of whisky bountifully supplied by the Very Reverend Sydney Evans, a former Dean of King's. In several ways Sydney Evans embodied tradition, and it is that topic which has provided a framework for this consideration of Michael's work.

2. A good example is G. W. Anderson, ed., *Tradition and Interpretation: Essays by Members of the Society for Old Testament Study* (Oxford: Clarendon, 1979).

3. The index to Anderson (*Tradition and Interpretation*, 459) gives some indication what such a survey might include: "Tradition: Complexes, Jerusalemite, Jewish, Local, Monarchical, Pre-Monarchical, Mosaic, Oral, Parallel, Transmission, Tribal, Reinterpretation, Sinai, Written." It is categories such as "transmission" and "reinterpretation" that I attempt to articulate in some form in this essay.

4. J. J. Collins, "Tradition and Innovation in the Dead Sea Scrolls," in *The Dead Sea Scrolls: Transmission of Traditions and Production of Texts* (ed. S. Metso, H. Najman, and E. M. Schuller; STDJ 92; Leiden: Brill, 2010), 1–23. Collins opens his essay by noting how the general definition of tradition in terms of practices as offered by Eric Hobsbawm (E. Hobsbawm and T. Ranger, eds., *The Invention of Tradition* [Past and Present Publications; Cambridge: Cambridge University Press, 1983], 1) is in need of refinement in relation to systems of thought and belief.

Judaism of the late Second Temple period, I attempt to associate Michael Knibb's research with the parameters of tradition as I see them.

2. Looking to the Past

2.1. Fascination

Almost as much as R. H. Charles, the name of Michael Knibb is associated with 1 Enoch.[5] As may become apparent in several parts of this essay, it is 1 Enoch that poses the conundrum of tradition as much as any set of compositions from the late Second Temple period. On the one hand, much that is associated with Enoch seems nonscriptural, but, on the other hand, it is obvious that Enoch is mentioned in the primeval history as seventh from Adam; he is part of Genesis, part of the Torah. To this extent he belongs somewhere among the lists of the great, even heading one such roll call in some versions of Sir 44:16: "Enoch pleased the Lord and was taken up, an example of repentance to all generations." A similar approbation is rehearsed at the end of the sequence: "Few have ever been created on earth like Enoch, for he was taken up from the earth" (Sir 49:14). Through this reference to authoritative Scripture, a case can be made for at least the Book of Watchers (1 En. 1–36) to be viewed as some form of rewritten Bible composition.[6] Knibb puts the same point in another way:

> the number of writings associated with the name of Enoch is an indication of the fascination which this figure held for later generations, a fascination aroused no doubt by the enigmatic statement of Gen. 5:24, "Having walked with God, Enoch was seen no more, because God had taken him away."

There is a straightforward fascination with some aspects of the past, which leads to reflection on their significance and importance for the reader or hearer. Fascination leads to the formation of tradition.

---

5. See the following works by Knibb, *A New Edition of the Ethiopic Enoch in the Light of the Aramaic Dead Sea Fragments* (Ph.D. diss., School of Oriental and African Studies, London, 1974); *The Ethiopic Book of Enoch: A New Edition in the Light of the Aramaic Dead Sea Fragments* (in consultation with E. Ullendorff; Oxford: Clarendon, 1978); *Het Boek Henoch: Het eerste of het Ethiopische boek van Henoch* (Deventer: Hermes, 1983); "1 Enoch," in *The Apocryphal Old Testament* (ed. Hedley F. D. Sparks; Oxford: Clarendon, 1984), 184–319; "The Ethiopic Book of Enoch," in *Outside the Old Testament* (ed. Marinus de Jonge; Cambridge: Cambridge University Press, 1985), 26–55.

6. See, e.g., D. Dimant, "1 Enoch 6–11: A Fragment of a Parabiblical Work," *JJS* 53 (2002): 223–37: "we may already assign *1 Enoch* 6–11 to the growing body of texts reworking the Bible to various degrees" (p. 237).

2.2. Aetiological Readings

A second aspect of the past that is present in Scripture as tradition but is present also in the conversion of Scripture into tradition is the search in the past for explanations for things. Two examples can be offered briefly from Knibb's discussion of sectarian compositions found in the Qumran library. First, the lessons of the past that are rehearsed in CD 2:14–3:12 are "a summary of some of the main events of Israel's past in which it is shown that by following the guilty inclination God's people had repeatedly brought punishment on themselves. The purpose of the summary governed the choice of the events and persons mentioned in that almost all are negative in character."[7] The rehearsal of scriptural traditions is a rhetorical device to explain why punishment overtakes God's people, who might have thought themselves in some way immune from divine wrath. The recitation of past punishments serves as an explanation for how and why the group reading the text can and should understand that the rest of Israel is still under punishment in some way.

Another aetiological reading of tradition can be observed in Knibb's description of part of the so-called Treatise on the Two Spirits in 1QS 3:13–4:1.

> The explanation of human behaviour in terms of an explicit dualism represents a new development in Judaism, but the background to the ideas of the Community Rule can be found in the Old Testament itself. The Old Testament often speaks of God's spirit which stirs men to action (cp. e.g. Judg. 14:6; 1 Sam. 10:10), but it also knows of spirits that are to some extent independent of him (cp. e.g. 2 Kings 19:7; Num. 27:16); it can even speak of God sending an evil (1 Sam. 16:14–16) or a lying (1 Kings 22:21–3) spirit. The doctrine of the two spirits in the Rule may be seen as a development of these Old Testament ideas, a development perhaps influenced by the dualistic beliefs of Zoroastrianism, the religion of ancient Iran.[8]

Scriptural traditions are seen to lie at the basis of the construction of an elaborate doctrine explaining why humans behave as they do.

2.3. Alternative Pasts

A particular interest in the past may result from awareness that there are alternative ways in which the past can be read and reconstructed. Authoritative versions of the past, however convoluted and multifaceted, such as those collections of definitive traditions to be found in the Torah, always represent the vision or

---

7. M. A. Knibb, *The Qumran Community* (Cambridge Commentaries on Writings of the Jewish and Christian World 200 BC to AD 200, 2; Cambridge: Cambridge University Press, 1987), 29.

8. Ibid., 95–96.

visions of one or a few sets of people; it is the victors who write the history. But there are always alternative pasts, and the writings compiled in 1 Enoch may be understood as much as an alternative version of the past as they can be comprehended as some kind of interpretation of what many may have thought was the authoritative or definitive vision as found in Genesis.

A significant set of alternative pasts can be found in the many different views in the late Second Temple period concerning the duration of the exile. In a significant article entitled "The Exile in the Literature of the Intertestamental Period,"[9] which has been much cited, Knibb has laid out some aspects of the views of the past that consideration of the motif of exile entails. Several groups seem to have held the common opinion that the exile did not finish in the sixth century, but that in some real sense Israel remained in exile beyond the time of Cyrus. For some, such as those responsible for parts of 1 Enoch and Daniel, the past was constructed on the basis of exegesis of various prophetic passages, most notably the seventy years of Jeremiah. For others there was an attempt to offer what might be called an integrated reading of the past based on the schematic application of a pattern, discernible elsewhere in the traditions of Israel's history, in which Israel goes repeatedly through the stages of sin, exile, and return.[10] Although those in power in Jerusalem from the fifth century B.C.E. onwards might have considered themselves to belong to the stage of return; others (for their own purposes) viewed themselves as belonging still to the period of exile.

But alternative pasts can also be created in minor and subtle ways (and often of course with an eye to the present). It is intriguing to observe in 2 Esd 1:38 that Ezra is designated as father. The title does not occur in the Hebrew Bible; for Ezra it occurs only in 2 Esd 1:38 and 2:5. "Perhaps the author's intention was to compare Ezra with Abraham who is more usually called 'father'; cp. Luke 16:24, 30."[11] By applying the designation of Abraham to Ezra, the author creates an affiliation in every sense of the word and maybe suggests by inference what he most certainly intends, that the church is the immediate heir to the promises given to Abraham; Ezra becomes a means of passing the divine promises given to Abraham directly to the readership of the adjusted 2 Esdras. The scriptural tradition is construed and appropriated in a way that is an alternative to the majority Jewish reading of the same scriptural source.

In the opening of 2 Esd 3 something similar happens. The prayer of Ezra opens with his setting himself in Babylon thirty years after the fall of Jerusa-

---

9. M. A. Knibb, "The Exile in the Literature of the Intertestamental Period," *HeyJ* 17 (1976): 253–72.

10. Knibb has further developed his interests in the conceptualization of the extent of the exile in his study "A Note on 4Q372 and 4Q390," in *The Scriptures and the Scrolls: Studies in Honour of A.S. van der Woude on the Occasion of His 65th Birthday* (ed. F. García Martínez, A. Hilhorst, and C.J. Labuschagne; VTSup 49; Leiden: Brill, 1992), 164–77.

11. M. A. Knibb, "Commentary on 2 Esdras," in *The First and Second Books of Esdras* (ed. R. J. Coggins and M. A. Knibb; CBC; Cambridge: Cambridge University Press, 1979), 87.

lem. Though many scholars have agonized over the datings of Ezra and Nehe-miah, none has taken the view that Ezra belongs actively to thirty years after the destruction of the first temple. The author knows it too and so has Ezra take the name of Salathiel, in Hebrew Shealtiel. Shealtiel was either the uncle (1 Chr 3:17–19) or father (Ezra 3:2) of Zerubbabel. Whatever the case, he is a suitable "link between the beginning and the end of the period of the exile, and a date thirty years after 587 B.C.E. is not inappropriate for him."[12] Through an ingenious device the author of 2 Esd 3 creates an alternative past that allows for a typologi-cal comparison between the time after the destruction of the first temple and the same time after the destruction of the second. A little bit of revision for suitable reasons can go a long way.

3. Looking to the Present

3.1. Making the Past Present

3.1.1. Translation

Translations, both ancient and modern, play their role in enhancing or inhibit-ing scriptural traditions, particularly in the ways in which they make texts from the past available to contemporary readers and listeners. Knibb has undertaken much translation work and commented on issues of method faced by the transla-tor.[13] His Schweich Lectures on the Ethiopic version of the Old Testament provide his keenest insights into the work of translators as the transmitters and adaptors of tradition.[14] In his first chapter he outlines many of the problems (and some of their solutions) that modern scholars face in the analysis of Bible translations in a language such as Geez. One of those problems might be the gap between the likely date of translation and the actual date of the earliest manuscript witnesses, so that it is not always clear whether one is reading the tradition as adapted by the translator or as transmitted and generated over generations through the minor adaptations of scribes. Nevertheless, it is clear that the Ethiopic version of the Old Testament was made primarily, if not necessarily exclusively, from the Septua-gint. However, it is equally clear that the whole was not completed from a single known text-type or recension,[15] although some books may be associated with individual manuscripts or text-types. In addition to the initial translations of

---

12. Ibid., 115.

13. E.g., M. A. Knibb, "The Translation of 1 Enoch 70.1: Some Methodological Issues," in *Biblical Hebrew, Biblical Texts: Essays in Memory of Michael P. Weitzman* (ed. Ada Rapoport-Albert and Gillian Greenberg; JSOTSup 333; The Hebrew Bible and Its Versions 2; Sheffield: Sheffield Academic Press, 2001), 340–54.

14. M. A. Knibb, *Translating the Bible: The Ethiopic Version of the Old Testament* (The Schweich Lectures of the British Academy 1995; Oxford: Oxford University Press for the Brit-ish Academy, 1999).

15. Ibid., 19.

individual books, there has been a more or less complicated process of revision, a process that may well have begun very shortly after the initial act of translation. Furthermore there is some debate concerning whether Syriac and Hebrew manuscripts were used at the time of the original translations or only subsequently, for the Syriac particularly through the Syro-Arabic text. Only detailed consideration of all the manuscript evidence permits modern readers to know which generation of traditors is responsible for what.

As far as the Ethiopic version is concerned, Knibb's detailed investigations, based particularly on Ezekiel, show that, though the restraints of the Ethiopic language require many minor adjustments as in general the Greek is rendered into Ethiopic, the version nevertheless provides not a literal rendering but a "faithful" translation.[16] This "faithfulness" is expressed in many minor deliberate additions and omissions and the use of free translation, which is usually the simplification of the underlying text but occasionally seems to suggest that the translator simply did not understand what he was reading. Part of the free translation is an apparent lack of consistency in the rendering of certain Greek words; it appears that consistency was not pursued for its own sake. Nevertheless, in the light of the variety of renderings of some words, which Knibb describes as "instinctive," it is difficult to "speak with any certainty of the intention of the translators."[17] Overall, understanding the place of translators of Scripture as transmitters and adaptors of tradition is returning to the scholarly agenda. In part this seems to be the result of the way in which the so-called biblical manuscripts from the Qumran caves have reinstated the ancient versions as witnesses to more than just dozens of scribal errors through which families of manuscripts can be stemmatically related.

As for modern translations, one example may be cited. In his comments on the New English Bible version of 2 Esdras, Knibb notes that the NEB version is often more paraphrastic than is helpful in revealing the background of several passages. In 2 Esd 6:1–5 the "description of the time before creation is similar to the description in Prov. 8:24–9 (although the N.E.B. translation does not fully bring out the points of contact), and Prov. 8 may have been in the mind of the author when he wrote this passage."[18] In this respect, because the NEB has an agenda other than the faithful representation of tradition, unlike those who rendered the Greek Old Testament into Ethiopic, it does not faithfully represent the tradition that is being developed from a scriptural source in an early Jewish text.

---

16. Ibid., 61.
17. Ibid., 110–12.
18. Knibb, "Commentary on 2 Esdras," 146.

3.1.2. EXEGESIS

In that significant article already mentioned, "The Exile in the Literature of the Intertestamental Period,"[19] Knibb not only suggests that there were alternative ways of constructing the past but also lays out some aspects of the role of exegesis in bridging the gap between the past and the present. In the article, he is particularly concerned with describing the various ways in which the exile is referred to in early Jewish literature. Overall he sees many common issues in the various early Jewish writings that he discusses: a shared view that Israel remained in a state of exile long after the sixth century and that the exile would be brought to an end only when God intervened in this world order to establish divine rule. But it is varieties of exegesis that particularly draws his attention. Daniel and 1 Enoch variously interpret and reuse the prophecies of Jeremiah, especially the seventy-year prophecy, in order to provide an overall periodized chronicle within which the authors stand at pivotal moments. The Assumption of Moses takes the exegesis of Jeremiah in Daniel yet a stage further, and the alternative traditional periodization of history, also represented in Daniel, of four world empires, is picked up and reworked in Enochic writings as well as in 4 Ezra and 2 Baruch. In many and various ways the prophets of old are interpreted; the interpretation obviously forms the basis of developing tradition.

Another example of exegesis at work is plain to see in the prayer in 2 Esd 6:38b–59. This is a reworking of the story of creation in order to state a problem of concern to the author, namely, that "if the world was created for Israel's sake, why is she ruled over by other nations and unable to enter into possession of the world (verses 55–9)?"[20] The creation story is not retold verbatim but adjusted in minor but significant ways. Some of the adjustments allow the modern reader to see that the author has introduced ideas that reflect some aspects of contemporary Jewish cosmology and its active spirits (2 Esd 6:41; cf. 1 En. 60:15–21). Other additions, such as the notion that the sea occupies one seventh of the world and the land six-sevenths are otherwise unknown, though seven is a common and significant number in other respects (see 1 En. 77:4–8).[21]

3.1.3. MAKING SENSE OF EXPERIENCE

Something of the significance of the role of translation and exegesis has already been indicated. Both activities, which may not in the end be entirely distinguishable from each other, are undertaken because translators and interpreters recognize the significance for themselves of the texts of another group and another time. Such texts are taken seriously, understood authoritatively, and brought into

---

19. See n. 9 above.
20. Knibb, "Commentary on 2 Esdras," 156.
21. For commentary on this section of 2 Esdras, see Knibb, "Commentary on 2 Esdras," 156–57.

the present to assist contemporary hearers or readers to make sense of their own experiences. But the process from text to tradition is far from straightforward; all manner of convoluted intervening stages are to be recognized, not least many of those now to be associated with the phenomenon of rewriting and reworking texts of emerging authority. Who suggests which texts will be relevant for making sense of the present? How is the interpretative process to work? Who will assess or recognize it as suitable interpretation?

There are indeed many instances when it is difficult for modern readers to understand the process of the creation of the literature before them. One such example can be seen in 2 Esd 1:26. Part of Israel's rejection as depicted in the passage is phrased as follows: "when you pray to me, I will not listen. You have stained your hands with blood." Apparently this is based on Isa 1:15: "When you lift your hands outspread in prayer, I will hide my eyes from you. Though you offer countless prayers, I will not listen. There is blood on your hands." In this way, the rejection of Israel seems to be the fulfillment of prophecy. But it could also be the case that such a reference to blood may rather "have been occasioned by Jewish ill-treatment of Christians."[22] Which came first, knowledge of the prophetic text that is selected for its negative picture of the relationship between God and Israel, or the experience of persecution at the hands of some Jews for which a suitable piece of prophetic tradition was sought by way of explanation? We can never know, nor do we need to, since commonly it is the two matters that work hand in hand: tradition, and the language it provides, and experience are formatively interwoven at all times. Occasionally, however, it is clearer which takes priority in the process.

3.1.4. Pluralism of Tradition

An important aspect of understanding the role of tradition in the late Second Temple period has become increasingly apparent as the entire corpus of extant compositions among the Dead Sea Scrolls has been published. It is no longer possible to argue that tradition is passed from one generation to another along single trajectories. Intelligent readings of the evidence from before the fall of the temple in 70 c.e. and even thereafter demand that the pluralities of early Jewish tradition be taken seriously. No longer is it possible, even if it ever was, to read back interpretative norms in a direct way from one age into another.

That the past, or traditions from the past, has more than one meaning is clear to see; there are as many pasts as there are observers in the present. We have already described and commented briefly on the range of views concerning the continuation of the exile in the Second Temple period. Another, but much smaller example of such diverse readings of the past can be seen in 2 Esd 5:7, in which a prophecy of fish in the Dead Sea is understood as a reversal of the natural order and as such an ominous portent of something destructive. The prophecy

---

22. Ibid., 84.

on which the idea may well be based, Ezek 47:7–10, portrays fish in the Dead Sea as one of the blessings of the new era[23] and such could also be envisaged in other more or less contemporary Jewish texts.[24] What is it to be, a blessing or a curse? Does it just depend on whether one likes fish?

3.1.5. THE PROCESS OF ACCRETION

For 1 Enoch it is clear that the earlier Enoch traditions develop and are elaborated through a process of formative accretion:

> the book of Watchers is, with the exception of the book of Astronomy, the oldest part of 1 Enoch and the basis upon which the other sections have been built; there are allusions to it and echoes of it in the Parables, the book of Dreams and the Epistle. It is not all of one piece, but acquired its present form by a process of accretion.[25]

Or, even within the book of Watchers,

> it would appear that chapters 12–16 stem from the author of the book of watchers himself; they serve as an elaboration of the material in chapters 6–11, which was probably taken over from the book of Noah. Much of what is said in the earlier chapters is repeated, but one significant new point is made: the continuing existence of evil in the world is attributed to the activities of the spirits which are held to have come from the giants (cp. 15:8–12).[26]

The same can be said of much of the literature that is found in the authoritative collections of Law, Prophets, and Writings, but also in many instances in the early Jewish literature of the Second Temple period.

A fine example of such a process of accretion is the growth of 2 Esdras. In his commentary on the work, Knibb offers a succinct summary of the process whereby the three constituent parts of this composite work have been put together: "2 Esdras 15–16 seems to have been written from the outset as an appendix to chs. 3–14 which was intended to make the earlier work relevant to a new situation, chs. 1–2 initially had an independent existence."[27] The different character of 2 Esd 1–2 is based on the presentation of Ezra as a prophetic inaugurator of a particular reading of the tradition with the thesis that Israel has

---

23. Ibid., 133.

24. See the references in G. J. Brooke, "4Q252 and the 153 Fish of John 21:11," in *Antikes Judentum und Frühes Christentum: Festschrift für Hartmut Stegemann zum 65. Geburtstag* (ed. B. Kollmann, W. Reinbold, and A. Steudel; BZNW 97; Berlin: de Gruyter, 1999), 253–65; reprinted in G. J. Brooke, *The Dead Sea Scrolls and the New Testament: Essays in Mutual Illumination* (London: SPCK; Minneapolis: Fortress, 2005), 282–97.

25. Knibb, "Ethiopic Book of Enoch," 29.

26. Ibid., 39.

27. Knibb, "Commentary on 2 Esdras," 76.

been rejected (2 Esd 1:1–2:9) and the church with her glorious future has taken Israel's place (2 Esd 2:10–48); the author of the two chapters draws "very heavily on the Old and New Testaments for the language and content of his work which in places has the appearance of being a mosaic of biblical quotations."[28]

3.2. IDENTITY

The traditions in which authors stand and to which they appeal betray something of their identity and social location.[29] Indeed, in the absence of passports and other documentation, it is through the correct reading of their traditions that authors may be most suitably identified. A simple but persuasive example makes the case. The character of the passage in 2 Esd 1:28–32 in which God expresses his concern for Israel emphasizes that Israel's rejection was very far from being God's original intention. The character of the passage is a strong indication that "the author was a Jewish, rather than a gentile, Christian."[30]

Much more complicated has been the scholarly discussion of the last thirty years concerning the identification of the traditors of the early Jewish apocalypses. Much ink has been spilled on this matter, but Knibb has attempted to shed some light on the complex issues involved. In his contribution to the Ackroyd Festschrift, a volume that he also co-edited, he considers the topic of prophecy and the emergence of the Jewish apocalypses. He discusses what might be known about those who developed the biblical traditions in the ways that are represented in the eschatologies and cosmologies of the apocalypses. In evaluating the place of wisdom as the source and context for the writing of the apocalypses over against those who were the heirs of the prophetic traditions, he characteristically and astutely describes the apocalypses as "a kind of interpretative literature," which is a significant feature of their character as learned writings. "The Jewish apocalypses," he concludes, "are properly to be regarded as a continuation of Old Testament prophecy, but they belong very firmly within a learned tradition."[31] This might seem very tentative, but discovering the identity of traditors from the traditions they pass on and develop is no easy matter; Knibb has been the master of resisting grand reconstructions that might fall once one fine detail of a text has been understood aright or which depend on extensive arguments from

---

28. Ibid., 77–78. Many of the likely Old Testament sources (from the Law, Prophets, and Psalms) are noted briefly by Knibb on p. 80.

29. Though it is also very easy to overinterpret matters; see, e.g., Knibb's criticism of George W. E. Nickelsburg's view, based on certain key geographical signals, that 1 En. 6–16 was composed in Galilee: M. A. Knibb, "Interpreting the Book of Enoch: Reflections on a Recently Published Commentary," *JSJ* 33 (2002): 450.

30. Knibb, "Commentary on 2 Esdras," 85.

31. M. A. Knibb, "Prophecy and the Emergence of the Jewish Apocalypses," in *Israel's Prophetic Tradition: Essays in Honour of Peter R. Ackroyd* (ed. R. Coggins, A. Phillips, and M.A. Knibb; Cambridge: Cambridge University Press, 1982), 169.

silence. For Daniel he has been able to argue that, while the vision reports in chs. 7 and 8 clearly show continuity with a literary genre familiar in prophetic literature, in fact it is plain that "there is overwhelming evidence which suggests that the Book of Daniel is rooted firmly in the traditions of wisdom."[32] Daniel is a book embedded in the mantological exegesis of oracles. Such a conclusion can be supported, furthermore, by consideration of other compositions: "the texts preserved in 4Q243–44, 4Q245, and 4Q246 all appear to represent a continuation of the tradition according to which Daniel was a mantic attached to the royal court, the mediator of divine revelations, just as he is in Dan 2, 4, and 5, and all probably are dependent on the biblical book."[33]

If the discussion of the identity of those who wrote and developed the traditions present in the early Jewish apocalypses is ongoing, so also is the debate about the origins of the Qumran community and more widely of the Essenes from which they came. In reaction against and in interaction with the proposals of Jerome Murphy-O'Connor in several articles, Knibb has investigated the parameters of the traditions to be found in the sectarian texts and found that claims for a Babylonian origin for the movement are unfounded. Whether it is in considering the motif of exile and the movement's self-understanding in their relation to its end,[34] or whether in terms of the role of the Book of Jubilees in the matter,[35] Knibb has repeatedly argued that the Essenes belong in Palestine. Through his handling of the traditions developed from such writings as parts of 1 Enoch, Daniel, Ben Sira, and especially Jubilees, he has concluded that "it seems entirely plausible to think of the Essenes—and the Qumran community— emerging in a Palestinian context from the movement that lies behind Jubilees."[36] Traditions create identity; identity reforms and renews tradition.

Another matter of identity that has taken Knibb's time concerns the Teacher of Righteousness. In discussing 1QH[a] 12:8b–9a ("They have banished me from my land like a bird from its nest") and 13:7b–8a ("You have placed me in a dwelling with many fishers who spread a net upon the face of the waters and with the hunters of the sons of iniquity"), Knibb declares that "the first passage quotes from Prov. 27.8, the second is built up from Jer. 16.16 and Isa. 19.8. In view of these considerations it is difficult to interpret the Qumran *Hymns* as referring to

32. M. A. Knibb, "'You are indeed wiser than Daniel': Reflections on the Character of the Book of Daniel," in *The Book of Daniel in the Light of New Findings* (ed. A. S. van der Woude; BETL 106; Leuven: Peeters, 1993), 403.

33. M. A. Knibb, "The Book of Daniel in Its Context," in *The Book of Daniel: Composition and Reception* (ed. John J. Collins and Peter W. Flint; 2 vols.; VTSup 83; Formation and Interpretation of Old Testament Literature 2; Leiden: Brill, 2001), 1:31.

34. M. A. Knibb, "Exile in the Damascus Document," *JSOT* 25 (1983): 99–117.

35. M. A. Knibb, "Jubilees and the Origins of the Qumran Community" (An Inaugural Lecture in the Department of Biblical Studies, King's College, London, 1989).

36. Knibb, "Exile in the Damascus Document," 114.

concrete experiences of a specific individual."[37] In this way, Knibb demonstrates that sometimes becoming aware of the scriptural traditions through which an individual is portrayed may obscure as much as reveal their identity.

3.3. INVENTING THE PAST

3.3.1. APOCALYPTIC

The invention of the past commonly belongs to innovators who claim authority for their utterances and understandings of the world in terms of the medium through which they have had access to the heavenly secrets. At its most extreme, this access to heaven reflects individual religious experience that cannot ultimately be verified. Most institutional religion is astutely suspicious of such experience and any claims based on it. Despite the continuing appearance of apocalyptic motifs in the sectarian scrolls from Qumran, it does not seem surprising to me that the sectarian compositions do not contain the description of any individualistic visions. The Qumran community was not an apocalyptic community, whatever that might mean, but a reforming one: nearly all the compositions in its library can be seen as developments of traditions found in one authoritative Scripture or another.[38] In the strict sense, the community and the movement of which it was a part, were traditional, as Knibb has pointed out most extensively in his book on the Qumran community.[39]

However, even apocalypses in their most explicit form as narrations of visions or auditions are caught out by the need to find a language in which their insights can be rendered meaningful. Most apocalypses depend on a standard set of literary tropes that have developed in various ways from prophetic and other traditions, as has been often observed, not least by Knibb himself.

3.3.2. EXPERIENCE

It is clear too that another cause of inventing a past may come from one's experiences in the present. The section of 1 Enoch known as the Book of Astronomy may well be the oldest part of 1 Enoch, in some form or other,[40] dating to the third century B.C.E. When considering the provenance of the Book of Astronomy, Knibb points out that the interest in astronomy reflects a concern over the calendar, and "underlying the material (as well as material in Jubilees and the

---

37. M. A. Knibb, "The Teacher of Righteousness–A Messianic Title?" in *A Tribute to Geza Vermes: Essays on Jewish and Christian Literature and History* (ed. P. R. Davies and R. T. White; JSOTSup 100; Sheffield: JSOT Press, 1990), 54.

38. As I have tried to argue explicitly in G. J. Brooke, "The Dead Sea Scrolls," in *The Biblical World* (ed. J. Barton; London: Routledge, 2002), 1.250–69.

39. Knibb, *Qumran Community*.

40. The differences between the calendrical information in the Aramaic forms of the Astronomical Book and that in the Ethiopic version are sometimes overlooked.

Qumran scrolls) is a dispute about the proper calendar to be followed."[41] Such a calendrical concern may well go back many years before the author of the Book of Astronomy set out his stall, but a significant motivating factor behind creating the Book and associating it with the knowledge with which Enoch was privileged according to tradition arises from a present uncertainty that required the author to take a point of view on the matter. Whatever the influences on the author may have been, part of the need for laying out the way it should be seen in relation to the practice of one calendar rather than another may well have been the very ambiguity of the tradition concerning the matter. Appeal to Enoch with regard to the solar calendar could at least take advantage of his age: 365 years.

3.3.3. Looking to the Future: Projection and Retrojection
Careful study of the literary compositions of early Judaism shows that in several instances traditions are projected into the future and then retrojected to the present in order, through expressions of hope and fear, to encourage a particular worldview in the here and now.

In a number of studies, Knibb has examined the messianism of the Second Temple period. One example of his cautious handling of text and tradition concerns his sensitivity toward the Ethiopic phraseology involved in the presentation of the Son of Man in 1 Enoch. Based in part on his analysis of the use of the demonstrative in Ethiopic Ezekiel, he concludes that the presence or absence of the demonstrative with reference to the angelic scribe (Ezek 9:2) "seems to have been entirely an arbitrary matter."[42] Therefore, in relation to the Son of Man in 1 Enoch nothing should be made of the presence or absence of the demonstrative as some scholars have proposed.[43]

More overtly in relation to the sectarian scrolls from Qumran, Knibb has proposed that any discussion of messianism should begin with the reference in 1QS 9:11 to "the coming of a prophet and the messiahs of Aaron and Israel" and the list of proof-texts in 4QTestimonia. His initial discussion of the importance of these texts in combination stresses that they reflect what has become known as a typical Qumran expectation of two messiahs, one a priest and the other a royal figure. For such an expectation Knibb has noted that "the roots of this belief in exilic and post-exilic texts are well known."[44] Knibb thus acknowledges that Qumran messianic belief is an expression for the future based on the developments of traditions from the past. He goes on to argue this in the particular case of the most suitable understanding of the figure of the Interpreter of the Law in

---

41. Knibb, "Ethiopic Book of Enoch," 28.

42. Knibb, *Translating the Bible*, 73.

43. Cf. M. A. Knibb, "Messianism in the Pseudepigrapha in the Light of the Scrolls," *DSD* 2 (1995): 179.

44. M. A. Knibb, "Eschatology and Messianism in the Dead Sea Scrolls," in *The Dead Sea Scrolls after Fifty Years: A Comprehensive Assessment* (ed. Peter W. Flint and James C. VanderKam; 2 vols.; Leiden: Brill, 1999), 2:385.

the Damascus Document. Since the Interpreter of the Law is a figure constructed from past tradition, it can be asked whether this figure is a priest or a prophet. By evaluating the various kinds of scriptural traditions that might be seen as having influenced the precise functions of the Interpreter of the Law, Knibb concludes—suitably to my mind[45]—that a background in Deut 33:8–11 and the attributes of Levi support viewing the eschatological interpreter as a priest. This view is well supported by other sectarian compositions at Qumran.

But there is more to Knibb's description of messianism at Qumran that is worth mentioning. He outlines the views of Hartmut Stegemann concerning the existence of three stages in the development of messianic beliefs among the community, part of which eventually came to occupy Qumran. For Stegemann, to begin with there was a collective view, as in Daniel; then an expression of a royal messianism (1QSa, 1QSb) developed in reaction against the priestly pretensions of Jonathan Maccabee; then followed a third stage, in which the expectations of a prophet and a priest were developed. For Stegemann, all comes about through the Essenes reflecting on certain deficits in their contemporary understandings of their experiences: the rejection of Jonathan's pretensions creates royal messianism, and the death of the Teacher produces yet further developments. Knibb's succinct comment on the view of Stegemann sums up neatly several aspects of what I have tried to present in this essay on the formation and renewal of scriptural tradition: "It is difficult to know," he states,

> how to balance the relative influence of tradition, as represented by the texts in the Hebrew Bible that were interpreted in a messianic sense, against the direct impact of events in the formation of messianic beliefs. But the messianic interpretation which is apparently given to Gen 49:10 and Num 24:17 in the Septuagint shows that these ideas were already traditional by the second century BCE, and at least to this extent Stegemann's emphasis on the creative role of the Essenes in the formation of messianic beliefs seems questionable.[46]

Just so. In addition, one may note that it is not just a question of modern readers trying to discern whether the development of tradition depends more on interpretative antecedents or more on actual life experiences; it is also worth noting that, however the tradition is being developed, in part its significance for making sense of the present derives from projecting matters into the future that, when suitably expressed, in some way bring illumination to the present in light of the past: projection and retrojection is what seems to take place in the development and expression of eschatological traditions.

A further example of this is presented by Knibb in his study of the Book

---

45. This agrees with what I have concluded: see G. J. Brooke, *Exegesis at Qumran: 4QFlorilegium in its Jewish Context* (JSOTSup 29; Sheffield: JSOT Press, 1985; repr., Atlanta: Society of Biblical Literature, 2006), 202–5.

46. Knibb, "Eschatology and Messianism in the Dead Sea Scrolls," 392.

of Enoch in the light of the Qumran wisdom literature. Knibb argues that the problematic phrase *raz nihyeh* "includes knowledge of past, present, and future (4Q418 123 i–ii 3–4), understanding of the present order of the world ('the ways of truth … all the roots of iniquity'; 4Q416 2 iii 14), and knowledge concerning the future judgement (4Q217 2 i 10c–11)."[47] Knibb notes that this speculation concerning wisdom has its background in texts like Prov 8:22–31 and Job 28. With regard to the Book of Remembrance of 4Q417 1 i 14–18, Knibb comments that "the reference to the 'vision of meditation' perhaps suggests that revelation is linked to the understanding of scripture."[48] Thus past, present, and future are brought together to illuminate the present in particular; all is based on scriptural tradition projected into the future and then retrojected into the present. Altogether Knibb notes that it is characteristic of the description of the divine descent for judgment referred to in 1 En. 17–19,[49]

> as of that in chapters 20–36, that it draws extensively on the Hebrew Bible for its content—not by way of direct quotation, but by incorporating and reworking material from relevant passages into the narrative. The way in which the narrative, from one point of view, represents the outcome of reflection upon, and interpretation of, scripture gives the narrative something of a learned character.[50]

3.3.4. The Demise of Tradition

This essay has focused on some of the ingredients that create and renew tradition over many generations, but consideration of the nature of such an amorphous phenomenon as scriptural tradition would not be complete without reflecting briefly on the demise of tradition.

Since the discovery of their absence among the Qumran finds, the Parables of Enoch (1 En. 37–71) have exercised not a few creative minds. As is well known, the Son of Man traditions are present in the Enoch materials exclusively in the Parables section. Of particular concern has been the dating of this section, not least because of the interest of many scholars in ascertaining whether the Enochic Son of Man traditions in any form have influenced either Jesus himself, in the way he chose to talk about himself, or those who talked and wrote about

---

47. M. A. Knibb, "The Book of Enoch in the Light of the Qumran Wisdom Literature," in *Wisdom and Apocalypticism in the Dead Sea Scrolls and in the Biblical Tradition* (ed. F. García Martínez; BETL 168; Leuven: Peeters, 2003), 202.

48. Ibid., 203.

49. Knibb has developed his ideas on the use of Scripture in 1 En. 17–19 in "The Use of Scripture in 1 Enoch 17–19," in *Jerusalem, Alexandria, Rome: Studies in Ancient Cultural Interaction in Honour of A. Hilhorst* (ed. F. García Martínez and G. P. Luttikhuizen; JSJSup 82; Leiden: Brill, 2003), 165–78. A somewhat different and less nuanced view of the use of Scripture in 1 En. 17–19 is taken by K. C. Bautch, *A Study of Geography of I Enoch 17–19: 'No One Has Seen What I Have Seen'* (JSJSup 81; Leiden: Brill, 2003).

50. Knibb, "Book of Enoch in the Light of the Qumran Wisdom Literature," 209.

him. When Józef T. Milik published his landmark preliminary edition of many of the Qumran Enoch fragments[51] with the proposal that the Parables section was likely to belong to the third century C.E. and to have been added to the corpus of 1 Enoch even later, there were several critical reactions. Among the most detailed was a critical review by Knibb, first delivered in draft at King's College in May 1978 and subsequently at the SNTS Pseudepigrapha Seminar in Paris the same year.[52]

Milik's proposals depend on a number of details that, when scrutinized closely, do not seem to be very strong arguments. His use of the early-third-century Sibylline literature as a source for some parts of the Parables, notably 1 En. 61:1 (Sib. Or. 2:233–37) and 1 En 56:5–7 (Sib. Or. 5:104–10) are not detailed enough to demonstrate securely dependence of the Parables on the Sibyllines. His similar insistence that 1 En. 51:1–3 depends on 2 Esd 7:32–33 and Pseudo-Philo's *Book of Biblical Antiquities* (L.A.B.) is more assertion than fact, since the dependence could well be the other way.

Two factors are used by Knibb to indicate a possible way forward. While acknowledging that the lack of the Parables among the Qumran Enoch fragments makes it unlikely that they were written and transmitted within broad Essene circles before the destruction of Qumran in 68 C.E., he uses our knowledge of the traditions in the *Parables* in two subtle ways that are exemplary for the mature handling of complex evidence such as is found in what survives of this literature. The most significant is his concern to argue that, where it is difficult or even impossible to show the literary dependence of one form of a tradition upon another, the first step should be to let the traditions stand in juxtaposition side by side. The similarities and differences between 1 En. 51:1–3, 2 Esd 7:32–33 and the L.A.B. 3:10, should encourage the reader to suppose their contemporaneity, rather than provoking insecure constructions of tradition history.

But a second factor supports the permission that Knibb gives for us to take these traditions together. Milik has argued for the late date of the Parables on the grounds of the absence of any interest in the Son of Man in Christian writers of the first to fourth centuries. Knibb turns the argument on its head and notes that interest in Son of Man Christology died out with the composition of the Gospels, so it is hardly surprising that there should be no quotations in early Christian literature from the Son of Man sections of the Enoch corpus, when there is so little concern for the title Son of Man in any case. The tradition that Jesus picks up from mixing the book of Daniel with common parlance and which is developed in sundry ways by the Gospel writers and their sources, comes to a noticeable end. This is not the place to attempt an explanation for the demise of a tradition,

---

51. J. T. Milik (with the collaboration of M. Black), *The Books of Enoch: Aramiac Fragments of Qumrân Cave 4* (Oxford: Clarendon, 1976); for a review, see E. Ullendorff and M. A. Knibb, *BSOAS* 40 (1977): 601–2.

52. M. A. Knibb, "The Date of the Parables of Enoch: A Critical Review," *NTS* 25 (1979): 345–59.

but to highlight the creative way in which the end of a tradition can be as significant as its formation and transmission.

3.3.5. What We Do Not Know

In several places in his writings Knibb confesses correctly that modern readers must remain in ignorance regarding certain matters. For example, in considering what traditions, scriptural and otherwise, might lie behind Jub. 4:16–25, he declares after detailed investigation that

> it is difficult to find unambiguous references in *Jubilees* to either the *Apocalypse of Weeks* or the *Epistle of Enoch*. It is in fact likely that both the *Apocalypse of Weeks* and the *Epistle* as a whole were in existence by the time *Jubilees* was composed, but that can neither be proved nor disproved from *Jubilees*.[53]

The close analysis of similar materials often reveals as many differences as similarities, so that the presentation of tradition is rarely a simple matter of one ancient text citing another. In most cases it is better to err on the side of caution and to be aware that there was more going on in antiquity than we will ever know. The transmission and development of tradition are a partial and problematic affair.

Another example of Knibb's reluctance to follow the crowd of scholarly opinion in oversimplifying lines of tradition can be seen in his treatment of the famous parable in 2 Esd 4:12–18, in which the trees plan to attack the sea and the waves plan to attack the forest. Neither plan comes to anything, and the point of the parable is that Ezra recognizes that everything is assigned to its proper place and that the place of humans is to understand earthly things and not the things of heaven. In commenting on the passage, Knibb observes suitably that "the imagery of the story reminds us in some ways of Jotham's fable (Judg 9:7–21), and the author of 2 Esd 3–14 may perhaps have drawn his inspiration from there. But it is also possible that the author has taken over from another source a fable that was already in existence."[54]

4. Conclusion

In this brief review we have noticed several intriguing phenomena. In writing this short essay in honor of Michael Knibb, I have convinced myself that the study of tradition is an all-encompassing task. His many fine studies on the literature of the Second Temple period have a coherence in them that is a mark not only of Michael's own scholarly integrity but also of the patterns of interwoven

---

53. M. A. Knibb, "Which Parts of *1 Enoch* Were Known to *Jubilees*? A Note on the Interpretation of *Jubilees* 4.16–25," in *Reading from Right to Left: Essays on the Hebrew Bible in Honour of David J.A. Clines* (ed. J. C. Exum and H. G. M. Williamson; JSOTSup 373; London: Sheffield Academic Press, 2003), 261.

54. Knibb, "Commentary on 2 Esdras," 123.

traditions and identities that are indeed discernible in these diverse compositions. Michael's part in illuminating what makes up the study of tradition in early Jewish literature and in demonstrating how such study should be done is a major contribution not only to the wider ambit of biblical studies but also to the humanities in general, because many disciplines face very similar issues.

To what tradition does Michael Knibb belong? To that tradition of precise scholarship which through its careful and helpful reading of the evidence displays a keen ability in letting texts and traditions speak for themselves.

THREE

Justifying Deviance: The Place of Scripture in Converting to the Qumran Self-Understanding

1. Introduction

Few nowadays would deny that the members of the Qumran community, and also probably of the wider movement of which that community was a part, were a minority in late Second Temple Judaism, even among the educated elites in Palestine. A case can be made that the Essenes were a well-recognized and widespread part of Judean society,[1] but it is unlikely that they should be seen as the main Jewish party of the time.[2] In short, the minority status of the Qumran group suggests that those who became members could well have been considered by others, or could have considered themselves, as deviating from normative Jewish behavior in certain ways. In part, I attempt in this essay to discover how those joining the Qumran group, or the Essene movement from which it had emerged, justified their behavior to themselves and to others.[3]

In addition to this concern with how new members justified their deviation from normative Jewish behavior, I present an additional thesis: that it is appropriate to describe the move made by those joining the Qumran community, or

---

1. See especially the writings of B. J. Capper, "The Palestinian Cultural Context of the Earliest Christian Community of Goods," in *The Book of Acts in Its Palestinian Setting* (ed. R. J. Bauckham; The Book of Acts in its First Century Setting 4; Grand Rapids, Mich.: Eerdmans, 1995), 323–56.

2. As H. Stegemann has argued, "The Qumran Essenes: Local Members of the Main Jewish Union in Late Second Temple Times," in *The Madrid Qumran Congress: Proceedings of the International Congress on the Dead Sea Scrolls, Madrid 18–21 March, 1991* (ed. J. Trebolle Barrera and L. Vegas Montaner; STDJ 11; Leiden: Brill, 1992), 83–166. His view depends on some considerable amount of special pleading and the identification of the "scribes" of the New Testament as Essenes.

3. Of course, people in any age seldom describe themselves as deviant; as has been pointed out, for example, by E. Goode, deviance neutralization by the deviant involves "the reflexivity of the self, the integrity of identity, and the need for a positive self-image" (see Goode, *Deviant Behavior: An Interactionist Approach* [Englewood Cliffs, N.J.: Prentice-Hall, 1978], 71).

Essenism in general, as one of conversion. This can be demonstrated from the fact that in the movement's own terms the root שוב plays a significant technical role: "The Priests are the converts of Israel who departed from the land of Judah, and (the Levites are) those who joined them" (CD 4:2–3).[4] The term also occurs in a less technical usage: "And this is the Rule for the men of the Community who have freely pledged themselves to be converted (*lšwb*) from all evil and to cling to all His commandments according to His will" (1QS 5:1).[5] And each member who approaches the Council of the Community is described as entering "the Covenant of God in the presence of all who have freely pledged themselves. He shall undertake by a binding oath to return (*lšwb*) with all his heart and soul to every commandment of the Law of Moses in accordance with all that has been revealed of it to the sons of Zadok" (1QS 5:8–9).[6]

The dominant motif of turning, of conversion, in those sectarian compositions that speak of new members, and even of the ongoing practices of existing members, can be taken as a signal that modern discussions of conversion may be applied to those joining the Qumran community in ways that might illuminate the processes of becoming a member. In particular, the general understanding of conversion put forward by Lewis Rambo in his landmark empathetic study, *Understanding Religious Conversion*,[7] seems to be relevant:

> Through conversion an individual may gain some sense of ultimate worth, and may participate in a community of faith that connects him or her to both a rich past and an ordered and exciting present which generates a vision of the future that mobilizes energy and inspires confidence. Affiliating with a group and subscribing to a philosophy may offer nurture, guidance, a focus for loyalty, and a framework for action. Involvement in mythic, ritual, and symbolic systems gives life order and meaning. Sharing those systems with like-minded people makes it possible to connect with other human beings on deeper intellectual and emotional levels.[8]

In his overarching description of the processes of conversion, Rambo acknowledges the insights of other analysts, notably John Lofland and Rodney Stark.[9] Lofland and Stark's work is based on the analysis of some of those who

---

4. G. Vermes, *The Complete Dead Sea Scrolls in English* (London: Penguin, 1998), 130; interpreting Ezek 44:15.

5. Ibid., 103.

6. Ibid., 104.

7. L. R. Rambo, *Understanding Religious Conversion* (New Haven: Yale University Press, 1993).

8. Ibid., 2.

9. Especially J. Lofland and R. Stark, "Becoming a World-Saver: A Theory of Conversion to a Deviant Perspective," *American Sociological Review* 30 (1965): 862–75; I am grateful to my colleague F. G. Downing, Honorary Research Fellow in the Centre for Biblical Studies at

converted to a small millenarian religious cult. This makes their insights all the more pertinent to some of the features of the sectarian compositions found at Qumran, which housed what some observers might well describe as a small millenarian religious cult. I shall use some aspects of the seven-stage framework of conversion proposed by Lofland and Stark to suggest that conversion theory may help us better understand how the Qumran community, and especially its new members, read the present. At several points Lofland and Stark's insights will, however, be modified by reference to Rambo's more nuanced and open-ended descriptions. In fact, Rambo's empathetic stance may be especially suited to the description of things concerning Qumran because he engages with his topic on the basis of his own personal experience in the Church of Christ, which he readily labels as a religious sect. "I found," he states, "that the Church of Christ stressed knowledge of the Bible and obedience to God's will: 'correct' knowledge and 'right' behavior were essential."[10] He goes on to observe that emotional issues were regarded as secondary or irrelevant alongside knowledge and action; he subsequently came to recognize that such knowledge and action are motivated by fear, self-loathing, and insecurity—emotional issues if ever there were any.

However, the straightforward application of theories of conversion is not the concern of this collection of essays. Rather, it is my task, in using such modern theories, to ask questions about the place of Scripture at each stage in the conversion process. I will look at how at each stage in that process converts may have justified their behavior or had it justified for them through appeal to Scripture. In what follows I suggest that various features of the use of the Jewish Scriptures in the sectarian compositions found at Qumran are illuminated when juxtaposed with some aspects of modern theories constructed for the better understanding of conversion, not least as those theories are suggestive of the move that is being made from the more normative to the less normative or deviant form of behavior.[11]

---

the University of Manchester, for indicating the value of Lofland and Stark's work and making other valuable bibliographical suggestions.

10. Rambo, *Understanding Religious Conversion*, xiii.

11. Sociological theories concerning deviance itself are not as helpful as conversion theory, largely because most deviance theory has been concerned with the causal explanation of crime, delinquency, and mental illness, and with discovering means for correcting deviant behavior; see the theoretical discussion of this by D. Matza, *Becoming Deviant* (Englewood Cliffs, N.J.: Prentice-Hall, 1969). Though attempting to describe the opponents of the author of the Pastoral Epistles, rather than the processes of conversion to a deviant form of religious behavior, L. K. Pietersen has suitably catalogued the various theoretical perspectives in the sociology of deviance and attempted to apply them to the reading of ancient texts: see L. K. Pietersen, "Teaching, Tradition and Thaumaturgy: A Sociological Examination of the Polemic of the Pastorals" (Ph.D. diss., University of Sheffield, 2000), 52–63.

2. The Seven Stages of Conversion

Lofland and Stark outline what they describe as seven necessary and sufficient factors for conversion. Converts must (1) experience enduring, acutely felt tensions (2) within a religious problem-solving perspective (3) which leads them to define themselves as religious seekers, (4) encountering the new group at a turning point in their lives, (5) wherein an affective bond is formed with one or more converts (6) where extracult attachments are absent or neutralized (7) and where, if they are to become deployable agents, they are exposed to intensive interaction. Let us consider each of these in turn.

2.1. Tension

At the outset Lofland and Stark observed that a potential convert must experience enduring, acutely felt tensions.[12] It is impossible to gauge what might best describe the tensions that could have characterized the circumstances of the average convert to Essenism or its Qumran form. Nevertheless, it may be assumed that there was a felt discrepancy between some imaginary, ideal state of affairs and the circumstances in which potential community members saw themselves as caught up. At least for some converts, as Lofland and Stark observed for the converts to the cult at the center of their investigation, there might be "a frustrated desire for a significant, even heroic, religious status, to 'know the word of God intimately,' and to be a famous agent for his divine purposes."[13] Lofland and Stark describe several kinds of preconversion tension experiences: notable among them were hallucinations of various kinds or speaking in tongues, trances, and so on—all factors that reinforced the experience of frustrated aspiration somewhat acutely, over long periods of time.

---

12. "Just as tension can have myriad consequences, its sources can also be exceedingly disparate. Some concrete varieties we discovered were: longing for unrealized wealth, fame, and prestige; hallucinatory activity for which the person lacked any successful definition; frustrated sexual and marital relations; homosexual guilt; acute fear of face-to-face interaction; disabling and disfiguring physical conditions; and—perhaps of a slightly different order—a frustrated desire for a significant, even heroic, religious status, to 'know the mind of God intimately,' and to be a famous agent for his divine purposes" (Lofland and Stark, "Becoming a World-Saver," 864–65). To what extent any of these bases of tension may have lain behind the motivation for individuals to begin their conversion process to the Qumran community will remain a secret, though presumably anyone with any kind of acute physical disfigurement would not have been able to proceed very far before finding themselves unwelcome. It is intriguing to note that two of the three nets of Belial described in CD cover wealth and sexual matters, items that feature significantly in Lofland and Stark's list here and that may have required explicit comment by the community's authorities not least because of the motivating experiences of new converts.

13. Lofland and Stark, "Becoming a World-Saver," 864–65.

Rambo is concerned to suggest that the context for the kinds of tension or crisis which Lofland and Stark describe as at the outset of the processes of conversion is extremely diverse and dynamic.[14] It seems to me that three features relating to the place of Scripture resonate with this stage of conversion. To begin with, it is commonly suggested that those particularly likely to engage on the journey to conversion will be experiencing some form of alienation and confusion. Such forms of tension are to be all the more readily experienced in settings characterized by pluralism of any sort. Perhaps the kinds of pluralism represented by the fragmentation of Judean society after the Maccabean revolt facilitated the moves to conversion that were needed to have new members sign up to a movement such as the one at Qumran. Intriguingly, the pluralism of the age is visible also in the variety of scriptural text-types attested at Qumran. Such variety is not the result of sectarian readings of the tradition,[15] like that found amoung Samaritan Jews, but is a reflection of what is available to elites more broadly.

But, second, while such pluralism in scriptural text-types might be a contributing factor to the kinds of pluralist experiences that create confusion and alienation and promote conversion to deviant groups, it is also the case that we know of such textual pluralism from within the movement to which converts were moving. Rambo observes that congruence is an important determinant of whether conversion will occur. In other words, it is possible to have one's cake and eat it too in this instance, because the same textual pluralism that is a feature of the confusion that motivates converts can also be found within the movement in a reassuring way. Rambo defines such congruence grandly: "elements of a new religion mesh with existing macro- and microcontextual factors."[16] This is not to insist that the Qumran community deliberately preserved diversity of text-types to encourage or facilitate the conversion process of new members, but it does not seem to have engaged in very careful restrictive practices.

A third feature of this initial stage of conversion to a deviant perspective becomes apparent through Peter Berger's analysis of the contemporary religious scene in *The Heretical Imperative*.[17] According to Rambo, Berger asserts that three religious options are available: deductive, reductive, and inductive.

---

14. Rambo, *Understanding Religious Conversion*, 44–55.

15. See G. J. Brooke, "*E pluribus unum*: Textual Variety and Definitive Interpretation in the Qumran Scrolls," in *The Dead Sea Scrolls in Their Historical Context* (ed. T. H. Lim et al.; Edinburgh: T&T Clark, 2000), 107–19, esp. 116–17; E. Ulrich, "The Absence of 'Sectarian Variants' in the Jewish Scriptural Scrolls Found at Qumran," in *The Bible as Book: The Hebrew Bible and the Judaean Desert Discoveries* (ed. E. D. Herbert and E. Tov; London: British Library; New Castle, Del.: Oak Knoll; Grand Haven: Scriptorium Center for Christian Antiquities, 2002), 179–95.

16. Rambo, *Understanding Religious Conversion*, 37.

17. P. L. Berger, *The Heretical Imperative: Contemporary Possibilities of Religious Affirmation* (Garden City, N.Y.: Doubleday, 1979).

> Deductive religiosity is based on some authority, such as the Bible or a religious leader, that provides "legitimate" interpretation of life and God. Followers acknowledge the revelation derived from these authorities and follow their dictates explicitly. In the deductive orientation, conversion is regulated by norms that delineate specific requirements for change in belief, behavior, and feeling.[18]

Though an analysis of the modern situation, Berger's viewpoint suggests that those most likely to start on the conversion process to the Qumran community or its parent group would already be inclined toward respect for authority of some sort, and among such authorities sacred text can claim pride of place. More can be said about this in relation to other stages of the conversion process, but this perception endorses the view that the lack of political or religious institutional power in Essenism generally was more than compensated for by the more highly developed place given to the authority of the Scriptures compared to other forms of contemporary Judaism. It was, therefore, not the case that Scripture just happened to play a significant role in the life of the Qumran community; rather, it played a necessary role as conveyer of authority, especially once the founding figure was no longer available.

2.2. Type of Problem-Solving Perspective

Converts to deviant religious groups also need to perceive that the perspective within which they can best make sense of the tensions in their lives are neither psychiatric nor political or sociopolitical, but rather religious. In understanding conversion in late antiquity it is not sensible to distinguish in an overly sophisticated way between these perspectives, since it is far from certain whether Jews of late Second Temple times would categorize their worldview as concerning religious and nonreligious matters. However, the important matter for our present purposes is to realize that converts do not seem to desire to manipulate the self or reorganize their immediate social surroundings. According to Lofland and Stark, they want to see "both sources and solutions as emanating from an unseen and, in principle, unseeable realm";[19] there is a "general propensity to impose religious meaning on events."[20]

Rambo proposes that, although it is not uncommon for converts to be largely passive in the face of missionary zeal, in many instances converts are active agents at the stage of crisis in their conversion process. It is, of course, impossible to interview new converts to the Qumran community, or to read the transcripts of such interviews. Rambo's experience, however, which is endorsed by other analysts, is that many conversions are based on the kind of extraordinary

---

18. Rambo, *Understanding Religious Conversion*, 29–30; summarizing and applying Berger's insight that the most important aspect of modern western secularization is pluralism.

19. Lofland and Stark, "Becoming a World-Saver," 867.

20. Ibid., 868.

experience that might be called mystical.[21] As some justification for his own conclusions he appeals to the Acts of the Apostles and the case of Saul of Tarsus. But
other kinds of experience can also be equally significant—such as recovery from
an illness—which may be irrelevant in considering conversion to a group apparently interested in healing. However, we cannot know precisely what kinds of
experiences a convert to the Qumran movement might have had. All that we can
stress at this stage is that at the base of the experiences of the modern converts
examined is the way in which they are all interpreted as providing a religious
perspective on life. They provide a basis for meaning in the transcendent.

What emerges as striking out of the sectarian documents found at Qumran
is that the sense of identity within the group seems to be very largely derived
from particular readings of Scripture. The community has no clearly identifiable founding moment that is celebrated in some way, and the founding figure
remains hidden behind an epithet. In other words, the religious perspective provided for the prospective convert is based on interpretations of Scripture rather
than on political events, historical moments, or founding figures. So, for example, the exhortations at the opening of the Damascus Document are epitomes
of scriptural narratives interpreted so as to provide the hearer or reader with
negative and positive examples from the past. Or again, the opening lines of the
Rule of the Community in its Cave 1 form recall the summary instruction of
Deut 6:4–5. The Scriptures and their suitable interpretation take pride of place in
the construction and reconstruction of the world. This provides the authoritative
religious perspective that enables the convert to move from crisis to quest. The
convert can transition from the experience of tension toward creative and active
agency in the move from one situation or group to another.

2.3. Seekership

The preconverts whom Lofland and Stark investigated all found conventional
religious institutions inadequate as a source of solutions. Each became a seeker,
a person searching for some satisfactory system of religious meaning to interpret
and resolve his or her discontent. Among the converts investigated there was a
persistent refusal to accept dogma but an equally persistent search for the truth in
personal experience, even in the mystical or occult realms. Intriguingly, Lofland
and Stark even record an interview with one pair of preconverts who described
their interest in the Dead Sea Scrolls as part of their own search for meaning.[22]

---

21. It could be that the quasi-mystical description of some worship at Qumran, which
might be implied through what is summarized in the Songs of the Sabbath Sacrifice, is indicative of the kinds of experience a member of the community might have continued to have
which would have been very largely congruent with his preconversion experiences.

22. Part of the interview runs: "My wife and I became interested in the revelation of
Edgar Cayce and the idea of reincarnation which seemed to answer so much, we read search-
ingly about the Dead Sea Scrolls, we decided to pursue Rosicrucianism, we read books on the

All preconverts believed that spirits of some variety came from an active supernatural realm to intervene in the material world. The supernatural realm might be experienced in the weather, in political affairs and national disasters, or in individual lives.[23] Such spirit entities could, sometimes at least, break through from the beyond and impart information, cause experiences, or take a hand in the course of events.[24] Furthermore, there is a persistent teleology among preconverts, an understanding that each person has a purpose within the overall purposes for which everything was created.

Rambo has underlined the importance of the quest: it is an ongoing process, but one that will greatly intensify during times of crisis. Rambo assumes that converts are commonly active agents in their own conversion. What might lead one to conclude that converts to the Qumran community were actively engaged in their own quests for meaning? One possible clue rests in the fact that, whereas most of the manuscripts containing sectarian compositions are penned in an orthography that has become identified as belonging to the Qumran scribal school, most of the manuscripts that contain copies of scriptural books are not penned in that way. This suggests that such manuscripts were brought to Qumran from elsewhere. Some of these copies of the Scriptures may have been brought by those joining the community. If that was the case, then it seems that at least some of those joining were already predisposed to constructing their outlook on the world on the basis of Scripture. That this may have been quantitatively and qualitatively different from many other Jews may be indicated by comparing Qumran ideology and use of Scripture with that of the Wisdom of Ben Sira. Ben Sira makes little explicit use of Scripture in his extensive writing and even comes to rely on non-Jewish sources for some of his instruction. Such is not the case at Qumran.

Three other matters involving Scripture may well be important at this stage in the move to deviancy through joining Essenism more generally, or the Qumran group in particular. Both these matters might also have had a role at other stages, but from a different perspective. In the first place, it is noteworthy that it is only Scripture as interpreted that offers a suitable religious construction of the world, but the really significant matter is that the interpretation is not plain to everyone but is divinely inspired. The skilled interpreter has to reveal the significance of the law. Some matters are indeed available to all, inasmuch as the text of the law is revealed (נגלה) but the interpretation exegetically discloses what is

---

secret disclosures to be gained from Yogi-type meditation" (Lofland and Stark, "Becoming a World-Saver," 868).

23. The presence at Qumran of compositions like 4QZodiology and Brontology ar (4Q318) may suggest that the outlook of some or many at Qumran was consonant with such a perspective that might have lain behind their conversion.

24. Lofland and Stark, "Becoming a World-Saver," 869.

hidden (נסתר). In relation to both the Damascus Document (CD 3:12–16) and the Rule of the Community (1QS 5:7–12; 8:15–16; 9:13–14, 18–20) the comments of Lawrence H. Schiffman are worth repeating in this context:

> The *nigleh*, then, is nothing more than Scripture, while the *nistar* is sectarian interpretation of it.… *nistar* is derived only through divinely inspired biblical exegesis. It would appear that, like the Sadducees and the later Karaites, the Qumran sect relied exclusively on interpretation of the Bible for the derivation of its *halakhah*.[25]

The same case can be made with regard to the interpretation of the prophets. According to the Habakkuk Commentary, the Teacher of Righteousness was the one "to whom God made known all the mysteries of the words of His servants the Prophets" (1QpHab 7:4–5).[26]

Second, the tendency toward a predestinarian outlook in the preconvert as observed by Lofland and Stark seems to correspond to some features of the sectarian compositions at Qumran. The notions of election and predestined membership of the covenant people resonate with scriptural allusions (1QS 9:14; 1QpHab 5:4; 1QH[a] 15:13–19). Converts actively engaged in their own quests, and those who were eventually admitted to the community would have understood themselves to be divinely preselected. Nevertheless, daily life within the new group would no doubt have been marked by all kinds of regular decision-making processes, which might indicate that God's hand did not control every action.[27]

Third, the standard ingredient in the convert's quest of recognizing that conventional religious institutions are inadequate as a source of solutions suggests that alternative sources of authority are commonly in the convert's outlook. Together with sensing the divine origin of the interpretations and perceiving themselves predestined in some way for their new lives, converts could well have acknowledged implicitly or explicitly that the texts of Scripture themselves were an increasingly significant authoritative institution. This authority could replace the temple or other political structures and the allegiances such institutions required. It is perhaps, then, no accident that the moves toward the institutionalization of Scripture are now best attested in this sectarian movement.

---

25. L. H. Schiffman, *The Halakhah at Qumran* (SJLA 16; Leiden: Brill, 1975), 32; the point remains valid, even if some of the terminology used to express the matter might now be different.

26. Vermes, *Complete Dead Sea Scrolls in English*, 481.

27. See the realistic assessment of this by E. P. Sanders, "The Dead Sea Sect and Other Jews: Commonalities, Overlaps and Differences," in *The Dead Sea Scrolls in Their Historical Context* (ed. T. H. Lim et al.; Edinburgh: T&T Clark, 2000), 7–43, esp. 29–30.

2.4. The Turning Point

The encounter with the new group occurs at what Lofland and Stark identify as a turning point for people, especially young adults. Old obligations and lines of action have diminished for various reasons, and new lines of involvement have become desirable and possible. It is impossible to say much about the moment of encounter, but it is clear from Rambo's nuancing of Lofland and Stark's work that the ways in which the advocate[28] of a particular group and the potential convert reciprocally meet each other's needs is an area that requires careful exploration. I have already suggested that in relation to the Qumran community and those who might be interested in joining, part of this reciprocity rests in a common interest in the Scriptures as a source of identity and of hope, as the agreed basis on which a perspective on the world can be suitably constructed. In the turning point, many other factors also need to be taken into account, such as commonalities in ethnicity, class, social background, economic status, lifestyle, and the like, as well as the way in which the community member might be able to offer inducements of various kinds to encourage the wavering convert.

It is not possible to outline in any significant way what part Scripture might have played at the turning point, but a few suggestions can indicate the sort of role the Scriptures could have occupied. It is clear that Scripture could have been a significant part of the missionary strategy of the advocate. Some particular piece of interpretation might have been found especially attractive by the prospective convert and been a major contributing factor at the turning point. Scripture could also have been part of the inducement to join. Perhaps rumors of long periods of extensive study of and deliberation about Scripture were seen as attractive. Maybe the prospect of possible involvement in the production of manuscripts of Scripture was also appealing.[29]

2.5. Cult Affective Bonds

The circumstances surrounding the fifth stage in the conversion process are particularly significant for its outcome. The important factor at this stage is the satisfaction derived from some form of personal encounter or connection with a member of the community or sect. Many converts reported intellectual reservations about the group but nevertheless developed strong personal bonds with members of the group.

---

28. Rambo (*Understanding Religions Conversion*, 66–86) devotes two chapters to outlining the role of advocates and their strategies.

29. This is the well-known understanding of the principal function of the Qumran settlement according to Hartmut Stegemann, *The Library of Qumran: On the Essenes, Qumran, John the Baptist, and Jesus* (Grand Rapids: Eerdmans, 1998), 51–55, esp. 52: "This construction plan reflects a clear center of interest: the *production of scrolls*, together with all preliminary stages of obtaining and working the leather from which the scrolls were made."

Again, it is impossible to gauge quite how a convert to the Qumran community might have developed strong personal bonds with members of the group. It
may be that in relation to Qumran it is incorrect to separate this stage from the
following stage inasmuch as it seems that the most obvious way in which personal
bonds were established between long-standing members and new converts was
through various forms of communal living, even if such living was often structured very hierarchically. Rambo provides a fuller understanding of this stage
by describing what Arthur Griel and David Rudy have labeled the encapsulation processes.[30] These processes involve four components (relationships, rituals,
rhetoric, and roles), but all four of these matters can also be as readily identified
as playing a significant part also in the sixth stage.[31] The pesharim and other
commentary sections could have been used to encourage identification with the
community and its supposed scripturally ordained history and circumstances in
this stage or in either of the subsequent ones, just as their divinely inspired exegesis might have played a role in convincing the potential convert of the heavenly
origin of the religious view of the world that they constructed.

2.6. EXTRACULT AFFECTIVE BONDS

At a sixth stage, extracult bonds are negated or neutralized and significant commitment is apparent. In Qumran it is not surprising that there is a fictive kinship
element[32] and a widespread disparagement of the temple cult as practiced by
others. Within a newly constituted Israel at the foot of Sinai, the convert joins
the community[33] and becomes variously part of both sanctuary and priesthood
as divinely intended. Although these scripturally based identity markers may
have been variously used during the history of the movement, the possibilities in
such phrases as "sanctuary of men/Adam" (מקדש אדם)[34] and "sons of Zadok" are

---

30. A. Griel and D. Rudy, "Social Cocoons: Encapsulation and Identity Transformation
Organizations," *Sociological Inquiry* 54 (1984): 260–78; as adapted by Rambo, *Understanding
Religious Conversion*, 103–8.

31. The extent to which the findings of C. Ullman ("Cognitive and Emotional Antecedents of Religious Conversion," *Journal of Personality and Social Psychology* 43 [1982]: 183–92),
that converts commonly had relational and emotional problems in childhood, adolescence,
and immediately prior to their conversion, especially that they had absent, weak, or abusive
fathers, can be translated to the circumstances of late antiquity is difficult to know; see the
discussion in Rambo, *Understanding Religious Conversion*, 111.

32. This is most obvious in the use of "fathers" and "mothers" in 4Q270 (4QD^e) 7 i
13–14.

33. As James C. VanderKam has recently suggested, even the language of the self-
designation of the community as *yaḥad* is derived as a neologism from Scripture: see J. C.
Vanderkam, "Sinai Revisited," in *Biblical Interpretation at Qumran* (ed. M. Henze; Studies in
the Dead Sea Scrolls and Related Literature; Grand Rapids: Eerdmans, 2005), 44–60.

34. See, e.g., G. J. Brooke, "Miqdash Adam, Eden and the Qumran Community," in
Gemeinde ohne Tempel—Community without Temple: Zur Substituierung und Transformation

manifold. In addition, as part of the use of such identity markers, there is a very strong rehearsal of purity regulations and a separatist ideology, endorsed not least by various statements from or the general ethos of Genesis, Deuteronomy, and Isaiah. It is this scripturally justified separation that apparently results in Jewish nonmembers of the community being labeled in ways similar to non-Israelites in Scripture. Thus, in the ceremony of admission, people are divided into those who are among the blessed and those who are cursed (1QS 1:21–2:18). The language pattern of the blessings and curses of Deuteronomy demarcate who is an insider and who an outsider. Once on the inside and adequately cleansed, the convert then can receive instruction that will enable a more profound understanding of the precepts of God. The separation from the habitation of the unjust is given a scriptural motivation; such separation is to enable the preparation of the way of the Lord in the wilderness. This is a way that is itself "the study of the Law which He [God] commanded by the hand of Moses, that they may do according to all that has been revealed from age to age, and as the Prophets have revealed by His Holy Spirit" (1QS 8:15–16).[35]

The rejection of others has its counterpart in a sense of rejection by others that can be confirmed in a number of ways. The ongoing use of the Hodayot within the community probably encouraged members to identify repeatedly with the persecution and rejection experienced by the author, readily recognized as a founding figure within the movement with an ongoing significance. In such a way, new converts and even long-standing members are equipped with and internalize a rhetoric that justifies their deviance. The hymnody that encapsulates such a sense of rejection is replete with scriptural allusion. Most obviously in 1QH[a] 12:7–9 we hear echoes of the servant song of Isaiah and the suffering motifs of the psalms of lament when we read:

> Teachers of lies [have smoothed] Thy people [with words], and [false prophets] have led them astray; they perish without understanding for their works are in folly. For I am despised by them and they have no esteem for me that Thou mayest manifest Thy might through me. They have banished me from my land like a bird from its nest; all my friends and brethren are driven far from me and hold me for a broken vessel.[36]

2.7. INTENSIVE INTERACTION

Total conversion, according to Lofland and Stark, comes about only after intensive interaction with full members. Such interaction, requiring physical proxim-

---

des Jerusalemer Tempels und seines Kults im Alten Testament, antiken Judentum und frühen Christentum (ed. B. Ego; WUNT 118; Tübingen: Mohr Siebeck, 1999), 285–301.

35. Vermes, *Complete Dead Sea Scrolls in English*, 109.
36. Ibid., 263.

ity, has to be concrete and may involve the daily or even hourly accessibility of full members. Such intensive interaction can take several forms. It can be based on continuous reminders and discussion about the need to make other converts. But this does not seem to have been the case at Qumran.

At Qumran total conversion is endorsed positively and negatively. On the positive side a year or two of probation pass in which the kind of association needed for total conversion is made entirely possible. Scripture plays its part: "and the Many shall be on watch together for a third of each night of the year in order to read the book, explain the regulation, and bless together" (1QS 6:7–8).[37] The study of Scripture and its correct interpretation do not seem to be undertaken solely for academic edification, but so that those of lesser rank or newer membership may have their allegiance constructed through Scripture. It is enough to regulate that it happens; the specific content does not need further definition.

On the negative side, this total conversion is endorsed through the careful repetition of the delimitation of the group, and particularly of those who can be full participants. Those who are excluded and those included are based on the repetition of scriptural models, interwoven in complex patterns.[38] As in Deut 23:2–4, so in 4QMMT restrictions are applied to the Ammonite, the Moabite, the bastard, the man whose testicles have been crushed or whose penis has been cut off. In 1QSa 2:4–9 restrictions based on Lev 5:3; 7:21; Deut 23:11–12; Exod 19:10–15; and Lev 21:16–24 are applied to any man smitten with any human uncleanness, any man smitten in his flesh, or paralyzed in his hands or feet, or lame, or blind, or deaf or dumb; the old and tottery are also carefully restricted. In 1QM 7 similar restrictions are applied to the community in its cosmic struggle. No man who is lame or blind or crippled or afflicted with a lasting bodily blemish or smitten with bodily impurity shall march out to war with them. In 4Q174, again following Deut 23:2–4, it is the unclean, the uncircumcised, the Ammonite, the Moabite, the half-breed, the foreigner, and the stranger who are refused access to the community because of the presence in it of holy ones (angels).

Initial tentative assent becomes a language device for interpreting everyday events in the convert's life. The convert is placed at the center of the battle between good and evil spirits. Lofland and Stark observe that the sect which the convert is joining "has a variety of resources for explicating everyday events in terms of a cosmic battle between good and evil spirits"; since all the cult's "interpretations pointed to the imminence of the end, to participate in these explications of daily life was to come more and more to see the necessity of one's personal participation as a totally committed agent in this cosmic struggle."[39]

---

37. F. García Martínez, ed., *The Dead Sea Scrolls Translated: The Qumran Texts in English* (2nd ed.; Leiden: Brill, 1996), 9.

38. As with all the lists of texts in this essay, it is unlikely that all were used at the same time; nevertheless, certain motifs are constantly repeated in various compositions and in various guises.

39. Lofland and Stark, "Becoming a World-Saver," 873.

A physical relocation, such as a move into communal buildings, often accompanies and endorses this move toward total conversion. On the basis of conversion theory it is likely that a very suitable understanding of the primary purpose of the Qumran buildings themselves is that they functioned as the place where new converts were made into total converts. Furthermore, it is perhaps no accident that in the form of the Rule of the Community found in the exemplar from Cave 1 (1QS), the ritual of admission is followed in cols. 3 and 4 by the so-called Treatise on the Two Spirits. In light of theories of conversion, it seems as if the editors of 1QS recognized that new members would need thorough cultural transformation within the cosmic dualism of the spiritual outlook of the community.

3. Conclusion

In this short study I have suggested that consideration of the processes of conversion as analyzed by recent theorists can help describe how a Jew might become a member of the Qumran community or the wider movement of which it was a part. Many factors would have been involved as a Jew moved from one form of Judaism to that found in the shifting sands of the sectarian writings of the Qumran community. Not all the factors involved would have been based in Scripture or justified scripturally. However, attention to these conversion processes enables modern readers of the sectarian compositions found in the Qumran caves to recognize that several features of the variety of ways in which Scripture was used in the Qumran community and the wider movement of which it was a part were perhaps in the form that they were, or functioned as they did, because they underlined the move from the moment of crisis or tension to the total conversion of the new member. Conversion theory contributes toward explaining in some cases why Scripture was used in the way that it was. Converts whose very conversion was a move toward deviancy found their move strategically supported by the ways in which they were encouraged to read the present through their use of Scripture. In many respects, for the convert to, and for the continuing member of, the Qumran community, Scripture justified deviance and endorsed a particular reading of present experience.

FOUR

MEMORY, CULTURAL MEMORY, AND REWRITING SCRIPTURE

1. INTRODUCTION

The study and analysis of rewritten Scripture, especially as exemplified by some compositions among the Dead Sea Scrolls, has become an increasingly debated and contested area. It is interesting to note immediately that the study of memory, either individual or collective or cultural, has played little or no part in the discussion; this may be somewhat surprising, since the rewritings to be found in works like Deuteronomy or 1–2 Chronicles can be fruitfully analyzed in such terms,[1] and remembrance plays a significant role in several compositions found in the caves at and near Qumran.[2] This paper attempts to start a conversation that gives some place to memory in the consideration of rewritten Scripture. Until now, for the rewritten Scripture compositions from the late Second Temple period, what might be loosely referred to as the precanonical period, at least three schools of thought seem to have emerged.

In the first school belong those who wish to retain the label "rewritten Scripture," or possibly even "rewritten Bible," as concerning matters of genre.[3] For such scholars there is some significant value in trying to articulate the literary features of such a genre. Commonly such features are to some extent predetermined by the selection and demarcation of those compositions that are widely considered as belonging to the genre, notably Jubilees, the Temple Scroll, the

---

1. J. W. Rogerson, *A Theology of the Old Testament: Cultural Memory, Communication and Being Human* (London: SPCK, 2009), 13–41.

2. B. G. Wold describes the use of זכר and related terms in relation to the recollection of the Exodus in 4Q185, 4Q370, 4Q462, 4Q463, 4Q504, and the *Damascus Document* ("Memory in the Dead Sea Scrolls: Exodus, Creation and Cosmos," in *Memory in the Bible and Antiquity: The Fifth Durham–Tübingen Research Symposium (Durham, September 2004)* [ed. S. C. Barton, L. T. Stuckenbruck, and B. G. Wold; WUNT 212; Tübingen: Mohr Siebeck, 2007], 50–63).

3. Of course most scholars resist categorization by others, but this group could include Philip S. Alexander ("Retelling the Old Testament," in *It Is Written: Scripture Citing Scripture. Essays in Honour of Barnabas Lindars, SSF* [ed. D. A. Carson and H. G. M. Williamson. Cambridge: Cambridge University Press], 99–121); and Moshe J. Bernstein ("'Rewritten Bible': A Generic Category Which Has Outlived Its Usefulness?" *Textus* 22 [2005]: 169–96).

Genesis Apocryphon[4] and the Reworked Pentateuch in its various manifesta-tions.[5] One feature of the approach of those scholars who might be allocated to this category is the assumption, sometimes unstated, that a more or less authori-tative form of the Torah has already come to be recognized, which such composi-tions are using as hypotext.

In the second school belong a group of scholars who also acknowledge the key role to be played by the analysis of such compositions as the four just men-tioned, but who have noticed that the literary exercise that such compositions represent is to be observed in a wide range of additional works. On the one hand, such attention to breadth undermines and challenges those approaches that are concerned with neat generic classification, since the larger the family of composi-tions to be considered, the less possible it is to insist on distinct family features in every case: very large literary families destabilize literary genres. On the other hand, broadening the basis of the discussion is commonly based on the obser-vation, analysis, and discussion of literary processes, so that the characteristic of this school of thought is attention to such processes.[6] From such a perspec-tive, rewritten Scripture loses its suitability as a literary genre tag and becomes a way of talking about a set of phenomena that are observable in various compo-sitions.[7] It is as if one is moving from the consideration of whether a particular composition can be labeled as rewritten Bible to consideration of whether certain compositions illustrate the processes of rewriting Scripture.[8]

In the third school we might put a smaller group of scholars who wish to

---

4. Some of the issues surrounding the discussion of the genre of the parts and whole of the Genesis Apocryphon, including the suitability of the term "rewritten Bible," are discussed in M. J. Bernstein, "The Genre(s) of the Genesis Apocryphon," in *Aramaica Qumranica: Pro-ceedings of the Conference on the Aramaic Texts from Qumran in Aix-en-Provence, 30 June–2 July 2008* (ed. K. Berthelot and D. Stökl Ben Ezra; STDJ 94; Leiden: Brill, 2010), 317–43.

5. Those four compositions are often mentioned as having become in some way nor-mative in scholarly discussion; see, e.g., M. M. Zahn, "Rewritten Scripture," in *The Oxford Handbook of the Dead Sea Scrolls* (ed. T. H. Lim and J. J. Collins; Oxford: Oxford University Press, 2010), 324–25; eadem, *Rethinking Rewritten Scripture: Composition and Exegesis in the 4QReworked Pentateuch Manuscripts* (STDJ 95; Leiden: Brill, 2011), 8.

6. Note, e.g., the contribution by Anders Klostergaard Petersen, "Rewritten Bible as a Borderline Phenomenon—Genre, Textual Strategy, or Canonical Anachronism?" in *Flores Florentino: Dead Sea Scrolls and Other Early Jewish Studies in Honour of Florentino García Martínez* (ed. A. Hilhorst, É. Puech, and E. Tigchelaar; JSJSup 122; Leiden: Brill, 2007), 285–306.

7. The breadth of discussion by scholars in the first volume of an ongoing project on rewritten Bible illustrates well how rewritten Bible can lose all sense of being a literary genre: A. Laato and J. van Ruiten, eds., *Rewritten Bible Reconsidered: Proceedings of the Conference in Karkku, Finland, August 24–26, 2006* (Studies in Rewritten Bible 1; Turku: Åbo Akademi University; Winona Lake, Ind.: Eisenbrauns, 2008).

8. Note the title of the book by Sidnie White Crawford, *Rewriting Scripture in Second Temple Times* (Studies in the Dead Sea Scrolls and Related Literature; Grand Rapids: Eerd-mans, 2008).

combine both perspectives, arguing for the existence of certain core literary or generic features but thinking more creatively about what such features seem to indicate about the character of the transmission of tradition or traditions in the Second Temple period. Thus, some who might be put in this group have tried to articulate what they consider to be characteristic features, for example, of Mosaic discourse.[9] More broadly others have sought to describe how a range of compositions enlarge and enhance the suitable description of scriptural exegesis in the Second Temple period.[10]

In this short contribution I wish to introduce into the discussion the concept of memory,[11] which I hope will illuminate as an etic analytical framework some further aspects of both particular literary compositions and also the phenomenon of rewriting Scripture more broadly. I am concerned with both individual and collective or cultural memory, a combination that has been briefly but persuasively exploited for the study of some New Testament texts by Markus Bockmuehl.[12]

2. Individual Memory

The various forms of the scriptural books that have come to light in the Qumran caves have encouraged a reconsideration of some of the canons of text criticism. It is clear that there is still a place for the analysis and explanation of shared errors, but it has also become increasingly acknowledged that many textual variants, both major and minor, are the result of intentional intervention with the text, of a mind at work. In talking of memory, that is, individual memory, I wish to draw attention to three phenomena that have a role in the better understanding of rewritten Scripture, namely, that an individual scribe is necessarily involved, that there is a varied set of motivating factors behind individual involvement in the transmission of texts, and that there is a complex network of practices, both mental and physical, through which the reproduction or representation of text takes place. Of course we should not forget the many-faceted problems associated with the study of individual memory as those have been highlighted in the

---

9. E.g., H. Najman, *Secondary Sinai: The Development of Mosaic Discourse in Second Temple Judaism* (JSJSup 77. Leiden: Brill, 2003). Najman looks mainly at Jubilees and the Temple Scroll and then uses Philo to articulate broader issues. For evaluation of some of Najman's ideas, see G. J. Brooke "Hypertextuality and the 'Parabiblical' Dead Sea Scrolls," in *In the Second Degree: Paratextual Literature in Ancient Near Eastern and Ancient Mediterranean Culture and Its Reflections in Medieval Literature* (ed. P. S. Alexander, A. Lange, and R. J. Pillinger; Leiden: Brill, 2010), 43–64.

10. See, e.g., Zahn, "Rewritten Scripture," 323–36.

11. A broad "history of memory" is provided by J. K. Olick and J. Robbins, "Social Memory Studies: From 'Collective Memory' to the Historical Sociology of Mnemonic Practices," *Annual Review of Sociology* 24 (1998): 112–22.

12. M. Bockmuehl, *Seeing the Word: Refocusing New Testament Study* (Studies in Theological Interpretation; Grand Rapids: Baker Academic, 2006), 173–88.

last one hundred years,[13] but it is possible to adopt a pragmatic approach and talk of the individual person's role in the transmission of tradition, to attempt to describe something of such a person's mental activities and mind's retention, some of which is textual.[14]

First, there is the role of the individual in the transmission of tradition. In whatever way scribal processes are construed, in any particular manuscript only one scribe, or perhaps only one scribe at a time, can hold the pen and craft the text. In other words, there has to be a place for the activity of the individual scribe. In postcanonical practices, the role of the scribe in the copying of authoritative compositions might be considered primarily and predominantly a matter of precise copying; the individual contribution of the copying scribe is strictly limited and put in the background. There has sometimes been a scholarly assumption that the role of scribes in earlier periods might have been similar, but more recent understanding of Jewish scribal practices in the Second Temple period has opened up the possibility for some consideration of the creative intervention of the scribe in the text that is being transmitted. There is such a thing as an exegetical variant; there are such things as literary editions of authoritative compositions, as Emanuel Tov and Eugene Ulrich would agree, though perhaps with varying degrees of enthusiasm.[15] All that means that an individual mind— what it remembers, how it articulates and rearticulates what it remembers, how it functions—needs to be considered as part of the process of the transmission (and development) of authoritative traditions. And by using the word "process," attention to the individual scribe in relation to rewritten Bible inevitably links these comments and observations with those who define rewriting in terms of processes.

Second, what is it that is motivating such interventions? As in so many matters in our understanding of rewritten Scripture, it is all too easy to put on anachronistic lenses to consider the evidence. Nevertheless, it certainly seems as if one motivating factor behind scribal intervention in the tradition was a felt desire for clarification of the plain meaning or simple sense of the text. But much more seems to be in play than simple sense exegesis. Among other factors, the contemporary life setting of the author of rewritten Scripture influences the combination of ideas that create the *Tendenz* of the adjustments to the underlying tradition; an earlier text is re-presented, that is, made present again, through

---

13. See, e.g., the psychological memory studies in A. Erll and A. Nünning, eds., *A Companion to Cultural Memory Studies* (Berlin: de Gruyter, 2010), 215–98.

14. P. Atkins, *Memory and Liturgy: The Place of Memory in the Composition and Practice of Liturgy* (Aldershot: Ashgate, 2004), 1–24. Atkins begins with the neurological understanding of the individual in his pragmatic consideration of the role of memory in liturgy.

15. See, e.g., the extended material on textual criticism and literary criticism in E. Tov, *Textual Criticism of the Hebrew Bible* (3rd rev. and expanded ed.; Minneapolis: Fortress, 2012), 283–326; E. C. Ulrich, *The Dead Sea Scrolls and the Origins of the Bible* (Studies in the Dead Sea Scrolls and Related Literature; Grand Rapids: Eerdmans, 1999), 99–120.

individual authors reflecting their own contexts of discourse[16] and attempting to meet the needs of their audiences as they perceive them or desire to mold them. Such adjustments of the received tradition might be principally halakhic or even more overtly theological as they reflect or create a way of looking at the world.[17] They might also indicate how an author considers his standing within a particular historical perspective and attempt to manipulate an audience toward a similar standing.[18] The motivations for adjusting the received traditions in the rewriting process are ideological in one way or another.

Third, there is a complex network of practices through which the reproduction or re-presentation of texts takes place. An understanding of scribes as copyists, perhaps as mere copyists, belongs in a world in which the precise forms of written texts have come to be normative in some way.[19] However, in an earlier period, which we might label "precanonical," in which there is still a substantial place for orality, in processes of both memorization and transmission, there is also some room for the toleration of textual variety, even contradictions.[20] Some theoreticians have even supposed a developmental history of memory in which antiquity is characterized by a move from "orality to writing, though writing never fully supplanted oral transmission. This new condition enabled two important practices—commemoration and documentary recording—associated with emerging city structures."[21] But the processes of textual production I am considering here are more basically a combination of wider sets of what has been remembered and the narrower set of vocalizations that are part of dictation or reading.

How might all this be pictured in practice? One possible model to aid understanding can be drawn from recent study of Jesus, Q, and the Gospels, especially the Synoptics.[22] The model is helpful in my view partly because it

---

16. For participating in ongoing Mosaic discourse, see Najman, *Seconding Sinai*, 41–69.

17. See, e.g., Wold, "Memory in the Dead Sea Scrolls."

18. E.g., in relation to the individual author's construction of the image of the Teacher of Righteousness and the need for the reader to engage in "mnemonic mimesis." See L. T. Stuckenbruck, "The Teacher of Righteousness Remembered: From Fragmentary Sources to Collective Memory in the Dead Sea Scrolls," in Barton et al., *Memory in the Bible and Antiquity*, 93.

19. "Only in a written culture could a concept such as verbatim memorization emerge" (A. I. Baumgarten, *The Flourishing of Jewish Sects in the Maccabean Era: An Interpretation* (JSJSup 55; Leiden: Brill, 1997), 123.

20. For some of the significance of the interface of orality and writing for the formation of new genres, see the collection of essays edited by A. Weissenrieder and R. B. Coote, *The Interface of Orality and Writing: Speaking, Seeing, Writing in the Shaping of New Genres* (WUNT 260; Tübingen: Mohr Siebeck, 2010).

21. Olick and Robbins, "Social Memory Studies," 105–40, summarizing the work of others.

22. For discussion of oral and written processes, see, e.g., the rich collection of essays edited by Werner Kelber and Samuel Byrskog (*Jesus in Memory: Traditions in Oral and Scribal Perspectives* [Waco: Baylor University Press, 2009]). Though there are traces of a historicist

allows for consideration of texts that can be widely acknowledged as exemplifying revisions of one another in some manner as such texts move toward ever-increasing authority. There are thus many parallels with the Jewish textual phenomena of the Second Temple period in which revisions and rewritings are taking place in a situation in which the developing authority of certain forms of the tradition is also an issue. There is no space here to delve in any depth into this complex material, but three features can be noticed especially, though in a general fashion.

First, there is the matter of the relationship between the Gospel of Mark and the subsequent Gospels that used it. All the lengthy debates about arguments from order are relevant not solely to constructions of Markan priority but also to whether the similarities and differences between Mark and its Synoptic counterparts express something that is essentially the same or things that are sufficiently different as to be separate compositions. With debates about rewritten Scripture as genre still ongoing, this parallel might be helpful in encouraging a more fruitful set of descriptors to be outlined than those so far put on the scholarly table.[23]

Second, there is the role of the individual Gospel writer. Though he might be inseparable from some communal context of discourse that provides the dominant parameters for what is remembered and recalled, nevertheless it is still possible to talk of an individual author or editor. For the understanding and analysis of rewritten Scripture, the role of the author and editor also needs to be acknowledged and given an appropriate setting, whether as redactor of the Temple Scroll or the Genesis Apocryphon or as the author of the Book of Jubilees.

Third, there is the relation of all three Gospels not just to one another but also to the ongoing forms of the Jesus traditions, not least in oral form.[24] This has been much debated in previous generations but has been repositioned in recent discussion in relation to everything from eyewitness testimony to the role of

---

agenda, Anthony Le Donne's work is rewarding theoretically (*The Historiographical Jesus: Memory, Typology, and the Son of David* [Waco: Baylor University Press, 2009], especially ch. 4, pp. 65–92). See also D. C. Allison, *Constructing Jesus: Memory, Imagination, and History* (Grand Rapids: Baker Academic, 2010).

23. Zahn (*Rethinking Rewritten Scripture*, 10) has argued that the "distinction between *quantity* of difference and *quality* of difference is critical to a proper understanding of the 4QRP MSS, as well as other similar works. If we classify the 4QRP MSS as copies of the Pentateuch, it should not be primarily because of their closeness to the pentateuchal text relative to other works, but because there is no *literary* or formal indication that they are anything other than pentateuchal" (italics hers).

24. See, e.g., J. D. G. Dunn, "Jesus in Oral Memory: The Initial Stages of the Jesus Tradition," *SBLSP* 39 (2000): 287–326; idem, *Jesus Remembered* (Christianity in the Making 1; Grand Rapids: Eerdmans, 2003). Dunn makes no use of the work of Maurice Halbwachs on collective memory, though much of Halbwachs seems to indirectly inform his approach (e.g., Halbwachs, *On Collective Memory* [ed., trans., and intro. L. A. Coser; Heritage of Sociology; Chicago: University of Chicago Press, 1992; French originals 1941 and 1952]).

memory in the citation of scriptural passages in other sources.[25] For rewritten Scripture the actual means of the transmission of text from one manuscript to another through oral or aural intermediate stages and the more general role of oral performance in the representation of tradition in any particular context, sectarian or not, needs to be set alongside the insights that can be derived from the New Testament analogies.

In this brief section I have attempted to suggest that it was indeed the case that individual authors and scribes participated in the re-presentation of the traditions that they inherited. Having admitted some of the problems of the recent study of individual memory from the outset, it is certainly time to acknowledge that some scholars have been concerned to argue over against the psychologists that "it is impossible for individuals to remember in any coherent and persistent fashion outside of the group contexts."[26] There is an individual memory, an individual scribal memory, but it is in large part socially and culturally constructed and operates within collective codes that can somehow define, endorse, and encourage certain processes and practices as normative. Individual memory and collective memory are entirely interdependent in some way.[27] Thus, although a suitable place must be given to the role of the individual's memory in the transmission of texts, there is a broader field of reference that also needs to be considered.

3. CULTURAL MEMORY

In recent years there has been some very helpful reflection on various methodological issues in relation to the analysis of the Dead Sea Scrolls.[28] It is interesting to note, however, that although there has been some increasing attention to sociological approaches,[29] little has appeared that directly addresses the explicit

---

25. A noteworthy repositioning for the purposes of this study is by Allison, *Constructing Jesus*, 1–30.

26. For a summary of the view of Halbwachs, see Olick and Robbins, "Social Memory Studies," 109.

27. Susan Sontag has, however, argued for the exclusive reality of individual memory ("all memory is individual"); for Sontag, cultural memory is a spurious notion, though she does admit that there is "collective instruction" through which individual memory is shaped or "stipulated" (*Representing the Pain of Others* [New York: Farrar, Straus & Giroux, 2003], 85–86). This is discussed and debated in Ron Eyerman, "The Past in the Present: Culture and the Transmission of Memory," *Acta Sociologica* 47/2 [2004]: 161–62). Furthermore, Peter Atkins (*Memory and Liturgy*, 69–82) seems to take a line similar to that of Sontag, noting how individuals learn from others, who collectively provide "corporate memory."

28. See, e.g., M. T. Davis and B. A. Strawn, eds., *Qumran Studies: New Approaches, New Questions* (Grand Rapids: Eerdmans, 2007); M. L. Grossman, ed., *Rediscovering the Dead Sea Scrolls: An Assessment of Old and New Approaches and Methods* (Grand Rapids: Eerdmans, 2010).

29. Most notable among these are Baumgarten, *Flourishing of Jewish Sects in the Mac-*

concern in other areas of the study of Judaism in antiquity[30] with collective or cultural memory.[31] There are some exceptions for the Dead Sea Scrolls, especially two contributions to the 2004 Durham–Tübingen symposium *Memory in the Bible and Antiquity*,[32] a short but insightful study by Jaime Vázquez Allegue,[33] and a notable essay by Philip Davies.[34]

The literature on collective or cultural memory is very extensive.[35] The major developments in biblical studies concerning collective or cultural memory that have developed from theories that trace their pedigrees back to Maurice Halbwachs have largely concentrated in various ways on issues having to do with historiography and narrative.[36] That is no accident, since Halbwachs himself was

cabean Era; D. J. Chalcraft, ed., *Sectarianism in Early Judaism: Sociological Advances* (London: Equinox, 2007); J. Jokiranta, "Social Scientific Approaches to the Dead Sea Scrolls," in Grossman, *Rediscovering the Dead Sea Scrolls*, 246–63; eadem, "Sociological Approaches to Qumran Sectarianism," in Lim and Collins, *Oxford Handbook of the Dead Sea Scrolls*, 200–231; and E. Regev, *Sectarianism in Qumran: A Cross-Cultural Perspective* (Religion and Society 45; Berlin: de Gruyter, 2007). In an evocative study on the culture and transmission of memory Ron Eyerman has noted wryly that "sociologists do not often think about memory and not often enough about history" ("Past in the Present," 160).

30. On memory in Judaism in antiquity, see especially D. Mendels, *Memory in Jewish, Pagan and Christian Societies of the Graeco-Roman World: Fragmented Memory–Comprehensive Memory–Collective Memory* (LSTS 45; London: T&T Clark International, 2004).

31. E.g., nowhere in the entry on collective memory in Lim and Collins, *Oxford Handbook of the Dead Sea Scrolls*, is there any mention of the work and influence of Halbwachs (*On Collective Memory*) or Jan Assmann (*Moses the Egyptian: The Memory of Egypt in Western Monotheism* [Cambridge, Mass.: Harvard University Press, 1997]; idem, *Religion and Cultural Memory: Ten Studies* [Cultural Memory in the Present; Stanford: Stanford University Press, 2006; German original 2000]).

32. Wold, "Memory in the Dead Sea Scrolls"; and Stuckenbuck, "Teacher of Righteousness Remembered" (see nn. 2 and 18 above).

33. J. Vázquez Allegue states, "Los autores de los textos de Qumrán recurren a la memoria para recrear tradiciones de la Biblia hebrea y, al mismo tiempo, interpretarla" ("Memoria colectiva e identidad de grupo en Qumrán," in Hilhorst et al., *Flores Florentino*, 91). However, although this statement would seem to be programmatic for our purposes, Vázquez Allegue moves in his article to consider several sites of memory apart from so-called rewritten Scripture compositions.

34. P. R. Davies, "What History Can We Get from the Scrolls, and How?" in *The Dead Sea Scrolls: Texts and Context* (ed. C. Hempel; STDJ 90; Leiden: Brill, 2010), 31–46.

35. A very helpful overview is presented by L. Weissberg ("Introduction," in *Cultural Memory and the Construction of Identity* [ed. D. Ben-Amos and L. Weissberg; Detroit: Wayne State University Press, 1999], 7–26), covering matters since the Enlightenment with deftness, such as the possible significance of the proliferation of museums, and discussing the agendas of Halbwachs and Pierre Nora. The category of "collective memory" is helpfully problematized by Noa Gedi and Yigal Elam, who see it as leading to lack of clarity in the consideration of both history and myth (Gedi and Elam, "Collective Memory—What Is It?" *History and Memory* 8 [1996]: 30–50).

36. See, e.g., Mark S. Smith provides some helpful overview with respect to Israelite religion in "Remembering God: Collective Memory in Israelite Religion," *CBQ* 64 (2002): 631–51;

concerned to construct a method that stood over against both the psychologists and psychoanalysts who had privatized memory[37] and also the historians who had objectified history, largely from elite perspectives. For those concerned with the study of the Hebrew Bible, the prioritization of collective memory as a way of understanding how Israel read its past has enabled the discussion of the text in the present of the authors to be asserted in a fresh manner. In particular that discussion has permitted and even encouraged the avoidance of issues concerning the historical veracity of what some texts purport to describe.[38] One need no longer be anxious about what happened, so much as concerned with how what is constructed as having happened is remembered and memorialized.[39] The remembrance of the past, its memorialization, can serve a variety of purposes; it is not value free.[40]

In the light of what has been taking place in the study of the Hebrew Bible, for the sectarian scrolls the study of collective memory has thus primarily been of assistance for tackling various vexed historical, or more properly historiographical, questions concerning the portrayal of the Teacher of Righteousness and his

---

see also A. Brenner and F. H. Polak, eds., *Performing Memory in Biblical Narrative and Beyond* (Bible in the Modern World 25; Amsterdam Studies in the Bible and Religion 3; Sheffield: Sheffield Phoenix, 2009). Perhaps the cultural memory's concern with history is because, as J. Wellhausen noted, "history, as it is well known, always has to be constructed" (R. G. Kratz, "Eyes and Spectacles: Wellhausen's Method of Higher Criticism," *JTS* 60 [2009]: 387; on why Wellhausen has not figured large in the study of cultural memory, see Kratz, 402).

37. In an attempt to use cultural trauma in relation to the construction of identity, Eyerman has also noted that "most often trauma is conceptualised on the individual level" ("Past in the Present," 160).

38. See the helpful comment of Konrad Schmid: "Many texts contain reworked traditions and memories that are older than themselves but did not exist in a fixed, written form. Committing them to writing was then more than and different from a mere codification of these traditions and memories. Instead, the act of writing was already an initial process of interpretation.... Thus Old Testament texts can be 'present' and literarily historically relevant in the modes of memory, tradition, and reception in different periods" (Schmid, *The Old Testament: A Literary History* [Minneapolis: Fortress, 2012], 46–47; see also the German original, *Literaturgeschichte des Alten Testaments* [Darmstadt: Wissenschaftliche Buchgesellschaft, 2008]). His combination of "reworked traditions" and "memories" is especially pertinent to the argument of this essay.

39. See, e.g., the valuable comments by Rogerson, *Theology of the Old Testament*, 1–41. Basing his ideas on those of C. Lévi-Strauss, Rogerson builds on the insights of others to distinguish among biblical texts between "cold" and "hot" reconstructions of the past, between those that are more interested in frigid stability in their present, continuity with the past for its own sake (e.g., 1–2 Chronicles), and those that are more concerned with the warmth of "positive" change in their present (e.g., the Deuteronomistic History), internalizing "the historical process in order to make it the moving power of its development" (Rogerson, 29).

40. This is illustrated trenchantly concerning the past in Israeli pioneering museums by Tamar Katriel in her article, "Sites of Memory: Discourses of the Past in Israeli Pioneering Settlement Museums," in Ben-Amos and Weissberg, *Cultural Memory and the Construction of Identity*, 118–22.

opponents in some compositions such as the Damascus Document and some of the so-called continuous pesharim.[41] Though some scholars still try to write the history of the second century B.C.E. from such compositions, there is acknowledgment even by them that there are major problems in undertaking such a task.[42] Others, notably Philip Davies himself, have even gone so far as to declare that "there is no real historiography at Qumran."[43] To my mind, Davies seems to make one kind of historiography normative, and he fails to find that; however, the texts from the Qumran caves actually present several different ways of doing history,[44] though it is true that none of them is akin to the sort of annalistic chronicling of events that characterize much of the historiography that became canonical.

Be that as it may, it seems to me that because scholars of the Bible have been able to see how cultural memory works most obviously in such texts as Deuteronomy (and its related histories) and 1–2 Chronicles, compositions that are most obviously rewritings of earlier traditions, so aspects of the study of cultural memory should be applied both to the so-called rewritten Scripture compositions and also to the processes of rewriting themselves. Along those lines Davies has drawn attention to several key features in the study of cultural memory that are in need of being applied to rewritten Scripture in some way. Davies has used the insights of Jan Assmann as a staring point for his own remarks. Assmann's words are worth rehearsing: "Seen as an individual and as a social capacity, memory is not simply the storage of past 'facts' but the ongoing work of reconstructive imagination. In other words, the past cannot be stored but always has to be 'processed' and mediated."[45] While it is widely acknowledged that cultural memory acts to create and strengthen social or group identity,[46] Davies has some helpful

---

41. See Stuckenbruck, "Teacher of Righteousness Remembered," 75–94; and also idem, "The Legacy of the Teacher of Righteousness in the Dead Sea Scrolls," in *New Perspectives on Old Texts: Proceedings of the Tenth International Symposium of the Orion Center for the Study of the Dead Sea Scrolls and Associated Literature, 9–11 January, 2005* (ed. E. G. Chazon, B. Halpern-Amaru, and R. A. Clements; STDJ 88; Leiden: Brill, 2010), 23–49, especially his overall comment: "the documents which referred to the Teacher were essentially *presentist*. Events in the Teacher's life were remembered because they were closely bound up with the community's self-understanding and activity. The 'collective memory' of the community about the Teacher was inextricably determined by *mimesis*" (p. 93).

42. See, e.g., J. H. Charlesworth, *The Pesharim and Qumran History: Chaos or Consensus?* (Grand Rapids: Eerdmans, 2002); H. Eshel, *The Dead Sea Scrolls and the Hasmonean State* (Studies in the Dead Sea Scrolls and Related Literature; Grand Rapids: Eerdmans, 2008).

43. This depends on how "real historiography" is defined, see Davies, "What History Can We Get from the Scrolls, and How?" 31.

44. See G. J. Brooke, "Types of Historiography in the Qumran Scrolls," in *Ancient and Modern Scriptural Historiography/L'historiographie biblique, ancienne et moderne* (ed. G. J. Brooke and T. Römer; BETL 207; Leuven: Peeters, 2007), 211–30.

45. Assmann, *Moses the Egyptian*, 14.

46. Wold ("Memory in the Dead Sea Scrolls") has outlined the role of the remembrance

comments to make about the workings of such cultural memory, comments that can in my opinion readily be applied to rewritten Scripture: "cultural memory, like personal memory, does of course contain a good deal of genuine recollection, but it also embellishes, distorts, invents and forgets the past."[47] There are four somewhat overlapping dimensions or processes: embellishment, distortion, invention, and forgetting.

Let us briefly consider each of these four dimensions as programmatic for thinking about the phenomenon of rewritten Scripture and its processes and attempt a crude alignment of these four strategies of rewriting with some of the characteristic principles of cultural memory as outlined by Assmann.[48] It is important to keep in mind that we are not interested in this kind of cultural memory for what we can learn about the historical circumstances of what earlier traditions purport to describe; rather we are concerned to notice how a community's memory works to handle the traditions it receives in recognizable ways by providing implicit commentary as cultural memories are changed and adjusted. The process as a whole can be understood in terms of what Assmann has labeled "the concretion of identity," the ways in which "the store of knowledge on the basis of which a group derives an awareness of its unity and peculiarity"[49] is reworked, normally so as to make a move that expresses the need for the strengthening or renewal of identity rather than merely a set of literary preferences.[50] The processes to which Davies has drawn attention are ways in which cultural memory works and has worked. They thus authenticate what is taking place in rewritten Scripture in fresh ways that are not matters to frustrate the text critic faced with yet more evidence for Samaritan readings in the Reworked Pentateuch or topics merely to entertain as in the Genesis Apocryphon, though both variant readings and audience enjoyment are possible side effects. Rather, as processes, they are not markers of literary genres, so much as indicators of the way texts are brought into their transmitter's present.[51] And again, such processes are not morally neutral, not value free.

First, embellishment and institutionalization. Numerous examples of the embellishment of received tradition in rewritten Scripture could be cited. In

---

of Exodus, creation, and cosmos for the construction of identity in some of the communities behind the scrolls.

47. Davies, "What History Can We Get from the Scrolls, and How?" 33.

48. I rely here on Assmann, "Collective Memory and Cultural Identity," 125–33. His ideas are also more fully worked out theoretically in *Religion and Cultural Memory*. The four aspects of cultural memory to be considered in the following paragraphs are institutionalization, obligation, organization, and the capacity for reconstruction.

49. J. Assmann, "Collective Memory and Cultural Identity," *New German Critique* 65 (1995): 130.

50. For general comments on the academic discussion of the place of identity in processes of social memory, see Olick and Robbins, "Social Memory Studies," 122–33.

51. This is why Zahn (*Rethinking Rewritten Scripture*, 229–36) is concerned foremost with "compositional techniques and interpretive goals" (233) rather than with genre definition.

many comments on rewritten Scripture scholars have noted the way that the authors and editors of such compositions extend the text on which they depend. The effect of embellishment is often to present a more rounded or coherent version of a textual tradition and in so doing to reflect some form of the institutionalization of a group's heritage.[52] Thus, embellishment is not just for literary effect but usually suggests other facets of the authoritative inheritance that are being made present to distinguish one group from another. An example of such embellishment in rewritten Scripture is the way in which in the Reworked Pentateuch there is a not infrequent supplementation of the base narratives either with the speeches of those whose commands have been carried out, or with the fulfillment narratives supplied for those commands that are given but that in the earlier sources are not recorded as carried out. These embellishments disclose a concern with narrative consistency and coherence, which no doubt earlier authors and editors shared but left discernibly incomplete. Especially in cases where God is a character in the narrative, such an approach reflects the kind of divine consistency that promotes "stability," both social and institutional. The rewritten Scripture crystallizes in a particular way at a particular time for a particular group what the tradition is understood as having sought to communicate.[53]

Second, distortion and obligation. An example of distortion might be detected in the calendrical and chronometric views of the writers of the Book of Jubilees. A particular system of measuring time within years and through many periods of years is imposed on the text. It is not the case that such things are not present in the base texts of Genesis and Exodus that the author of Jubilees uses, but rather that such matters are "cultivated" in ways that are determined externally. The overall approach in Jubilees is a further example of such distortion of what is re-presented; for example, according to the narrative fiction of the text, various patriarchal figures observe some of the halakhic implications of the Sinaitic Law before ever it was made known. Assmann has been concerned to show how cultural memory is set firmly against historicism but rather creates "a normative self-image of the group" and "engenders a clear system of values."[54] Thus, one does not turn to Jubilees to discover what happened in Eden or at the flood or when Abraham entered the land, but rather to discern the value system of its author. Such values are most readily discernible when rewritten Scripture "distorts" its base text.

Third, invention and organization. An example of invention would seem to be the literary construction of Abram's dream in the Genesis Apocryphon 19:14–23. Although Joseph Fitzmyer describes the text as "a lengthy embellish-

---

52. Assmann, "Collective Memory and Cultural Identity," 130–31.
53. Another clear example of such a process and its purpose is the embellishment of the law of the king of Deut 17 in 11QT 56–59.
54. Assmann, "Collective Memory and Cultural Identity," 131.

ment of the biblical story,"[55] I am inclined to read this as invention. There is no precedent for this expansion of the text and no hint of a dream at this place in what we should probably justifiably take as the scriptural base text. This is not an extension of the text, but, as Fitzmyer himself acknowledges, this seems to be an invention that is "intended to be an explanation of the lie that Sarai will have to tell to cover up the real identity of Abram, her husband. The lie is to be told in conformity with a dream accorded to Abram, and though the origin of the dream is never ascribed to God, this is certainly the implication."[56] The invention contributes to the creation of a social identity through the enhancement of Abram's role as a patriarchal hero; the invented text frames him in the context of a view of the world in which divine intentions can be known to individuals through dreams and visions. It is in such inventions that what Assmann has called "the institutional buttressing of communication"[57] can be readily perceived. One of the principal ways in which such buttressing support takes shape is through explanation and exegesis, through commentary which in this case is implicit in the narrative reworking (as is usual in rewritten Scripture). Invention and organization are also readily apparent in the extensions to the scriptural material that are evident in the Temple Scroll but also in the compositions that seem to be variously related to the Temple Scroll in part, such as 4Q365.[58]

Fourth, forgetting and the capacity for reconstruction. Forgetting should not be construed principally as negative, though some ways of presenting the past that deliberately deny what took place in order to undermine some group or other can be exceedingly destructive. Forgetting is the most notable and obvious means through which memory reconstructs the past.[59] For the most part in these few comments I am thinking of selective forgetting, rather than of some kinds of overall historical amnesia that are sometimes considered to be a feature of the contemporary twenty-first-century Western worldview propagated in the media and popular culture. Developing the thinking of Halbwachs, Assmann has noted that "no memory can preserve the past. What remains is only that 'which society in each era can reconstruct within its contemporary frame of reference.'"[60] Cultural memory works by selected reconstruction of the past into some kind of

---

55. J. A. Fitzmyer, *The Genesis Apocryphon of Qumran Cave 1 (1Q20): A Commentary* (3rd ed.; BibOr 18B; Rome: Pontifical Biblical Institute, 2004), 184.

56. Ibid., 184.

57. Assmann, "Collective Memory and Cultural Identity," 131: a principle that Assmann labels as "Organization."

58. On this, see, e.g., Dwight D. Swanson, who asks questions about both the processes behind the production of additional material and also its authoritative status ("How Scriptural Is Re-Written Bible?" *RevQ* 21.83 [2004]: 418–24).

59. Mark S. Smith ("Remembering God," 649–51) has made some intriguing observations about how and why various discourses about the divine were "forgotten" in later compositions, notably the memory of El's family and the memory of the female side of divinity.

60. Assmann, "Collective Memory and Cultural Identity," 130.

unified or focalized pattern to which each contemporary situation relates in its own way, sometimes "by appropriation, sometimes by criticism, sometimes by preservation or by transformation." Rewritten Scripture as the artefactual textual evidence of particular groups at particular times discloses how such groups had a rich capacity for reconstructing the past. Abbreviation and forgetting are exemplary techniques of such reconstruction. Two examples can be briefly mentioned. First, in Jubilees, Sarai's cruel treatment of Hagar as in Gen 16:4–14 is entirely omitted from the description in Jub. 14:21–24 of how Sarai offers Hagar to Abram and she conceives by him. The politics of the degradation of Hagar and Ishmael serves some purpose in one generation and its circumstances, but not in another. Second, it is well known that in his rewriting of the events at Sinai (*Ant.* 3.101–2) Josephus forgets to mention the incident of the golden calf. The politics of the people's disobedience serves in one generation and its circumstances, but not in another.

It is commonly noted among those who have paid attention to the workings of cultural memory that groups, communities, peoples, and nations have systems of reflexivity through which all that is remembered is appropriated. Where religion is part and parcel of social self-expression, so it is in myth and ritual in particular that cultural memory is appropriated.[61] Two further observations that are related to each other seem significant at this point. The first concerns the apparent absence of those compositions commonly labeled as rewritten Scripture either generically or phenomenologically in what survives of the rules and rituals of the movement of which the Qumran community was a part. The second concerns the wealth of what survives among the manuscripts collected together in the Qumran caves; there is rewritten Scripture in abundance. How are these two related matters to be explained? I suspect that an answer might be found in the complex character of the kind of sectarianism to be observed in this group, but that is the subject for another essay.

4. Conclusion

In this chapter I have tried to raise the profile of memory in the consideration and evaluation of the phenomenon of rewritten Scripture. Because of the way in which we are fortunate to have individual manuscript copies of many of the compositions with which we are concerned, it seems to me dangerous to suppose that we can explain the phenomenon of rewritten Scripture by referring to literary works solely as abstract entities that somehow reflect the changing moods of the cultural complexities of Second Temple Judaism. Individual manuscripts require that some attention be given to individual scribes, authors, and editors. In so doing it is important to reckon with the mental processes of the individual

---

61. Hence it is important to pay attention to the role of memory in prayer and worship: see, e.g., Atkins, *Memory and Liturgy*.

in several ways, at least trying to take account of matters such as how individuals have their memories constructed by those they encounter and how scribes work to re-present compositions in ways that reflect how their own identities have been formed.

Nevertheless, for all that it is important to describe and discuss the particulars of the individual manuscripts within which rewritten Scripture can be found and the individual scribes behind them, so it is also worthwhile to indicate how collective or cultural memory might be understood as illuminating the phenomenon of rewritten Scripture. I have tried to indicate this by paying attention to four features in which particular rewriting strategies reflect some of the various aspects of how cultural memory works: embellishment and institutionalization, distortion and obligation, invention and organization, and forgetting and the capacity for reconstruction. These aspects do not define rewritten Bible more closely as a textual genre, but I believe that in some measure they improve our understanding of the processes at work in the rewriting of authoritative texts and traditions. It is still possible to endorse the need to be concerned with the analysis of a certain group of texts that clearly rewrite earlier traditions in a systematic, even sequential fashion. However, the appeal to various views about the role of cultural memory can help in describing the character of the processes of rewriting. Those processes involve a wide range of matters from attention to very specific exegetical issues to the construction and presentation of group identities.

Memory needs to be carefully defined and to be understood as including both individual and social dimensions in constructive dialogue, but it might offer one among several overarching categories that can describe both the minutiae of textual developments and the larger framing motivational issues that provoke full-scale rewritings.

We are left with many questions about how the movement that preserved all these compositions in their caves actually used them, but it seems to me that the phenomenon of rewritten Scripture is indeed partially better informed when it is recalled, in the words of Assmann, that "being that *can be remembered* is text."[62]

---

62. Assmann, *Religion and Cultural Memory*, ix (italics mine).

FIVE

Hypertextuality and the "Parabiblical" Dead Sea Scrolls

In memoriam Kurt Schubert (1923–2007)[1]

1. What Labels Are We Using?

The volume in which this essay first appeared was intended to include the word "palimpsests" in its title; thus, the thinking behind this essay began with reference to the work of Gérard Genette, who has used the term most provocatively. Although in codicology a palimpsest is simply a recycled manuscript in which the most recent text does not necessarily have any relationship to the text over which it is written, the term helpfully suggests how one text may lie on top of another text that has not been entirely erased. Genette used the term metaphorically to express how the text written on top was "literature of the second degree."

Nevertheless, for the purposes of this study I have been on the quest for a more suitable term that, without metaphor, might describe something of the relationships between the texts of my concern. In relation to much of what is presented in the Dead Sea Scrolls, the Second Temple period Jewish collection of literature from the caves at and near Qumran on the northwest shore of the Dead Sea, my preferred term has become "hypertext." This choice is indicated trivially by the spell-checker on my word-processing software. The spell-checker does not recognize intertext, paratext, peritext, epitext, metatext, cotext, transtext, architext, or hypotext, but it does seem to know what a hypertext is, suggesting that it knows, for example, of the relationship between James Joyce's *Ulysses* (the hypertext) and Homer's *Odyssey* (the hypotext).[2] The spell-checker is clearly not

---

1. Professor Kurt Schubert was the leading Dead Sea Scrolls scholar of the first generation in Vienna and established the University of Vienna's Institut für Judaistik in 1966; he kindly attended and commented on the first lecture on the scrolls that I gave in Vienna in May 2005 and died shortly before the meeting of the Palimpsests symposium.

2. Richard Macksey points out that "the hypertextual relationship of *Ulysses* to Homer's epic is less than obvious without the novelist's chapter titles, which Joyce suppressed in the published version of the book. Genette works out the complex network of correspond-

at the cutting edge of research into the character of much of the literature that I wish to consider, but it seems to recognize through its lack of erudition that I have a significant problem in labeling that has to be addressed in some way. The accepted significance of long-standing descriptors has to be stretched or qualified in several ways to account adequately for some of the kinds of literary compositions that I will consider in what follows, so it seems preferable to adopt the term hypertext as a useful term because while it forces its user to keep in mind that the text under discussion is dependent in some way on others, it also does not make unnecessary claims about the kind of authority the hypotext might have had.

Let us clear the ground immediately. The term "paratext," preferred by some scholars,[3] might be suitable for speaking of some kinds of literary activity, but it is not really adequate for the task of categorizing literary activity that is imitation and dependence of one sort or another. Although it is certainly the case that it is difficult to describe the many forms of Jewish scriptural rewriting as "parabiblical" because for compositions from the Second Temple period the "biblical" part of the compound descriptor is clearly anachronistic, it is equally problematic to move to the term "paratextual" since that term has been coined by others for other purposes. By paratextuality Genette indicates all the "liminal devices and conventions, both within the book (peritext) and outside it (epitext), that mediate the book to the reader: titles and subtitles, pseudonyms, forewords, dedications, epigraphs, prefaces, intertitles, notes, epilogues, and afterwords."[4] Some of these items are indeed preserved in the Dead Sea Scrolls, but it is wrong to suggest that the move from parabiblical to paratextual can be made by the scholar of ancient Jewish texts without causing confusion. Thus, the label to be preferred is "hypertext"; it is this term that seems to be useful for insisting that texts are related to other texts interpretatively, a fact that can easily be forgotten, as will be indicated in what follows. Hypertexts form the subject of Genette's *Palimpsestes*, the "literature of the second degree," though I do not intend to agree with or

---

ences between the eighteen chapters of the novel and Homer's original narrative in a detailed diagram; see *Palimpsestes* (Paris: Éditions du Seuil, 1982), 356" (Macksey, "Foreword," in *Paratexts: Thresholds of Interpretation* [ed. G. Genette; trans. J. E. Lewin; Literature, Culture, Theory 20; Cambridge: Cambridge University Press, 1997], xv).

3. Armin Lange helpfully outlines the development of the terminology in "In the Second Degree: Ancient Jewish Paratextual Literature in the Context of Graeco-Roman and Ancient Near Eastern Literature," in *In the Second Degree: Paratextual Literature in Ancient Near Eastern and Ancient Mediterranean Culture and Its Reflections in Medieval Literature* (ed. P. S. Alexander, A. Lange, and R. J. Pillinger; Leiden: Brill, 2010), 3-40, esp. 13-20. He seems to have developed his own usage of the term as preferable to the somewhat anachronistic "parabiblical" that he has used in several contexts: see, e.g., A. Lange, "From Literature to Scripture: The Unity and Plurality of the Hebrew Scriptures in Light of the Qumran Library," in *One Scripture or Many? Canon from Biblical, Theological, and Philosophical Perspectives* (ed. C. Helmer and C. Landmesser; Oxford: Oxford University Press, 2004), 84.

4. Macksey, "Foreword," xviii.

adhere to Genette's detailed categorization of the relationships between "hypertexts" and "hypotexts."[5]

2. What Literary Corpus Is Being Discussed?

In addition to searching for suitable labels, we need to be careful to outline the kind of literary corpus that the labels will serve to illuminate. Which literary compositions are we talking about as literature of the second degree? It can be asserted that all texts are related to other texts in one way or another, so it is necessary to limit the scope of this study by proposing that our principal concern will be with some of those compositions in which there was probably a deliberate intention to be interpretative. For the Dead Sea Scrolls, the specific concern of this study, a suitable place to start is the Index volume of Discoveries in the Judaean Desert (DJD). That volume has a fascinating section that presents a taxonomy by Armin Lange and Ulrike Mittmann-Richert of the genres of the compositions found in the Qumran corpus.[6] They describe what they label "parabiblical texts" as follows:

> This term as used in DJD, refers to literature "closely related to texts or themes of the Hebrew Bible."[7] On the basis of biblical texts or themes, the authors of parabiblical texts employ exegetical techniques to provide answers to questions of their own time, phrased as answers by God through Moses or the prophets. The result of their exegetical effort is communicated in the form of a new book. Therefore, parabiblical literature should not be understood as a pseudepigraphic phenomenon, i.e. the ascription of a literary work to a biblical author, but as a form of scriptural revelation, comparable to the phenomenon of literary prophecy. For this purpose, the authors of parabiblical literature used different genres: rewritten Bible, new stories or novellas created on the basis of biblical items or topics, different types of apocalypses, and testaments. In addition, parabiblical texts combining different genres can be found. However, it should be noted that a single biblical quotation or allusion, elaborated on in the context, does not necessarily indicate the parabiblical character of a fragmentary manuscript since implicit quotations are also extant in other genres of ancient Jewish literature (e.g. the Damascus Document). Because of these uncertainties, the classification of parabiblical literature is more restrictive than that proposed by the editors in the respective DJD volumes.[8]

---

5. See the suitable problematization of Genette's grid of relation and mood by Armin Lange, "In the Second Degree" (n. 3 above), 16–19. For example, it is immediately difficult to suppose that all "serious imitation" of a hypotext must be described as forgery.

6. A. Lange and U. Mittmann-Richert, "Annotated List of the Texts from the Judaean Desert Classified," in *The Texts from the Judaean Desert: Indices and an Introduction to the Discoveries in the Judaean Desert Series* (ed. E. Tov; DJD 39; Oxford: Clarendon, 2002), 115–64.

7. E. Tov, "Foreword," in *Qumran Cave 4.VIII: Parabiblical Texts, Part 1* (ed. J. C. VanderKam; DJD 13; Oxford: Clarendon, 1994), ix.

8. Lange and Mittmann-Richert, "Annotated List of the Texts," 117–18.

The DJD classification is circumscribed by three factors. First, it is constrained by the fact that already in 1994 the label "parabiblical" has been determined largely in relation to the Reworked Pentateuch manuscripts.[9] For continuity's sake the same label has been retained in the DJD series by the editors of manuscripts of a wide range of subgenres. Second, even if the label is in some ways unsatisfactory, it is defined in a somewhat more restricted way than many contributors to the DJD series have felt bound by. Third, its use makes assumptions about what was of primary authority, especially in the middle of the Second Temple period; one wonders, for example, whether the books of Chronicles should be better perceived as some kind of rewritten composition, whereas paleo ParaJoshua, not least because of its paleo-Hebrew script, was being presented as significantly authoritative by its scribal transmitters. Some rewritten texts, such as Deuteronomy, were clearly already authoritative by the second century B.C.E.; others, such as the books of Chronicles also eventually became part of the canon.[10] The use of the label "hypertext" enables us to avoid all these problems and to begin from the larger perspective of how texts depend on earlier or contemporary compositions.

Whatever the labels, in general we seem to know what kinds of composition we are talking about. I side with Lange and Mittmann-Richert in supposing that, until there is greater clarification through better understanding of what we are considering, it is safe to err on the side of inclusion, rather to think that we should immediately group texts in smaller well-defined categories. For me this means that even the label "rewritten Bible" should be conceived broadly.[11] But also, for now, leaving behind the label rewritten Bible and talking rather of hypertexts, we may still seem to know what we are talking about in relation to the Jewish literary corpus that has survived in the Qumran caves.[12]

In the first place, almost all the Pentateuch is represented extensively in these kinds of rewritten paraphrases preserved in the caves. Generally these hypertextual compositions follow the order of the source and often stay very close to its

---

9. See E. Tov and S. White, "Reworked Pentateuch," in VanderKam, *Qumran Cave 4.VIII: Parabiblical Texts, Part 1* (DJD 13), 187–351, for 4Q364–367. 4Q158 is also regularly included as an exemplar of this composition: see G. J. Brooke, "4Q158: Reworked Pentateuch[a] or 4QReworked Pentateuch A?" *DSD* 8 (2001): 219–41.

10. On how Chronicles may have been perceived by those at Qumran, see G. J. Brooke, "The Books of Chronicles and the Scrolls from Qumran," in *Reflection and Refraction: Studies in Biblical Historiography in Honour of A. Graeme Auld* (ed. R. Rezetko et al.; VTSup 113; Leiden: Brill, 2007), 35–48.

11. See G. J. Brooke, "Rewritten Bible," in *Encyclopedia of the Dead Sea Scrolls* (ed. L. H. Schiffman and J. C. VanderKam; New York: Oxford University Press, 2000), 777–81, where I argue for the use of the term as an overarching category. Among those who prefer a stricter use of the label for a narrower, more closely defined genre are M. J. Bernstein, "'Rewritten Bible': A Generic Category Which Has Outlived Its Usefulness?" *Textus* 22 (2005): 169–96.

12. To find information on the compositions mentioned in what follows see the various reference contributions in Tov, *Texts from the Judaean Desert: Indices* (DJD 39).

phraseology; sometimes there is greater divergence. For Genesis several compositions belong in this category, such as the Genesis Apocryphon (1QapGen), an Aramaic narrative retelling of large sections of Genesis, whose extant portions are mostly concerned with Noah and Abraham. The fragments of the Exposition on the Patriarchs (4Q464) are probably another such retelling, but in Hebrew, as also the Paraphrase of Genesis and Exodus (4Q422), and the Text Mentioning the Flood (4Q577) and the presentation of the flood in Commentary on Genesis A (4Q252 i–ii). Testamentary literature, such as the Testament of Judah (3Q7; 4Q484) and related compositions such as the Aramaic Levi Document (1Q21; 4Q213–214) can also be classified as sapiential or eschatological hypertextual literature. There also seems to be a similar literary phenomenon in Greek (4Qpap paraExod gr).[13] Association with particular patriarchs is common.

For Genesis and Exodus it is widely acknowledged that the most throughgoing hypertextual reworking is to be found in the book of Jubilees; this is a Hebrew narrative retelling of Gen 1–Exod 15 that introduces various halakhot, notably on the Sabbath, so that the patriarchs are seen to be law-abiding before ever the Law was given. To assert its own authority Jubilees declares that its content was revealed to Moses from the heavenly tablets by the angel of the presence. Also in Cave 4 were up to three manuscripts that contained a composition closely related to Jubilees (4Q225–227).

For other parts of the Pentateuch the classic example of so-called rewritten Bible is the Temple Scroll, known in three or more manuscripts (4Q524; 11Q19; 11Q20; 11Q21?); rather than being revealed to Moses by an angel as is the case in Jubilees, the Temple Scroll is made up of speeches addressed to Moses by God himself. The content of the Temple Scroll is of two sorts: in the first part, various pentateuchal laws concerning the tabernacle and sacrifice are arranged and supplemented with texts from Ezekiel, 1–2 Kings, and 1–2 Chronicles (and other sources); in the second part there is an abbreviated hypertextual presentation of Deut 12 onwards, the law for those who live in the land, which has an expanded section that corresponds to Deut 17:14–20, the law for the king, perhaps an expansion whose contents are directed against some contemporary ruler. Jubilees and the Temple Scroll could also be classed as nonsectarian religious law, though their outlook is taken up in several sectarian compositions; the same goes for the Apocryphon of Moses (1Q22; 4Q375–376; 4Q408).

There are rewritten or hypertextual forms for several of the history books too, what later became the Former Prophets. Dependent in some way on the book of Joshua are the Apocryphon of Joshua (4Q378–379; also found at Masada [Mas apocrJosh]), and the Prophecy of Joshua (4Q522). A form of the Apocryphon of Joshua seems to be cited as a scriptural authority in the sectarian Testimonia

---

13. See E. C. Ulrich, "A Greek Paraphrase of Exodus on Papyrus from Qumran Cave 4," in *Studien zur Septuaginta—Robert Hanhart zu Ehren: Aus Anlaß seines 65. Geburtstages* (ed. D. Fraenkel et al.; MSU 20; Göttingen: Vandenhoeck & Ruprecht, 1990), 287–98.

(4Q175) and so should perhaps be added to the list of books that were deemed of primary authority at Qumran but that did not make it into subsequent Jewish or Christian canon lists. For Samuel there is hypertextual material in the Vision of Samuel (4Q160) and for Kings a paraphrase in the Paraphrase of Kings et al. (4Q382). In some instances it is difficult to tell whether the form in the Qumran library is secondary in every respect. It is possible that the freedom with which the Gospel writers rework their narrative sources is a reflection of the same scribal attitude.

There are some hypertextual forms of the prophetic books too, notably the three forms of the Apocryphon of Jeremiah (4Q383; 4Q384; 4Q385a; 4Q387; 4Q388a; 4Q389–390; 4Q387a), the five or six copies of Pseudo-Ezekiel (4Q385; 4Q386; 4Q385b; 4Q388; 4Q391; 4Q385c), and the Daniel Apocalypse (4Q246), Pseudo-Daniel (4Q243–244) and the Four Kingdoms (4Q552–553). Some poetic materials that are akin to the scriptural psalms could also be categorized as hypertextual or rewritten Bible (such as 2Q22; 4Q371–373; 4Q460). The List of False Prophets (4Q339), the Biblical Chronology (4Q559), and various Narrative works (e.g., 4Q462) can also be classed as nonsectarian hypertextual compositions. I further consider that in its widest usage hypertextuality applies also to a number of poetic and liturgical texts, for which Genette's understanding of imitation by pastiche is significant as a way of understanding compositional method.[14] Among such compositions can be put the Apocryphal Psalms, the Non-Canonical Psalms, and even the Hodayot.

3. Hypertextuality in the Qumran Library

What are we to do to make sense of this range of compositions that many have called parabiblical or paratextual but which I am labeling now as hypertextual? With one eye on Genette, I want to concentrate on what I will distinguish as four kinds of hypertextuality, though the issues to be discussed overlap considerably. In a more recent work, L'Œuvre de l'art, Genette has considered the aesthetic status of a work of art, such as a piece of literature, but also has played on his own title to consider how such artistic pieces "work." Without reducing the implications of his insights, Genette nevertheless has come to see that "a work of art is an intentional aesthetic object, or, which amounts to the same thing: a work of art is an artifact (or human product) [enlisted] to an aesthetic function."[15] In this, as Richard Macksey points out, Genette underscores the viewer's or reader's share in the intentional process. "The work is never reducible to its immanent object,

---

14. By pastiche Genette implies both multiplicity and playfulness in the relation of the hypertext to its hypotexts (plural).

15. G. Genette, L'Œuvre de l'art: immanence et transcendance (Paris: Éditions du Seuil, 1994), 10; Macksey, "Foreword," xvii, n. 2.

because its being is inseparable from its action."[16] Thus, it is to the mixture of form and function that we should turn. Consideration of function takes us away from considering Jewish hypertexts in a political and social vacuum. Since we know that texts demand to have readers and hearers and are not entities sufficient in themselves, it is necessary to take into account that they "have ways of existing that even in their most rarified form are always enmeshed in circumstance, time, place, and society—in short, they are in the world, and hence worldly,"[17] as Edward Said has remarked. Texts disclose power relationships.

3.1. Seconding Sinai Primordially

My first set of hypertext comments refers particularly to those compositions related to the Torah—what can be labeled as Mosaic discourse. I have elsewhere tried to describe how a large proportion of the works in the Qumran library seem to depend in one way or another on scriptural antecedents.[18] Even a cursory look at a collection of compositions from the library, such as can be seen in Geza Vermes's *The Complete Dead Sea Scrolls in English*, reveals that the largest listings are for "Bible Interpretation" and "Biblically Based Apocryphal Works,"[19] though even that conceals just how often many of the other compositions in the library are literature in the second degree. Within this literature pride of place both in terms of quantity of compositions and also in terms of quality of interaction with the hypotext goes to works based on the Torah.

What is taking place in this Mosaic literature? The model I adopt here is a brief adaptation of some insightful ideas put together very suggestively by Hindy Najman; her ideas have to be adapted somewhat because they do not anchor the text in its function, as Genette demands. Najman has proposed that there are four indispensable features of Mosaic discourse in the Second Temple period. (1) "By reworking and expanding older traditions through interpretation, a new text claims for itself the authority that already attaches to those traditions." (2) Such new texts ascribe to themselves the status of Torah, as either heavenly or earthly in origin but, in any event, "an authentic expression of the Torah of Moses." (3) "The new text is said to be a re-presentation of the revelation at Sinai." There is a recreation of the Sinai experience to emphasize "the presentness of the Sinai event." (4) "The new text is said to be associated with, or produced by, the founding figure, Moses," a claim that serves to authorize the new interpretations as

---

16. From Genette's *prière d'insérer* for *L'Œuvre de l'art*.

17. E. Said, *The World, the Text, and the Critic* (1983; repr., London: Vintage, 1991), 35.

18. G. J. Brooke, "The Dead Sea Scrolls," in *The Biblical World* (ed. J. Barton; London: Routledge, 2002), 1:250–69.

19. G. Vermes, *The Complete Dead Sea Scrolls in English* (5th rev. ed.; London: Penguin2004), vii–xii. One could equally well look at the list in Lange and Mittmann-Richert, "Annotated List of the Texts."

divine revelation, dictation, prophecy, or inspired interpretation, and so to show that the new text is an extension of earlier ancestral discourse.[20] For Najman, the key to Mosaic hypertexts is a heady mixture of matters to do with authority, authenticity, immediacy, and continuity.

I will make a few comments on each of these topics. First, authority: To my mind Najman makes an assumption, perhaps partially unwarranted, about the status of the Mosaic Torah as an authoritative, that is, for her, an authorizing text in the Second Temple period. There can be little doubt that the five books of the Torah occupy some preeminent position for many Jews in the immediate post-Ezra period, but this preeminence is not of the sort that the same text comes to occupy in the canonical period. I have argued elsewhere that one interesting factor in appreciating rewritten texts is the way they not only receive authority from the texts they rework, but they also give it.[21] In other words, the very activity of hypertextual rewriting is a bestowal of authority, perhaps where such authority needed to be asserted because in some way it was lacking. So ongoing Mosaic discourse in the rewritten Torah texts may well be an acknowledgment of the Torah's authority, but it is also an assertion of it, perhaps in the face of those who would challenge it. This is how one can justify the conclusion, correct in my view, that the rewritten compositions were not designed to replace the hypotexts for which they are the hypertexts.[22] They are not palimpsests in the sense that they are written over, erased, or barely legible hypotexts; nevertheless the hypotext would lose what authority it ever had without the presence of hypertexts.

Second, authenticity: For Najman, authenticity is a matter of status, defined in large part by origin, whether heavenly or earthly. It seems to me that the issue may be more complex. Authenticity in texts would seem to have to do with integrity and truth claims. The authenticity of rewritten Torah texts is represented in the ways that they offer their own inherently consistent integrity. This is something that belongs where it is brought to birth; it cannot be passed on. It has to be learned anew in each successive generation; hypertexts enable the authentic renewal of their hypotexts. From one generation to another this might be achieved through redaction. Sometimes such textual redaction creates a system of literary coherence where such was somewhat lacking; compositions may then

---

20. H. Najman, *Seconding Sinai: The Development of Mosaic Discourse in Second Temple Judaism* (JSJSup 77; Leiden: Brill, 2003), 16–17.

21. G. J. Brooke, "The Rewritten Law, Prophets and Psalms: Issues for Understanding the Text of the Bible," in *The Bible as Book: The Hebrew Bible and the Judaean Desert Discoveries* (ed. E. D. Herbert and E. Tov; London: British Library; New Castle, Del.: Oak Knoll; Grand Haven: Scriptorium Center for Christian Antiquities, 2002), 31–40.

22. See, e.g., P. S. Alexander, "Retelling the Old Testament" in *It Is Written: Scripture Citing Scripture: Essays in Honour of Barnabas Lindars, SSF* (ed. D. A. Carson and H. G. M. Williamson; Cambridge: Cambridge University Press, 1987), 99–121, esp. 116: "despite the superficial independence of form, these texts are not intended to replace, or to supersede the Bible."

spawn recensions in textual production. There are also full-blown rewritings and pseudepigraphs. But in any new generation it seems to me that authenticity must be rediscovered. An authentic voice in the Mosaic discourse is one that is in some way limited to a particular setting, in which it is produced and to which it speaks.

Third, immediacy: Genette comments that paratextual elements are one of the key ways in which a text is promoted: "Although we do not always know whether these productions are to be regarded as belonging to the text, in any case they surround it and extend it, precisely in order to present it, in the usual sense of this verb but also in the strongest sense: to make present, to ensure the text's presence in the world, its 'reception.'"[23] In stressing the presentness of the textuality of the Sinai event, a significant characteristic of rewritten or hypertextual Torah is its contribution to and enabling of the making contemporary of the Torah, and through such a process facilitating its appropriation by the audience, even if the fiction of Israel at Sinai sits uneasily with the realities of the reader's circumstances. In the postcanonical period it seems to be explicit commentary on the Torah that normally serves this function; in the precanonical period it seems as if rewritten scriptural texts were one of the ways in which, through their very authenticity, authentic experience of one particular understanding of the past was created in the present. But this function of making Sinai present is also the undoing of the ongoing authority of these so-called rewritten Bible texts, since their very contemporaneity soon becomes dated. They are like workers on a short-term contract; without a permanent contract in the community based in other matters they are soon replaced with other rewritings. If authenticity is something that cannot be passed on but has to be learned again in each generation, then immediacy, like Moses' shining face, soon fades.

Fourth, continuity: Authenticity in particular is discovered and rediscovered in each generation, but in Mosaic discourse and in other discourses too it depends on being recognized as authentic by virtue of its character as hypertext. In other words, it stands in relation to a hypotext, namely, the Mosaic Torah. Thus, part of the character of the rewritten hypertextual Torah compositions is their being recognizable as continuous with the Torah itself. But in fact again, it is often and usually more complex than that. The relation of hypertext to hypotext is not a straightforward one in which the hypertext is the literature of the second degree, as Genette would have us believe, since the trick of continuity is often played out in the way that the hypertext might claim to be prior to the text on whose authority it is overlaid. This is what Najman ingeniously calls primordial writing: the book of Jubilees re-presents what is on the heavenly tablets; the Temple Scroll is constructed with God as the voice of the narrator; and the Reworked Pentateuch manuscripts reflect a redactional coherence that is surely more akin to the character of God himself than the muddle that now makes up the Torah.

---

23. Genette, *Paratexts*, 1.

Another feature of the continuity that is characteristic of the way these rewritten texts take part in the representation of their hypotexts is the way in which by comparison with the closed Torah they retain the character of being open-ended, of being part of a "rolling corpus."[24] The rewriting process goes on from generation to generation and the variety of forms, for example, of the Reworked Pentateuch reflects this ongoing activity. From this point of view, to ask whether, for instance, 4Q158 is a version of the same composition as 4Q365 somewhat misses the point. The corpus is on a roll.

3.2. The Place of the Deuteronomistic Metanarrative

The second category of hypertexts in the Qumran collection that I wish to consider briefly are those that are primarily rewritten narrative compositions apart from those that use the narratives of the Torah. As mentioned in relation to those compositions which engage in ongoing Mosaic discourse, I have surmised elsewhere that the existence of rewritten forms of texts, the existence of hypertexts, is one indication among others of the emerging authority of the hypotexts upon which they depend. It is intriguing in the Qumran library to notice what is present and seemingly absent in relation to what we now regard as the scriptural narrative materials. An immediate first impression is that there is more extant that relates to prophetic activity than there is in relation to the history of Israel from Joshua to the exile.

The Deuteronomistic History from the early postexilic period, whatever its precise extent and contents, represents a major attempt at offering Second Temple Israel, emerging Judaism, a metanarrative for explaining principally the exile itself and Israel's relation to the land. For those who collected the Qumran library together, it seems that this metanarrative was both recognized as a suitable theological reading of exile, since the theology of Deuteronomy is omnipresent in many of the sectarian compositions such as MMT[25] or even, as I have written elsewhere,[26] in the Commentary on Genesis A. Its presence can be felt too in the community's rule books of all sorts and in the way it is programmatic in such presectarian compositions as the Temple Scroll.

But it seems that, while the Deuteronomistic metanarrative was known by those who collected together the Qumran library, it was no longer in wide use; the theology of Deuteronomy persisted in other guises, and historiography was

---

24. To adopt a descriptor used for the development of the book(s) of Jeremiah by William McKane, *A Critical and Exegetical Commentary on Jeremiah* (2 vols; ICC; Edinburgh: T&T Clark, 1986–96).

25. "And the curses [that] came from in the days of Jeroboam the son of Nebat until Jerusalem and Zedekiah king of Judah were exiled" (MMT: 4Q398 frgs. 11–13, lines 18–20).

26. G. J. Brooke, "The Deuteronomic Character of 4Q252," in *Pursuing the Text: Studies in Honor of Ben Zion Wacholder on the Occasion of his Seventieth Birthday* (ed. J. C. Reeves and J. Kampen; JSOTSup 184; Sheffield: Sheffield Academic Press, 1994), 121–35.

pursued in other ways.[27] The Qumran community and the wider movement of which it was a part seem to have considered itself as barely coming out of exile. Although clearly in the land in the late second and first centuries B.C.E., it is widely thought that the community felt dis-ease with regard to Jerusalem and its temple. The community and movement were in a kind of liminal borderline state between exile and occupation. Perhaps for some reason the Deuteronomistic metanarrative might not have seemed to be the most suitable paradigm for such a state of liminality. Rather the prophetic reading of history in a variety of forms, periodized and on the way to fulfillment, was what the community looked to for illumination and identity. Thus, although there do seem to be paraphrases of the books from Joshua to Kings in the library, it is the hypertextual prophetic texts for Jeremiah and Ezekiel, even for Samuel and Daniel, that are better preserved and seem more prominent. Such an observation suggests the unsuitability of the Deuteronomistic metanarrative for the community; perhaps part of that unsuitability arose because other sections of Judaism in the late Second Temple period had appropriated that reading of events to assert their own contemporary authoritative positions.

Something of the avoidance of such chronicled metanarratives by the collectors of the Qumran library might also be discernible in their attitude to the books of Chronicles, itself a hypertext in some way related to the Deuteronomistic hypotext. For the books of Chronicles the situation in what survives from the library is stark.[28] One manuscript (4Q118) has been labeled as a copy of Chronicles;[29] it contains remains of two columns of writing. The contents of the second column correspond to 2 Chr 28:27–29:3, but the contents of the first have no parallel in Chronicles, Kings, or what may be reconstructed as a Hebrew text based on the Greek translation of Chronicles. It is thus unlikely that 4Q118 is a straightforward copy of the books of Chronicles. Alexander Rofé has wondered whether in fact 4Q118, like 4Q382 (Paraphrase of Kings), contains "a homiletical revision of the Book of Kings that included a psalm of entreaty similar to the one attributed to Hezekiah in Isa 38:9–20."[30]

Beyond the circumstances of the accidents of preservation, what expla-

---

27. See G. J. Brooke, "Types of Historiography in the Qumran Scrolls," in *Ancient and Modern Scriptural Historiography/L'historiographie biblique, ancienne et moderne* (ed. G. J. Brooke and T. Römer; BETL 207; Leuven: Peeters, 2007), 211–30.

28. J. Trebolle Barrera ("Chronicles, First and Second Books of," in Schiffman and VanderKam, *Encyclopedia of the Dead Sea Scrolls*, 129) offers a concise note on Chronicles in the Dead Sea Scrolls but with little explanation or interpretation.

29. See J. Trebolle Barrera, "4QChr," in *Qumran Cave 4.XI: Psalms to Chronicles* (ed. E. Ulrich et al.; DJD 16; Oxford: Clarendon, 2000), 295–97.

30. A. Rofé, "'No *Ephod* or *Teraphim'—oude hierateias oude dēlōn*: Hosea 3:4 in the LXX and in the Paraphrases of Chronicles and the *Damascus Document*," in *Sefer Moshe: The Moshe Weinfeld Jubilee Volume. Studies in the Bible and the Ancient Near East, Qumran, and Post-Biblical Judaism* (ed. C. Cohen et al.; Winona Lake, Ind.: Eisenbrauns, 2004), 135–49, esp. 143 n. 22.

nations might be offered for this lack of concern for Chronicles at Qumran and in its parent movement? A general answer might consider that the type of chronicling of events that is to be found in Chronicles was of little concern to these Jews. A more specific answer should consider that there was a deliberate avoidance of such historiography. "The scarcity of Chronicles at Qumran could be by chance, with several other manuscripts being lost. More likely, however, the small number of scrolls is by design, since Chronicles has a strong focus on Jerusalem and the temple, from which the Qumran community had removed itself."[31] The reasons for such avoidance might be very complicated but, in addition to its overt emphasis on Jerusalem and the temple, could include the real likelihood that works like Chronicles were being adopted and promoted by the Hasmonean priest-kings, for whose outlook the majority of those at Qumran seem to have had considerable antagonism. More particularly, the concern in Chronicles for a chastened Davidic model of kingship might have proved an attractive model and tradition to support the Hasmonean rulers; there is nothing in the sectarian compositions at Qumran to suggest that the members of the community supported a reestablished monarchy in any form in the pre-messianic era. Thus, the absence of obvious manuscript copies of the books of Chronicles from the Qumran library can be understood in two ways.[32] On the one hand, the community that preserved the scrolls may well have been antipathetic to the probable Hasmonean claims to be heirs to the Davidic tradition.[33] On the other, over against Hasmonean Davidic aspirations, the community kept silent about the Davidic identification of its Messiah of Israel until the end of the first century B.C.E.[34] The slender presence of some kinds of historical narrative hypertext in the Qumran library allows us to surmise that indeed a composition's function was so important that the hypotextual preferences of the community and the movement of which it was a part are revealed in what is preserved of its own hypertexual output.

---

31. J. C. VanderKam and P. W. Flint, *The Meaning of the Dead Sea Scrolls: Their Significance for Understanding the Bible, Judaism, Jesus, and Christianity* (San Francisco: HarperSanFrancisco, 2002), 118.

32. G. J. Brooke, "Between Authority and Canon: The Significance of Reworking the Bible for Understanding the Canonical Process," in *Reworking the Bible: Apocryphal and Related Texts at Qumran. Proceedings of a Joint Symposium by the Orion Center for the Study of the Dead Sea Scrolls and Associated Literature and the Hebrew University Institute for Advanced Studies Research Group on Qumran, 15–17 January, 2002* (ed. E. G. Chazon, D. Dimant, and R. A. Clements; STDJ 58; Leiden: Brill, 2005), 85–104, here 88–89.

33. Cf. 1 Macc 2:57, which can be read as shifting the Davidic inheritance to the Hasmonean dynasty. See J. Goldstein, *1 Maccabees: A New Translation with Introduction and Commentary* (AB 41; New York: Doubleday, 1976), 240.

34. A more extensive treatment of this can be found in Brooke, "Books of Chronicles and the Scrolls from Qumran," 35–48.

3.3. Identity as "Pastiche"

The third kind of hypertext for brief consideration is the poetry of a wide range of compositions in the Non-Canonical and Apocryphal Psalms as well as the Hodayot. Of those, I shall focus in particular on the Hodayot. Here Genette's label "pastiche," a kind of imaginatively creative and playful imitation through anthologization, seems particularly suitable. Even if one does not subscribe to the approach of Svend Holm-Nielsen, who proposed a very extensive list of scriptural allusions in the Hodayot without asking whether they were either intended or discernible to all readers,[35] nevertheless it is clear that there is much scriptural phraseology in these anthologies. They are imitative pastiches of anthological allusion. Here, I think, is a matter of moving poetically from the universal to the particular. Although this was happening in any case for the Psalms themselves as the paratextual data in the superscriptions was added to the poems themselves, in the Hodayot, without such overt paratextual paraphernalia, there is a move toward the widely used poetry of others for the construction of particular identities.

The specific hypertextual function of the Hodayot has been discussed recently in several works. In particular the analyses of Carol Newsom and Julie Hughes highlight what imitative pastiche may be about. In her study *The Self as Symbolic Space*,[36] Newsom has provided, among many other things, a fascinating reading of 1QH^a 12:5–13:4.[37] It is intriguing that in attempting to describe and define the meaning and significance of the poem Newsom has presented it through an analysis that is both literary and psychological, rather than hypertextual or psychological. It is unclear whether this is a deliberate attempt by her at secularizing the poetry to enable its broader universally illuminating human insights to emerge from the dark caves of Qumran or an unintended avoidance of theology to preserve the text from falling into abuse. Nevertheless, Newsom's descriptions have disclosed much of the meaning of the hymn in terms of its social function in the formation of self-identity. As has been noted, it is the exposure of the function of texts that is a key role of hypertextual awareness; Newsom intriguingly reaches her functional conclusions without much appreciation of hypotexts and hypertexts.

---

35. S. Holm-Nielsen, *Hodayot: Psalms from Qumran* (ATDan 2; Aarhus: Universitets-forlaget, 1960).

36. C. A. Newsom, *The Self as Symbolic Space: Constructing Identity and Community at Qumran* (STDJ 52; Leiden: Brill, 2004).

37. I have engaged with Newsom's reading in G. J. Brooke, "The Structure of 1QH^a XII 5–XIII 4 and the Meaning of Resurrection," in *From 4QMMT to Resurrection: Mélanges qumraniens en hommage à Émile Puech* (ed. F. García Martínez et al.; STDJ 61; Leiden: Brill, 2006), 15–33.

Newsom has recognized that 1QH[a] contains a complex sequence of poems, each of which has distinctive traits, although there are many shared items as well. For 1QH[a] 12:5–13:4 she has noted that it is particularly closely related, in terms of its "projection of antithetical rival discourses" and its striking similarities of diction, to 1QH[a] 10:3–19, which puts the leader at the center of things in not initiating conflict with outsiders but in concentrating "on the cultivation of a closed community of truth."[38] Newsom has wondered whether 1QH[a] 12:5–13:4 was conceived as a programmatic development of the closing ideas of 1QH[a] 10:3–19, but because of its ambition she has defined it as "the map of truth," an attempt to sketch out "a map of an ideology of truth and the kind of identities implied by such an ideology."[39] Here the poem is clearly conceived of as more significant for its function for its contemporary reader than in terms of the poetic pieces that make it up. In fact this is so much the case in Newsom's reading that she has barely mentioned the way the Hodayot are hypertexts based on other literary sources in many ways.

In the first part of the poem Newsom has proposed that the overriding concern is a poetic attempt to account for the sectarian community's rejection by the larger society. The rejection is portrayed in part as nonsensical or irrational (1QH[a] 12:8), but mostly as the result of seductive villainy perpetrated by those false teachers who are the mirror image of the implied speaker himself. Newsom has understood this as primarily symbolic, though she has not denied the possibility that the poet envisaged actual social rivals. In the first part of the poem the actors are the speaker and his false opponents and the people of God they have led astray. In the second part of the poem the speaker's own community comes into the frame as a counterbalance to the straying people of God of the first part.[40] The strategy of the poem is thus to expose the impossibility of resolving the contradictions between the speaker and the false teachers, between the speaker and the seduced people of God, and between the speaker's followers and the false teachers; the only viable relationship is between the speaker and his followers ("through me you have caused light to shine upon the faces of the many"; 1QH[a] 12:27). Newsom has then described the consequence of this viability as "eschatological salvation,"[41] which has its counterpart in the eschatological destruction of the false teachers and the people they have led astray. There is thus a present contradiction projected in the poem that is resolved by means of an eschatological perspective; intriguingly, Newsom has demonstrated how the poem makes sense of contemporary issues by reference to the eschaton.

---

38. Newsom, *Self as Symbolic Space*, 311.

39. Ibid.

40. Newsom comments appealingly that "the little drama described in this hodayah is one that in romance novels one would recognize as seduction and betrayal versus redemption through true love" (*Self as Symbolic Space*, 320).

41. Ibid., 321, referring to 1QH[a] 12:24–25.

Newsom's reading of the poem is intensified through her keen observation that the poem is mostly about a polarization between the material attached to the use of the two pronouns, predominantly "they/them" in the first half of the poem and "I" in the second half. The opposition is not one of ignorance and knowledge, because "they" are characterized not as the ignorant but as liars, those who understand but who deliberately pervert knowledge, those who know the truth of God but assert their own autonomy over against it (1QH[a] 12:17–18).[42] Over against such double dealing the speaker asserts a kind of self-denial, the recognition of the worthlessness of every being unless fashioned anew through the recognition of God's power and compassion; such self-abnegation is an act of empowerment as long as strength and comfort are derived from the assertion of divine sovereignty rather than from any sense of self-righteousness.

Newsom has caught the force of the final form of the poem in a largely convincing manner, but, apart from the motif of "eschatological salvation," her theological reticence requires some supplementation, not least because it does not disclose how the poem is hypertextual. In part the necessary hypertextual supplementation is provided by the recent analysis by Julie Hughes, whose overall assessment of this poem is based largely on appreciating its allusions to scriptural passages.[43] Hughes has divided the poem into two sections:[44] first, an introduction and complaint against enemies (1QH[a] 12:5–29a), which has four subunits (an introductory stanza, 12:5–6; two sections on the speaker and his enemies, 12:6–13 and 14–22, which have together have four "and they" units; and a climactic conclusion, 12:22–29); second, a prayer of confession and commitment (12:29b–13:5), whose chief characteristic is the four "and I" subsections.[45] Hughes has used two features to discern how the poem is organized and to describe its significance: the poetics of the poem, which includes a range of markers, such as the frequent use of pronouns,[46] and the use of scriptural allusions, its hypertextuality. For the first section she has noted that the conjunction with the third person plural pronoun is used four times (12:6, 9, 13, 16); for her second section she has noted the balancing use of the first person pronoun four times (12:30, 33, 35, and probably 39), though she resists seeing anything

---

42. Ibid., 324.

43. J. A. Hughes, *Scriptural Allusions and Exegesis in the Hodayot* (STDJ 59; Leiden: Brill, 2006), 95–134.

44. In the Ph.D. dissertation form of her work, Hughes presented a structural analysis closer to the three parts indicated by Jacob Licht, *The Thanksgiving Scroll: A Scroll from the Wilderness of Judaea, Text, Introduction, Commentary and Glossary* (in Hebrew; Jerusalem: Bialik Institute, 1957), 91–98: 1QH[a] 12:5–22, 22–29; 12:29–13:4.

45. I have adjusted Hughes's numbering of lines to agree with that which is popularly available in F. García Martínez and E. J. C. Tigchelaar, eds., *The Dead Sea Scrolls Study Edition*, vol. 1, *1Q1–4Q273* (Leiden: Brill, 1997), 166–71.

46. In fact, in anticipating the insights of Newsom (*Self as Symbolic Space*, 322–25), Hughes has nicely labeled the poem "'I' and 'They'" (*Scriptural Allusions and Exegesis in the Hodayot*, 95).

chiastic in the balancing construction. The mixture of explicit pronouns produces less structural clarity in what she has labeled a "climactic conclusion" to the first part (12:22b–29a).

For scriptural background Hughes has noted a wide range of texts, distinguishing between those that are very likely to have been in the mind of the poet and those that might possibly also be present. The most likely allusions include the probable appeals to Hos 6:3 in 1QH^a 12:6 and Hos 4:14, with its context of God holding the priests and prophets culpable for the people's lack of knowledge, in 1QH^a 12:7. Also highly probable are allusions to Exod 34:29 (1QH^a 12:5); Deut 33:2 (1QH^a 12:6); Jer 2:11 (1QH^a 12:10, with the theme of plotting); Ps 69:21 (1QH^a 12:11); Hab 2:15 (1QH^a 12:11); Jer 23:9 (1QH^a 12:12); Prov 19:21 (1QH^a 12:13); Ps 33:11 (1QH^a 12:13); Deut 29:17–20 (1QH^a 12:14; a key Deuteronomic passage for providing both terms and themes for this poem); Ezek 14:3–7 (1QH^a 12:15); Ezek 13:6 (1QH^a 12:16); Isa 28:11 (1QH^a 12:16); Jer 23:20 (1QH^a 12:21); and Ezek 13:10 (1QH^a 12:24). In addition to Deuteronomy, Hughes has thus identified a number of allusions to covenantal passages in Hos 4:1–6:3; Jer 23:9–40; and Ezek 13:1–14:11 as structurally significant. This is hypertextual pastiche with a purpose.

Given the overall unity of the poem, it is worth noting the way in which not only certain scriptural books are alluded to more than once, but also certain verses recur in the poem. Like others before her, Hughes has noted the hint of Isa 53:3 in 1QH^a 12:8 and 23. Other passages alluded to more than once are Isa 30:10 in 1QH^a 12:7 and 10; Isa 57:17 in 1QH^a 12:17, 18, 21, and 24;[47] Ps 20:8 in 1QH^a 12:22 and 36; and Isa 42:6 in 1QH^a 12:5 and 42:3 in 1QH^a 12:25. These may be more important structurally than Hughes has allowed, since she has been guided primarily by the recurrence of pronouns and what she has assessed to be dominant passages of Scripture that shape the covenantal concerns of the poem.

A combination of the insights of Newsom and Hughes permits the modern reader to appreciate the hypertextual character of the pastiche that makes up much of the Hodayot to be concerned with the construction of identity by the poet through the carefully structured use of allusion—this is Scripture rewritten poetically, anthologically, hypertextually. Identifying the Hodayot, and by implication most of the poetic and liturgical compositions at Qumran, as hypertextual enables one to appreciate how these texts function as part of an ongoing discourse in ways that are not unlike the key motifs of discourse identified with respect to Moses by Najman.[48]

---

47. Menahem Kister has indicated that Isa 57:14–21 provides several items of sectarian terminology ("Biblical Phrases and Hidden Biblical Interpretations and *Pesharim*," in *The Dead Sea Scrolls: Forty Years of Research* [ed. D. Dimant and U. Rappaport; STDJ 10; Leiden: Brill; Jerusalem: Magnes Press and Yad Izhak Ben-Zvi, 1992], 32–34).

48. One might consider this discourse to be as poetically inspired and as revelatory as anything in Mosaic discourse.

3.4. The Liminality of Texts

Having considered some aspects of hypertextuality for the Torah, the Former and Latter Prophets, and the Psalms in the three previous subsections of this essay, my final category covers all three in a general way and can be put briefly. Genette has used the notion of paratextual liminality entirely appropriately to describe all the elements in a literary work that are on the edges, the items that intervene between the reader and the text and often serve to interpret the text: titles, sub-headings, marginalia, colophons, even pagination. My sense is that many texts themselves function as a whole liminally, both spatially and temporally. They are on the borders between states, they are the markers of the transformational processes that are the character of much human existence, they articulate relationship, not least relationships of power. Indeed, as written artefacts they stand at the border between the act of speech and the act of reading, between orality and appropriation. Or, as written artefacts they stand between the author and the reader or hearer. They can even stand between the cooked and the raw, to pick up on Claude Lévi-Strauss.[49] There is not space to mine this rich seam of interpretative possibilities.

For "rewritten" scriptural hypertexts, this liminality can be seen in the way that they seem to function necessarily as mediating the hypotext to a new audience. Hypertexts stand between the increasingly authoritative hypotext and the community of readers or hearers that through them is enabled to receive the contemporary significance of the earlier signified through the mediating signifier. As such, in terms of the Qumran community and the wider movement of which it was or had been a part, "rewritten" compositions stand intriguingly between the widely accepted text and sectarian identity. It seems, for example, as if most of the hypertextual texts that I have listed or discussed in this essay are not replete with sectarian traits, though there may be some few of them, such as the jubilee periodization in the Apocryphon of Jeremiah. If this is accurate as a description of the liminal state of the hypertexts in the Qumran library, as somehow between the general and the particular, then the compositions considered here may be among the most important markers for the reconstruction of the historical circumstances of the movement whose identity is expressed in the library, circumstances in the fourth to second centuries B.C.E. when much of this material is being composed.

And these "rewritten" hypertexts are liminal in another way as indicated in the earlier subsections of this paper. They facilitate the transformation of their hypotexts from an authoritative to a quasi-canonical status.[50] It can easily be

---

49. See, e.g., the reading of the story of Joseph and Aseneth this way in G. J. Brooke, "Joseph, Aseneth, and Lévi-Strauss," in *Narrativity in Biblical and Related Texts/La narrativité dans la Bible et les textes apparentés* (ed. G. J. Brooke and J. -D. Kaestli; BETL 149; Leuven: Leuven University Press, 2000), 185–200.

50. See again Brooke, "Between Authority and Canon," 35–48.

recognized that the production of these compositions belongs to the period when this hypotextual development is taking place. Although it is certainly the case that hypertexts of all sorts continue to be produced after texts become canonically fixed in the form of their text, the liminal character of such hypertexts is one of maintaining rather than producing canonical authority in the hypotext. In the precanonical period, these hypertexts give authoritative identity both to the hypotexts on which they depend and to the community of readers and hearers that adopt and preserve them, perhaps for yet further rewriting.

4. Conclusion

In sum, as we reflect on the relationship between hypertext and hypotext in the Qumran library, I propose that scholars need to consider the issues of how hypertexts illuminate matters to do with primordial authority, how they can expose hypotextual preferences not least through the selection of alternative metanarrative, how they function to offer identity through pastiche, and how they work as liminal artefacts. In keeping those kinds of issues on the modern scholarly interpretative agenda, the label "hypertext" is more useful than some of the proposed alternatives.

SIX

Controlling Intertexts and Hierarchies of Echo in Two Thematic Eschatological Commentaries from Qumran

1. Introduction

Since Julia Kristeva first introduced the concept of intertextuality and Gérard Genette adapted it for use in literary as well as linguistic contexts,[1] the term has been used very widely, not least in biblical studies.[2] For some, it applies precisely to the very explicit use of earlier literary traditions, the dependence of one author on another; in such contexts intertextuality is akin to literary influence, and discussion may still revolve around authorial intention and the use of sources. Susan Graham has summed up neatly Kristeva's reaction to such a use: "Strictly speaking, Kristeva rejects the 'banal' misreading of her term 'intertextuality' as 'the study of sources,' now preferring the term 'transposition' and restricting intentional literary references to what she calls influence."[3] For others, the concern of intertextuality is to be conceived more broadly as having to do with the way in which the readers or hearers of a text, especially ones near the initial stages of a composition's existence, would be able to locate it in a field of references;[4] some of those references might indeed be deliberate on behalf of the author of the text,

---

1. In D. Marguerat and A. Curtis, eds., *Intertextualités: La Bible en échos* (Le monde de la Bible 40; Geneva: Labor et Fides, 2000), it is interesting to note how some studies depend on the terminology of Kristeva while others make more reference to Genette.

2. For a recent collection of studies with some contributions that position the papers in the broader discourse, see S. Alkier and R. B. Hays, eds., *Die Bibel im Dialog der Schriften: Konzepte intertextueller Bibellektüre* (Neutestamentliche Entwürfe zur Theologie 10; Tübingen: Francke, 2005); in English as Richard B. Hays, Stefan Alkier, and Leroy A. Huizenga, eds., *Reading the Bible Intertextually* (Waco: Baylor University Press, 2009).

3. S. L. Graham, "Intertextual Trekking: Visiting the Iniquity of the Fathers upon 'The Next Generation,'" *Semeia* 69–70 (1995): 195–219, here 199. Graham is referring to Julia Kristeva, *La révolution du langage poétique: L'avant-garde à la fin du XIXe siècle, Lautréamont et Mallarmé* (Paris: Éditions du Seuil, 1976), 59–60.

4. This approach is taken, for example, by J. Frow, "Intertextuality and Ontology," in *Intertextuality: Theories and Practices* (ed. M. Worton and J. Still; Manchester: Manchester University Press, 1990), 4–46.

but many more would belong to a field of language use resonant with traditions of numerous kinds better described as echoes, many of which were probably far less self-consciously produced.[5] Such fields of reference are distinctive for each reader, since each reader brings different experiences to the reading of the text.

The purpose of this short paper is to take both aspects of intertextual study, to suggest that any text may well contain controlling intertexts and a hierarchy of other echoes. In a commentary it is clear that this is the case, since for the commentary to make sense, the hypotext, that which is being commented upon, needs to be recognizable whether explicitly or implicitly; and the hypertext, the commentary proper, will necessarily have its own set of references.[6] A commentary is normally the attempt of the commentator to "produce unifying and clarifying explanations."[7] This study will make explicit what has long been recognized in various ways about the use of and appeal to other textual traditions in two of the better preserved thematic Eschatological Commentaries found in Qumran's Cave 4, 4Q174 and 4Q177, commonly known as Florilegium and Catena A respectively.

2. The Texts and Their Intertexts

2.1. Eschatological Commentary A (4Q174)

2.1.1. The Text

To my mind it is clear that both aspects of the dynamic of intertextuality are apparent in Eschatological Commentary A. To exemplify this I cite here a translation of the most extensive fragment of the Commentary, now widely labeled as forming parts of cols. 3 and 4. The paragraph divisions belong to the way the scribe has set out the composition on the manuscript; at the least, they indicate how one person construed the principal sections and subsections of the composition.

> (iii 1) "and his enemies will not disturb him any more; neither will a son of wickedness afflict him anymore as formerly and as from the day that (2) I commanded judges to be over my people Israel" (2 Sam 7:10–11aᵃ). That is the house

---

5. The descriptive category of echo has been exploited very productively by R. B. Hays, *Echoes of Scripture in the Letters of Paul* (New Haven: Yale University Press, 1989).

6. On hypertexts and hypotexts in the Qumran commentary literature, see G. J. Brooke, "Hypertextuality and the 'Parabiblical' Dead Sea Scrolls," in *In the Second Degree: Paratextual Literature in Ancient Near Eastern and Ancient Mediterranean Culture and Its Reflections in Medieval Literature* (ed. P. S. Alexander, A. Lange and R. J. Pillinger; Leiden: Brill, 2010), 43–64.

7. Graham, "Intertextual Trekking," 199; Graham is describing the activity of any reader, and especially academic readers, who are often unconsciously responding "to a desire to repress a frightening sense of fragmentation" so as to impose "unifying and totalising interpretations" often with theological purposes.

which [he will build] for himself in the latter days, as it is written in the book of (3) [Moses], "The sanctuary of the Lord which thy hands have established; The Lord will reign for ever and ever" (Exod 15:17b–18): that is the house to which shall not come (4) [even to the tenth generation and for] ever, Ammonite nor Moabite (cf. Deut 23:3–4) nor bastard nor stranger nor proselyte for ever, for his holy ones are there. (5) [His glory shall] be revealed for ever; continually it shall be seen over it. And foreigners shall not make it desolate again, as they desolated formerly (6) the sanctuary of Israel because of their sin. And he promised to build for himself a sanctuary of Adam/men, for there to be in it for him smoking offerings (7) before him, works of thanksgiving. And that he said to David, "And I will give you rest from all your enemies" (2 Sam 7:11aᵝ) that means that he will give rest to them for all (8) the sons of Belial who cause them to stumble in order to destroy them [through their errors], just as they came with the plots of Belial to cause to stumble the sons of (9) light, and in order to devise against them plots of wickedness so that they [might be caught] by Belial through their [wicked] error.

(10) "And the Lord declares to you that he will build you a house. And I will raise up your seed after you, and I will establish the throne of his kingdom (11) for ever. I will be to him as a father, and he will be to me as a son" (2 Sam 7:11b, 12aᵝ, 13b, 14a): He is the shoot of David who will stand with the Interpreter of the Law, who (12) [will rule] in Zion in the latter days as it is written, "And I will raise up the booth of David which is fallen" (Amos 9:11): he is the booth/branch of (13) David which was fallen, who will take office to save Israel.

(14) Midrash of "Happy is the man who does not walk in the counsel of the wicked" (Ps 1:1aᵃ); the interpretation of the matter concerns those who turn aside from the way of [sinners concerning] (15) whom it is written in the book of Isaiah the prophet for the latter days, "And it will be that as with a strong [hand he will cause us to turn away from walking in the way] (16) of this people" (Isa 8:11); and they are those concerning whom it is written in the book of Ezekiel the prophet that "they shall not [defile themselves any more] (17) with their idols" (Ezek 37:23). They are the Sons of Zadok and the m[e]n of their cou[nc]il who keep fa[r from evil ...] and after them [...] a community.

(18) "Why do the nations rage and the peoples meditate on a vain thing, the kings of the earth set themselves and the rulers take counsel together against the Lord and against (19) his anointed?" (Ps 2:1–2). The interpretation of the matter [is that "the nations" are the Kitt]im and "those who take [refuge in Him" are] the chosen ones of Israel in the latter days; (iv 1) that is the time of refining which is coming [upon the house of] Judah to complete [...] (2) of Belial and a remnant of [the people] Israel will be left, and they will do all the Law [...] (3) Moses; that is [the time as] it is written in the book of Daniel the prophet, "For the wicked to act wickedly but they do not understand" (Dan 12:10) (4a) — "but the righteous [shall purify themselves] and make themselves white and refine themselves, and a people knowing God will be strong" (Dan 11:35, 32b),—they are—(4) the wise will understand" [...].⁸

---

8. Translation adapted slightly from G. J. Brooke, *Exegesis at Qumran: 4QFlorilegium in*

2.1.2. THE INTERTEXTS

2.1.2.1. The Authoritative Scriptural Collection.   The top layer of concern in Eschatological Commentary A is reflected in those scriptural passages that have been selected for consideration. In what survives, three compositions can be so identified: Deut 33, 2 Sam 7, and some of the Psalms. From the best reconstruction of the fragmentary manuscript[9] it is likely that those texts (and possibly others) were interpreted in that order. As a result the question arises concerning whether there is any significance in the order. Not surprisingly, the suggestion has been made that the order reflects that of the emerging Jewish canon[10] in which, by the end of the first century B.C.E., it seems that the Torah has become preeminent and the prophets function as an open-ended secondary category, a category that might on some occasions include or at least be juxtaposed with other writings, including the Psalms.[11]

But if the order is a reflection of something quasi-canonical, is the selection of those three books or parts of them indicative of something else, perhaps a particular theological topic or a circumstantial perspective? Perhaps it is the case that the very selection of three (or more) items from the authoritative collection of scriptural traditions indicates not only some kind of affirmation of the authoritative collection as a whole but also the need for the collection always to be read and appropriated selectively. In this way the selection sets up two kinds of intertextual relation at the same time: on the one hand, it hints at its dependence on the authoritative ordered collection of Scriptures in which the Law and the Prophets have a range of overarching relationships determined through texts being in context, and, on the other hand, through the selection process a differ-

Its Jewish Context (JSOTSup 29; Sheffield: JSOT Press, 1985; repr., Atlanta: Society of Biblical Literature, 2006), 91–93.

9. See A. Steudel, *Der Midrasch zur Eschatologie aus der Qumrangemeinde (4QMidrEschat^{a.b}): Materielle Rekonstruktion, Textbestand, Gattung und traditionsgeschichtliche Einordnung des durch 4Q174 ("Florilegium") und 4Q177 ("Catena A") repräsentierten Werkes aus den Qumranfunden* (STDJ 13; Leiden: Brill, 1994).

10. See É. Puech, *La croyance des Esséniens en la vie future: Immortalité, resurrection, vie éternelle? Histoire d'une croyance dans le Judaïsme ancien* (EBib 22; Paris: J. Gabalda, 1993), 573 n. 20; because of the interest in 1Q30 in numbering books and "their interpretations," Puech also wonders whether 1Q30 refers to this Eschatological Commentary.

11. The very fragmentary reference to Moses, the prophets, and David in MMT C has resulted in a flurry of studies that suggest that MMT forms a missing and early link between the statements in the Greek Prologue to Ben Sira ("the Law, the Prophets, and the other books") and the tripartite delineation of Luke 24:44 ("the law of Moses, the prophets, and the psalms"). For a recent survey of some of the views on bipartitite and tripartite authoritative scriptural collections in the light of MMT, see G. J. Brooke, "'Canon' in the Light of the Qumran Scrolls," in *The Canon of Scripture in Jewish and Christian Tradition/Le canon des Écritures dans les traditions juive et chrétienne* (ed. P. S. Alexander and J. -D. Kaestli; Publications de l'institut romand des sciences bibliques 4; Lausanne: Éditions du Zèbre, 2007), 81–98.

ent set of relationships is created through the authoritative texts being presented out of context.[12]

One further comment also needs to be made. In this principal fragment that contains the end of the interpretation of Nathan's oracle from 2 Sam 7 and then the start of a commentary on at least some of the Psalms, it is noticeable that most of the interpretation of 2 Sam 7 is presented through the use of pronouns through which particular and specific identifications are made. In addition, part of 2 Sam 7 (vv. 11b–14a) is presented in an abbreviated form, as if there are items that the commentator wants the reader to avoid. However, in the Eschatological Commentary A the commentary on the Psalms is presented somewhat differently. On the one hand, the commentary on the principal verses from the Psalms is introduced through a technical formula involving the word "pesher"; this might indicate something particular about the status or genre of the text on which comment is being made. On the other hand, only the opening verses of the Psalms are given, and the reader is assumed to know the rest of the text. Thus, whereas the lemma of 2 Sam 7 is deliberately abbreviated to direct the reader's attention away from what might distract, the use of incipits for the Psalms operates in the reverse way to encourage the reader or hearer to recall the whole Psalm. And whereas the identificatory pronouns encourage an atomistic reading of the base text, the use of incipits encourages the reader to take the Psalm as a whole; thus, pesher exegesis in this instance might be other than atomistic. It is likely that these hermeneutical differences indicate that the two subsections come from different sources or originate in slightly different circles, but they have possibly been collocated as intertexts in their own right because they suggest each other, not least through the common interest of 2 Sam 7 and Ps 2 in the sonship of the king.[13] The editorial process of combining these two distinct pieces of commentary is evident not only in their shared subject matter but also in the use in both parts of the phrase "in the latter days" (באחרית הימים; iii 2, 12, 15, 19).[14]

2.1.2.2. Explicit Supportive Authoritative Intertexts. Within the exegetical discussion of each scriptural text several other scriptural sources are used. In what

---

12. I am struck by Daniel Boyarin's observation that texts can subvert their own consciously intended meanings and so indeed do more than one thing with the texts that they relate to; see Boyarin, "Issues for Further Discussion: A Response," *Semeia* 69–70 (1995): 296.

13. I first suggested this in G. J. Brooke, "Shared Intertextual Interpretations in the Dead Sea Scrolls and the New Testament," in *Biblical Perspectives: Early Use and Interpretation of the Bible in Light of the Dead Sea Scrolls: Proceedings of the First International Symposium of the Orion Center for the Study of the Dead Sea Scrolls and Associated Literature, 12–14 May 1996* (ed. M. E. Stone and E. G. Chazon; STDJ 28; Leiden: Brill, 1998), 35–57, here 39–42, 55–57.

14. On this phrase, see A. Steudel, "*b'ḥryt hymym* in the Texts from Qumran," *RevQ* 16 (1993–94): 225–46.

survives it is possible to see five of these supportive authoritative intertexts: Exod 15:17b–18 (iii 2–3); Amos 9:11 (iii 12); Isa 8:11 (iii 15–16); Ezek 37:23 (iii 16–17); and Dan 11:35, 32a; 12:10 (iv 4–4a). The selection of these supportive secondary intertexts is not arbitrary. On the one hand, their selection depends on their fit with an overall thematic conception concerning what the author is trying to say in general and specifically about the latter days. On the other hand, as several scholars have shown,[15] they are linked with the primary controlling base text through an intricate use of catchwords and other exegetical techniques which display the erudition and subtlety of the interpreter and which go a long way toward demonstrating to an audience that the interpretation is indeed correct. Interpretation in these sectarian compositions does not simply derive from some kind of divine inspiration, but comes about through the exquisite application of much learning that is demonstrable in its technical agility. Sadly, in many cases that agility lies beneath the surface and has to be dug up by the modern commentator, often with difficulty, to show how the commentary was woven together.

2.1.2.3. Intertextual Echoes from Authoritative Traditions.   Then there is a third intertextual layer in which various matters can be differentiated. This third layer is constituted mostly of implicit echoes of other texts. Perhaps the most obvious item that falls into this category in the part of Eschatological Commentary A that has been cited occurs in iii 3–4 in the phrases "that is the house to which shall not come (4) [even to the tenth generation and for] ever, Ammonite nor Moabite that is the house to which shall not come (4) [even to the tenth generation and for] ever, Ammonite nor Moabite." The language of Deut 23:3–4 is clear here, and the scriptural passage is extended with other categories of people who are to be excluded from the community gathered for worship. The allusion to Deuteronomy is not formulaically introduced and it could well have been that some readers or listeners in antiquity could have missed the allusion.

Something similar might be the case with another phrase that possibly resonates with other traditions. There is a striking wordplay used to describe the interim penultimate sanctuary as מקדש אדם: is this idiom to be translated as "sanctuary of Adam," or as "sanctuary of man/human sanctuary"? I consider that it is not necessary to choose between these two renderings, but to let the ambiguity stand.[16] In this way various fields of reference can be opened up for the ancient reader or listener. The striking possibility that in some way the community can understand itself as the kind of sanctuary that has hints of Eden opens up not only possibilities of links with the narratives of the opening chapters of

---

15. Notably E. Slomovic, "Toward an Understanding of the Exegesis in the Dead Sea Scrolls," *RevQ* 7 (1969–71): 3–15.

16. As I have argued in G. J. Brooke, "Miqdash Adam, Eden and the Qumran Community," in *Gemeinde ohne Tempel–Community without Temple: Zur Substituierung und Transformation des Jerusalemer Tempels und seines Kults im Alten Testament, antiken Judentum und frühen Christentum* (ed. B. Ego et al.; WUNT 118; Tübingen: Mohr Siebeck, 1999), 285–301.

Genesis and their cultic significance, but more promisingly it draws attention to the mediation of ideas from those chapters in other textual traditions, not least the book of Jubilees and the Temple Scroll. At the opening of Jubilees God commands the angel of the presence: "Write for Moses from the first creation until my sanctuary is built in their midst forever and ever. And the Lord will appear in the sight of all. And everyone will know that I am the God of Israel and the father of all the children of Jacob and king upon Mount Zion forever. And Zion and Jerusalem shall be holy" (Jub. 1:27–28).[17] That the compiler of Eschatological Commentary A could be interacting with such a tradition is not unlikely, especially given the concern of both texts with the sovereignty of God in relation to his sanctuary. A passage in the Temple Scroll might also be part of this wider intertextual field of reference:

> ... in regard to all that they offer, their drink-offerings and all their gifts that they shall bring to me in order to be acceptable. I shall accept them and they shall be my people and I shall be for them forever. I will dwell with them for ever and ever and will sanctify my [sa]nctuary by my glory. I will cause my glory to rest on it until the day of creation on which I shall create my sanctuary, establishing it for myself for all time according to the covenant which I made with Jacob in Bethel. (11Q19 29:5–10)[18]

Here there is an understanding that the penultimate sanctuary will be a place where the divine glory dwells and there is some reflection on the ultimate sanctuary that will not be made by human hands, but at a time of creation. These are the kinds of intertexts that a learned reader or listener might have recognized as enhancing the significance of the wordplay in Eschatological Commentary A.

2.1.2.4. Intertextual Echoes of Other Literary Traditions. There is at least a fourth level of intertextuality in Eschatological Commentary A. This is the intertextuality that can be found almost coincidentally in the author's selection of language, from the technical terminology of the text, some of which may also contain resonances of specific literary traditions. The quality of these echoes varies in intriguing ways. For example, it has long seemed to me that much of the vocabulary and idiom of Eschatological Commentary A echoes that of the so-called Admonition of the Damascus Document.[19] In fact an indication that this is so rests not just in the various items of vocabulary but in certain shared intertextual matters: both compositions cite Amos 9:11 (CD 7:16; 4Q174 iii 12). Several other matters can be mentioned very briefly: the sons of Zadok as the chosen ones of Israel (CD 4:3–4); "the latter days" (CD 4:4; 6:11); the use of the term

---

17. *OTP* 2.54.

18. Translation from G. Vermes, trans., *The Complete Dead Sea Scrolls in English* (5th rev. ed.; London: Penguin, 2004), 201.

19. Brooke, *Exegesis at Qumran*, 205–9.

"pesher" (CD 4:14); the saving of Israel (CD 5:19); the Interpreter of the Law (CD 6:7; 7:18)—these items are, of course, not exclusive to the Damascus Document and Eschatological Commentary A, but together with several others they form a collection of shared vocabulary, some of it markedly technical. This is a shared vocabulary that is indicative of a literary tradition. It does not seem to be the case that the author of Eschatological Commentary A is alluding to the Damascus Document; it is not a matter of literary dependence or influence. Rather here are intertextual echoes that identify the literary tradition to which the author of Eschatological Commentary A belongs.

2.1.2.5. Echoes of Possible Textual Worlds.   There is a remarkable interpretative juxtaposition in Eschatological Commentary A. It is noticeable that the "house" of the oracle of Nathan is interpreted as in the oracle itself as having a double meaning. In Eschatological Commentary A that double meaning is expounded in relation to the community as sanctuary and the Davidic Messiah. However, in the interpretation of Ps 2 it seems as if the individual anointed royal figure of Ps 2:7 is understood collectively rather than individualistically: the interpretation speaks of "the chosen ones of Israel." This could be an intertextual echo of a tradition of interpretation emerging out of some kind of dissatisfaction with expectations of an individual messianic savior in favor of locating the divine promise of such a figure in the community itself. Such a literary tradition has been found in other more or less contemporary texts and could have been known to the author of the exegetical insights of Eschatological Commentary A.[20] This kind of intertextuality is less tangible than deliberate or unconscious allusions or the shared use of technical vocabulary, but ancient readers or listeners could well have known in other texts the kinds of concern the text before them was expressing.

2.2. Eschatological Commentary B (4Q177)

2.2.1. The Text

Although more fragmentary than the principal extant piece of Eschatological Commentary A, Eschatological Commentary B is more extensively preserved, with parts of five columns capable of extensive reconstruction. For the purposes of this short study I will focus briefly on the quotations and interpretations of Psalms 16 and 17 in col. x.

> (x 1) [... al]l their words [...] [... pr]aises of the glory that he say[s ...] (2) [...
> "and the Lord will take away] from you all (your) sickness" (Deut 7:15a). "To

---

20. See the evidence put together, for example, by S. Ruzer, "Who Was Unhappy with the Davidic Messiah?" and "The New Covenant, the Reinterpretation of Scripture and Collective Messiahship," in *Mapping the New Testament: Early Christian Writings as a Witness for Jewish Biblical Exegesis* (Jewish and Christian Perspectives 13; Leiden: Brill, 2007), 101–29, 215–37, respectively.

the ho[ly ones that] are in the la[nd] and my nobles in [whom] is all my delight (Ps 16:3a). [...] (3) [...] will we be like it (cf. Joel 2:2b). [... and] tottering of the knees and anguish in all loin[s (Nah 2:11b). ...] (4) [...] ... Hear, [O Lord, (what is) just], heed my cry, give ear to [my prayer (Ps 17:1a) ...] (5) [...] in the latter days, in the time when he will seek [...] the Council of the Community. That (is) the [...] (6) [...] The interpretation of the passage (is) that a man shall arise from the hou[se of ...] (7) [... and] they shall be as fire to the whole world; and they (are) those about whom it is written in the latter [days " ...] ... are reck[less" (Zeph 3:4?)] (8) [... s]aid concerning the [l]ot of light that was to be in mourning during the dominion of Bel[ial and concerning the lot of darkness] that was to be in mourning [...] (9) [...] ... from it and [...] to the heads of mourning. Return, O Lor[d ... G]od of mercies and to Israe[l re]ward ... [...] (10) [...] that have d[e]filed themselves with the spirit[s of Be]lial, but let them be forgiven forever and bless them [...] yet. He shall bless them forever [... the w]onders of the[ir] periods [...] (11) [...] ... of their fathers, according to the number of the[ir] names, clearly set out by names, for each man [...] their [y]ears and the period of their existence and [...] ... of their language [...] (12) [...] ... the offspring of Judah. [And] now behold all is written on the tablets that [...] God, and he informed him of the number of [...] ... and .. [...] (13) [...] to [him] and to his seed [for]ever. And he arose from there to go to Aram. "Blow the horn in Gibeah" (Hos 5:8a^a). The "horn" (is) the book of [...] (14) [(Hos 5:8a$^\beta$?) ... th]is (is) the book of the Torah again/Second Torah that a[ll the m]en oh his Council have despised, and they spoke rebelliously against him, and th[ey] sen[t ...] (15) [...] great [sig]ns concerning the ... [...] and Jacob shall stand on the winepresses, and rejoice over th[eir] downfall [...] (16) [...] chosen .. [...] to the men of his Council. They (are) the sword. And which [...][21]

2.2.2. The Intertexts

2.2.2.1. The Authoritative Scriptural Collection. It seems that what remains of Eschatological Commentary B contains a thematic commentary on selected Psalms from the first book of the Psalter.[22] The large number of Psalms manuscripts that have survived in the Qumran caves and their rich variety[23] make it difficult to demonstrate precisely what might have been the Psalter that lies

21. Translation based on J. Milgrom and L. Novakovic, "Catena A (4Q177=4QCat^a)," in *The Dead Sea Scrolls: Hebrew, Aramaic, and Greek Texts with English Translations*, vol. 6B, *Pesharim, Other Commentaries, and Related Documents* (ed. James H. Charlesworth and Frank Moore Cross; Princeton Theological Seminary Dead Sea Scrolls Project; Tübingen: Mohr Siebeck; Louisville: Westminster John Knox Press, 2002), 286–303, here 289–91.

22. On the theological perspective of the composition as a whole, see A. Steudel, "Eschatological Interpretation of Scripture in 4Q177 (4QCatena^a)," RevQ 14/55 (1989–90): 473–81.

23. See especially, P. W. Flint, *The Dead Sea Psalms Scrolls and the Book of Psalms* (STDJ 17; Leiden: Brill, 1997); on pp. 135–49 he considers the stabilization of the Psalter, especially Pss 1–89.

behind the commentary, especially since some kind of selection process seems likely. This is a subject that still requires further study, but with the extant columns in the order now agreed[24] the following citations are extant: Ps 11:1a, 2 (viii 7–8); 12:1a (viii 12); 12:7 (ix 1); 13:2–3 (ix 8–9); 13:5a (ix 11–12); 16:3 (x 2); 17:1a (x 4); 6:2a, 3a (xi 7); 6:4–5a (xi 8); 6:6a (xi 10–11).

Apart from the order of the Psalms, which appears to be distinctive, three other facts can be noted. The first is that, as in Eschatological Commentary A, the majority of the references to the Psalms are to their opening verses. For those concerned with how authoritative texts might be cited and used in late Second Temple Judaism it is important to observe that the use of incipits in this way seems to indicate that the remainder of the Psalm is to be understood as read. The use of incipits makes an assumption about the reader's knowledge of the Psalms, their primary field of reference for appreciating the commentary. The second is that the technical term "pesher," extant but twice in all the fragments of the manuscript (ix 9; x 6), seems in both instances to be used solely of the Psalm base text and never as a technical signal for the interpretation of supportive authoritative citations. Therefore, it seems to indicate something about the status and perception of the Psalms being interpreted as in the section of Eschatological Commentary A where the Psalms are interpreted. Third, it is likely that the Psalms in this commentary have been selected for some reason, possibly because of their being predominantly individual laments or pleas for salvation; as such they fit with the concerns of the commentator, concerns that are all the more explicit when the supportive citations are considered.[25]

2.2.2.2. Explicit Supportive Authoritative Intertexts.   Sadly, the text of Eschatological Commentary B is not as well preserved as that of the largest surviving fragment of Eschatological Commentary A, in which it is possible to see clearly the way in which supportive authoritative texts are identified with introductory formulae ("in the book of Isaiah the prophet" [iii 15]; "in the book of Ezekiel the prophet" [iii 16]; etc.). Nevertheless, it is likely, given the way that pronouns are used after the citation of Hos 5:8a, for example, that the secondary citations from Nahum, Zephaniah,[26] and Hosea in this section of the composition were probably given some kind of introduction, however brief. Such introduction would signal that the choice of supportive intertext was deliberate.

---

24. See the arguments in Steudel, *Der Midrasch zur Eschatologie aus der Qumrangemeinde*, 62–70. It is to be noted that except in 4Q177 Ps 6 does not seem to occur out of order, though in some instances there is not enough data to be certain.

25. These insights are made explicit by S. Tzoref with M. Laughlin, "Theme and Genre in 4Q177 and Its Scriptural Selections," in *The Mermaid and the Partridge: Essays from the Copenhagen Conference on Revising Texts from Cave Four* (ed. J. Høgenhaven and G. J. Brooke; STDJ 96; Leiden: Brill, 2011), 169–89.

26. On the probability that Zeph 3:4 is explicitly cited here, see Steudel, *Der Midrasch zur Eschatologie aus der Qumrangemeinde*, 104.

Intriguingly, these supportive intertexts come predominantly from the Twelve Minor Prophets. There is also an allusion to Joel 2:2 in line 3 and Mic 2:10b–11 is used in col. viii 10 and Zech 3:9 is used in col. ix 2. It seems as if the author of Eschatological Commentary B was particularly concerned to interpret the Psalms by means of explicit references to the Twelve. The manuscripts of the Twelve from the Qumran caves and the existence of running commentaries on several of their constituent books, most famously on Habakkuk, strongly suggest that the collection of the Twelve as a whole should be understood as a key second-ary intertext for the right interpretation of the Psalms and not just the few chosen verses that are made explicit.[27]

In addition, there are several references to the books of Isaiah, Jeremiah, and Ezekiel: Isa 37:30 (viii 2); 32:7a (viii 5); 32:7b (viii 6–7); 27:11b (viii 12–13); 22:13b (viii 15); Jer 6:14 (viii 14); 18:18 (xi 6); Ezek 25:8[28] (ix 13–14); 22:20 (xi 4). There is also a citation of Deut 7:15.

2.2.2.3. Intertextual Echoes from Authoritative Traditions.   In two places what survives of the commentary in col. x makes references to other items of literature as if the reader is expected to know what is being talked about. First, in x 12 there is a reference to all that "is written on the tablets." The text seems to proceed to indicate a role for God in relation to the tablets. Is this a simple reference to the tablets of the Law given to Moses on Sinai or is there a reference to some other tablets made known through divine disclosure, such as the heavenly tablets known from other literature, such as the book of Jubilees? At least it seems that they are not the writings engraved on stone that contained the teachings of the Watchers that Cainan transcribed (Jub. 8:3). Second, in x 14 there is the intrigu-ing phrase הואה ספר התורה שנית, which has been variously rendered. Since the work of John Strugnell,[29] several scholars prefer to read this phrase as "this is the book of the Torah again" as if there is a second reference to the Torah in the appeal to Hos 5:8a. More commonly the Hebrew has been understood as "this is the book of the Second Law."[30] In the latter case, the search is then on for identi-fying the Second Law, whether as the Temple Scroll,[31] Miqṣat Maʿaśê Ha-Torah, or something else.

27. On the Twelve Minor Prophets in the scrolls, see G. J. Brooke, "The Twelve Minor Prophets and the Dead Sea Scrolls," in *Congress Volume: Leiden 2004* (ed. A. Lemaire; VTSup 109; Leiden: Brill, 2006), 19–43.

28. With a full explicit introduction: "as it is written in the book of the prophet Ezekiel."

29. J. Strugnell, "Notes en marge du volume V des «Discoveries in the Judaean Desert of Jordan»," *RevQ* 7 (1969–70): 163–276, here 241.

30. E.g., F. García Martínez, ed., *The Dead Sea Scrolls Translated: The Qumran Texts in English* (2nd ed.; Leiden: Brill, 1996), 211.

31. E.g., Y. Yadin, *The Temple Scroll: The Hidden Law of the Dead Sea Sect* (London: Wei-denfeld & Nicolson, 1985), 226–28; note also the reference to the "Law" that the Teacher sent to the Wicked Priest according to 4QpPsᵃ, the pesher on on Ps 37:32 (4Q171 3–10 iv 7–9).

In the *Eschatological Commentary A* it seems as if scriptural texts could be alluded to either in their own terms or through other authoritative compositions; in the *Eschatological Commentary B* that pattern continues, but with explicit reference to other authoritative writings, perhaps indicating that readers and listeners needed some prompting to make the correct intertextual connections.

2.2.2.4. Intertextual Echoes of Other Literary Traditions.   As has been widely pointed out, not least by Lidija Novakovic, Eschatological Commentary B contains "numerous expressions that are characteristic of the Qumran sectarian documents."[32] From the passage cited above, it is easy to recognize, for example, an idiom "the lot of light" (x 8) and the technical terms "the Council of the Community" (x 5) and the "men of his Council" (x 16) as three such items; other examples could be cited. This would locate Eschatological Commentary B firmly within the linguistic and literary world of the sect,[33] and it might be possible with closer scrutiny to discern whether there was a particular literary tradition within the sectarian compositions that was echoed more than others; this would require us to move beyond the sample of text given in this short study and so cannot be taken forward here.

2.2.2.5. Echoes of Possible Textual Worlds.   The wider echoes that might be contained in the text of Eschatological Commentary B are difficult to discern from this cursory glance at col. x by itself. Nevertheless, there are several possible indications that there were other matters at stake. First, there are the traditions associated with mourning, not least during the "dominion of Belial" (x 8–9).[34] Second, there is the allusory reference to the "offspring of Judah." To whom might this be a reference? In some sectarian compositions, such as Pesher Habakkuk (8:1), there are positive references to the "house of Judah" which suggest that Judahite literary traditions were self-referential for some part of the Qumran community or even for the wider movement of which it was a part. Third, similar but more broadly based assertions can be made concerning the role of Jacob (x 15).

3. Conclusions

In this brief study of two sectarian Eschatological Commentaries, I have tried to indicate that there is an intertextual hierarchy. In first place, there is the authori-

---

32. Milgrom and Novakovic, "Catena A (4Q177=4QCatᵃ)," 286.

33. On the possibilities for and the significance of identifying a composition as sectarian, see D. Dimant, "Sectarian and Non-Sectarian Texts from Qumran: The Pertinence and Usage of a Taxonomy," *RevQ* 24/93 (2009): 7–18.

34. Such mourning might be associated especially with Zion, though no reference to the place occurs in 4Q177 col. x. Steudel ("Eschatological Interpretation of Scripture in 4Q177 (4QCatenaᵃ)," 478) rightly states that "Zion and Jerusalem are the centre of the author's eschatological hope."

tative base text selected by the author of the commentary; its order seems largely to control the structure of the commentary itself. Second, the author of the commentary (or his sources) makes explicit reference to other authoritative texts that are used to support the interpretation. So far all is deliberate. In third place, however, there are echoes of yet other authoritative traditions; from the author's perspective these may be deliberate or not and from the reader's perspective they might or might not be recognized. Fourth, there are intertextual echoes of other literary traditions. Last, there are echoes of possible textual worlds.

The Jewish commentary traditions from antiquity permit the modern reader to see a place both for the author and the reader. Through selected controlling primary texts, secondary supportive texts and a hierarchy of echoes the rich intertextual character of the interpretative tradition becomes all the more apparent when described and analyzed through the application of intertextuality as a somewhat loosely defined modern reading strategy.

SEVEN

PEŠER AND MIDRAŠ IN QUMRAN LITERATURE: ISSUES FOR LEXICOGRAPHY

1. INTRODUCTION

This short study examines again the uses of the two terms *pēšer* (pesher) and *midrāš* (midrash) in the Qumran sectarian literature, paying particular attention to the issues the terms provoke for lexicographical work such as that proposed for the *Theologisches Wörterbuch zu den Qumranschriften* (= ThWQ). Of particular note are the ways in which compilers of entries on the range of forms and uses of terms such as these need to consider the role of Semitic philology, the place of context in determining meaning, and the ongoing tension between diachronic and synchronic evidence in the construction of semantic fields.

It is difficult to know how to delimit the topic of this short study.[1] In terms of textual profile, I will consider principally vocabulary from texts within those compositions that are commonly identified with the Qumran community or the parent or broader movement of which it was a part; this will enable some specialized and particular uses of terms to be discussed, though restricting comments on a wider range of contexts. In terms of lexical choices, I will consider principally two terms that seem to serve rather different semantic functions, both having a discernible technicality, but one apparently having a more restricted use than the other; this will facilitate discussion of several linguistic issues that creators of dictionaries, and theological ones at that, need to keep in mind.

To some extent the purpose of this paper is not so much to give a complete and thorough survey of lexemes concerned with interpretation[2] as to indi-

---

1. For an early study on the range of possibilities, see M. Gertner, "Terms of Scriptural Interpretation: A Study in Hebrew Semantics," *BSOAS* 25 (1962): 1–27.

2. It would be difficult to know where to begin in defining a list of interpretative vocabulary. Perhaps one might start with the verbs in Sir 39:1–3 and their possible Hebrew equivalents. On some of the implications of this passage of Sirach for the definition of the scholarly interpretative activity of the sage, see S. G. Dempster, "Torah, Torah, Torah: The Emergence of the Tripartite Canon," in *Exploring the Origins of the Bible: Canon Formation in Historical, Literary, and Theological Perspective* (ed. C. A. Evans and E. Tov; Grand Rapids: Baker Academic, 2008), 87–127, esp. p. 111.

cate through some comments on two particular items what some of the issues involved in the study of such vocabulary can be. However, in some ways, perhaps the most important items concerning interpretation in the Qumran literature, as elsewhere, are the third person pronouns that, when used demonstratively, permit the identification of one thing with another and produce a wonderful range of "this" is "that" possibilities, interpretative moves that are highly significant when the dominant exegetical strategy is the making contemporary of earlier traditions. A whole study could be devoted to demonstratives and the various ways they function in particular contexts in the Qumran literature.[3] The interpretative function of those little words would indeed seem to deserve some attention in a separate entry in *ThWQ*, but these pronouns have not been listed for separate treatment.

In addition, it has long been acknowledged that context determines meaning.[4] For the members of the Qumran community or its wider movement, such contexts were far more than the written data that now survive for scholars to peruse and confuse. It is clear too that words have ranges of meaning in differing contexts, semantic fields that overlap with those of other like-minded words. Nearly fifty years ago, Frederick F. Bruce noted that "while the root *p-sh-r* is not found in the Hebrew part of *Daniel*, the same idea is conveyed there by such common roots as *byn, yd‘, skl* and *ngd* – in reference, for example, to the angelic interpretation of the seventy years of *Jer.* 25:11f. (29:10) as seventy heptads of years (*Dan.* 9:2, 24ff.)."[5] A full study of exegetical terminology should indeed take account of this range of terms and others that have some aspect of the grasping, decoding, and transferring of meaning from text to text or from text to audience or reader. The issue in this case is that entries in *ThWQ* should allow space for semantic fields explained through context, space for synonyms derived from word chains and in particular from word pairs. To illustrate some of the issues associated with the study of the technical terminology associated with interpretation the essay that follows focuses on the two well-known terms, "pesher" and "midrash."

---

3. E. Qimron (*The Hebrew of the Dead Sea Scrolls* [HSS 29; Atlanta: Scholars Press], 57–64) outlines the pronominal phenomenon in Qumran literature largely in terms of morphology; he notes that "the outstanding morphological feature of the personal pronouns and pronominal suffixes is the presence of pronoun doublets" (p. 64). On the other hand, a significant start in terms of syntactical analysis is made by M. F. J. Baasten, "Nominal Clauses Containing a Personal Pronoun in Qumran Hebrew," in *The Hebrew of the Dead Sea Scrolls and Ben Sira: Proceedings of a Symposium Held at Leiden University, 11–14 December 1995* (ed. T. Muraoka and J. F. Elwolde; STDJ 26; Leiden: Brill, 1997), 1–16.

4. There are many ways of presenting what now seems to be a truism, but the widely published and discussed work of Algirdas J. Greimas has been fundamental to the discipline.

5. F. F. Bruce, *Biblical Exegesis in the Qumran Texts* (Grand Rapids: Eerdmans, 1956).

2. PESHER

The obvious place to begin the more precise journey of this paper is with the term *pšr*, since this is a term used in various technical formulae and it is largely distinctive of the Qumran sectarian literature,[6] though not restricted to it alone. In addition, the comprehensive discussion of this term has been conducted in a previous generation and the complete release of the previously unpublished scrolls in 1991 has not offered new data to demand any significant review of the term. This was partly the result of the original categorization of the finds from Cave 4 in the 1950s. Those manuscripts containing the word *pšr* were put together as a set, grouped after the scriptural scrolls and very closely related texts, and assigned to John M. Allegro. The way this was done can be illustrated from the composition originally known as Patriarchal Blessings (now part of 4Q252). Because the principal fragment thus designated contained extracts from the blessings of Jacob in Genesis 49 followed in at least one place by interpretation introduced with a formula containing the word *pšr*, so the manuscript was assigned to Allegro.[7] But after a while Józef Milik came to realize that the fragment that Allegro had called Patriarchal Blessings was in fact part of a commentary on selected passages of Genesis;[8] Milik agreed a swap with Allegro and in place of the fragment that contained the term *pšr*, Allegro was assigned 4Q341.[9] My introductory point

---

6. D. Dimant sees the term *pšr* as most characteristic of the peculiar biblical exegesis espoused by the community ("The Qumran Manuscripts: Contents and Significance," in *Time to Prepare the Way in the Wilderness: Papers on the Qumran Scrolls by Fellows of the Institute for Advanced Studies of the Hebrew University, Jerusalem, 1989–1990* [ed. D. Dimant and L. H. Schiffman; STDJ 16; Leiden: Brill, 1995], 27–28 and n. 13). This aspect of Qumran distinctiveness is developed in Shani Berrin, "Qumran Pesharim," in *Biblical Interpretation at Qumran* (ed. M. Henze; Studies in the Dead Sea Scrolls and Related Literature; Grand Rapids: Eerdmans, 2005), 110–33.

7. Allegro published a preliminary edition of the fragment in "Further Messianic References in Qumran Literature," *JBL* 75 (1956): 174–87.

8. Eventually all the fragments assigned to this scroll were published in a principal edition by G. J. Brooke, "252. Commentary on Genesis A," in *Qumran Cave 4.XVII: Parabiblical Texts Part 3* (ed. J. C. VanderKam; DJD 22; Oxford: Clarendon, 1996), 185–207. Milik had labeled the composition *pGenᵃ*, but only one section of the composition is pesher in a technical sense. It has taken several years of patient insistence, but now Milik's name for the composition has been generally discarded and supplanted by the more neutral and all-embracing Commentary on Genesis.

9. Originally published in J. M. Allegro, *The Dead Sea Scrolls and the Christian Myth* (Newton Abbot: Westbridge Books, 1979), 235–40. Published in its principal edition by J. Naveh, "341. 4QExercitium Calami C," in *Qumran Cave 4.XXVI: Cryptic Texts and Miscellanea, Part 1* (ed. S. J. Pfann et al.; DJD 36; Oxford: Clarendon, 2000), 291–93; plate xviii. See also G. J. Brooke, "4Q341: An Exercise for Spelling and for Spells?" in *Writing and Ancient Near Eastern Society: Papers in Honour of Alan R. Millard* (ed. P. Bienkowski, C. B. Mee, and E. A. Slater; LHBOTS 426; London: T&T Clark International, 2005), 271–82.

here is that lexicographers must take into account the scholarly epoch when the principal discussion of certain terms was undertaken.

In the first decade of scholarly work on the scrolls and under the influence in particular of Pesher Habakkuk from Cave 1, the term *pšr* had come to be used as a genre label. The term had achieved notoriety well beyond its humble origins. But what were those origins? By the time Maurya P. Horgan came to present her revised dissertation on all the pesharim, she was able to offer a review of the evidence concerning the term that has served well for nearly thirty years.[10] Horgan began her collection of mini-editions of the pesharim by noting that the fifteen texts that she was presenting together were "neither the only texts in which the key word 'pesher' occurs, nor are they the only texts that reflect aspects of biblical interpretation and study among the members of the Qumran community."[11] Horgan offered a word study with the aim of arriving at a translation of the term that would suitably "reflect the correct meaning of the word."[12] She discussed the four terms *pṭr*, *pšr*, *ptr*, and *pṭr*, the first of which is a common root meaning "separate," "set free," or "loosen,"[13] and has nothing to do etymologically with *pšr*. The semioticians of the last generation have surely taught us that it is problematic to engage on a quest as if words have "correct meanings," since there is so much range in any one example of word use as the signifier and the signified are interwoven in multiple ways in practice and are also disentangled in multiple ways by those who observe linguistic phenomena.[14]

For Horgan, the starting point for appreciating the meaning of *pšr* is its Semitic etymology: this is a fundamentally significant matter for those who have been and are involved in writing articles for the *ThWQ*—what is the correct place for Semitic philology in the entries in the *Wörterbuch*? One senses in Horgan's use of Semitic philology the end of an era in Hebrew and Aramaic linguistics and lexicography for students trained in the Western tradition of Biblical Stud-

---

10. That little concerning the word *pšr* was advanced between her monograph in 1979 and her comprehensive re-presentation of her work in 2002 is in evidence inasmuch as she simply refers to the discussion of the terminology in her earlier work: M. P. Horgan, "Pesharim," in *The Dead Sea Scrolls: Hebrew, Aramaic, and Greek Texts with English Translations. Pesharim, Other Commentaries, and Related Documents,* vol. 6B, *Pesharim, Other Commentaries, and Related Documents* (ed. J. H. Charlesworth et al.; Princeton Theological Seminary Dead Sea Scrolls Project 6B; Tübingen: Mohr Siebeck; Louisville: Westminster John Knox, 2002), 1 and n. 3.

11. M. P. Horgan, *Pesharim: Qumran Interpretations of Biblical Books* (CBQMS 8; Washington, D.C.: Catholic Biblical Association of America, 1979), 1.

12. Ibid., 230.

13. Cf. Akkadian *paṭāru*, Hebrew *pāṭar*, Aramaic *pĕṭar*.

14. There are many helpful studies of semiotics in relation to Biblical Studies. In English I mention only a beautifully crafted short guide by J. Cook, "Semiotics," in *Dictionary of Biblical Interpretation* (ed. J. H. Hayes; 2 vols.; Nashville: Abingdon, 1999), 2.454–56; B. S. Jackson, *Studies in the Semiotics of Biblical Law* (JSOTSup 314; Sheffield: Sheffield Academic Press, 2000).

ies. In the nineteenth century and earlier, the majority of professors of Hebrew Bible were trained first in Semitic languages as these were available. To begin with, there were Aramaic, Syriac, and Rabbinic Hebrew, but the predominant cognate language was Arabic;[15] subsequently the languages of earlier times and more distant places written in signal or alphabetic cuneiform were the dominant cognate languages to be mastered. There are many classic examples of this phenomenon, ranging, just in England, from the inclusion of an Arabic version in Walton's seventeenth-century polyglot Bible to the fact that in Manchester to this day the full professorial chair in Hebrew and other Semitic Languages is in the Department of Near Eastern Studies, while the Professor of Bible, required to cover Greek as well as Hebrew Scriptures, is in the Department of Religions and Theology. Shortly before the twenty-nine-year-old Maurya Horgan submitted her dissertation in 1976 at Fordham University, in the United Kingdom the Old Testament section of the *New English Bible* had been published (1970); Godfrey Driver had been the editor of the translation committee and it is well known that the translation contains many Arabisms, perhaps the most famous of which is the rendering of *tiṣnaḥ* in Judg 1:14: as Achsah sat on the donkey, "she broke wind," and Caleb not surprisingly said, *ma lāk*, rendered in the NEB as "What did you mean by that?" Semitic philology can run wild when unleashed! It needs to be applied with adequate methodological controls.

To some extent Horgan's philological starting point for *pšr*, namely, her grappling with the root *pšr*, is fully warranted and remains so.[16] When there is little in contemporary Hebrew to assist in the explanation of what seems to be both a borrowing from Aramaic and a sociolectal lexeme that is a neologism with technical usage, it seems appropriate to turn to cognate languages for help. The danger in the application of Semitic philology to the comprehension of individual lexemes is that what Ferdinand de Saussure distinguished as *langue* and *parole* can be confused: the use of language in a given situation (*parole*; the use of *pšr* in the Qumran literature) is replaced by the system of language itself (*langue*; the supposed root meaning of *pšr*).[17] Nevertheless, the root *pšr* is known in Akkadian of the Old Babylonian period, Aramaic, Hebrew, and Arabic and has the fundamental meaning of "loosen" or "dissolve." The Akkadian idioms that permit a consideration of the term's semantic field include "release prisoners," "settle a dispute," "loose an oath," "report or explain dreams"; furthermore, in the intensive conjugation there is evidence for "unravel thread," "loosen an evil spell," and "interpret dreams, especially by magic." Horgan depends on the work of A. Leo

15. P. R. Weis ("The Date of the Habakkuk Scroll," *JQR* 41 [1950]: 137–42) identified *pšr* as a medieval Arabic term, though obviously his lexicography was caught up in the debates about the dating of the scrolls.

16. Very similar philological points are made by Berrin, "Qumran Pesharim," 113.

17. Horgan is well aware of this risk in her comments on the possible existence of a proto-Semitic *ptr* that could explain both Hebrew *ptr* and Aramaic *pšr* (Horgan, *Pesharim: Qumran Interpretations of Biblical Books*, 234–37).

Oppenheim, an Assyriologist of the first rank, to show that the term can refer to the reporting of a dream, namely, translating the symbols of the dream into language; it can refer to the interpreting of a dream for the dreaming person, not so much an exposition as a therapeutic release of meaning, so that it can also refer to the process of dispelling or removing the evil consequences of a dream.[18]

As is well known, the root *pšr* appears in the Hebrew Bible only in Qoh 8:1: "Who is like the wise one, and who knows the interpretation of a thing (*pēšer dābār*)?" The Greek translator rendered this precisely as λύσιν ῥήματος, apparently reflecting the root meaning of *pšr* as "loosen." Horgan has pointed out that the feminine form *pišrâ* occurs in Sir 38:14 in a discourse on the role of the physician. In the light of the Akkadian data, she proposes as a translation of the verse: "for he too will pray to God that *pšrh* [a release] will avail him, and healing in order to preserve his life." In that way the sense of dispelling evil omens is retained. The Greek has ἀνάπαυσις, "rest, repose, ease."[19]

In the Aramaic of Daniel, the root *pšr* occurs both verbally and nominally. It is used in relation to the interpretation of dreams, especially in Dan 2 and 4, and in connection with the analysis of the writing on the wall during Belshazzar's feast in Dan 5. In Aramaic in manuscripts from the Qumran caves, the verb is now discernible in the Book of Giants (4Q530 2 ii + 6–12, 14): "The dream which you will give to Enoch, the scribe of discernment (*spr prš*'), and he will interpret (*ypšwr*) for us the dream."[20] The context of dream interpretation fits precisely with what has long been suggested for the principal ingredient of the use of *pšr* in Qumran Hebrew where the verbal use of *pšr* is also rare. Indeed, the situation remains the same as when Horgan wrote: there seems to be only one certain occurrence of the verb, namely, that in 1QpHab 2:8, the use of the infinitive *lpšwr* referring to the interpretation of the words of the prophets.[21]

As for the noun in Qumran Hebrew, it is nearly always used as the key semantic element in a range of formulae that introduce the interpretation of a scriptural text. Most scholars have stopped agonizing about the precise meaning of the term[22] and render it simply as "interpretation" or, with a past participle,

---

18. A. Leo Oppenheim, *The Interpretation of Dreams in the Ancient Near East: With a Translation of an Assyrian Dream Book* (Transactions of the American Philosophical Society 46/3; Philadelphia: American Philosophical Society, 1956), 217–25.

19. Though it also has been wondered whether the uncial ΑΝΑΛΥΣΙΝ was misread as ΑΝΑΠΑΥΣΙΝ: see Horgan, *Pesharim: Qumran Interpretations of Biblical Books*, 232 n. 10.

20. See É. Puech, *Qumrân Grotte 4.XXII: Textes araméens, première partie 4Q529–549* (DJD 31; Oxford: Clarendon, 2001), 28. There are three or four uses of the Aramaic noun: 4Q203 frg. 8, line 13; 4Q530 2 ii + 6–12, 23; 7 ii 7 and 10. For frg. 7, Puech restores the context to refer to the interpretation of two dreams—probably not inappropriate, but fairly extensive restoration.

21. A verbal form is restored in 1Q22 1 i 3.

22. See, in particular, the helpful study by I. Rabinowitz, "*Pêsher/Pittârôn*: Its Biblical Meaning and Its Significance in Qumran Literature," *RevQ* 8/30 (1973): 219–32: "The term

as "interpreted,"[23] though to my mind there is still some room for contextual precision.[24] Several significant issues arise that need to be kept in mind by lexicographers. First, one can legitimately ask what the use of the term *pšr* implies about the object of interpretation: is it to be understood as like a dream? So, second, what does the use of the term in the light of such a context, imply about the method of interpretation: should the modern interpreter look to oneirocriticism in late antiquity or to parallels in scriptural exegesis to be found in authors like Philo or Matthew or indeed elsewhere, such as to omen interpretation? And third, what does the use of the term imply about the status of the interpretation? Is it bound to come to pass, just as the interpretations offered by Joseph in Genesis came to pass? Is it to be understood in some way in the light of speech-act theory as performative speech?

Some of the key issues to note in all this for the conceptualization of a reference tool like *ThWQ* are the following. First, it is not inappropriate to consider etymological matters, though these need to be controlled in some measure in terms of time and space: etymological observations need to be contemporary and local for best effect. The demonstrable borrowing from Aramaic, even if a generation or two removed from subsequent usage, is to be preferred to analysis in terms of Akkadian precedents. Nevertheless, wider etymological considerations raise a second matter, namely, that the wider cultural context can be very significant for a full appreciation of the semantic range of any particular term. This may be especially notable in a scribal culture whose parameters are not restricted. The lesson of Ben Sira is often repeated; the sign of a least one kind of wise literate Jew was international travel and cross-cultural exposure. To confine an understanding of *pšr* to the internal data of the Qumran literature alone is not appropriate, but how wide and far the modern lexicographer should travel to unravel the meaning of the term is a matter for debate and discernment. Third, what is at stake particularly in a work like *ThWQ*? Horgan concluded her reading of the use of the term in Daniel with the following observation: "Daniel is called the chief of the magicians (4:6); the mystery (*rāzā*) of the dream and the interpretation were revealed to Daniel in a vision of the night (2:19). It is clear, however, that the notion of interpreting dreams by magic has been theologized; the interpretation is revealed by God."[25] It is thus to be noted that the function of the technical term introduces or rather conveys theological assumptions and meanings that the theological lexicographer should be poised to disclose.

---

pēsher, in fine, never denotes just an explanation or an exposition, but always a presaged reality, either envisaged or emergent or else observed as already actualised" (pp. 225–26).

23. The preferred rendering of various formulations by G. Vermes, *The Complete Dead Sea Scrolls in English* (5th rev. ed.; London: Penguin, 2004).

24. This kind of precision is offered by W. H. Brownlee, *The Midrash Pesher of Habakkuk: Text, Translation, Exposition with an Introduction* (SBLMS 24; Missoula, Mont.: Scholars Press, 1979), in his preferred translation, "prophetic meaning."

25. Horgan, *Pesharim: Qumran Interpretations of Biblical Books*, 234.

Before concluding this brief discussion of *pšr*, it is important to recall the several uses that imply a wider function of the term than its use as "presage," "prophetic meaning," or "interpretation." In 1Q30, perhaps a fragmentary part of a liturgical document,[26] the term occurs with a plural suffix, *pšryhm*, "their interpretations." In the light of the damaged but wider context that speaks of the books in five parts, Horgan comments that "here the noun *pēšer* may refer to some distinct works, possibly written commentaries."[27] Does this indicate that the modern use of the term as a generic label is at least in part justified from ancient usage? At the least the grammatical shift from singular to plural permits a collective referent to be envisaged, and it is a small step from there to the identification of the content of the interpretation with the container through which it is conveyed. The move is implied furthermore in 4Q180 where the distinctive idiomatic phrase *pšr ʿl* occurs twice (4Q180 frg. 1 lines 1 and 7).[28]

In addition the term occurs, apparently in its regular singular formulaic patterns, in 4Q159 frg. 5, a small piece that has been the subject of a detailed study by Moshe Bernstein.[29] The words preceding the *pšr* formula do not correspond to any known form of the scriptural text of Exod 33 to which some phraseology in the fragment most closely corresponds. Against the background of Israel's experience in the wilderness after the event of the golden calf, Bernstein suggests that "the pesher is not the interpretation of a text, but of an historical event, treating the event as prefiguring or typologizing an event in the future. I suggest that the Qumranites … may have seen in this pentateuchal passage a model or precedent in Moses' separation of himself from the Israelite camp, after the biblical Israelites had sinned with the golden calf, for their own departure to the desert to isolate themselves from the sinful remainder of contemporary Israel."[30] Here a suitable lexical view of *pšr* has enabled a modern reader to overcome the problem of how a difficult fragment might best be understood. Fragmentary texts force their modern readers to leave much unanswered, but a plausible suggestion is facilitated by knowledge of idiomatic usage in other compositions.[31] At the least

---

26. See J. T. Milik, *Qumran Cave I* (DJD 1; Oxford: Clarendon, 1955), 132.

27. Horgan, *Pesharim: Qumran Interpretations of Biblical Books*, 233.

28. Elsewhere the use is always *pšrw ʿl*, the third person suffix implying only a reference to the interpretation at hand.

29. M. J. Bernstein, "4Q159 Fragment 5 and the 'Desert Theology' of the Qumran Sect," in *Emanuel: Studies in Hebrew Bible, Septuagint and Dead Sea Scrolls in Honor of Emanuel Tov* (ed. S. M. Paul et al.; VTSup 94; Leiden: Brill, 2003), 43–56.

30. Ibid., 53.

31. Bernstein's imaginative reconstruction of an actual separation in the wilderness is probably preferable to that of D. Dimant, "Not Exile in the Desert but Exile in the Spirit: The Pesher of Isa. 40:3 in the *Rule of the Community*," *Meghillot: Studies in the Dead Sea Scrolls* 2 (2004): 21–36 (English summary, ii–iii); eadem, "Non pas l'exil au desert mais l'exil spirituel: L'interprétation d'Isaïe 40, 3 dans la *Règle de la Communauté*," in *Qoumrân et le Judaïsme du tournant de notre ère: Actes de la Table Ronde, Collège de France, 16 novembre 2004* (ed. A. Lemaire and S. C. Mimouni; Collection de la *REJ* 40; Paris: Peeters, 2006), 17–36.

these last few paragraphs indicate that it is important to take the full range of data into account. A lexicographical question arises: should the surviving majority usage be preferred to other less common uses? In other words, in the light of the data being partial and fragmentary, how do the authors of discursive dictionary entries make decisions about which text or group of texts to prioritize in their presentation of individual lexemes?

3. MIDRASH

As with the term *pšr*, so with the term *mdrš*, much ink has been spilled. However, whereas the debate about the likely significance of *pšr* had largely been concluded in the first thirty years after the scrolls came to light, the debate concerning midrash has only really taken off in the last two decades, spurred in part by a rediscovery of the possible significance of the scrolls within the broader fields of the study of rabbinic literature and hermeneutics.[32]

Much of the debate in the last twenty years can be characterized in terms of whether the term *mdrš* should be understood in the light of earlier tradition read forward, in relation to rather limited contemporary evidence, or in terms of later materials read backward.[33] Whereas the chief characteristic of the discussion of *pšr* is the place of Semitic philology and the suitable cultural contextualization of usage, for *mdrš* the major characteristic of the discussion has to do with the appropriate use of diachronic data, discussion that has the determination of relevance as a significant part of its profile. From the pre-Qumran period the issue is how closely, or even whether, the term *mdrš* should be associated with exegetical *study*. From the later rabbinic perspective questions arise concerning whether the term has as a significant part of its referent, even in the Qumran period, either certain elements of hermeneutical method or particular features of certain later literary genres containing Jewish interpretation.[34]

Another matter that setting discussion of *pšr* alongside *mdrš* brings into focus is whether nominal or verbal forms of a lexeme should be given priority. Whereas for *pšr* there is virtually no presentation in the Qumran literature of

---

32. See the helpful summary of this recent orientation around the concept of midrash by P. S. Alexander, "The Bible in Qumran and Early Judaism," in *Text in Context: Essays by Members of the Society for Old Testament Study* (ed. A. D. H. Mayes; Oxford: Clarendon Press, 2000), 35–62, esp. 35–40, 44–46.

33. For this approach to debates about interpretation in the Qumran scrolls, see G. J. Brooke, "From Bible to Midrash: Approaches to Biblical Interpretation in the Dead Sea Scrolls by Modern Interpreters," in *Northern Lights on the Dead Sea Scrolls: Proceedings of the Nordic Qumran Network 2003–2006* (ed. A. Klostergaard Petersen et al.; STDJ 80; Leiden: Brill, 2009), 1–19.

34. A good survey of several key modern commentators on rabbinic midrash is provided by S. E. Docherty, *The Use of the Old Testament in Hebrews: A Case Study in Early Jewish Bible Interpretation* (WUNT 2/260; Tübingen: Mohr Siebeck, 2009), 83–120.

the root as a verb (as indicated above), for *mdrš* there are a few nominal uses but, including a few parallel examples, over 135 uses of the verb in the corpus. For *mem*-preformative nouns such as *mdrš*, there is a debate in any case. Some lexicons list them under the verbal stem, while others list them separately, in effect as distinct words.[35]

Before commenting briefly on some of the diachronic issues, let us look at the contemporary evidence first, and the nominal before the verbal. The nominal form *mdrš* occurs but eleven times in the extant nonscriptural scrolls; all its uses are in what most would acknowledge as sectarian compositions. There are two (three, if parallels are counted) occurrences in the Damascus Document. CD 10:6 is part of a context in which the judgment of the community is described against one who is slack in fulfilling the instructions of the upright: "But when his deeds are evident, according to the *explanation* of the law (*mdrš htwrh*) in which the men of perfect holiness walked, no-one should associate with him in wealth or work."[36] In 4Q266 frg. 11, lines 18–20 (// 4Q270 7 ii 12–15), J. M. Baumgarten restores and reads, "This is the elaboration (*prwš*) of the laws (*mšptym*) to be followed during the entire period of visitation, that which will be visited upon them during the periods of wrath and their journeys, for all who dwell in their camps and all who dwell in their towns. Behold, it is all in accordance with the final *interpretation* of the Law (*mdrš htwrh h'hrwn*)."[37]

There are three occurrences of the term in 1QS. In 1QS 6:24 we read, "And these are the regulations (*hmšptym*) by which they shall judge in an examination of the Community (*bmdrš yhd*) depending on the case."[38] This is in effect the title of a subsection of the Rule of the Community, which is followed by a long list of offenses and misdemeanors and their appropriate punishments, a section with parallels in some Cave 4 versions of the Rule of the Community, but also in 4Q259 and some extant copies of the Damascus Document (4Q266; 4Q270). In 1QS 8:15, the term *mdrš* is used in the comment after the citation of Isa 40:3: "This is the study of the law (*mdrš htwrh*) which he commanded through the hand of Moses, in order to act in compliance with all that has been revealed from age to age, and according to what the prophets have revealed through his holy spirit."[39] The preparation of the way of the Lord is the *mdrš htwrh*, both in this text and in the parallel passage in 4Q259 3:6: "This is the study of the law ([*md*]*r*[*š htwrh*])

---

35. This is one of the classic differences, for example, between BDB and *The Dictionary of Classical Hebrew* (ed. D. J. A. Clines; 8 vols.; Sheffield: Sheffield Academic Press, 1993–2012). The latter defines *mdrš* as "study, inquiry, interpretation, midrash, ... written discourse, ... perh. explanation, development of existing data" (5:150).

36. Translation from F. García Martínez and E. J. C. Tigchelaar, *The Dead Sea Scrolls Study Edition* (2 vols.; Leiden: Brill; Grand Rapids: Eerdmans, 2000), 1:579.

37. J. M. Baumgarten, ed., *Qumran Cave 4.XII: The Damascus Document (4Q266–273)* (DJD 18; Oxford: Clarendon, 1996), 76–77.

38. García Martínez and Tigchelaar, *Dead Sea Scrolls Study Edition*, 1:85.

39. Ibid., 1:89–91.

which he commanded through the hand of Moses. These are the regulations for the Instructor ..."[40] 1QS 8:26 is part of a passage in which the regulations for the men of perfect holiness are laid out, especially as they form a council, including what should be done if one of them errs inadvertently: "If his conduct is perfect in the session, in the investigation (*bmdrš*), and in the council according to the Many, if he has not sinned again through oversight until two full years have passed." Here the object of the *mdrš* is not made explicit, but the context implies that it refers not to the exegesis of Scripture, or even of a nonscriptural law, but to the examination of other members of the community. This last text has a partial parallel in 4Q258 7:1–3: "he should be excluded from pure food and from the council and the judgment for two full years. And he may return to the interpretation (*bmdrš*) and to the council if he does not go sinning through oversight until two years have passed."[41] Apart from 1QS 8:15 and its parallel in 4Q259, *mdrš* in the Rule of the Community seems to refer primarily to the examination of fellow members of the community. It is the interpretation of people as much as it is the study of texts.

The other occurrences of the term *mdrš* in the Rule of the Community occur in 4Q256 9:1, which has a verbatim parallel in 4Q258 1:1: "Midrash for the Instructor concerning the men of the law who freely volunteer ... "[42] This titular usage of the term is reflected also in two other texts. On the verso of 4Q249, a title or incipit is preserved: "Interpretation of the Book of Moses (*mdrš spr mwšh*)."[43] In the principal fragment of 4Q174, the term is used to introduce a new section of interpretation. After the commentary on the oracle of Nathan has been completed, the new section begins with the term *mdrš* followed by the preposition *mn* and the first verse of Ps 1: "Midrash of Ps 1:1 «Blessed [the] man who does not walk in the counsel of the wicked». The interpretation of this word (*pšr hdbr*)...."[44] This use in 4Q174 has been particularly significant in some discussions about how the term *mdrš* might function technically as denoting a literary genre or as belonging on a semantic trajectory between describing an interpretative approach or set of techniques that in later terms were understood as belonging archetypically to particular genres of scriptural interpretation.[45]

---

40. Ibid., 1:531.

41. Ibid., 1:523.

42. Ibid., 1:513. P. S. Alexander and G. Vermes translate *mdrš lmśkyl* here as "Instruction for the Maskil" (*Qumran Cave 4.XIX: Serekh Ha-Yaḥad and Two Related Texts* [DJD 26; Oxford: Clarendon, 1998], 54). In relation to the parallel in 4Q258 they state baldly (p. 96): "*mdrš* has the meaning of teaching, instruction, or interpretation, as in *1QS* VI, 24; VII [*sic*] 15, 26; *CD* XX 6; *4QFl* 1 i 14."

43. García Martínez and Tigchelaar, *Dead Sea Scrolls Study Edition*, 1:497.

44. Ibid., 1:353.

45. Note, for example, how 4Q174 is the starting point in the significant article on midrash by P. S. Alexander, "Midrash," in *A Dictionary of Biblical Interpretation* (ed. R. J. Coggins and J. L. Houlden; London: SCM Press, 1990), 452–59.

What is one to make of these dozen uses of the term *mdrš* in the Qumran sectarian manuscripts? Since the object of the nominal activity is sometimes undefined, sometimes a person (perhaps as a subjective genitive), and sometimes a text (as an objective genitive), it might seem suitable to attempt to use the same word in translation to represent all the various uses, a term in English such as "examination." The rarity of entirely congruent semantic fields for words in different languages makes such strictures in translation undesirable, and this is indicated by the way that it is very difficult to find any single term that will also be able to cover the titular uses of the term in the 4Q256 and 4Q258 occurrences.

Timothy Lim has proposed that for the term *mdrš* there are four broad categories of referents.[46] First, there are references to "communal study" as in 1QS 8:14–16, 26; it is interesting to see the order in which Lim lists his meanings. Second, some uses are best rendered as "inquiry," that is, "a judicial inquiry"; such is the case for 1QS 6:24, where the term occurs in the construct with *yḥd*, "an inquiry of the community." Third, Lim understands *mdrš* in CD 20:6 as "communal regulation": no member of the congregation shall have any dealings with a fellow member "when his deeds become apparent according to the midrash of the Torah in which the men of perfection walk." Lim proposes, "'Midrash' here has the sense of communal regulation based upon the content of the Torah."[47] Fourth, the term is used in a titular sense in 4Q258 1 i 1, 4Q256 5 i 1, and 4Q249, but Lim insists that the titular usage is not a reference to a genre of biblical exegesis, "but 'instruction' or 'rule' which the Wise Teacher will impart to the sectarians,"[48] since in the longer corresponding passage in 1QS 5:1 the term *serek* is used synonymously for *mdrš*. In the joint use of *mdrš* with *pšr* in 4Q174, Lim concludes, *mdrš* should be translated as "a study of" or "an instruction deriving from" Ps 1:1 rather than as a reference to a genre of biblical exegesis that is the direct precursor of the rabbinic midrashim.

Lim is right to be cautious about whether the term *mdrš* in 4Q174 could refer to a piece of literature. The occurrence of *mdrš* with *pšr* in 4Q174 prompted William Brownlee to consider that here was the possibility of identifying a genre of interpretation other than midrash haggadah or halakhah; thus, he took over the term coined apparently by E. Earle Ellis and applied it to a whole genre: midrash pesher.[49] Although it is not used clearly to define a literary genre, just as we have noted that *pšr* can possibly refer in the plural to written collections of interpreta-

---

46. T. H. Lim, "Midrash Pesher in the Pauline Letters," in *The Scrolls and the Scriptures: Qumran Fifty Years After* (ed. S. E. Porter and C. A. Evans; JSPSup 26; Roehampton Institute London Papers 3; Sheffield: Sheffield Academic Press, 1997), 280–92.

47. Ibid., 287.

48. Ibid., 288.

49. E. E. Ellis, "Midrash Pesher in Pauline Hermeneutics," *NTS* 2 (1955–56): 127–33; republished in *Prophecy and Hermeneutics in Early Christianity: New Testament Essays* (WUNT 18; Tübingen: Mohr Siebeck, 1978), 173–81.

tions, so *mdrš* in 4Q174, and even more so in 4Q249, could refer to the group of *pšr* interpretations that are to follow, not just to the commentary on Ps 1:1.

Having considered the nominal form of the root, let us turn briefly to the verb. While the consideration of the verbal evidence for *drš* in the Qumran collection is seldom directly applied to this problem, it is the verb that has taken priority in diachronic discussions. No doubt this is because the substantive *mdrš* occurs only twice in the Hebrew Scriptures, in 2 Chr 13:22, "the midrash of the prophet Iddo," and in 2 Chr 24:27, "written in the midrash of the book of the kings." In the former the term seems to designate the literary source from which the Chronicler took his account, whereas in the latter the NRSV renders the term not unsuitably as "Commentary."

The shortage of *mdrš* as a substantive noun in the Hebrew Scriptures leads this paper directly to the point of contrast I wish to make in terms of lexical comprehension within the diachronic treatment of words. The question emerges: how can criteria be constructed that enable the modern reader to determine when words widen their semantic fields and take on new meanings? In a widely cited study, Johann Maier turns to the verb *drš* to trace the trajectory of development. He is concerned to show that "scarcely sufficient evidence exists for a connotation of the verb *drš* like 'to interpret' or 'to expound' in early Jewish literature."[50] Maier is particularly concerned to suggest that Lawrence Schiffman's views on scriptural exegesis at Qumran depend on understanding the verb *drš* in the Qumran sectarian literature as "to study."[51] He disagrees and argues instead that a key text and context, 1QS 6:6–8, should be translated as: "In the place where these ten (members) are (living) must not be missing a man advising/instructing/enacting the law, day and night, concerning good relations each one with his companion."[52]

Maier supports his view that *drš* cannot mean "to study" in the Qumran literature by referring to the Greek Bible, where the translators did not use terms of interpretation to render the Hebrew and by appeal to the targumim, where the consistent rendering of *drš* is with forms of the verb *ṭbʿ* ("to demand," "to summon").[53] Maier then offers a detailed study of pentateuchal and prophetic

---

50. J. Maier, "Early Jewish Biblical Interpretation in the Qumran Literature," in *Hebrew Bible/Old Testament: The History of Its Interpretation*. Vol. 1, *From the Beginnings to the Middle Ages (Until 1300)* (ed. M. Sæbø; Göttingen: Vandenhoeck & Ruprecht, 1996), 113.

51. L. H. Schiffman, *Sectarian Law in the Dead Sea Scrolls: Courts, Testimony and the Penal Code* (BJS 33; Chico, Calif.: Scholars Press, 1983), 14–17. Schiffman's understanding of *drš* as "study" is supported by many others, e.g., Alexander, "Bible in Qumran and Early Judaism," 40 (for 1QS 6:6–8).

52. Maier, "Early Jewish Biblical Interpretation in the Qumran Literature," 114–15. Maier's German translation of the passage is: "Und nicht weiche von einem Ort, wo sich die Zehn befinden, ein Mann, der in bezug auf Torah Anweisung(en) erteilt, (und zwar) tagsüber und nachts, ständig, bezüglich des guten (verhaltens) eines jeden zu seinem Nächsten" (*Die Qumran Essener: Die Texte vom Toten Meer I* [UTB 224; Munich: Reinhardt, 1995], 182).

53. P. Heger argues that the targum is not quite so monolithic in its renderings as Maier

uses of *drš* to support his argument. He is particularly concerned to show that the verb *drš* becomes a technical term in requesting an oracle and being told what such an oracle might contain, and a technical term in another way in juridical contexts, meaning "to summon for interrogation." Through a presentation of Deut 17:8–12 and its parallel in the Temple Scroll (11Q19 56:1–11), Maier argues that *drš* is priestly activity in legal declaration. He concludes that "there is no reason to assume for Qumran *drš* / *mdrš* a connotation like 'to expound' or 'to derive from scripture'. Some of the hermeneutical devices ascribed to the Qumran community do not fit the Qumran concept of revelation and authority at all, but correspond more or less to Christian or/and orthodox Jewish Biblical canon theology and hermeneutics."[54] I do not intend to declare whether Maier or Schiffman should be preferred, but my point is to draw attention to Maier's procedure. On the basis of pre-Qumran Hebrew usage, as he understands it, and in light of how Jewish Greek- and Aramaic-speaking interpreters have subsequently understood their Hebrew base text, so the connotational use of terms in the sectarian Qumran literature is contextualized and determined. But the question remains for Maier: at what point and on what grounds might he be willing to permit a widening of the semantic field so that Qumran *drš* / *mdrš* could be conceived of as having a connotation like "to expound" or "to derive from scripture."[55]

Paul Mandel seems to agree with Maier. In assessing the origins of midrash in the Second Temple period he concludes that "the word *darash* retained a decidedly non-textual connotation throughout the Second Temple period, and it is this connotation that is also evident in texts from the early rabbinic period. An analysis of the relevant evidence shows that the Jewish scholar, who was indeed named *sofer*, was involved not so much in the *interpretation of a text* (the Bible) but in the *instruction in law*."[56] For Mandel, the *doresh ha-Torah* is the expounder of the Law, not its senior student, and the community's activity as described in 1QS 8:12–16 is "instruction of the Law."

<EXT>The essence of the activity designated by the term *darash* is primarily one of instruction, delivered and revealed by one who has knowledge to one who does not. Of course such instruction may include passages of Scripture,

---

supposes ("The Development of Qumran Law: Nistarot, Niglot and the Issue of 'Contemporization,'" *RevQ* 23 [2007–8]: 174).

54. Maier, "Early Jewish Biblical Interpretation in the Qumran Literature," 119–20.

55. On some aspects of the rabbinic use of *mdrš*, see, among others, M. I. Gruber, "Biblical Interpretation in Rabbinic Literature: Historical and Philological Aspects," in *The Encyclopedia of Judaism*, vol. 1, *A–E* (ed. Jacob Neusner, Alan J. Avery-Peck, and William Scott Green; 2nd ed.; Leiden: Brill, 2005), 217–34.

56. P. Mandel, "The Origins of Midrash in the Second Temple Period," in *Current Trends in the Study of Midrash* (ed. C. Bakhos; JSJSup 106; Leiden: Brill, 2006), 13–14 (italics his). Among others, Mandel is arguing against Gertner ("Terms of Scriptural Interpretation," 5), who proposed that *darash* in the sense of study and investigation was a conceptual transformation attributable to the times of Ezra the Scribe.

and so midrash as a scriptural activity is not precluded. Indeed, the exposition of passages from Scripture occupies a formidable place in Jewish instruction. But these form only a subset of topics that may be expounded (taught).[57]

As with Maier, so Mandel's argument runs from materials that predate the Qumran sectarian literature and follow on after it: the debate is a diachronic one.

Among those who have had problems with the approaches represented by both Maier and Schiffman is Paul Heger.[58] Heger's explicit assumption is that various terms, including *drš*, are highly nuanced and "that their meanings in any particular instance can be derived only from their contexts."[59] Heger's overall thesis is that the Qumran sages did indeed use exegesis to develop their law, and that their literature mirrors the same tension between the "eternal" text of the law and its interpretation as is to be found in rabbinic literature. He has argued, furthermore, that "a difference was maintained in Qumran between inspiration, whereby earnest study of the Torah would lead to correct interpretation, and revelation, which was limited to non-halakhic matters and to a select number of people."[60] Of interest in the context of this brief study is Heger's approach: the matter of diachronicity for him is one of reading back an understanding from the rabbinic materials to the earlier Second Temple period data and of differentiating between prophecy and halakhah in a rigid fashion; in that way he appears to construct context anachronistically.

Heger proposes that indeed in Deuteronomy and other scriptural contexts *drš* must be understood as "to investigate" the facts or the correct law, but he prefers to read Ezra 7:10 as concerning how the leader "interpreted" or "studied"[61] the law of the Lord. And for many of the uses of *drš* or *mdrš* in the Qumran scrolls he asserts that in most instances the verb must be understood as "interpret." Heger suitably determines the meaning of the term *drš* on the basis of its object; he argues that *drš* is used extensively for the interpretation of the law, an activity that any devout Israelite can engage in, but it is not used for the exposition of the mystical hidden things in the prophecies that he claims were revealed in visions to the Teacher of Righteousness. But there are always exceptions to these kinds of general assertions, such as the use of *mdrš* to introduce the pesher exegesis of the Psalms in 4Q174. More worryingly, Heger builds a large edifice with significant theological ramifications on the distinctions that he asserts rather than demonstrates. At least part of the edifice is based on assumptions about the authority and status of the Torah as eternal and unchangeable in the Second Temple period, assumptions that to me are largely those of a later period or of none at all.

57. Maier, "Early Jewish Biblical Interpretation in the Qumran Literature," 29.
58. Heger, "Development of Qumran Law," 167–206.
59. Ibid., 169.
60. Ibid.
61. Ibid., 173–74. Here Heger oscillates between these translations for *drš* in Ezra 7:10.

This is not the place to sort out the debate, but it is important to note how the various participants construct their approaches, to try to unravel some of their assumptions and to appreciate the complexity of what is at stake for anybody who might try to construct a lexical entry for *drš* or *mdrš* in the Qumran literature, and a lexical entry with a theological dimension too. For these terms, as probably for others, the key issues of definition remain in the tension between, on the one hand, the likely senses of the uses of the words in certain significant contexts and, on the other, the appropriate use of diachronic data.

4. Conclusion

In this paper, largely focused on *pšr* and *mdrš*, I have attempted briefly to disclose some of the issues involved in the handling of any lexeme. I hope that through the discussion of some aspects of the history of scholarship on these terms to have shed some light on what linguistic assumptions are sometimes made by scholars and to encourage the thought that there can be no single template for what is presented in a work such as *ThWQ* since variety is present in the data at many levels. Of particular significance for those charged with compiling entries for a work such as *ThWQ* are the controlled uses of philological insights, well-wrought arguments from context, and a constant awareness of the tension between diachronic and synchronic data in establishing semantic fields.

EIGHT

GENRE THEORY, REWRITTEN BIBLE, AND PESHER

1. THE PROBLEM

The purpose of this short study is to try to clarify a problem that in various ways has already been widely discussed. In particular, the problem concerns how the wide range of compositions from the Second Temple period that represent or depend implicitly or explicitly on some form of authoritative Jewish Scripture should be suitably described and categorized; what might make for the better reading of all this literature, especially in terms of what is now known of it from the Qumran caves? I am not concerned with offering any solutions to the problem, though along the way there might be some indications of what kinds of solutions could be more rather than less appropriate; rather, this essay will search for some explanatory dynamism by attempting to lay out several of the issues that need to be addressed by all those who are concerned to find answers to what is best understood as a matter of genre analysis. To take the discussion forward I have sought some suggestive clarification of the issues concerned from some few of those literary theorists who have been concerned with genre in recent decades, theorists whose work is not regularly part of the scholarly discourse concerning the Dead Sea Scrolls, though many of their insights have indeed, directly or indirectly, come into play in the fields of biblical studies and Jewish studies.[1]

2. WHY IS THERE A PROBLEM?

The problem concerning the categorization of the wide range of compositions from the Second Temple period that represent or depend implicitly or explicitly on some form of authoritative Jewish Scripture has arisen because the publication of the Dead Sea Scrolls has enabled us to see into the literary world of Juda-

---

1. For an accessible introduction to genre analysis among literary theorists, see, e.g., J. Frow, *Genre* (New Critical Idiom; London: Routledge, 2006); easy access to key thinkers is provided by D. Duff (ed.), *Modern Genre Theory* (London: Pearson Education, 2000), whose own "Introduction" (pp. 1–24) is an excellent survey of the modern field. The classic survey and exposition in English is by A. Fowler, *Kinds of Literature: An Introduction to the Theory of Genres and Modes* (Oxford: Clarendon, 1982).

ism of the second half of the Second Temple period in ways that had previously been thought impossible. In the first decade after the initial discoveries in the Qumran caves, the publication of Pesher Habakkuk from Cave 1 and preliminary editions of some similar commentary texts from Cave 4 set in motion a series of investigations on the nature of those distinctive sectarian commentaries; the question was posed many times in different ways whether the so-called pesharim were continuous with other forms of Jewish scriptural commentary or should rather be considered as something strangely *sui generis*. The publication of less clearly sectarian compositions such as the Genesis Apocryphon provoked a somewhat different scholarly response but also opened up the possibility for the construction of a new literary category, "Rewritten Bible."[2] However, it has been the release of all the unpublished Cave 4 manuscripts in 1991 and the subsequent publication of their contents in editions and translations that have most acutely demanded some fresh reconsideration of the character of the transmission of authoritative traditions in early Judaism.

For some literary theorists the definition of the corpus of texts that might deserve the label "literature" has produced a wide-ranging set of critical points of view, based on the evaluation of such topics as the delineation of literary canons, the consideration of elitism, the role of orality, the nature of "discourse," whether there is such a thing as "bad literature," indeed whether texts exist at all apart from the assumptions and prejudices of their readers.[3] However, for the student of the written remains of early Judaism, texts fall readily into two groups, the documentary and the literary. Although there can be overlap even between two large groups such as those, overwhelmingly it is clearly literary texts that have survived from the Qumran caves. Among the literary texts, those that re-present earlier compositions of emerging and increasing authority (broadly or narrowly conceived), or that interpret them implicitly or explicitly, form a very substantial group of compositions.[4]

For that group of texts three interpretative cruxes emerge at the outset. First, how should the "authority" of texts or textual traditions within particular groups of texts be articulated suitably? Whatever might be the creative and hermeneutically strong ways of answering that question, the question itself brings to the fore the issue of the primacy of a text's status and function, matters that could well seem to have more controlling force in generic discussion than a text's form or content but are often assumed or ignored in debates about genre.[5] Second, in

---

2. A genre label launched by G. Vermes, *Scripture and Tradition in Judaism: Haggadic Studies* (2nd ed.; StPB 4; Leiden: Brill, 1973; 1st ed. 1961).

3. See, e.g., the sample of issues outlined by Fowler, *Kinds of Literature*, 1–6.

4. I have even suggested that all the literature from the Qumran caves might be seen as relating to earlier authoritative Scriptures in one way or another: G. J. Brooke, "The Dead Sea Scrolls," in *The Biblical World* (ed. J. Barton; London: Routledge, 2002), 1:250–69.

5. An exception is the consideration of Mosaic discourse by H. Najman, *Seconding Sinai: The Development of Mosaic Discourse in Second Temple Judaism* (JSJSup 77; Leiden: Brill,

what ways is it appropriate and justifiable to distinguish earlier from later, or authoritative from dependent, primary from secondary? And what might such distinctions suggest about the place for considering the hierarchy of genres, generic instability, and evolutionary models of genre construction? Third, what labels might suitably be imposed on this broad range of literature, a breadth of literary compositions that seldom makes plain how it understands itself? It is these questions in particular that show why there is a problem with the appreciation of the genres of much of this literature. In what follows I will try to pay attention to those questions by addressing issues surrounding the definition of the corpus to be studied, the problems surrounding the criteria for generic definition, the perspective of the evolution of genres (continuities and discontinuities, shifting hierarchies, inherent instability, etc.), and the need for cross-cultural analogies.

3. The Issue: Defining the Corpus

As has already been implied in the previous paragraphs, the definition of the literary corpus to be discussed is a key matter. The first issue to be decided concerns what literary compositions are to be discussed. I consider it appropriate to include within the corpus at the outset all those compositions that seem to have some kind of authority for Jews in general in the second half of the Second Temple period or that are concerned to present or re-present such compositions in some way, even if only for a particular segment of Judaism. The starting point for understanding works that might be described as rewritten Bible or pesher is the group of texts that includes both what they rewrite or comment upon as well as the rewritings and explicit commentaries.[6] In relation to the so-called "parabiblical texts" about which he writes, Daniel Falk notes at the outset, that "lying between 'biblical' text and commentary as this category does, it greatly complicates the matter of identifying what is a 'biblical' text."[7]

On the basis of the evidence of the scrolls from the Qumran caves this has been clear for some time, at least since it became evident that several of the so-called "biblical" manuscripts actually allowed the modern reader to see interpretative activity at work. In some cases this was very obvious, such as when 4QDeut^n was classed as "biblical," but on further reflection was seen to contain an excerpted

---

2003); see also E. Ulrich, "From Literature to Scripture: The Growth of a Text's Authoritativeness," *DSD* 10 (2003): 3–25; and D. K. Falk, *The Parabiblical Texts: Strategies for Extending the Scriptures in the Dead Sea Scrolls* (LSTS 63; CQS 8; London: T&T Clark, 2007), 14–15.

6. I take this to be part of what is intended by S. White Crawford when she spends her introduction discussing issues of authority and canon before embarking on helpful descriptions of what is taking place in the Reworked Pentateuch, Jubilees, the Temple Scroll, the Genesis Apocryphon, and Commentary on Genesis A (see Crawford, *Rewriting Scripture in Second Temple Times* [Studies in the Dead Sea Scrolls and Related Literature; Grand Rapids: Eerdmans, 2008], 1–18).

7. Falk, *Parabiblical Texts*, 1.

text (as may also be the case, for example, with 4QDeut[j]).[8] However, in other cases it is less clear how one distinguishes between what might be classed as variant editions of a scriptural work and what might be better understood as interpretative adjustments, either major or minor. To which subgroup should 4QJudg[a] be assigned? Is it an early form of the text of Judges of emerging authority or is it a later adjustment, perhaps even an accidental adjustment, of an earlier form of the text? Julio Trebolle Barrera has noted how biblical scholarship, even before the evidence from Qumran came to light, had thought of 6:7–10 as a literary insertion, and he has concluded that "4QJudg[a] can confidently be seen as an earlier literary form of the book than our traditional texts."[9] Some scholars have urged caution before using such small pieces as evidence for constructing theories of the textual history of Judges;[10] Natalio Fernández Marcos has argued that "the omission of 6:7–10 in 4QJudg[a] does not belong to an original stage of the book but it constitutes an accidental or intentional abbreviation."[11] Others have argued that the convergence of earlier literary-critical insights and the textual data from the Qumran caves "strongly argues that 4QJudg[a] displays, if not an earlier edition of the *entire* book of Judges, at least an 'earlier literary form' for this passage,"[12] or that "it is reasonable

---

8. 4QDeut[j] and 4QDeut[n] are both still presented as biblical scrolls in E. Ulrich, *The Biblical Qumran Scrolls: Transcriptions and Textual Variants* (VTSup 134; Leiden: Brill, 2010), 184–240. On excerpted texts, see L. Doering, "Excerpted Texts in Second Temple Judaism: A Survey of the Evidence," in *Selecta colligere II: Beiträge zur Technik des Sammelung und Kompilierung griechischer Texte von der Antiker bis zum Humanismus* (ed. R. M. Piccione and M. Perkams; Hellenica 18; Alessandria: Editioni dell'Orso, 2005), 1–38. Doering's study is particularly important for considering the practice of excerpting in non-Jewish literature, a point to be made below in the discussion of genres as cross-cultural phenomena.

9. J. Trebolle Barrera, "49. 4QJudg[a]," in *Qumran Cave 4.IX: Deuteronomy, Joshua, Judges, Kings* (ed. E. Ulrich et al.; DJD 14; Oxford: Clarendon, 1995), 161–64.

10. See, e.g., R. S. Hess, who thinks of the variant as a later abbreviation ("The Dead Sea Scrolls and Higher Criticism of the Hebrew Bible: The Case of 4QJudg[a]," in *The Scrolls and the Scriptures: Qumran Fifty Years After* [ed. S. E. Porter and C. A. Evans; JSPSup 26; Sheffield: Sheffield Academic Press, 1997], 122–28); N. Fernández Marcos prefers to view the variant as an accidental or intentional omission ("The Hebrew and Greek Text of Judges," in *The Earliest Text of the Hebrew Bible: The Relationship between the Masoretic Text and the Hebrew Base of the Septuagint Reconsidered* [ed. A. Schenker; SBLSCS 52; Atlanta: Society of Biblical Literature, 2003], 1–16).

11. N. Fernández Marcos, "The Genuine Text of Judges," in *Sôfer Mahîr: Essays in Honour of Adrian Schenker Offered by Editors of Biblia Hebraica Quinta* (ed. Y. A. P. Goldman, A. van der Kooij, and R. D. Weis; VTSup 110; Leiden: Brill, 2006), 33–45, here 42. Cf. the similar reasoning of A. Rofé, "The Biblical Text in Light of Historico-Literary Criticism: The Reproach of the Prophet-Man in Judg 6:7–10 and 4QJudg[a]" (in Hebrew), in *On the Border Line: Textual Meets Literary Criticism* (ed. Z. Talshir and D. Amara; Beer-Sheva 18; Beersheva: Ben-Gurion University of the Negev Press, 2005), 33–44, x (English summary): "It is not plausible that 4QJudg[a] preserved a text that preceded that old edition [of the eighth century B.C.E.]."

12. E. C. Ulrich, "Deuteronomistically Inspired Scribal Insertions into the Developing Biblical Texts: 4QJudg[a] and 4QJer[a]," in *Houses Full of All Good Things: Essays in Memory of Timo Veijola* (ed. J. Pakkala and M. Nissinen; Publications of the Finnish Exegetical Society 95;

to assume that the shorter text without this theological pattern represents an earlier edition of the book."[13]

Put summarily, it seems to be the case that careful consideration of the manuscripts from the Qumran caves at least allows the possibility that much more of the continuity between earlier and later copies of the same scriptural work should be recognized than is sometimes assumed. Nevertheless, it is also the case that, once the underlying authoritative texts (hypotexts) are put together with the overlaying interpretations that they provoke (hypertexts),[14] it is also possible to discern that authoritative hypotexts can be distinguished, more often than not, from their interpretative hypertexts, even if some manuscript copies of a hypotext contain interpretative hypertextual features, and some hypertexts sometimes obtain authoritative status, such as is most commonly recognized for the book of Deuteronomy or for the books of Chronicles and is also the case for some of its readers for the book of Jubilees.

For attempting to define the scope of the group of texts that are concerned with deliberately interpreting earlier authoritative Scriptures, a suitable place to start is the Index volume of Discoveries in the Judaean Desert.[15] That volume has a fascinating section that presents a provisional taxonomy by Armin Lange and Ulrike Mittmann-Richert of the genres of the compositions found in the Qumran corpus.[16] They classify the compositions found in the caves at and near Qumran under fifteen headings. The first two are described as "parabiblical texts" and "exegetical texts." They define what is included under "parabiblical texts" as follows:

> This term as used in DJD, refers to literature "closely related to texts or themes of the Hebrew Bible."[17] On the basis of biblical texts or themes, the authors of parabiblical texts employ exegetical techniques to provide answers to questions

---

Helsinki: Finnish Exegetical Society; Göttingen: Vandenhoeck & Ruprecht, 2008), 489–506, here 492. Ulrich's approach to 4QJudg[a] is supported by the wider contextual study of long additions by M. M. Zahn, "The Problem of Characterizing the Reworked Pentateuch Manuscripts: Bible, Rewritten Bible, or None of the Above?" *DSD* 15 (2008): 315–39, esp. 323.

13. R. Sollamo, "Panegyric on Redaction Criticism," in Pakkala and Nissinen, *Houses Full of All Good Things,* 684–96, here 694.

14. I have tried to expound the significance of these terms in G. J. Brooke, "Hypertextuality and the 'Parabiblical' Dead Sea Scrolls," in *In the Second Degree: Paratextual Literature in Ancient Near Eastern and Ancient Mediterranean Culture and Its Reflections in Medieval Literature* (ed. P.S. Alexander, A. Lange, and R. Pillinger; Leiden: Brill, 2010), 43–64 (included in this volume).

15. Falk (*Parabiblical Texts,* 3–17) has provided an intriguing survey of what different scholars have included within the categories his study is concerned with.

16. A. Lange and U. Mittmann-Richert, "Annotated List of the Texts from the Judaean Desert Classified," in *The Texts from the Judaean Desert: Indices and an Introduction to the Discoveries in the Judaean Desert Series* (ed. E. Tov; DJD 39; Oxford, Clarendon, 2002), 115–64.

17. E. Tov, "Foreword," in *Qumran Cave 4.VIII: Parabiblical Texts, Part 1* (ed. J. C. VanderKam; DJD 13; Oxford: Clarendon, 1994), ix.

of their own time, phrased as answers by God through Moses or the prophets. The result of their exegetical effort is communicated in the form of a new book. Therefore, parabiblical literature should not be understood as a pseudepigraphic phenomenon, i.e. the ascription of a literary work to a biblical author, but as a form of scriptural revelation, comparable to the phenomenon of literary prophecy. For this purpose, the authors of parabiblical literature used different genres: rewritten Bible, new stories or novellas created on the basis of biblical items or topics, different types of apocalypses, and testaments. In addition, parabiblical texts combining different genres can be found. However, it should be noted that a single biblical quotation or allusion, elaborated on in the context, does not necessarily indicate the parabiblical character of a fragmentary manuscript since implicit quotations are also extant in other genres of ancient Jewish literature (e.g. the Damascus Document). Because of these uncertainties, the classification of parabiblical literature is more restrictive than that proposed by the editors in the respective DJD volumes.[18]

Three issues immediately become apparent from this definition. First, it is clear that Lange and Mittmann-Richert are aware that they have constructed a category in a way more limited than might sometimes be supposed. To some extent the constraint has been imposed by the fact that already in 1994 the label "parabiblical" had been defined largely in relation to the Reworked Pentateuch manuscripts.[19] This means that the category, broad as it may at first seem, is largely restricted to compositions with some kind of narrative prose basis to them. Second, the classification is acknowledged to have counterparts in other compositions; it is likely that Lange and Mittmann-Richert allude here to passages of implicit interpretation and reuse of authoritative Scriptures in a wide range of compositions, not just in the Damascus Document, to which they make explicit reference, but notably also in various poetic compositions. Third, the category of "parabiblical texts" is constructed as an overarching umbrella term that is actually not a narrowly defined genre itself.[20] Its use in this general and plausible way shows that other scholars, in using the same term but as a genre label of a specific set of texts, have often not been aware of the issue of the hierarchy of genres in the way that they have approached the generic description of the compositions with which they work.

---

18. Lange and Mittmann-Richert, "Annotated List of the Texts," 117–18.

19. E. Tov and S. White, "Reworked Pentateuch," in VanderKam, *Qumran Cave 4.VIII: Parabiblical Texts, Part 1* (DJD 13), 187–351, for 4Q364–367. 4Q158 is also regularly included as an exemplar of this composition: see G. J. Brooke, "4Q158: Reworked Pentateuchᵃ or 4QReworked Pentateuch A?" *DSD* 8 (2001): 219–41.

20. The designation "rewritten Bible" has also been considered as an umbrella term: see, e.g., E. Koskenniemi and P. Lindqvist, "Rewritten Bible, Rewritten Stories: Methodological Aspects," in *Rewritten Bible Reconsidered: Proceedings of the Conference in Karkku, Finland, August 24–26 2006* (ed. A. Laato and J. van Ruiten; Studies in Rewritten Bible 1; Turku: Åbo Akademi University; Winona Lake, Ind.: Eisenbrauns, 2008), 11–39, here 16.

A fourth issue is in fact also apparent, namely, that the classification makes certain assumptions about what was of primary authority, especially in the middle of the Second Temple period; one wonders, for example, whether the books of Chronicles should be better perceived as some kind of rewritten composition, whereas paleo paraJoshua, not least because of its paleo-Hebrew script, was being presented as significantly authoritative by its scribal transmitters.[21] Some rewritten texts, such as Deuteronomy, were clearly already authoritative by the second century B.C.E.; others, such as the books of Chronicles, also eventually became part of the canon.[22]

Partly because of that I am inclined to think that an even larger category of textual compositions should be the starting point for any kind of generic taxonomy that includes rewritten Bible and pesher. This larger category should include all texts that are concerned directly with the transmission of authoritative tradition. In other words, the scriptural texts should not be automatically distinguished from those compositions that interpret them, either implicitly or explicitly. I have commented elsewhere on how the scrolls from the Qumran caves have provoked those who study them to reconsider the boundaries between text and interpretation.[23] As part of this broad spectrum of compositions, it matters little for our immediate purposes whether we define a term like "Rewritten Bible" narrowly or more broadly.[24] What I am proposing here as the first issue that needs to be addressed is that, just as genre theorists will often begin solely with prose and poetry, so a broadly based starting point for the category of material to be discussed permits us to see similarities and continuities between vari-

---

21. Lange and Mittmann-Richert, "Annotated List of the Texts," 126 n. 8: "4Qpaleo para-Josh (4Q123) should not be understood as an additional manuscript of the Apocryphon of Joshua, because the paleo-Hebrew script in which it is written suggests the Biblical character of this manuscript." Lange has since noted that definitive classification of this manuscript is not possible: A. Lange, *Handbuch der Textfunde vom Toten Meert*, Band 1, *Die Handschriften biblischer Bücher von Qumran und den anderen Fundorten* (Tübingen: Mohr Siebeck, 2009), 189.

22. On how Chronicles may have been perceived by those at Qumran, see G. J. Brooke, "The Books of Chronicles and the Scrolls from Qumran," in *Reflection and Refraction: Studies in Biblical Historiography in Honour of A. Graeme Auld* (ed. R. Rezetko, T. H. Lim, W. B. Aucker; VTSup 113; Leiden: Brill, 2007), 35–48.

23. G. J. Brooke, "New Perspectives on the Bible and Its Interpretation in the Dead Sea Scrolls," in *The Dynamics of Language and Exegesis at Qumran* (ed. D. Dimant and R. G. Kratz; FAT 2/35; Tübingen: Mohr Siebeck, 2009), 19–37, esp. 19–21.

24. See G. J. Brooke, "Rewritten Bible," in *Encyclopedia of the Dead Sea Scrolls* (ed. L. H. Schiffman and J. C. VanderKam; New York: Oxford University Press, 2000), 777–81, where I argue for the use of the term as an overarching category. Among those who prefer a stricter use of the label for a narrower, more closely defined genre are M. J. Bernstein, "'Rewritten Bible': A Generic Category Which Has Outlived Its Usefulness?" *Textus* 22 (2005): 169–96. See also M. Segal, "Between Bible and Rewritten Bible," in *Biblical Interpretation at Qumran* (ed. M. Henze; Studies in the Dead Sea Scrolls and Related Literature; Grand Rapids: Eerdmans, 2005), 10–28.

ous compositions; the prioritizing of smaller categories at the outset tends toward asserting and prioritizing difference and discontinuity.

The need for breadth at the outset is brought into focus sharply by a deconstructionist hypothesis put forward by Jacques Derrida. He has asserted that "every text participates in one or several genres, there is no genreless text; there is always a genre and genres, yet such participation never amounts to belonging. And not because of an abundant overflowing or a free, anarchic, and unclassifiable productivity, but because of the trait of participation itself."[25] That assertion has been helpfully expounded by Marjorie Perloff as containing two particular points.[26] First, there is the idea that no single text will ever contain all the characteristics of a particular genre; thus, no single text by itself can ever act as the defining work of a kind of literature. Second, once a particular composition is seen as belonging to a particular genre and is allowed to participate in that genre, the genre inevitably changes, even if only in relatively minor ways.

If these points are applied, for example, to the supposed genre of "Rewritten Bible," it can immediately be seen that, even if the range of compositions so named and sorted is limited to just the Genesis Apocryphon, the book of Jubilees, parts of Josephus's *Antiquities*, and the Liber antiquitatum biblicarum, then no single one of them can be held up as definitive of the genre. But, second, a real problem arises for the value of the generic label if other compositions, such as the Temple Scroll or the Reworked Pentateuch(s) are also assigned to the genre. The participation of such texts in the definition of the genre changes it so that it becomes unclear even if some of the other texts previously or originally assigned to the genre should remain part of it.

To clarify the character of "Rewritten Bible" and pesher, the scholar needs to begin with a wide set of literary compositions, at least all those in early Judaism concerned with the transmission of authoritative traditions, both those that might be labeled as Scripture and those that interpret them implicitly or explicitly.

4. Determining Genre: Morphology and More

Having addressed in a limited way the issue concerning what compositions are to be considered, the next issue concerns how the genres of such compositions are to be described. The starting point for most genre definition in biblical studies has been, not inappropriately, the text itself, its structure or shape, its morphology, determined in large manner on the basis of a close reading of a composition's content. To this end it has often been the application of form-critical insights that

---

25. J. Derrida, "The Law of Genre," *Glyph: Johns Hopkins Textual Studies* 7 (1980): 172–97; repr., *Critical Inquiry* 7 (1980): 55–81, here 65.

26. M. Perloff, "Introduction," in *Postmodern Genres* (ed. M. Perloff; Oklahoma Project for Discourse and Theory 5; Norman: University of Oklahoma Press, 1989), 4.

has resulted in, among other things, conclusions concerning generic definition.[27] There are two matters to be addressed in this brief section of this essay. First, there needs to be some discussion of the basis on which genre is determined. Second, it is important also to consider how the determination of genre assists in the transmission of text from author(s) to reader(s).

For the first point, it is clear, for example, that the most succinct but thoroughgoing definition of rewritten Bible is principally based on content. Whereas Geza Vermes seems to have understood rewritten Bible as haggadic development of biblical narrative (to some extent both content and process, though the focus is really on content),[28] Philip Alexander has outlined the key features of the genre largely in terms of both form and content.[29] For my part, as I have indicated above, I consider that in addition to such key items in the generic definition there has also to be some way in which the generic definition takes account of the role of authority in the whole process inasmuch as rewritten Bible compositions seem both to confer and to receive authority from the scriptural text that they seek to elucidate, re-present, or rewrite. Such compositions confer authority on the scriptural texts by showing that they are worth updating and interpreting, even if that is only done on an implicit level, and they also themselves receive authority from the scriptural text they seek to represent insofar as they themselves are part of the ongoing voice or function of the texts they rewrite. For his own purposes but in a not entirely unrelated way, Falk has described rewritten Bible as concerned with creative imitation through which the authority of various traditions is extended.[30]

In the same way, the pesharim, both the continuous and the thematic ones, have a particular form and content. Basically the form is of scriptural quotation followed by an interpretation regularly introduced by a formula including the word "pesher," and the content is equally of two parts, the scripture being some unfulfilled scriptural text, such as a prophetic oracle, a blessing, a curse, even a psalm, followed by actualizing exegesis in which the text is identified as referring to the present circumstances of the implied readers or the happenings in

---

27. For the Hebrew Bible this is most thoroughly represented recently in the Forms of the Old Testament Literature series published by Eerdmans; see also the recent comments by a co-editor of the series, M. A. Sweeney, "Form Criticism: The Question of the Endangered Matriarchs in Genesis," in *Method Matters: Essays on the Interpretation of the Hebrew Bible in Honor of David L. Petersen* (ed. J. M. LeMon and K. H. Richards; SBLRBS 56; Atlanta: Society of Biblical Literature, 2009), 17–38, esp. 18–21.

28. Vermes, *Scripture and Tradition*, 95.

29. P. S. Alexander, "Retelling the Old Testament," in *It Is Written: Scripture Citing Scripture. Essays in Honour of Barnabas Lindars, SSF* (ed. D. A. Carson and H. G. M. Williamson; Cambridge: Cambridge University Press, 1987), 99–121.

30. Falk, *Parabiblical Texts*, 16. Because of the breadth of the compositions he considers, Falk declares that rewritten Bible is not a genre but a strategy; perhaps, however, we need to talk about hierarchies of genre more explicitly and perceive that, for some, the label will suit one level in the hierarchy and, for others, it will work better at another level.

their imminent future. Again, I am interested to ask questions of authority, as indeed seems to be the case with some of these compositions themselves. However, whereas the text declaims authority in terms of the status of the Teacher of Righteousness, the one to whom God has made known all the mysteries of his servants the prophets (1QpHab 7:4–5), it has become increasingly clear to those who have studied the pesharim closely that the scriptural text and the interpretation are tied together in an exegetically intricate fashion through the application of a wide range of hermeneutical techniques.[31] It is thus the case that, for any who might wonder about the status of the Teacher as implied author, the skillfulness of the interpretation would provide independent attestation of the veracity of the exegesis.

In considering the first issue, the extent of the literary corpus to be considered, I have tried briefly above to justify the inclusion of a wide range of scriptural and interpretative compositions under one umbrella. In so doing, at least insofar as rewritten Bible and the pesharim are concerned, it becomes possible to notice one feature that might possibly explain in part the differences in form and content that they have. At the risk of a broad overgeneralization, the rewritten Bible compositions are concerned to bring into the present those authoritative texts that narrate or legislate for past events and in so doing they incorporate their interpretations into the texts themselves; such contemporization of an authoritative text does not undermine its authority but rather enhances it, making it relevant for new readers and audiences. The pesharim of various shapes and sizes are concerned not with modernizing pastness but with realizing things perceived to be as yet unfulfilled. To have incorporated the actualizations into the authoritative oracle, blessing, or curse would obviously compromise the divine voice as "originally" heard, and so the fulfilment of the text had to be presented authoritatively apart from the authoritative text being fulfilled. The authoritative past can be rewritten (indeed, must be rewritten in each generation), but the imminent divinely voiced future can logically only be restated.[32]

Second, there needs to be some brief posing of the question concerning for whom genre labels are supposed to function. For whom do generic labels provide assistance? Are they just for the better understanding of the text itself or

---

31. For the continuous pesharim, see especially the monographs by W. H. Brownlee, *The Midrash Pesher of Habakkuk: Text, Translation, Exposition with an Introduction* (SBLMS 24; Missoula, Mont.: Scholars Press, 1979); and S. L. Berrin, *The Pesher Nahum Scroll from Qumran: An Exegetical Study of 4Q169* (STDJ 53; Leiden: Brill, 2004). For comments on a thematic commentary, see G. J. Brooke, *Exegesis at Qumran: 4QFlorilegium in Its Jewish Context* (JSOT-Sup 29; Sheffield: JSOT Press, 1985; repr., Atlanta: Scholars Press, 2006).

32. For all that on occasion the restatement may involve some alteration of the authoritative text; see, e.g., G. J. Brooke, "The Biblical Texts in the Qumran Commentaries: Scribal Errors or Exegetical Variants?" in *Early Jewish and Christian Exegesis: Studies in Memory of William Hugh Brownlee* (ed. C. A. Evans and W. F. Stinespring; SBL Homage Series 10; Atlanta: Scholars Press, 1987), 85–100; Berrin, *Pesher Nahum Scroll*, 12–19 and throughout.

for some other purpose? Eric Hirsch in his quest for validity in interpretation gives some priority to generic labels being principally helpful to the reader: "an interpreter's preliminary generic conception of a text is constitutive of everything that he subsequently understands;"[33] or again, "without helpful orientations like titles and attributions, readers are likely to gain widely different generic conceptions of a text, and these conceptions will be constitutive of their subsequent understanding."[34] Sadly, it is certainly the case that few authors in antiquity explicitly and consistently name the genres of their compositions in their compositions.

I am struck by the way in which Thomas Beebee has crisply identified four stages of generic criticism: "genre as rules, genre as species, genre as patterns of textual features, and genre as reader conventions," which for him correspond more or less to "the four positions in the great debate about the location of textual meaning: in authorial intention, in the work's historical or literary context, in the text itself, or in the reader."[35] As with Hirsch, for Beebee genres are principally of use to readers; for him generic differences "are grounded in the 'use-value' of a discourse rather than in its content, formal features, or its rules of production."[36] Not surprisingly, Beebee's work is principally in the area of reader-response.

If in fact the appreciation of genre is a major way in which texts are mediated from author to reader or hearer, then in addition to matters of form and content, the way texts work for their first or implied readers and hearers, their function, also needs to be considered.[37] The suggestion in this chapter is that the construction and construal of authority in textual tradition is a factor in the definition of both rewritten Bible and pesher, and also in other genres and subgenres that are transmitting authoritative texts in a variety of other ways. All this is to say that in generic definition a place has to be made for the role of a text's setting(s) and function(s).[38]

---

33. E. D. Hirsch, *Validity in Interpretation* (New Haven: Yale University Press, 1967), 74.

34. Ibid., 74. Cited in relation to the definition of pesher by G. J. Brooke, "Qumran Pesher: Towards the Redefinition of a Genre," *RevQ* 10/40 (1981): 483–503, here 492.

35. T. O. Beebee, *The Ideology of Genre: A Comparative Study of Generic Instability* (University Park: Pennsylvania State University Press, 1994), 3.

36. Ibid., 7.

37. Probably also to be considered for a more rounded appreciation are issues concerning how texts render gender issues, construct the gender of their readers, or have their meaning constructed by the gendered reader; see, e.g., M. Gerhart, *Genre Choices, Gender Questions* (Oklahoma Project for Discourse and Theory 9; Norman: University of Oklahoma Press, 1992), esp. ch. 3, "Genre and Gender in the Biblical Hermeneutical Tradition."

38. Important aspects of function not touched upon here are considered, for example, by R. L. Colie, *The Resources of Kind: Genre-Theory in the Renaissance* (Una's Lectures 1; Berkeley: University of California Press, 1973), 1–31; she has considered at one level how genre theory works to connect literary kinds with kinds of knowledge and experience, and at another level how genre works for booksellers and librarians. Just how and for whom were all those scrolls catalogued and stored in Cave 4?

5. The Evolution and Instability of Genres

In whatever way a genre comes to be defined, whether largely in terms of form or content, or through those in combination with consideration of setting and function, and the analysis of a wide range of comparative material, most generic labels are often understood primarily as aspects of synchronic taxonomy, for all that it must be acknowledged that genres change every time a new text is added as an illustration of a particular genre.[39] However, it is equally important that any understanding or definition of genre provides some account of where any particular text stands diachronically. Diachronicity is important not only for showing that all genres change and develop but also for indicating that all genres are inherently unstable.[40] It also encourages the analyst to consider how hierarchies of genres are also susceptible to change.

Whatever system of description and classification is adopted by those engaged in the analysis of implicit and explicit exegetical literature of the late Second Temple period, it is becoming increasingly clear that over the centuries there seems to be a gradual shift from the implicit to the explicit. Daniel Machiela has recently expressed this somewhat romantically as follows: "Rewritten Bible seems to be an interpretive genre standing between the halcyon days of 'inner-biblical exegesis,' when the scriptures were still relatively open to change, and the dawn of lemmatised commentary with *pesharim*-type texts."[41] The latter does not displace the former entirely, but in relation to trying to take account of theories of the hierarchy of genres, neither is it merely an innovative subgenre. As a result, there is a need for a generic point of view that gives some place to change and development in how authoritative traditions are re-presented in early Jewish texts.

For some genre theorists the biological analogy is the best way to factor in the evolution of genres,[42] but for others the evolutionary model moves too slowly. Tzvetan Todorov, the famous formalist, has commented as follows:

> Being familiar with the species tiger, we can deduce from it the properties of each individual tiger; the birth of a new tiger does not modify the species or its definition. The impact of individual organisms on the evolution of the species is so slow that we can discount it in practice.... The same is not the case in the realm of art or science. Here evolution operates with an altogether differ-

---

39. For general comments on diachronic and synchronic description, see Fowler, *Kinds of Literature*, 48–52.

40. On generic instability, see ibid., 45–48.

41. D. A. Machiela, *The Dead Sea Genesis Apocryphon: A New Text and Translation with Introduction and Special Treatment of Columns 13–17* (STDJ 79; Leiden: Brill, 2009), 134.

42. See D. Fishelov, *Metaphors of Genre: The Role of Analogies in Genre Theory* (University Park: Pennsylvania State University Press, 1993), 20.

ent rhythm: every work modifies the sum of possible works, each new example alters the species.[43]

But provided the evolutionary analogy is not applied rigidly, it can encourage change and development to be factored into any generic description. The literary analyst then needs to find reasons why genres change, and beyond that why hierarchies of genres can also change. There seems to be no necessity or inevitability to the process. But as with the biological evolution of a species, outside factors often promote such changes. To my mind there are at least two interrelated outside factors motivating the general move to explicit commentary in Judaism. One of these concerns the shift from temple to text as the primary location for the divine voice. If such is the case, then the evidence of the Dead Sea Scrolls in late Second Temple Judaism is a significant portent for what is to happen after 70 C.E. The sect represented in many of the compositions found in the Qumran caves projects itself as having withdrawn from several, many, or all of the institutional practices of the temple; the divine voice becomes predominantly scriptural before its time and as the authority of certain textual traditions is enhanced in a compensatory fashion, so it becomes less adaptable. The inherent instability of the tradition's adaptability becomes a matter of angst, the text generally stabilizes, and the appropriation subsequently comes through explicit commentary.[44]

But a second diachronic factor needs also to be considered alongside the shift from temple to text as the primary location of the divine voice. It so happens that when all the compositions that offer re-presentations of authoritative traditions are set on some kind of continuous spectrum, from works like Chronicles at one end to the explicit commentaries on the other,[45] then if placed in some supposed chronological order, there seems to be a tendency, as Machiela and many others before him have pointed out, toward increasing amounts of lemmatized explicit commentary on scriptural texts from the second century B.C.E. onward. To my mind this is both a reflection and function of the increasing authority of some scriptural compositions in this same period, but also stimulation for the growth of that authority, both effect and cause. It is no accident that the four-hundred-year move from authority to canon more or less coincides with this same gradual shift toward the predominance of lemmatized commentary. If the Hasmoneans

---

43. T. Todorov, *The Fantastic: A Structural Approach to a Literary Genre* (trans. R. Howard; Ithaca, N.Y.: Cornell University Press, 1975), 6

44. The institutionalization of the text may be reflected also in the fixity of its official Hebrew language; perhaps it is no accident that the most obvious way in which implicit exegesis of the text continues in Judaism is in the Aramaic targumim.

45. As in the lists of Lange and Mittmann-Richert (see n. 16 above), something of the range of compositions is provided in the description offered by M. J. Bernstein, "The Contribution of the Qumran Discoveries to the History of Early Jewish Biblical Interpretation," in *The Idea of Biblical Interpretation: Essays in Honor of James L. Kugel* (ed. H. Najman and J. H. Newman; JSJSup 83; Leiden: Brill, 2004), 226–37.

can be implicated as prime movers in that process, so also the shift to explicit commentary, notably in the sectarian compositions, is also in no small part a political move.

As to the matter of the changing hierarchies of genre, for the twentieth century, this is brought out most strikingly by Moshe Bernstein's observation that before the discovery of the Dead Sea Scrolls there was plenty of scholarly comment on wisdom, history, fiction, legend, apocalypse, testament, and polemic, but virtually no recognition of biblical interpretation as a literary phenomenon in late Second Temple Judaism; Bernstein explains this in part by the scholarly "failure to recognize the variety of generic forms which biblical interpretation could adopt."[46] Although one should naturally be cautious in allowing the partial evidence from the Qumran caves to control the agenda, it is nevertheless the case that the wide range of both sectarian, but especially nonsectarian, compositions has enabled scholars to see the dominant place of scriptural interpretation in late Second Temple times. As a result, the scholarly understanding of the hierarchy of genres has changed. Rather than scriptural genres continuing with some changes and adaptations, such as with the increasing writing of apocalypses, it is now possible to discuss more energetically and in a more informed way an enormous range of materials in which both the continuities and discontinuities with earlier literary forms and fashions can be discussed. But, beyond this change in scholarly perception, it is also possible now for scholars to notice changes over time within the broad spectrum of all that now passes for scriptural interpretation in early Judaism. Since the publication of all the scrolls, the taxonomic understanding of interpretative compositions has changed.

Let us say a little more about the instability of genres. The feature of instability in most forms of rewritten Bible is that they make the text present to a particular community, large or small. In so doing, the relevance of the text is to be found in the re-presentation. The authenticity of the re-presentation is to be discerned particularly in the contemporary reader's appropriation of the authoritative text through the re-presentation. Since each generation will require the re-presentation to be made afresh for its own particular circumstances, so the genre, like most others, is inherently unstable. Indeed, the same can be said for all commentary, whether implicit or explicit. Resistance to its instability, as in some traditions of Orthodox Judaism, where little or nothing modern is admitted, demands *force majeure*. The plethora of commentaries in most Christian communities is a sure sign of the impermanence of the exercise and so of the genre of commentary writing as part of the wider practice of scriptural interpretation.

Perhaps somewhat ironically, the instability of a contemporary genre can lead to the stabilization of others. As has often been noted, the dominant aspect of the development of pesher interpretations, whether formally identified through the use of the term pesher or more informally presented, is that the object of

---

46. Bernstein, "Contribution of the Qumran Discoveries," 217.

interpretation is some kind of prophetic text. I have elsewhere tried to indicate that among such prophetic texts should be included not only those visions and auditions that belong to the literary prophets but also such texts as unfulfilled blessings and curses, dreams yet to be realized, and poetry conceived of as oracular in some way. Perhaps it is no accident that the earliest form of explicit running commentary in Judaism in Palestine of the late Second Temple period concerns these unfulfilled prophetic texts. Whereas rewriting could dominate in terms of how authoritative texts that spoke to the past could be brought into the present, texts that spoke to the future could be brought back into the present only through being restated in a more or less stable form and given explicit interpretation that identified its features with elements of present or imminent experience. This was especially the case for a community that found itself caught with two identities, the identity of Israel of old and the identity of special election. For the former it seemed possible to talk in terms of continuity with the past, but for the latter a problem arose. The problem rested in the way in which election was not brought about through any new visionary experience of a prophetic sort but through how a particular group of Jews sought to understand itself by standing under the authority of earlier tradition.

6. Cross-Cultural Analogies

David Fishelov has defined genre as "a combination of prototypical, representative members, and a flexible set of constitutive rules that apply to some levels of literary texts, to some individual writers, usually to more than one literary period, and to more than one language and culture."[47] That definition is designed to distinguish categorization by genre from categorization by period, school, style, or author. As such it suggests that genre is categorization across literary periods, and that genre should make reference to a "dynamic cluster of formal, stylistic, and thematic features."[48] He is also concerned to adopt a pragmatic approach that works against essentialism in genre analysis; a cross-cultural approach to genre certainly inhibits essentialist descriptions of the evidence.

It is probably fair to say that most literary theorists would argue that those discussions of genre that work across cultural boundaries are more likely to lead to a better understanding of what any particular culturally specific group of compositions may be about than discussions that remain restricted solely to a single cultural context alone. Many pertinent examples might be cited in relation to the history of interpretation of authoritative traditions in Judaism. I cite just one. Although he was writing in somewhat general terms and without detailed awareness of the wide range of interpretative rewriting processes that the scrolls from the Qumran caves now offer us, Henning Graf Reventlow has insisted that there

---

47. Fishelov, *Metaphors of Genre*, 8.
48. Ibid.

was little value in describing what was taking place in Judaism in the centuries either side of the turn of the era unless one also took into account the wider context of processes of interpretation in the Hellenistic world:

> It is important that the contemporary reader not view the means of understanding and the methods that emerged in an isolated manner.... The biblical interpreters only put to use the methods that were generally practiced in their own time.[49]

That is, those of the Hellenistic philosophical schools. To this could also be added the need for Jewish interpretation to be contextualized in terms of interpretative traditions of various kinds as those are reflected in Mesopotamian writings of the second half of the first millennium B.C.E.[50]

A more directly relevant example comes from the recent telling observation made insightfully by Markus Bockmuehl that it seems odd how little attention Qumran scholars who are interested in the interpretation of scriptural texts have paid to developing commentary traditions in the Greco-Roman world.[51] The term "commentary" has been widely used by Qumran scholars. For 4Q252 and its related texts, I opted for the term "commentary" largely for etic reasons on the basis of its modern and somewhat neutral usage: modern, because biblical commentaries embrace both the scriptural passages, usually in sequence,

---

49. H. G. Reventlow, *History of Biblical Interpretation*, vol. 1, *From the Old Testament to Origen* (SBLRBS 50; Atlanta: Society of Biblical Literature, 2009), 33.

50. See, e.g., J. C. VanderKam, *Enoch and the Growth of an Apocalyptic Tradition* (CBQMS 16; Washington, D.C.: Catholic Biblical Association of America, 1984); A. Lange, "The Determination of Fate by the Oracle of Lot in the Dead Sea Scrolls, the Hebrew Bible and Ancient Mesopotamian Literature," in *Sapiential, Liturgical and Poetical Texts from Qumran: Proceedings of the Third Meeting of the International Organization for Qumran Studies, Oslo 1998. Published in Memory of Maurice Baillet* (STDJ 35; Leiden: Brill, 2000), 39–48; M. Nissinen, "*Pesharim* as Divination: Qumran Exegesis, Omen Interpretation and Literary Prophecy," in *Prophecy after the Prophets? The Contribution of the Dead Sea Scrolls to the Understanding of Biblical and Extra-Biblical Prophecy* (ed. K. De Toyer, A. Lange, and L. L. Schulte; CBET 52; Leuven: Peeters, 2009), 43–60.

51. On the similarities between the commentary techniques and forms of commentary in the Hellenistic and Qumran continuous pesharim, see M. Bockmuehl, "The Dead Sea Scrolls and the Origins of Biblical Commentary," in *Text, Thought and Practice in Qumran and Early Christianity: Proceedings of the Ninth International Symposium of the Orion Center for the Study of the Dead Sea Scrolls and Associated Literature, Jointly Sponsored by the Hebrew University Center for the Study of Christianity, 11–13 January, 2004* (ed. R. A. Clements and D. R. Schwartz; STDJ 84; Leiden: Brill, 2009), 3–29. Bockmuehl's study has extensive notes on relevant secondary literature. He permits himself some "genetic" speculation, wondering about the suitability of setting the Qumran continuous pesharim in the context of its contemporary Hellenistic commentary tradition in terms of (1) its attention to citing the source in sequence, (2) lemmatization, (3) the implied claims to authority in the comments, and (4) the move beyond the plain sense through something akin to allegorization.

and the interpretative comments upon them, and neutral, because the term is sufficiently general in terms of generic hierarchy as to include a wide range of compositions. But "commentary" is a Latin term (*commentarius*), and as a literary phenomenon the Latin *commentarius* is the heir to much Hellenistic practice, evident in various *hypomnēmata*, that might go back to as early as the fifth century B.C.E., but which flourished from the second century B.C.E. onward, not least in Alexandria.[52] The early use of the Latin term implies a wide range of written records such as a sketch, notebook, or memorandum, but it has acquired a more technical sense by the second century of "commentary, brief explanation, annotation,"[53] even though first-century commentaries exist such as that by Asconius on Cicero's speeches.

The modern discussion of Latin commentaries and the literary traditions to which they belong has been developing apace in recent years.[54] Most scholars are agreed that this tradition begins to take shape in the first centuries B.C.E. and C.E., which is also the time of the Jewish traditions that we see in the sectarian literature found at Qumran.[55] There is as yet little agreement among classical scholars about the evolution of the commentary or the forms it might suitably take.[56] In fact, Qumran scholars are similarly engaged in attempts at adequate description and classification. Perhaps it is no surprise that in their translation of the Dead Sea Scrolls, a translation that has paid particular attention to the naming of texts (sometimes problematically so), Michael O. Wise, Martin G. Abegg, and Edward M. Cook opt to call both the continuous and the thematic pesharim

---

52. There may also be elements in the earlier and contemporary Greek commentary tradition that make the generic comparison suitable too: see Bockmuehl, "Dead Sea Scrolls and the Origins of the Biblical Commentary," 6–13.

53. C. T. Lewis and C. Short, *A Latin Dictionary* (Oxford: Clarendon, 1962), 377. In the Latin tradition Aulus Gellius, the late-second-century C.E. grammarian, uses the term *commentarius* in association with *liber* ("book"), and Suetonius, his contemporary, uses the term of a written journal.

54. See, e.g., in general, R. K. Gibson and C. Shuttleworth Kraus, ed., *The Classical Commentary: Histories, Practices, Theory* (Mnemosyne Supplements 232; Leiden: Brill, 2002); especially C. S. Kraus, "Introduction: Reading Commentaries/Commentaries as Reading," 10–20. Kraus tries to tie textual production with textual reception in her title. She has identified three features of commentary: "segmentation," the act of dividing up the text that is being commented upon, "tralaticiousness," the fact that commentaries tend to repeat issues from other commentaries and their predecessors, and "lemmatisation," the use in commentaries ancient and modern of parallels that offer both a single line of thought and polyphony (this is a different understanding of lemmatization from that normally applied by students of early Jewish scriptural interpretation).

55. On the history of literary development in the sectarian commentary literature, see the preliminary and stimulating analytical work of A. Steudel, "Dating Exegetical Texts from Qumran," in Dimant and Kratz, *Dynamics of Language*, 39–53.

56. J. J. O'Donnell, review of Glenn W. Most, ed., *Commentaries—Kommentare* (Aporemata: Kritische Studien zur Philologiegeschichte 4; Göttingen: Vandenhoeck & Ruprecht, 1999), *Bryn Mawr Classical Review* 19 (2000): 468.

"commentaries," though for 4Q174 the content is given priority: "The Last Days: A Commentary on Selected Verses."[57]

7. THE MATTER IN A NUTSHELL:
ANTHOLOGIES AND EXCERPTED TEXTS

Under the consideration of how the literary corpus to be discussed in this article might be defined, it was noted, on the one hand, that no single composition can ever define a genre and, on the other, that every composition that is encouraged to join a particular kind of text immediately alters the understanding of the group to which it might be assigned. The purpose of this closing section is to offer some brief comments on one text, Commentary on Genesis A, in the light of the previous discussion in order for the reader to see how addressing some of the issues mentioned might illuminate a single composition that also happens to be compiled from sources. Commentary on Genesis A is an anthology.

Several manuscripts from the Qumran caves have been recognized as anthological, containing collections of excerpts or extracts of larger compositions. The dominant form of what has been labeled so far as "excerpted" is to be found among those compositions that seem to depend on a single authoritative source, such as 4QDeut[j] and 4QDeut[n] or 4QCant[a] and 4QCant[b]. There are some exceptions, such as the Testimonia document (4Q175), which contains extracts from four sources. However, it is likely that many more texts should be included under this heading. For example, since the work of Andrew Wilson and Lawrence Wills, the anthological character of the Temple Scroll has been obvious.[58] Or again, the Genesis Apocryphon is probably an anthology of some kind too.[59]

The Commentary on Genesis A has received much attention, both as a whole and in its various parts.[60] As a whole, its modern interpreters have wondered extensively whether it has its overall focus on answering questions that arise from the reading of the plain meaning of the text of Genesis, or rather that the selection of passages for comment in some form is based on some single or complex thematic concern. Whatever the case, it cannot be doubted that the forms in which the written commentary is given range from what might readily be labeled

---

57. M. O. Wise, M. G. Abegg, E. M. Cook, *The Dead Sea Scrolls: A New Translation* (San Francisco: HarperSanFrancisco, 1996), viii.

58. A. M. Wilson and L. M. Wills, "Literary Sources of the Temple Scroll," *HTR* 75 (1982): 275–88.

59. See, e.g., M. J. Bernstein, "Divine Titles and Epithets and the Sources of the *Genesis Apocryphon*," *JBL* 128 (2009): 291–310.

60. See, e.g., Bernstein, "Contribution of the Qumran Discoveries to the History of Early Biblical Interpretation," 233–34; J. Saukkonen, "The Story behind the Text: Scriptural Interpretation in 4Q252" (Ph.D. diss., University of Helsinki, 2005); and G. J. Brooke, "Genesis Commentaries (4Q252–254)," in *The Eerdmans Dictionary of Early Judaism* (ed. J. J. Collins and D. C. Harlow; Grand Rapids: Eerdmans, 2010), 667–68.

rewritten Bible to pesher. It is no accident that this collection plays a significant role in the recent studies by Daniel Falk and Sidnie White Crawford.[61] The contribution of the Commentary on Genesis A to the ongoing representation of the text of Genesis has been covered elsewhere[62] and the cross-cultural understanding of excerpted or anthological compositions for antiquity has been undertaken to some extent by Lutz Doering.[63] As a collection of sources, a multigenre compilation, Commentary on Genesis A might be subjected to genre evaluation of a kind that takes seriously not just its constituent parts but the overall anthological presentation.

In the few paragraphs that follow I will consider how viewing the work as an anthology might have explanatory power. If it is granted that Commentary on Genesis A is indeed some kind of anthology, then there may be some value in considering the issues of diachronic and synchronic readings together with a cross-cultural perspective from modern anthological literature. In modern literary theory there is not much discussion of anthology as a genre, but a distinction can be made between those anthologies that are assembled in an attempt to represent some kind of canonical view of a topic whose sources come from a wide range of time periods and whose ideological point of view is largely implicit, and those that are deliberately put together synchronically with an explicit agenda in mind. Whether the following paragraphs throw any new light on Commentary on Genesis A, I leave the reader to judge.

First, a diachronic perspective. If Commentary on Genesis A is complied from a number of sources, it could be that those sources come from different times and places. There are at least two ways of reading that diachronic viewpoint, ways that are not mutually exclusive. On the one hand, one can wonder whether the compilation is indicative, almost in a paradigmatic but largely unintentional way, of the transition that is already under way from (earlier) implicit interpretation as found in rewritten scriptural texts to the (later) explicit interpretation of the pesharim, especially the so-called continuous ones. Its contents may be coincidental, not least as its compiler might be collecting different solutions to problems in the plain meaning of Genesis. Its agenda is largely implicit and undeclared.

Whether it is addressing issues in the plain meaning of the text of Genesis or presenting topics on the basis of some coherent theme, is it in effect creating a (canonical?) set of reading strategies for the sectarian commentator to emulate as appropriate? The type of modern anthology that tries to establish a "canonical" set of texts about a particular topic is commonly aimed for use in the delivery of educational curricula. If that approach is applied to the understanding of a

---

61. Falk, *Parabiblical Texts*, 120–39; Crawford, *Rewriting Scripture in Second Temple Times*, 130–43.

62. G. J. Brooke, "Some Comments on 4Q252 and the Text of Genesis," *Textus* 19 (1998): 1–25.

63. Doering, "Excerpted Texts in Second Temple Judaism," 1–38.

composite work such as Commentary on Genesis A, one can legitimately ask whether it intended to offer those who read and studied it a range, perhaps even a definitive range, of possibilities for the reading of Genesis.[64] But the diversity of genres of commentary in Commentary on Genesis A may have been determined in some way by the character of the base text being commented upon. In that way the diversity of genres of commentary was an expression of sensitivity toward the generic variety of the materials selected for comment, little more. Whatever the case, this is a definition of anthology on the basis of content, content from a variety of times and places.

However, second, there is also the other kind of anthology, predominantly a synchronic construction, and defined largely by function: this is anthology that seeks to address an agenda more or less explicitly and to offer a critique of other points of view, to support a particular set of ideas and to subvert others. Cynthia Franklin has described these kinds of modern anthologies as concerned principally with issues of identity and community—matters that have also been discerned in the various sections of Commentary on Genesis A, however it is construed. Franklin has noted how the editors of these kinds of anthologies "generally begin with a section focused on contributors' experiences of oppression. They then create sections in which contributors assert and celebrate their identities, and they conclude with a section that predicts and explores ways the community they have created can lead to social change or revolution. They carefully craft the anthologies between narrative, identity, community, and activism."[65] Though this is a description based on the reading of many anthologies of women's writing since 1980, it is quite possibly a fine summary of the function of Commentary on Genesis A.[66] Perhaps at the outset the experience of oppression is left unstated, but through attention to the careful delineation of the calendar, self-definition over against the sons of Ham and Japhet, and the application of the blessings of Jacob to the community and its eschatological aspirations "narrative, identity, community, and activism" are presented, perhaps as a deliberate challenge to other readings of Genesis. Franklin also suggests that a "multi-genre format is intimately connected to the contributors' minority status."[67] By this she intends to indicate that marginalized voices require a multiplicity of genres in order to be heard, but it is clear that the multiple forms of the content in an anthology of synchronic sources has a function beyond that of the mere repetition of those sources. For Commentary on Genesis A, perhaps it is no surprise

---

64. Falk (*Parabiblical Texts*, 139) has concluded, "It seems to be intended for internal use by the community to reinforce its identity and ideology. Some sort of study setting is most likely."

65. C. G. Franklin, *Writing Women's Communities: The Politics and Poetics of Contemporary Multi-Genre Anthologies* (Madison: University of Wisconsin Press, 1997), 10.

66. Falk (*Parabiblical Texts*, 139) concludes that Commentary on Genesis A is concerned with identity and ideology.

67. Franklin, *Writing Women's Communities*, 12.

that Sidnie White Crawford concludes that the interpretative goal was more important than the diversity of exegetical techniques displayed in the various sources that the compiler used.[68]

Here, then, is an example of how some reflection on genre theory can provide questions and raise issues that in themselves might cast new light on the whole topic investigated in this chapter.

---

68. Crawford, *Rewriting Scripture in Second Temple Times*, 141–42.

NINE

Room for Interpretation: An Analysis of Spatial Imagery in the Qumran Pesharim

1. Spatial Perspectives

1.1. Introduction

Within the theme of "Texts and Context" this paper investigates whether there is any information in the Qumran pesharim that might indicate where they were created and used. The principal concern, then, is to reconsider most of the obvious spatial language in the pesharim to discern what sense of space and place they might disclose.

The sense of space and place, which was variously stressed by Michel Foucault,[1] and then popularized for the English-speaking world by Edward Soja, especially through his writings on thirdspace,[2] has provided a welcome balance to two or more centuries of scholarship that prioritized time over space, chronology over place, history over territory, and eschatology over immanence. Though the terms "space" and "place" are commonly used interchangeably as virtual synonyms, several thinkers have tried to differentiate them or have defined them in terms of a spectrum of meaning, in particular suggesting that "space" refers to the undifferentiated infinite, whereas "place" refers to a particular locality or spot.[3]

---

1. M. Foucault, *Power Knowledge: Selected Interviews and Other Writings 1972–77* (New York: Pantheon, 1980).

2. E. Soja, *Thirdspace: Journeys to Los Angeles and Other Real-and-Imagined Places* (Cambridge, Mass: Blackwell, 1996).

3. See the helpful summary of the debate about definitions in J. Inge, *A Christian Theology of Place* (Explorations in Practical, Pastoral and Empirical Theology; Aldershot: Ashgate, 2003), 1–13. In addition to Foucault, Inge cites M. de Certeau, *The Practice of Everyday Life* (trans. Steven Rendall; Berkeley: University of California Press, 1984), 117 ("places" have a multitude of particular "spaces") and J. -Y. Lacoste, *Expérience et absolu: Questions disputées sur l'humanité de l'homme* (Epiméthée; Paris: Presses universitaires de France, 1994), 8 ("space" is geometric; "place" gives us the coordinates).

1.2. Aspects of Spatial Awareness in Qumran Studies

In this short study I am concerned to ask briefly how spatial language is used in one particular genre of sectarian texts found in the caves at and near Qumran. For Qumran itself the study of space and place has had three aspects. In the first place, there has been some reflection on various significant spatial motifs, most notably the "wilderness" language used by the community. In a landmark study, Shemaryahu Talmon addressed the topic in a summary fashion.[4] The particular use of wilderness and exile language in the Rule of the Community has likewise occupied several commentators.[5] For my own part I still consider that the terminology was understood initially as a scriptural designation for the place from which divine salvation would appear, but that subsequently the actual move by some members of the sectarian group caused the scriptural typology to be taken literally, so that in the final form of the Rule of the Community the motif has been transformed from referring to the space of salvation into the concrete place where salvation might first become a reality.[6]

The second aspect of place in some scholarly discussion has been a focus on the archaeology of the Qumran site. Some interpreters have insisted on divorcing the finds of scrolls from the finds at the site, despite the discovery of ostraca and writing implements among the ruins themselves, and despite some manuscript caves being accessible only through the Qumran site and others being on the very next marl promontory. But for the majority of interpreters the caves and their contents are to be associated with the site of Qumran, even if only in terms of the majority of the manuscripts having been brought to the caves by those who occupied the site itself. In several cases various suggestions have been made about how the features of the site might reflect aspects of the life of the community referred to in some of the sectarian scrolls. I made some suggestions in this direction myself twenty years ago,[7] but the most extensive recent description that relates

4. S. Talmon, "The 'Desert' Motif in the Bible and in Qumran Literature," in *Biblical Motifs: Origins and Transformations* (ed. A. Altmann; Philip W. Lown Institute of Advanced Judaic Studies, Brandeis University, Studies and Texts 3; Cambridge, Mass.: Harvard University Press, 1966), 31–63.

5. E.g., see recently D. Dimant, "Non pas l'exil au desert mais l'exil spirituel: L'interprétation d'Isaïe 40,3 dans la *Règle de la Communauté*," in *Qoumrân et le Judaïsme du tournant de notre ère: Actes de la Table Ronde, Collège de France, 16 Novembre 2004* (ed. A. Lemaire and S. C. Mimouni; Collection de la Revue des études juives 40; Paris: Peeters, 2006), 17–36; H. Najman, "Towards a Study of the Uses of the Concept of Wilderness in Ancient Judaism," *DSD* 13 (2006): 99–113.

6. See G. J. Brooke, "Isaiah 40:3 and the Wilderness Community," in *New Qumran Texts and Studies: Proceedings of the First Meeting of the International Organization for Qumran Studies, Paris 1992* (ed. G. J. Brooke with the assistance of F. García Martínez; STDJ 15; Leiden: Brill, 1994), 117–32.

7. G. J. Brooke, "The Temple Scroll and the Archaeology of Qumran, 'Ain Feshkha and Masada," *RevQ* 13 (1988): 225–37.

the site to various aspects of the contents of the scrolls is that by Jodi Magness.[8] In particular, the water system of the site most readily lends itself to juxtaposition with the several textual descriptions of the important place that water played in the life of the sectarians.

The third aspect of the consideration of space and place in the scrolls and at Qumran has been a series of studies that have variously engaged with spatial theory to assist in the better understanding of both scrolls and site. Among these have been the studies by Jean-Baptiste Humbert on sacred space at Qumran,[9] by Magness on communal meals and sacred space,[10] and by Stephen Pfann on similar topics.[11] More challenging theoretically in its readings of the site, the texts, and the ideologies of the communities represented by them has been the analysis by Philip Davies in which he has argued that physical and metaphorical spatial terminology variously reflect sectarian self-understandings and their implied boundaries.[12] Joan Branham has taken up one aspect of the topic of liminality, namely, physical boundary marking, in relation to the Qumran site,[13] which includes the demarcation of cemeteries. Liv Lied, who has applied "thirdspace" ideas to the unresolved conundrum concerning the location of Damascus,[14] and Jorunn Øklund, who has tried to mark out sacred space in the Temple Scroll,[15]

---

8. J. Magness, *The Archaeology of Qumran and the Dead Sea Scrolls* (Studies in the Dead Sea Scrolls and Related Literature; Grand Rapids: Eerdmans, 2002), 32–46 and throughout.

9. J. -B. Humbert, "L'espace sacré à Qumrân: propositions pour l'archéologie," *RB* 101 (1994): 161–214.

10. J. Magness, "Communal Meals and Sacred Space at Qumran," in *Shaping Community: The Art and Archaeology of Monasticism. Papers from a Symposium Held at the Frederick R. Weisman Museum, University of Minnesota, March 10–12, 2000* (ed. S. McNally; BAR International Series 941; Oxford: Archaeopress, 2001), 15–28; reprinted as ch. 6 in J. Magness, *Debating Qumran: Collected Essays on Its Archaeology* (Interdisciplinary Studies in Ancient Culture and Religion 4; Leuven: Peeters, 2004).

11. S. J. Pfann, "A Table in the Wilderness: Pantries and Tables, Pure Food and Sacred Space," in *Qumran, the Site of the Dead Sea Scrolls: Archaeological Interpretations and Debates. Proceedings of a Conference held at Brown University, November 17–19, 2002* (ed. K. Galor et al.; STDJ 57; Leiden: Brill, 2006), 159–78.

12. P. R. Davies, "Space and Sects in the Qumran Scrolls," in *"Imagining" Biblical Worlds: Studies in Spatial, Social and Historical Constructs in Honor of James W. Flanagan* (ed. D. M. Gunn and P. M. McNutt; JSOTSup 359; London: Sheffield Academic Press, 2002), 81–98.

13. J. Branham, "Hedging the Holy at Qumran: Walls as Symbolic Devices," in Galor et al., *Qumran, the Site of the Dead Sea Scrolls*, 117–31.

14. L. I. Lied, "Another Look at the Land of Damascus: The Spaces of the *Damascus Document* in the Light of Edward W. Soja's Thirdspace Approach," in *New Directions in Qumran Studies: Proceedings of the Bristol Colloquium on the Dead Sea Scrolls, 8–10 September 2003* (ed. J. G. Campbell, W. J. Lyons, and L. K. Pietersen; LSTS 52; London: T&T Clark International, 2005), 101–25.

15. J. Øklund, "The Language of Gates and Entering: On Sacred Space in the *Temple Scroll*," in Campbell et al., *New Directions in Qumran Studies*, 149–65.

are among those who have undertaken the analysis of spatial terminology and perspectives in the study of specific texts.

1.3. Purpose of This Study

Although there are warnings about undertaking the spatial analysis of texts,[16] my concern is to ignore them partially and to take some texts that are widely agreed to have belonged to the community that lived at Qumran itself to see what is said in them about space and place. I have chosen the so-called continuous pesharim[17] for this short study because it is indeed quite likely that they were composed at Qumran and so might be construed as reflecting the ideology of those who lived there more than some of the other sectarian community texts that could have had an extensive pre-Qumran life or extensive use outside Qumran. These texts, more than any other form of scriptural interpretation found in manuscripts from the Qumran caves stand a chance of reflecting their immediate context in the running commentary. Furthermore, there has as yet been no spatial analysis of this subgenre of biblical commentary from the Qumran caves. Davies has rightly noted that the spatiality of the *yaḥad* community can be conceived quite apart from whether it occupied the Qumran site.[18] It is certainly appropriate not to tie the concepts of the Rule of the Community exclusively to Qumran, since much in that composition probably belongs to pre-Qumran times by one or two genera-tions. But the quest of this investigation is an analysis of the spatial terminology of the continuous pesharim because they can be taken as contemporary with the Qumran site itself and might well be the products of the community that lived there.[19]

---

16. See H. Lefebvre, *The Production of Space* (trans. D. Nicholson-Smith; Oxford: Basil Blackwell, 1991), 15: "[A]ny search for space in literary texts will find it everywhere and in every guise: encoded, projected, dreamt of, speculated about" (cited by Davies, "Space and Sects in the Qumran Scrolls," 81 n. 1).

17. Distinguishing the so-called continuous pesharim as a group for investigation is somewhat problematic, since scholars now acknowledge that there were not simply two types of sectarian commentary, thematic and continuous, but that there was a range of commentary types in several of which the technical term "pesher" occurs.

18. Davies, "Space and Sects in the Qumran Scrolls," 97: "Whether or not this space was conceived at Qumran is really somewhat irrelevant." This point has been developed in a some-what different historical fashion by J. J. Collins, "The Yahad and 'The Qumran Community," in *Biblical Traditions in Transmission: Essays in Honour of Michael A. Knibb* (ed. C. Hempel and J. M. Lieu; JSJSup 111; Leiden: Brill, 2006), 81–96: "The settlement at Qumran may well have been occupied by members of the yahad, but the yahad cannot be equated with 'the Qumran com-munity'" (p. 96). In the same volume, similar matters are debated by S. Metso, "Whom Does the Term Yahad Identify?" 213–35; reprinted in *Defining Identities: We, You, and the Other in the Dead Sea Scrolls: Proceedings of the Fifth Meeting of the IOQS in Groningen* (ed. F. García Martínez and M. Popović; STDJ 70; Leiden: Brill, 2008), 63–84.

19. The assertion by some that the continuous pesharim are autographs is highly prob-

2. Space and Place in the Continuous Pesharim

2.1. Qumran Commentaries?

If indeed the continuous pesharim are contemporary with the occupation of the Qumran site by a sectarian community and were possibly the product of that same community,[20] then one can suitably ask how they deserve the label "*Qumran* commentaries," indicating not just the place of their discovery but also how they might reflect the life, beliefs, and practices of the community that lived there. Before attempting to answer the question, it is important to bear in mind three factors. First, it is clear that in the so-called continuous pesharim the scriptural text exercises a controlling role, often providing much of the vocabulary of the commentary and certainly playing a part in what was being selected as worthy of comment in the commentator's present experience or eschatological hope. Thus, the vocabulary of the pesharim is not entirely an independent witness to contemporary contexts. Second, it is widely acknowledged that the language of the pesharim is notoriously and probably deliberately nonspecific. The widespread use of sobriquets throughout the genre has resulted in an extensive scholarly literature dedicated to the specific identity of certain individuals and groups. Third, the discourse of the pesharim is focused on people rather than places; the rhetorical strategies of the pesharim are designed to construct social identity in various ways rather than to endorse the priority of a particular sectarian location.[21] Thus, in several ways the very character of the language of the commentaries inhibits our quest from the start.

Perhaps because of the nonspecificity of the language of the pesharim, the first striking phenomenon to notice is that there is virtually nothing in the spatial language of the commentaries that can be clearly identified with Qumran in any explicit or direct fashion. There is no reference to Secacah. Just as for the individuals and groups, so for the possible places, the nonspecificity and polyvalence of the terminology make it difficult to link the distinctive commentary activity with any particular aspect of the Qumran site. There are no references to the room for interpretation where the study of the prophets might have taken place. One possible explanation for this rests in the descriptions of communal study themselves. Three texts come to mind: in the somewhat idealistic Rule of the Congregation

---

lematic, not least because there are five manuscripts that contain pesharim on Isaiah and because there are two scribal hands in 1QpHab.

20. The continuous pesharim reflect most of the same scribal practices as can be found in many of the manuscripts containing sectarian compositions. This has led to their being viewed as products of the so-called Qumran scribal school, but not with a complete homogeneity of scribal practice. See E. Tov, *Scribal Practices and Approaches Reflected in the Texts Found in the Judean Desert* (STDJ 54; Leiden: Brill, 2004), 258–59.

21. See, e.g., J. Jokiranta, "Social Identity Approach: Identity-Constructing Elements in the Psalms Pesher," in García Martínez and Popović, *Defining Identities*, 85–109.

(1QSa) there is some information: "From his yo[uth they shall instru]ct him (ילמ[דהו)] in the Book of Hagi/u, and according to his age they shall enlighten him (ישכילהו) in the law[s of] the covenant. [And according to his understanding they shall] teach him (יי[סרו]) their regulations" (1QSa 1:6–8). Lawrence Schiffman has argued that the three elements of the curriculum here are the Book of Hagi/u, that is, the Torah; the laws of the covenant, that is, "practical application of the commandments"; and the regulations of the sect.[22] The identification of the Book of Hagi/u with the Torah has not been universally accepted, but it is quite likely, given the parallel between CD 13:2–3, "And in a place of ten, there shall not be lacking a priest learned in the Book of Meditation," and 1QS 6:6–8, "And in the place where there are ten, there shall not be lacking a man who studies the Torah day and night continually."[23] It is the study of the Law and its various extensions in community life that is the focus of this communal task, not the study of the prophets. Perhaps the study of the unfulfilled prophecies, blessings, curses, promises, and other topics was undertaken in a solitary fashion by a particularly gifted or inspired interpreter. As such he might still have referred to the cave or room where he undertook this activity or used it analogously in his interpretations, but it so happens that such evidence does not survive.

2.2. Some Specific Locations?

To my mind, perhaps the closest that the continuous pesharim come to naming an actual place is in 4QpPs^a (4Q171) 1–10 iii 15–16, where the person described in Ps 37:23–24 as "the one whom the Lord supports" is described as la'amôd. Maurya Horgan has taken this nominally and translated the phrase, which seems to refer to the Teacher of Righteousness, "as a pillar."[24] Obviously this is metaphorical, but one wonders whether the interpreter could point to an actual pillar as he spoke; in which case does that limit the number of rooms at Qumran where such a statement might have been made most forcefully? Florentino García Martínez and Eibert Tigchelaar take it as a verbal form and speak rather of the one whom "God [ch]ose to stand."[25] The nominal translation might seem preferable,

22. L. H. Schiffman, *The Eschatological Community of the Dead Sea Scrolls: A Study of the Rule of the Congregation* (SBLMS 38; Atlanta, Ga.: Scholars Press, 1989), 14–15.

23. As pointed out by S. D. Fraade, "Hagu, Book of," in *Encyclopedia of the Dead Sea Scrolls* (ed. L. H. Schiffman and J. C. VanderKam; 2 vols. New York: Oxford University Press, 2000), 1:327, who also writes, "Both passages are commonly understood to be reworkings of Joshua 1:8 (with an echo of Psalm 1:2), in which God charges Joshua: 'Let this Book of Torah not cease (*lo' yamush*) from your lips, but recite (*hagita*) it day and night, so that you may observe faithfully all that is written in it.'"

24. M. P. Horgan, "Pesharim," in *The Dead Sea Scrolls: Hebrew, Aramaic, and Greek Texts with English Translations*, vol. 6B, *Pesharim, Other Commentaries, and Related Documents* (ed. J. H. Charlesworth et al.; Princeton Theological Seminary Dead Sea Scrolls Project 6B; Tübingen: Mohr Siebeck; Louisville: Westminster John Knox, 2002), 17.

25. F. García Martínez and E. Tigchelaar, *The Dead Sea Scrolls Study Edition* (2 vols.;

since the interpretation continues by describing how this figure was established to build (*lbnwt*) a congregation for him; but the verbal translation shows that the two infinitives in the interpretation form a neat literary balance. Whatever the case, it is possible to see here some construction language,[26] and buildings need locations; if the allusion is to an actual pillar at Qumran, then the possibilities for the site of such communal interpretative activity are restricted to locus 77.

A second term for consideration is "wilderness." I have already mentioned the way in which the liminal motif of the wilderness has played a specific role in understanding the location of the Qumran community, particularly as that is played out in the Rule of the Community. The term occurs twice in the continuous pesharim and therefore might be taken as confirming the interpretation given it in the Rule of the Community. In 4QpPs[a] 1–10 iii 1–2, the interpretation of the blameless of Ps 37:18–19a identifies them as the "returnees of the wilderness (*šby hmdbr*)," either those who "return to the wilderness"[27] or those "who have returned from the wilderness"[28] to whom will be given all the inheritance of Adam. The unlocated group of the Psalm is located firmly in the wilderness. It is possible to think that the inheritance of Adam has a geographical implication. The only other occurrence of *mdbr* in the continuous pesharim is in a very broken interpretation of Isa 10:24–27 in 4QpIsa[a] 4–6 ii 18: "when they return from the wilderness of the peoples." The implication of the interpretation is that the term "wilderness" describes the place of exile and oppression, whether in Assyria or Egypt, from which the Prince of the Congregation will have a role in delivering the people. It is unlikely that this can be conceived as a reference, however oblique, to Qumran.[29]

A third term deserves a little consideration. The phrase "house of Judah" occurs twice in the extant portions of the continuous pesharim. In 1QpHab 8:1, the righteous of Hab 2:4 are "those who do the Law in the House of Judah" (cf. CD 4:11). It would be nice if a lintel had been found at Qumran with בית יהודה inscribed on it, but the options for the best understanding of the label are either as a designation that distinguishes the community from the house of Israel for some reason, or as a self-reference for the sect itself, or as a definition of the group as the party of the Teacher whose name may have been Judah.[30] In 4QpPs[a] 1–10

Leiden: Brill; Grand Rapids: Eerdmans, 2000), 1:345.

26. I am grateful to H. Eshel for also observing that in several instances Hebrew vocabulary referring to buildings was subsequently adapted metaphorically and applied to aspects of literary activity.

27. As Horgan, "Pesharim," 15.

28. As García Martínez and Tigchelaar, *Dead Sea Scrolls Study Edition*, 1:345.

29. E. Regev supposes helpfully that ideas such as "exile" serve a thematic rather than geographical function and as such are essentially alocative (*Sectarianism in Qumran: A Cross-Cultural Perspective* [Religion and Society 45; Berlin: de Gruyter, 2007], 45–46).

30. The options are laid out by W. H. Brownlee, *The Midrash Pesher of Habakkuk: Text, Translation, Exposition with an Introduction* (SBLMS 24; Missoula, Mont.: Scholars Press,

ii 13–14, Ps 37:12–13 is interpreted to refer to those in the "house of Judah" who plot against those who do the Torah. The phrase "house of Judah" also occurs in Hos 5:14a in 4QpHos[b] (4Q167) frg. 2, line 3, but the comment is too fragmentary to discern how it is interpreted. The widespread metaphorical use of the term "house" makes the identification of a specific location with the "house of Judah" virtually impossible.[31] The same has to be said for the "house of Absalom" of 1QpHab 5:9.

Lastly, the designation "house of his exile (*byt glwtw*)" (1QpHab 10:6) has commonly been supposed to be a reference to Qumran. To my mind this is only possible by way of transfer. If the Teacher had never actually been to Qumran, because he was active in the movement before it was established, then the referent of this phrase is certainly unknown.

2.3. Qumran as a Holy Place?

If there is little or nothing in the spatial language of the continuous pesharim that can be associated with the physical location of Qumran and its spatiality, one can nevertheless ask whether there is anything in the imagery of the commentaries that might indirectly refer to the site and the manner of its occupation. If indeed the Rule of the Community has been correctly identified as reflecting in some way the *yaḥad* of Qumran, and even the changes that that community underwent as it apparently moved from being highly priestly and hierarchical toward being something more egalitarian in outlook,[32] then one might expect the commentaries to reflect, even if only indirectly, such hierarchical priestliness and gradual changes away from that. Perhaps, even in a much more general way, if the site functioned as a temporary substitute for or extension of the temple in Jerusalem or as a place of purification,[33] then maybe such concepts should be reflected in the continuous pesharim. However, perhaps somewhat surprisingly, a term such as *mqdš* occurs but twice in the continuous pesharim. In 1QpHab 12:9 it refers to the divine sanctuary in Jerusalem, and in 4Q167 frg. 20, line 1 the context is too broken for interpretation to be sure, but the phrase "sanctuary of Israel" probably also implies a reference to Jerusalem. The term *hykl* does not occur in the commentary sections of the continuous pesharim.

1979), 126. In addition, it should be noted that 4QpNah, which otherwise does not speak of the Righteous Teacher, nevertheless talks of the time "when the glory of Judah is revealed" (4Q169 3–4 iii 4).

31. 1QpMic frgs. 20–21, line 2 refers to the "men of his house," but the context is too small to know if this is a reference to a particular building.

32. See, e.g., G. J. Brooke, "From 'Assembly of Supreme Holiness for Aaron' to 'Sanctuary of Adam': The Laicization of Temple Ideology in the Qumran Scrolls and Its Wider Implications," *Journal for Semitics* 8/2 (1996): 119–45.

33. As suggested by E. M. Cook, "What Was Qumran? A Ritual Purification Centre," *BARev* 22/6 (1996): 39, 48–51, 73–75.

At best, for my purposes, the commentaries reflect various boundary distinctions that may have been particularly pertinent at the Qumran site but that cannot be demonstrated as needing Qumran (or any other particular site for that matter) for their suitable understanding.

Perhaps we should not be searching for horizontal spatiality in the pesharim. After all, the continuous pesharim can themselves be understood as some kind of prophecy. The interpretations that they contain are understood as God-given like the prophetic texts that are the basis of the commentary: the interpreter is the one to whom "God made known all the mysteries of his servants the prophets" (1QpHab 7:5).

This reflects the kind of vertical spatiality to which Davies has drawn attention as characteristic of the *yaḥad*'s conceptualization of space and place,[34] rather than the horizontal sense of place we could use to identify a particular location.

2.4. Actual Place-Names in the Pesharim

From what has been indicated so far, it seems unlikely that there is any direct reference in the continuous commentaries to the Qumran site and its role in framing the prophetic interpretative practices of the community. It is natural, then, that we should turn our attention to the actual geographical place-names that feature in the commentaries.

In several instances places are named in the scriptural lemmata.[35] A few examples can be mentioned, such as 4QpPs^a 13, a fragment that contains a quotation of Ps 60:8–9, which speaks of Shechem and the Valley of Succoth. 4QpIsa^c 6–7 ii 1–6 provides a fragmentary reading of Isa 10:12–19b, in which the king of Assyria, against whose arrogance Isaiah's text is directed, seems to be interpreted as king of Babylon, since the region is mentioned in the comment. This transfer from Assyria to Babylon does not seem to have been difficult for the commentator. The returning remnant of the house of Jacob of Isa 10:22–23 is identified with the penitents or returnees of Israel (*šby yśr'l*). 4QpIsa^c frg. 21, lines 2–3 mentions Lebanon and Carmel in the fragmentary interpretation, probably of Isa 29:17, that precedes the citation of Isa 30:1–5. It is not possible to comprehend precisely what the interpretation is about, though the geographical labels appear to be given human referents. The same is more certain in 4Q169 frgs. 1–2, lines 5–9,

---

34. Davies, "Space and Sects in the Qumran Scrolls," 97: "Internally, then, the space of the society is unique, entirely different from the space of the rest of the world; it is shared, it is single, it is vertically oriented." The vertical orientation can be best discerned in some of the community's worship texts in which the commingling of heaven and earth through the presence of angels in the worshiping community is clear.

35. I am grateful to H. Eshel for observing during the discussion of this paper that the place-names that survive in the Isaiah pesharim in particular are all a long way from Qumran and so it is not altogether surprising that the interpretations discuss matters geographically distant from the site.

where Carmel and the blossoms of Lebanon are almost certainly identified as the leaders of particular groups. Egypt figures prominently in 4Q163 frg. 21, lines 11–13; frg. 25, line 5; frg. 28, line 1; as well as in 4Q167 frg. 17, line 1.

4QpIsa^c 23 ii 3–10 contains a citation of Isa 30:15–18, which describes those left as a flagstaff on a mountaintop and as a standard on a hill.[36] In the only line of the interpretation that follows, there is the identification of the principal characters of the passage with the "Seekers-after-Smooth-Things" who are in Jerusalem. In 1QpPs 9, part of a very fragmentary manuscript, there is one place where Ps 68:30 is cited; the verse can be restored with confidence with its reference to Jerusalem, because the interpretation seems to keep a literal reference to Jerusalem. In col. 2 of 4QpIsa^b the woe of Isa 5:11–14 and its follow-up in Isa 5:24c–25 are both interpreted explicitly as referring to the congregation of the men of mockery who are in Jerusalem; the interpreter has taken his cue from the prophecy's address in Isa 5:3 to the inhabitants of Jerusalem, to identify the wicked there. Indeed, it is Jerusalem that is mentioned more than any other place in the continuous pesharim.[37] The important matter to note is that in the more complete commentaries the name Jerusalem is introduced in the comment where it is not to be found in the scriptural lemma.[38] This happens twice in the Habakkuk commentary: 1QpHab 9:4 and 12:7. In 4Q169 3–4 i 2, 10–11 there are three mentions of Jerusalem in the comments where there are none in the scriptural lemmata. All this reinforces the view that the community at Qumran was more focused on Jerusalem than on its own immediate surroundings.[39]

The designation "Israel" presents a peculiar problem, since it can refer to either people or land, or one by virtue of the other.[40] It tells us little or nothing about the relationship between the continuous pesharim and the Qumran context, even though it might be convenient to argue that Qumran was either clearly

---

36. It would certainly seem inappropriate to think of such images as assisting in the identification of the settlements on the hilltops above Ein Gedi as the principal Essene settlement, "below (infra)" which was Ein Gedi as Pliny describes (*Nat.* 5.73). See Y. Hirschfeld, "A Community of Hermits above Ein Gedi" (in Hebrew), *Cathedra* 96 (2000): 8–40.

37. 1QpHab 9:4; 12:7; 1Q14 frgs. 8–10, line 3; frg. 11, line 1; 1Q16 frgs. 9–10, line 2; 4Q161 frgs. 5–6, lines 9 and 13; 4Q162 ii 7 and 10; 4Q163 23 ii 11; 4Q165 frgs. 1–2, line 2; 4Q168 frg. 1, line 1; 4Q169 3–4 i 2, 10–11.

38. I am grateful to A. I. Baumgarten for observing during the discussion of this paper that in some similar ways some aspects of Zionism paid particular attention to how certain attitudes to the land might be validated.

39. See, e.g., G. J. Brooke, "Moving Mountains: From Sinai to Jerusalem," in *The Significance of Sinai: Traditions about Divine Revelation in Judaism and Christianity* (ed. G. J. Brooke, H. Najman and L. T. Stuckenbruck; TBN 12; Leiden: Brill, 2008).

40. It occurs in 1QpHab 8:10; 4Q161 frg. 1, line 2; frgs. 8–10, line 3; 4Q162 ii 8; 4Q163 4–7 i 3; ii, 7, 12–13; 23 ii 2–3; frg. 25, line 7; 4Q164 frg. 1, lines 1 and 7; 4Q165 frg. 6, line 1; 4Q167 frg. 10, line 2; 4Q169 3–4 i 8 and 12; iii 3 and 5; iv 3; frg. 5, line 2; 4Q171 1–10 iii 11–12; 3–10 iv 24; frg. 11, line 2.

understood as within the land, as on the west side of the Jordan, or as outside the
land in exile, as some of the sectarian writings might imply.

2.5. GENERAL LOCATIVE TERMINOLOGY

In addition to the specific geographical place-names that are mentioned in the
continuous pesharim, there are a number of general terms such as *'rṣ* (ארץ) and
mqwm (מקום) that do occur. What is the referent of these terms?

In fact *mqwm* occurs but twice. In 1Q14 frgs. 1–5, line 2 the context is too
broken to permit comment. In 4Q171 1–2 ii 6 (Ps 37:10b), "When I look carefully at his territory (*mqwmw*), he will not be there," speaks of the wicked and is
interpreted as concerning what takes place at the end of forty years: "they will be
consumed, and there will not be found on earth any [wi]cked man." This reads
as the opposite of the rapture theology of some modern apocalypticists; it is the
wicked who will disappear so that the righteous inherit the earth, as the subsequent interpretation of Ps 37:11 makes clear. The referent of *'rṣ* seems to be the
land of Israel, rather than the whole earth, since the interpretation contains Deuteronomic echoes that relate to the promised land.

In 4QpPs^a 1–10 iii 8–11, Ps 37:21–22 describes those blessed as inheriting
the land. In the interpretation of this verse the "high mountain of Isra[el]," on
which the blessed will delight, is famously substituted for the land. The word *'rṣ*
is very widely used in the Qumran corpus. In Pesher Habakkuk alone it occurs
eleven times.[41] In 1QpHab 3:1, for example, the comment speaks of the "cities
of the land" by way of describing the extent of the devastation to be wrought by
the Chaldeans, namely, the Kittim; it is entirely appropriate to take the referent
of "cities of the land" in its plain sense and not to try to see it as a cipher for the
camps of the movement of which the Qumran community was a part. The subsequent verse, Hab 1:6b, which speaks of "dwelling places (*mšknwt*)" is interpreted
simply of the cunning and deceit by which the Kittim will deal with all peoples,
and the land in the comment on Hab 1:8–9 is best understood as a reference to
the land of Israel.[42]

As for other general locative terms, there are several references to mountain.
The word *hr* occurs in 1Q14 frgs. 1–5, line 3; 4Q161 frgs. 5–6, line 9; 4Q162 ii 9;
4Q163 23 ii 7; frg. 24, line 1; frg. 57, line 1; 4Q169 frgs. 1–2, line 9; and 4Q171
1+3–4 iii 11. The fortress (*mbṣr*) of Hab 1:10 is not understood to refer to the for-
tifications of Qumran, since in the comment it is generalized into "the fortifica-
tions of the peoples (*mbṣry h'mym*)" (1QpHab 4:4–6). The word *mqwh*, possibly

---

41. 1QpHab 3:1, 10; 4:13; 6:8; 9:8; 10:14; 12:1, 7, 9; 13:1 and 4.
42. It features too in 1Q14 frgs. 1–5, line 3; 1Q15 lines 2 and 5; 4Q161 frgs. 2–4, line 5;
4Q162 ii 1–2; 4Q163 frgs. 2–3, line 3; frgs. 8–10, line 5; frg. 31, line 5; 4Q165 frgs. 1–2, line 4;
4Q169 frgs. 1–2, lines 2 and 10; 4Q171 1–2 ii 4, 7–8, 10; 1+3–4 iii 9; 3–10 iv 11.

referring to a reservoir or ritual bath, sadly never occurs in extant parts of the continuous pesharim.

As for 4QpIsa[b] ii 1–2, the spatial images of Isa 5:5b–6a, the hedge being removed, the wall broken down, etc., appear to be interpreted simply in an abstract fashion in terms of divine abandonment. Not enough text survives to say more, but this seems to correspond to several other places where spatial images are taken abstractly rather than related to concrete surroundings.

2.6. Places as People

The Israelite tribal designations encourage the close association of people with particular places or regions. In the late Second Temple period these are transferred to Israel as a whole. In sectarian texts the assumption is that the promises made to Israel are the inheritance of the sectarian movement alone.

In several texts it is clear that the location of divine promises or indeed of the covenant is with people. In 4QpPs[a] 1–10 ii 4–5, Ps 37:9b describes those who wait for the Lord as those who will inherit the land. Intriguingly this is interpreted in the commentary without any reference to territory as simply being about "the congregation of his chosen ones, those who do his will." In 1QpMic, Mic 1:5c, "And what are the high places of Judah? Is it not Jerusalem?," is interpreted as a reference to the "Righteous Teac[h]er, who is the one [. . .]w and to a[l]l who volunteer to be added to the chosen ones of [. . .] in the Council of the Community."[43] Perhaps Judah is understood as the name of the Righteous Teacher; whatever the case might be, the places of Mic 1:5 are identified with the Teacher and the chosen community. The community is in some sense a restored Jerusalem in anticipation. Famously, in 1QpHab 12:3–4, "Lebanon is the Council of the Community."[44]

In 4QpPs[a] 1–10 iv 13–15, Ps 37:35–36 speaks of the place of the wicked, but the interpretation does not seem to pick up on the spatial image at all, simply condemning the Man of the Lie to judgment. In 4Q169 3–4 ii 1–2, the "city of Ephraim" is identified as "the Seekers-After-Smooth-Things at the latter days." In 4Q169 Manasseh and Ephraim are identified with their supposed inhabitants as ciphers for opponents of those to whom the commentary is addressed. Most explicitly, in 1QpHab 10:5–13 there is the quotation of Hab 2:12–13 concerning the one who builds a city. This is interpreted in an extensive comment of the "Spouter of the Lie" who has built a "city of emptiness" and a "congregation of falsehood." The place is made into a group of people.

A closing comment to this subsection is possibly pertinent. Those who

---

43. Horgan, "Pesharim," 135.

44. G. Vermes, "Lebanon – The Historical Development of an Exegetical Tradition," in idem, *Scripture and Tradition in Judaism: Haggadic Studies* (2nd ed.; SPB 4; Leiden: Brill, 1983), 26–39.

describe the phenomenon of Christian monasticism commonly note that the monastery is not just an alternative place to which the members of an order can retreat. Rather, it is a place of social and political statement where a new community is established to replace the inadequacies of the world that the rest of the population inhabit. In the monastery the community of fictive kinship is a substitute for the sinful urban culture of others and a proleptic place where the focus is on perfection. Though there are obvious differences between the Qumran community (and the movement of which it was a part) and later Christian monasticism, such as the relative paucity of the language of fictive kinship, nevertheless, the transformation of space into community renders the bounded place of restricted access useful but essentially transient, as place for those with such commitment is actually "the whole inhabited world."[45]

3. CONCLUSION

Perhaps the journey of this short study has been largely a negative one. There seems little or nothing in the continuous pesharim that can be used to locate them or the practice of prophetic interpretation to which they attest at the Qumran site. We cannot locate where there was a room for interpretation. Their point of reference is not the wilderness location or the walled enclosure erected there.

Nevertheless, this observation in itself allows us to affirm several things about the continuous pesharim. First, their structure displays the fact that they are put together in many ways under the control of the scriptural text; it is that which most commonly provides the language of the commentary, not the immediate spatial environment of the commentator. Second, the dominant self-reference in the commentaries is to the community in some form. It is people who localize many of the spatial referents of the scriptural texts. Third, where there are specific places named in the commentary sections, it is Jerusalem that dominates in the discourse. Jerusalem is the place where the ideological battle is being fought out; this is probably an accurate reflection of circumstances in the first century when the continuous pesharim were being composed. Jerusalem, purified and cleansed, is the place to which the community aspires in the imminent future. In the continuous pesharim the room for interpretation is the scripturally rooted longing of the community to which they are addressed.

---

45. See the helpful comments of P. Sheldrake, *Spaces for the Sacred: Place, Memory, and Identity* (London: SCM, 2001), esp. ch. 4, "The Practice of Place: Monasteries and Utopias," 90–118, here 118.

TEN

THE SILENT GOD, THE ABUSED MOTHER, AND THE SELF-JUSTIFYING SONS: A PSYCHODYNAMIC READING OF SCRIPTURAL EXEGESIS IN THE PESHARIM

1. INTRODUCTION

This essay has its origins in my initial reactions to a very stimulating interdisciplinary study of the book of Lamentations by Hugh Pyper.[1] Pyper begins his reading of Lamentations with a stark quotation from a modern Jewish writer as she struggles with the experience of sitting through the hearing of Lamentations in synagogue on the Ninth of Av:

> Whatever the Babylonians did to turn Jerusalem the city to rubble, it is the Jewish poet, I can't help feeling, who rips the bride Jerusalem's jewelled veil from her forehead, stripping her embroidered robes to flash us a glimpse of her genitals: 'ervatah' translated by the squeamish or modest translator as her nakedness.[2]

Pyper's concern is to reflect on why the poet of Lamentations "has chosen to centre the book round this strange, abhorrent metaphor of Zion as the raped woman, or, even more loadedly, the raped mother."[3] His approach is literary and psychological, with attention to significant aspects of gender. His argument is that the text might best be understood "as a symptom of melancholia and so the ambivalence which turns the anger of the survivor against the dead victim."[4]

---

1. H. S. Pyper, *An Unsuitable Book: The Bible as Scandalous Text* (The Bible in the Modern World 7; Sheffield: Sheffield Phoenix Press, 2005), 89–101. Pyper acknowledges his own indebtedness to the work of T. Linafelt, "Surviving Lamentations," *HBT* 17 (1995): 45–61; idem, *Surviving Lamentations: Catastrophe, Lament, and Protest in the Afterlife of a Biblical Book* (Chicago: University of Chicago Press, 2000).

2. N. Seidman, "Burning the Book of Lamentations," in *Out of the Garden: Women Writers on the Bible* (ed. C. Büchmann and C. Spiegel; New York: Fawcett Columbine, 1994), 278–88, here 282.

3. Pyper, *Unsuitable Book*, 89.

4. Ibid., 90. Pyper sees ambivalence in the text's compassion for Zion as a victim, on the

-151-

Using Freud's distinction between mourning, which is considered a healthy process leading to closure,[5] and melancholia, which is unhealthily persistent, leaving the melancholic trapped in an unresolved experience of abandonment that becomes turned in upon the self, Pyper wonders whether Lamentations as a symptom of the melancholic might not also contain in the very persistence of the dis-ease the seeds of some kind of hope for the restoration of the beloved.[6]

Pyper pays particular attention to the way Lamentations presents the tripartite relationship between the survivors of the destruction of Jerusalem, the supposedly nurturing maternal Jerusalem herself, and the God who has declared judgment against Jerusalem. For Pyper, Lamentations seems to play out the survivors' melancholic resentment at survival. He understands that resentment as ambivalent, on the one hand being notionally directed against the figure of the mother, Jerusalem, who is perceived as having abandoned her children through the abuse heaped upon her and yet permitting their survival in her very abandonment of them; but on the other hand the anger and resentment are actually turned inward and directed against the self. The abused Jerusalem also surprisingly enables the anger that might otherwise be directed at God (for not intervening on behalf of the survivors) to be directed elsewhere; in this way the silent God can be perceived as turning the destruction that the mother has experienced into divine judgment. That judgment is experienced from the past in the present by the resentful and angry survivors but is also a matter for being fully worked out in the future.

Something of this kind of reading of Lamentations seems to resonate with some aspects of the purpose and function of the pesharim, especially the so-called continuous ones.[7] They envisage a ravaged Jerusalem, a place of abominations and impurity (1QpHab 12:8–9), a city that continues to be abused by those in power, especially those to be associated with the Wicked Priest. They try to address the problem of the silence of God, in minor ways by addressing the divine delay, but largely by projecting divine judgment into the future. They present a self-justification for the community of their readers, by among other things masochistically insisting on the value of enduring persecution in the hope of some ultimate restoration; the grief of the present circumstances of the

---

one hand, and, on the other, the text's justification for the punishment of Zion for her lasciviousness.

5. Lamentations has been understood in terms of this positive view of the grief process of mourning by P. Joyce, "Lamentations and the Grief Process: A Psychological Reading," *BibInt* 1 (1993): 304–20.

6. Pyper, *Unsuitable Book*, 90; here Pyper is building on the proposals concerning the positive aspects of melancholia proposed by Linafelt, "Surviving Lamentations"; and idem, *Surviving Lamentations: Catastrophe, Lament, and Protest*.

7. Although the so-called continuous pesharim include among them compositions of several different sorts, as a group they can be distinguished more or less satisfactorily from the much more obviously thematic sectarian commentaries.

community is melancholically turned in on the community members, and the chief compensation for their current circumstances is future divine intervention—though perhaps there is some occasional relief in the community support network.[8] However, over and above this set of general parallels that I will attempt to work through in the body of this essay, in the sectarian scrolls there are direct continuities with ideas of mourning in many guises. For example, for the root *'bl* in particular, although 4QpHos[a] (ii 17 on Hos 2:13)[9] projects the notion of mourning onto those who have abused the calendar, "And [all]/[joy] has been turned for them into mourning (*l'bl*)," for the most part the destructive element of mourning is taken up by the members of the community.[10] In an overall context of eventual divine consolation, this sense of brokenness is picked up quite explicitly in 4QTanh frg.14 line 3: "he has hated us, he has broken us."

This psychodynamic approach to texts in the hands of someone not widely read or deeply trained in psychology or the psychology of religion can swiftly lead to inappropriate analysis.[11] I am not qualified to offer a psychological profile of the authors of the pesharim nor a psychoanalysis of their first readers; all that could only be partial in any case because of the distance in time and place between analyst and patient. All we have to put on the couch are some fragmentary texts and archaeological reconstructions. It thus seems unlikely that we should attempt to see something deeply problematically psychotic or pathological in the way the continuous pesharim are composed and presented, particularly if the whole of the evidence of the sectarian compositions in the Qumran library is kept in mind. Nevertheless, I am concerned to take advantage of the sugges-

---

8. And, as I will suggest below based on compositions other than the pesharim, in the present experience of the silent God in the worship entered into by the community.

9. Unless otherwise indicated all references to and translations of the pesharim are taken from M. P. Horgan, "Pesharim," in *The Dead Sea Scrolls: Hebrew, Aramaic, and Greek texts with English Translations*, vol. 6B, *Pesharim, Other Commentaries, and Related Documents* (ed. James H. Charlesworth et al.; Princeton Theological Seminary Dead Sea Scrolls Project 6B; Tübingen: Mohr Siebeck; Louisville, Westminster John Knox, 2002).

10. For *'bl* the poet has his mourning turned to joy (1QH[a] 10:5 = 4Q432 frg. 3, line 4), though he returns to the theme again (1QH[a] 19:22; 4QH[a] frg. 1, line 3); he also looks to a future when mourning and anguish flee (4Q427 7 ii 5). The "lot of light" is in mourning during the reign of Belial (4Q177 1–4 x 8); indeed there are chiefs of mourning (4Q177 1–4 x 9). The wicked are condemned to mourning in 1QS 4:13 (= 4Q257 5:12).

11. It is noticeable how tentative are many of the contributions to J. H. Ellens and W. G. Rollins, eds., *Psychology and the Bible: A New Way to Read the Scriptures* (4 vols.; Praeger Perspectives; Psychology, Religion, and Spirituality; Westport, Conn.: Praeger, 2004), simply because of the obvious lack of multidisciplinary competence acknowledged by many of the authors. The contribution to the four-volume set of essays that comes closest to the concerns of this paper is that by K. Syreeni, "Coping with the Death of Jesus: The Gospels and the Theory of Grief Work," in *From Gospel to Gnostics*, vol. 3 of Ellens and Rollins, *Psychology and the Bible*, 63–86. Syreeni considers the Gospels as grief work, including the role of the mother figure as part of the consideration of the management of attachment in the grief process.

tiveness of Pyper's study to allow a reconfiguration of some of the issues that are reflected in the contents of the pesharim. I wonder in particular if some of the discussion may have implications for the better understanding of the function of the pesharim as a genre—perhaps they serve in some way to help community patients to work through the grief of their circumstances by telling and hearing the story again, a story that is a creative mixture of past circumstances, present experiences, and future hopes, often arranged in an apparently disordered fashion.[12]

Because of my own methodological ineptitude, I appreciate the firm insistence from the expert practitioners that "psychological biblical criticism is not a method. It is a way of reading the biblical text that is sensitive to the psychological factors that may be at play."[13] Although I am aware of a century and more of psychology, psychiatry, and psychoanalysis, this paper is a glimpse at "the interaction of psychological factors, especially unconscious factors, in shaping both internal and external behavior,"[14] inasmuch as those can be discerned in the close reading of texts and the imaginatively controlled recreation of their social environments. I am also acutely aware, as Walter Brueggemann has noted, that "there is a danger, in the eclectic enterprise of psychological criticism, to impose a psychological theory on the text in a way that overrides the specificity of the text itself and distorts the text in order to serve the theory that an interpreter may advocate."[15] Because of that I turn immediately to describe some aspects of the specificity of the texts themselves.

---

12. Though we might need to qualify his use of both "apocalyptic" and "Essene," something of this is caught for the pesharim by J. T. Milik, *Ten Years of Discovery in the Wilderness of Judaea* (SBT 26; London: SCM, 1959), 65: "The apocalyptic Essene *mind*, especially when obliged to give a continuous exposition of a prophetic text, cannot be expected either to confine itself to the events of one period, or to separate out different events into clear groups" (italics mine). Horgan (*Pesharim: Qumran Interpretations of Biblical Books* [CBQMS 8; Washington, D.C.: Catholic Biblical Association of America, 1979], 6–8) has made a similar point.

13. D. A. Kille, "Psychology and Biblical Studies," *NIDB* 4:684. On the numerous possibilities of reading strategies opened up by psychological sensitivity to scriptural (and other) texts see the wide range of essays in Ellens and Rollins, *Psychology and the Bible*, especially the very positive appreciation of G. Theissen *Psychologische Aspekte paulinischer Theologie* (Göttingen: Vandenhoeck & Ruprecht, 1983). Cf. D. Mitternacht, "Theissen's Integration of Psychology and New Testament Studies: Learning Theory, Psychodynamics, and Cognitive Psychology," in *From Freud to Kohut*, vol. 1 of Ellens and Rollins, *Psychology and the Bible*, 101–17.

14. The concise definition of psychodynamics provided by W. G. Rollins and D. A. Kille, eds., *Psychological Insight into the Bible: Texts and Readings* (Grand Rapids: Eerdmans, 2007), 271.

15. W. Brueggemann, "Psychological Criticism: Exploring the Self in the Text," in *Method Matters: Essays on the Interpretation of the Hebrew Bible in Honor of David L. Petersen* (ed. J. M. LeMon and K. H. Richards; SBLRBS 56; Atlanta: Society of Biblical Literature, 2009), 213–32, here 215.

2. The Pesharim

With some of these ideas from Pyper's reading of Lamentations in mind, and with the cautionary notes from those concerned with the approach of psychological criticism ringing in our ears, let us move to consider the specificity of the texts, as Brueggemann has demanded,[16] in this case the pesharim themselves. It is important to consider these compositions in their own right at the outset. Too often they have been analyzed and assessed, pillaged, and plundered, solely with the reconstruction of the founding moments of the community in mind;[17] the discovery of such early community history may be an indirect result of the study of the pesharim so cannot be entirely dismissed, but primacy should really be given to how the pesharim reflect and construct their present.[18]

A highly suitable starting point for this appreciation of the continuous pesharim in their own right has been provided recently by Annette Steudel. She has offered some important comments on the likely relative dates of several sectarian exegetical compositions, including the continuous pesharim.[19] Once the likely date of the extant copies of the continuous pesharim is noticed, it is immediately apparent that the more immediate background of the events of the mid-first century B.C.E. should be used to explain some of their contents rather than the events of a century earlier. Most notably, the dating profile would strongly suggest that, with the possible exception of 4QpIsa^c, the circumstances lying behind the pesharim are the political terror and religious turmoil that runs from the Jewish civil war that eventually was ended by Pompey's troops and their trampling on the altar in 63 B.C.E. to the establishment of the control of Herod the Great[20] as one result of the emergence of the Roman Empire after the defeat of Mark Antony. It cannot be stated too often that it is against the background of that period that their composition and certainly their copying need principally to

---

16. Ibid., 215–16.

17. See H. Stegemann, *Die Entstehung der Qumrangemeinde* (Inaugural-Dissertation, Bonn, 1971); J. H. Charlesworth, *The Pesharim and Qumran History: Chaos or Consensus?* (Grand Rapids: Eerdmans, 2002), 67–118; H. Eshel *The Dead Sea Scrolls and the Hasmonean State* (Studies in the Dead Sea Scrolls and Related Literature; Grand Rapids; Eerdmans, 2008), 32–46 (Eshel tries to exercise considerable caution in his reconstructions). A summary of some earlier views is presented by Horgan, *Pesharim*, 6–8.

18. As well argued by J. Jokiranta, "Pesharim: A Mirror of Self-Understanding," in *Reading the Present in the Qumran Library: The Perception of the Contemporary by Means of Scriptural Interpretation* (ed. K. De Troyer and A. Lange; SBLSymS 30; Atlanta: Society of Biblical Literature, 2005), 23–34, esp. 30–34.

19. A. Steudel, "Dating Exegetical Texts from Qumran," in *The Dynamics of Language and Exegesis at Qumran* (ed. D. Dimant and R. G. Kratz; FAT 2/35; Tübingen: Mohr Siebeck, 2009), 39–53, esp. 46–52.

20. K. Elliger associates Pesher Habakkuk with "vielleicht Anfangszeit des Herodes" (*Studien zum Habakuk-Kommentar vom Toten Meer* [BHT 15; Tübingen: J. C. B. Mohr, 1953], 273–74).

be set, not some supposed activity of a Teacher who might have been active a century or more earlier in the middle of the second century B.C.E.[21] Scholars studying the relationship between the pesharim and historical events and circumstances should begin with Pesher Nahum, since what survives of it lacks any reference to the Teacher and clearly signals that it was composed during or after the reign of Demetrius, widely understood to be Demetrius III Eukarios (95–88 B.C.E.).

The second point to note about the pesharim, not least the continuous pesharim, is their form and structure. In the continuous pesharim it is clear that the scriptural text is distinguished from the interpretation that is given to it in two ways, in the variable use of spaces and through the employment of a technical formula introducing each section of interpretation. These markers serve to distinguish the prophetic text from the comment and so may be construed as indicative of hermeneutical discontinuity between the two. However, continuity is indicated in some ways too.[22] Most notably, the interpreter is described as the one to whom God made known all the mysteries of the words of his servants the prophets (1QpHab 7:4–5), just as God was also the source of the unfulfilled and incomprehensible oracles. In addition, continuity is identifiable in the way the vocabulary of the prophetic oracles is often reused in the interpretation, not just in terms of those items in the oracle that require identification but also as the principal source of the vocabulary of the interpretation itself, sometimes with the involvement of extensive wordplay.[23] The interpretation is distinct from but also coherent with the oracle it expounds.

A third point concerns genre. The form of both the continuous and the thematic pesharim as some kind of combination of explicit prophetic scriptural citation followed by interpretation clearly enables these compositions to be seen as

---

21. See especially the landmark study of P. R. Davies "History and Hagiography," in *Behind the Essenes: History and Ideology in the Dead Sea Scrolls* (BJS 94; Atlanta: Scholars Press, 1987), 87–105, which argued that it was very likely that earlier rhetorical traditions in the Hodayot were probably taken up in a hagiographical manner in later historicizing compositions such as Pesher Habakkuk. See also G. J. Brooke, "The Pesharim and the Origin of the Dead Sea Scrolls," in *Methods of Investigation of the Dead Sea Scrolls and the Khirbet Qumran Site: Present Realities and Future Prospects* (ed. M. O. Wise et al.; Annals of the New York Academy of Sciences 722; New York: New York Academy of Sciences, 1994), 339–54. Something of the force of this argument is recognized, but inappropriately, by those who would rather date the Teacher in the first century B.C.E.

22. In general see the comments on dismantling the distinction between text and interpretation by Brooke, "New Perspectives on the Bible and Its Interpretation in the Dead Sea Scrolls," in Dimant and Kratz, *Dynamics of Language*, 19–37, esp. 19–21.

23. See Horgan, *Pesharim*, 244–45, for a brief outline of how vocabulary from the scriptural lemma can be variously used in the interpretation; the commentaries of W. H. Brownlee (*The Midrash Pesher of Habakkuk: Text, Translation, Exposition with an Introduction* [SBLMS 24; Missoula, Mont.: Scholars Press, 1979]) and S. L. Berrin (*The Pesher Nahum Scroll from Qumran: An Exegetical Study of 4Q169* [STDJ 53; Leiden: Brill, 2004]) expound the subtleties by which the lemma and comment are linked.

part of two trajectories. On the one hand, from earlier times to their present, the pesharim are in some way continuous with forms of prophecy; they are not prophecy in a straightforward sense but are a textualized literary form of it.[24] On the other hand, the pesharim belong to the developing trajectory of Jewish Bible interpretation.[25] Taking both perspectives into account, the pesharim merit the label prophetic commentary, and there can then be some discussion as to how they might best be understood within those broad traditions, especially whether they deserve to be considered some kind of early form of midrash. In addition, more specifically, it has long been widely acknowledged that the way in which the pesharim focus on what are perceived to be unfulfilled oracles, divine promises, blessings, and curses gives them a divinatory quality.[26] The unfulfilled prophetic text is to be understood as if it was like an omen text or dream.[27] The skilled interpreter, like a Joseph or a Daniel, knows both the dream and the interpretation. The scriptural text becomes a symbolic repository.[28]

A fourth matter to note involves the character of the texts of the pesharim. It has often been stated that the continuous pesharim may be one-off autographs.[29]

---

24. Continuity with the prophetic past has been enunciated, e.g., by G. J. Brooke, "Prophecy and Prophets in the Dead Sea Scrolls: Looking Backwards and Forwards," in *Prophets, Prophecy and Prophetic Texts in the Second Temple Period* (LHBOTS 427; ed. by M. H. Floyd and R. D. Haak, London: T&T Clark, 2006), 151–65, and most extensively by A. P. Jassen, *Mediating the Divine: Prophecy and Revelation in the Dead Sea Scrolls and Second Temple Judaism* (STDJ 68; Leiden: Brill, 2007). Among those who have also urged care in how the terms "prophet" and "prophecy" are used in relation to the sectarian compositions are H. Barstad, "Prophecy at Qumran?" in *In the Last Days: On Jewish and Christian Apocalyptic and Its Period* (ed. K. Jeppesen, K. Nielsen, and B. Rosendal; Aarhus: Aarhus University Press, 1994), 104–20; and G. J. Brooke, "Was the Teacher of Righteousness Considered to Be a Prophet?" in *Prophecy after the Prophets? The Contribution of the Dead Sea Scrolls to the Understanding of Biblical and Extra-Biblical Prophecy* (ed. K. De Troyer and A. Lange, with L. L. Schulte; CBET 52; Leuven: Peeters, 2009), 77–97.

25. As contextualized neatly by M. J. Bernstein, "The Contribution of the Qumran Discoveries to the History of Early Jewish Biblical Interpretation," in *The Idea of Biblical Interpretation: Essays in Honor of James L. Kugel* (ed. H. Najman and J. H. Newman; JSJSup 83; Leiden: Brill, 2004), 215–38, esp. 222–23, 226.

26. See especially M. Nissinen, "*Pesharim* as Divination: Qumran Exegesis, Omen Interpretation and Literary Prophecy," in De Troyer and Lange, *Prophecy after the Prophets?* 43–60.

27. And so, as dream, perhaps particularly suitable for psychodynamic interpretation. Kille ("Psychology and Biblical Studies," 685) has noted specifically that "psychological perspectives can shed light on biblical experiences of healing, dreams, or speaking in tongues." Surprisingly, dreams are only intermittently discussed in Ellens and Rollins, *Psychology and the Bible*.

28. On the pesharim as being commentaries akin to dream interpretation, see the summary remarks of Horgan (*Pesharim*, 231–37) concerning the etymology of the technical terminology and the suitability of Daniel as the closest co-text for the pesharim. The discussion was brought into focus first by A. Finkel, "The Pesher of Dreams and Scriptures," *RevQ* 4 (1963–64): 357–70.

29. See the brief discussion by Horgan, *Pesharim*, 3–4; she has rightly concluded that "at

In discussing the symptomatic melancholia of Lamentations, Pyper notes that, even though there might be some positive value in the persistence of the melancholic condition, persistence that might lead to the hope of restoration, the very fact that Lamentations exists as a fixed text tips the scales toward noting that persistence of dis-ease always outweighs the positive hope. Hence, Lamentations is used and reused in Jewish liturgy to this day. How should the fixity of the pesharim be suitably conceptualized? Were the pesharim fixed autographs? It seems to me that that is very unlikely. Several of the individual manuscripts, not least Pesher Habakkuk, contain scribal features that seem to indicate that the texts were copied and even possibly amended as they were copied, perhaps so as to include further exegetical insight as that had become clear in the use and study of the pesher in a community gathering of some sort. Even if the texts of the pesharim were not fixed, nevertheless, the ongoing use of the pesharim, as their presence in at least three caves implies, would seem to indicate something of their persistence, as also for the ongoing continuing circumstances of their sectarian movement. They might indeed be viewed as symptomatic of the condition of the community.

A fifth matter for consideration is the character of much of the language of the pesharim. As is well known, for the most part the characters in the interpretations are represented in the code of sobriquets.[30] Some brief attention must be paid to why this mode of discourse is used. A weak view would be that the sectarian commentators were exercising caution lest their writings fall into the wrong hands. More pertinently, it might readily be appreciated that the representation of one's opposition in figurative stereotype was and remains a standard tactic in their de-humanization, a linguistic strategy for reinforcing distance.[31] But why should the in-group use coded terminology to refer to its own past leaders and membership? There seem to be three options for understanding this, options that are not necessarily mutually exclusive. One way of viewing the matter is that the use of sobriquets all round enables the interpretation to remain polyvalent, capable of changing referent and thus remaining continually valid at whatever point in the story of the community the text is read. Another view might be that some kind of quasi-dualistic rhetorical balance was considered necessary; just as the community's opponents are stereotyped so that they can be brutalized, so are the community members so that they can be protected. Yet a third way is to

---

least some of the manuscripts containing pesharim are not autographs."

30. See H. Bengtsson, *What's in a Name? A Study of Sobriquets in the Pesharim* (Ph.D. diss., Uppsala, 2000); M. A. Collins, *The Use of Sobriquets in the Qumran Dead Sea Scrolls* (LSTS 67; London; New York: T & T Clark, 2009).

31. See the comments by P. S. Alexander, "Insider/Outsider Labelling and the Struggle for Power in Early Judaism," in *Religion, Language, and Power* (ed. N. Green and M. Searle-Chatterjee; Routledge Studies in Religion 10; New York: Routledge, 2008), 83–100; see 93–95 on the power-plays implied in this stereotypical language.

suggest that this was not just a matter of rhetorical balance but of hyperbole.[32] I take hyperbolic usage to imply that the stereotypical language offers a coping mechanism for those faced with the circumstances in which at least some of the readers of the pesharim seem to have found themselves.

With this brief description of these five important aspects of the pesharim in mind, I now move to consider some elements of how Pyper's melancholic reading of Lamentations might shed some light on the continuous pesharim from the Qumran caves.

3. Father, Mother, Sons

3.1. The Silent God

There has been some considerable debate concerning how the understanding of prophecy in the sectarian compositions from Qumran allows or even encourages the modern reader of these texts to assert that in many ways there is much in the pesharim in particular that is continuous with earlier prophetic traditions. As mentioned above, there are continuities and discontinuities. One element of the discontinuity seems to concern the severe restriction of the hearing of the divine voice. Even in the works associated with Enoch and Daniel, there is much of God to be seen, but little that is directly heard. The group that collected the library of the Qumran caves together does not preserve for us the narration of visions or auditions. For them, as probably for their contemporaries, God's voice was to be heard indirectly. God has fallen silent.[33]

The pesharim make explicit two aspects of the silence of God that resonate with the way in which Pyper describes the supposed absence of God at the moment of destruction and thereafter. First, the community attests to the impurity of Jerusalem and its cultic practitioners by withdrawing from full participation in the temple cult. As a result, the community seems to be experiencing some measure of ongoing persecution. In some ways the community seems to have brought this upon itself through its withdrawal and its somewhat aggressive stance toward those who are still participating in what is taking place in Jerusalem. The silence of God can be heard in the way that he is understood to have

---

32. Suggested by Alexander, "Insider/Outsider Labelling," 95, on the insightful grounds that the assertions about the community were so counterfactual that they could be sustained only by such use of hyperbole.

33. Not only does this apply also to the reading of Lamentations by Pyper, but also it is an idea intriguingly developed in the context of psychological interpretation of messianism by I. Gruenwald, "Jewish and Christian Messianism: The Psychoanalytic Approach of Heinz Kohut," in Ellens and Rollins, *From Freud to Kohut*, 247–75. Gruenwald has commented that "when in a number of places in the Temple Scroll the third-person form of speech used in the scriptural references to God changes into the first person, this change evidently signals a dramatic attempt at reversing the ongoing trend towards God's voicelessness" (p. 266).

"abandoned" the vineyard (4QpIsaᵇ 1:2 [on Isa 5:5b–6a]); he is the one who hides his face from the land (4QpHosᵇ frg. 2, line 6). It can also be heard in the way that ongoing persecution, real or imagined, accompanies the withdrawal from the temple. Indeed, such persecution is a hallmark of community membership and identity according to the pesharim.

Second, because of the ongoing persecution, it is clear that God does not seem to be active on behalf of the community now in its daily protection. That divine inactivity, the silence of God's judgment of the community's opponents, is explained in terms of deferral: "the fulfilment of the period he did not make known to them" (1QpHab 7:2). Notably in Pesher Habakkuk, the interpretation of the appointed time of Hab 2:3a is that "the last period will be prolonged, and it will be greater than anything of which the prophets spoke" (1QpHab 7:7–8). Likewise the interpretation of the phrases that stand in poetic parallelism with Hab 2:3a in Hab 2:3b are understood as a last period that is drawn out for the community (1QpHab 7:12), a matter that has to do with a predetermined divine plan, the timing of which God seems either unable or unwilling to share.

These two aspects to the divine silence are both tied to the figure of the Teacher of Righteousness. In the pesharim there may be some construction or possibly some recollection of the original persecutions of the Teacher of Righteousness in order to provide for the ongoing identity of the community through its collective memory in some way.[34] But the use of the Teacher to assist identity formation is not a matter of celebration; those moments of the community's founding are not marked with cultic anamnesis in any way in the liturgical life of the movement as far as is known. Rather, the pesharim introduce the Teacher of Righteousness into their exegesis not least because in the construction of how the divine voice is mediated into the community, the Teacher seems to have played a very significant role and to have continued to do so as the sectarian movement, or at least the part of it responsible for the pesharim, sought to maintain its identity. The teacher is the one to whom God has made known all the mysteries of his servants the prophets.[35]

It is easy enough to notice how the Teacher functions in the Damascus Document, by implication in the Hodayot, as well as in the pesharim. The Teacher acts, on the one hand, as the priestly Interpreter of the Law and, on the other, as the wise poet, the implied (or actual) author of at least some of the Hodayot. As priestly Interpreter of the Law, he represents continuity with the temple and the suitable construction of halakhic regulations for every aspect

---

34. As demonstrated by Jokiranta, "Pesharim: A Mirror of Self-Understanding," 23–34.

35. Among others, O. Betz has shown in detail that whatever might be made of this revealed insight, the pesharim and other sectarian compositions do not disclose how the revelation of new meaning was experienced or received (*Offenbarung und Schriftforschung in der Qumransekte* [WUNT 6; Tübingen: Mohr Siebeck, 1960]).

of daily life within the movement. As specified for one form of the movement in the Rule of the Community, those regulations especially reflect the need for purity, as if the community was a group of priests functioning in the temple. On the other hand, as wise poet, he represents the focus of identity formation; he can label those whom God has chosen to be with him and those who are false prophets and lying teachers.[36] But the Teacher is also constructed as the interpreter of unfulfilled prophetic texts; he is the diviner of oracles who is able "to find new meanings that displace old meanings, and to assert that the new meanings are not imposed but have been there in the texts all along."[37] As Susan Handelman has written of Freud, "the interpreter's job is to reveal, eluci- date, and construct for conscious awareness those hidden unities that contain a core of definite historical truth. Interpretation is not, in the Aristotelian sense, the distinguishing of truth from falsehood, but the relationship of hidden to shown: not appearance to reality, but manifest to latent."[38] The Teacher extends the significance and application of what was revealed (nigleh), and he reveals what was hidden (nistar). In all he does he is configured as allowing the com- munity to hear the voice of the silent God.

In relation to the pesharim in particular, in some way it seems as if the unful- filled prophetic text and its revealed interpretation become both an extended echo of the divine voice and a substitute for God's auditory institutional presence in the city of the sanctuary, in the holy of holies. The oracle can be understood as akin to a dream, and the skilled interpreter can both retell the dream and provide its interpretation through a range of hermeneutical moves that release both its symbolic and its actual meaning. God is silent in the community in the sense that the recording of the divine voice of old has to be replayed afresh; but he is also present, displaced from his place in the holy of holies, yet vital in the texture of the text. The Teacher's teaching is that the silent God will indeed be heard loudly again, at a future unknown moment of judgment.

Although the hearing of the divine voice may be recognized once more

---

36. As construed insightfully by C. A. Newsom, *The Self as Symbolic Space: Constructing Identity and Community at Qumran* (STDJ 52; Leiden: Brill, 2004).

37. Brueggemann, *Psychological Criticism*, 218. Brueggemann's full sentence here has to do with Freud as interpreter and reads: "Freud's work, like that of the rabbis, is to read and interpret texts, to find new meanings that displace old meanings, and to assert that the new meanings are not imposed but have been there in the texts all along."

38. S. Handelman, *The Slayers of Moses: The Emergence of Rabbinic Interpretation in Modern Literary Theory* (SUNY Series on Modern Jewish Literature and Culture; Albany: State University of New York Press, 1982), 148; cited by Brueggemann, *Psychological Criticism*, 218. Handelman has attempted to explain how Freud was often thinking in intriguing continuity with rabbinic modes of thought; for her, like the rabbis, Freud was deconstructing "Moses" to find new readings, just as subsequent Jewish thinkers, like Jacques Lacan, Jacques Derrida, and Harold Bloom, have also done.

as only indirect and therefore inaudible in itself, the immediate and imminent experience of the silent divine in the community is nevertheless retained. It is inappropriate to read the pesharim as if they somehow represent exclusively the psyche (whether as super-ego, ego, or id) of the community membership. In particular, alongside these exegetical works it is important to place various liturgical and poetic texts, not least on the one hand the Hodayot, which embody in their use the Teacher's construction of the identity of the community and, on the other hand, the Songs of the Sabbath Sacrifice, which so very well describe the inability of even the purest members of the community to cause the enduring presence of the divine. God can indeed be known and experienced, but he cannot be controlled or possessed. God is silent in the community in the sense that even if the community member caught up in the ecstatic experience of worship in the midst of the angels were to catch a glimpse of the divine radiance, he would hear nothing from the throne itself, partly because the volume of praise somehow inhibits the terrifying threat of the divine word itself.

In all this, a striking feature is that the community's identity is not constructed by association with the metanarrative of Israel as expressed in the books from Joshua to 2 Kings.[39] The story to be identified with seems to be one that conflates the wilderness experience of Israel at Sinai with the ongoing sense that the exile might just be coming to an end. The city of the sanctuary is still ravaged, as it was before by the Babylonians. However, the ongoing anger of the melancholic is directed not at the silent God but, in texts like the pesharim, at those who continue to ravage the land and its principal city. The melancholia of the suffering and persecuted community member is relieved through the Teacher's model interpretations of unfulfilled prophetic texts through which the community can hear the future divine voice in judgment, if not the immediacy of the divine voice in the present. The silent God remains part of the community's experience and the community's story is wrapped up in promise.

3.2. The Abused Mother

Pyper's point is that in some way the melancholic author of Lamentations projects his anger for his condition back on the maternal figure, the victim, in a self-destructive way. So, what of Jerusalem, the city of the sanctuary, in the pesharim? As has become well known, Jerusalem is the place to which reference is made most often in the sectarian scrolls from the Qumran caves. The wilderness ideology of the Rule of the Community, whether ideal or real, does not lead to any significant role for Sinai in the spatial self-definition of the

---

39. Though these books were indeed known to the community, they are not cited often nor used extensively as a source for positive definition of what it is to be Israel with a renewed covenant. The exceptions may be those parts that were deemed to be prophetic and unfulfilled, such as the oracle of Nathan (2 Sam 7; cf. 4Q174).

movement. Even though the very term *yaḥad* might be derived from the Sinai narrative,[40] all eyes remain on Jerusalem.[41] This is certainly the case for the topography of the pesharim.

Jerusalem seems to be named explicitly fourteen times in what survives of the continuous pesharim. In 4QpIsa[a] frgs. 2–6, line 25, Jerusalem is in parallel with Zion in the quotation of Isa 10:28–32; and in the interpretation of those verses that survives (line 29) Jerusalem is explicitly mentioned as the goal of the one who "goes up from the Valley of Acco." In 4QpIsa[b] ii 7 and 10, Jerusalem is named in two separate pieces of interpretation, the first on Isa 5:11–14 and the second on Isa 5:24c–25; in both instances the interpretation concerns "the men of mockery who are in Jerusalem." In a similar way in 4QpIsa[c] 23 ii 11, the "Seekers-After-Smooth-Things" are identified as "in Jerusalem." In 4QpIsa[e] frgs. 1–2, line 2, the context is too fragmentary to be reconstructed, though it seems as if the city's name belongs in an interpretation of a text of Isaiah that precedes the citation of Isa 40:12 that follows in lines 3–4 of the fragments. In 1QpMic, Jerusalem can readily be restored twice, once in frg. 10, line 4, in the citation of Mic 1:5, and once in frg. 11, line 3, in the citation of Mic 1:9. In 4QpMic, Jerusalem occurs in the citation of Mic 4:8c–12; nothing of the comment survives, but, as with 1QpMic, the selection of the passage might itself be indicative of a concern with Jerusalem. There are three occurrences in Pesher Nahum: in 4QpNah 3–4 i 2, Demetrius is described as the one "who sought to enter Jerusalem"; in 3–4 i 10, there is mention of an army that is in Jerusalem; and in 3–4 i 11, there is a reference to the "priests of Jerusalem." In Pesher Habakkuk there are two references: in 1QpHab 9:4 there is reference to "the last priests who are in Jerusalem," and in 1QpHab 12:7 Jerusalem is explicitly named as the place where the "Wicked Priest committed abominable deeds and defiled God's sanctuary." In 1QpPs there are a quotation and an interpretation of Ps 68:30, both of which mention Jerusalem. In addition, various epithets also occur, such as "the high mountain of Israel, his holy mountain" (4QpPs[a] 1–10 iii 11), and Zion is mentioned in the continuous pesharim three times, all in scriptural citations: twice in 4QpIsa[a] (in Isa 10:24–27 in 4QpIsa[a] frgs. 2–4, line 7; in Isa 10:28–32 in 4QpIsa[a] frgs. 5–6, line 9) and once in 4QpIsa[c] 23 ii 15 (in the quotation of Isa 30:19–21). It is quite clear that the direction of vision in the continuous pesharim is toward Jerusalem.

In several of the texts just listed, Jerusalem is portrayed negatively by association and also quite openly. Most explicitly the abuse of Jerusalem is laid out in the interpretation of Hab 2:17b in 1QpHab 12:6–9: "And when it says, On account of the bloodshed of the town and violence done to the land, its interpretation:

---

40. See J. C. Vanderkam, "Sinai Revisited," in *Biblical Interpretation at Qumran* (ed. M. Henze; Studies in the Dead Sea Scrolls and Related Literature; Grand Rapids: Eerdmans, 2005), 44–60.

41. See G. J. Brooke, "Moving Mountains: From Sinai to Jerusalem," in *The Significance of Sinai: Traditions about Divine Revelation in Judaism and Christianity* (ed. G. J. Brooke, H. Najman, and L. T. Stuckenbruck; TBN 12; Leiden: Brill, 2008), 73–89.

the 'town' is Jerusalem, where the Wicked Priest committed abominable deeds and defiled God's sanctuary." 4QpNah 3–4 iii 1 also mentions the abominations. The term is frequent in the sectarian literature and closely related texts such as the Temple Scroll. Those texts that implicate Jerusalem by association might include 4QpNah 3–4 i 2–3, in which the gentile Demetrius is defined as the one who sought to enter Jerusalem on the advice of the "Seekers-After-Smooth-Things." In addition, the priests who have amassed wealth are specifically named as the "priests of Jerusalem" (4QpNah 3–4 i 11) or "the last priests of Jerusalem" (1QpHab 9:4–5). Jerusalem is probably the reference of the "city of emptiness" built with bloodshed (1QpHab 10:10). The desolation of Jerusalem is echoed in the destruction of the "young men, strong men, and old men, women and toddlers," who are all victims in 1QpHab 6:11. However, despite all this negative description, in the pesharim Jerusalem does not seem to be the focus of the anger of the sectarian commentators. Their anger and aggressive militancy are directed rather against those who have and continue to plunder and defile the city and the metropolitan land, especially the Wicked Priest, the "Seekers-After-Smooth-Things," and "the priests of Jerusalem."

Three further comments, however, might suitably be made. First, it is clear from the Rule of the Community (1QS 8:5–10) that the community has transferred the key imagery of the temple to itself and has set itself up as the place where atonement for the land might be possible. Through this metaphorical transfer, the community indicates that it has in effect abandoned the city of the sanctuary, if only temporarily. In some way this can be understood as making the community complicit in the abuse of the city and its sanctuary. The safe place to be has become the *yaḥad* in its various permutations; the community has turned in on itself to recover some sense of well-being, and in so doing it negates the very aspiration of open inclusiveness with which the Isaianic poems of consolation resonate. Behind a façade of cultic sensitivity, there is a manipulative exclusiveness that is truly sectarian. Furthermore, there is a sense in which the repetitive strains of the pesharim with their various tellings and retellings of the abuse and desolation of Jerusalem in a limited number of literary tropes are voyeuristic as the city is objectified by association. Overall, this attitude to Jerusalem and the significance of its temple hardly seems healthy.[42]

Second, the replacement of the temple by the community itself has to be facilitated somehow. In the second half of the first century B.C.E. it seems as if this was made possible, at least in part, by the pesharim themselves. The pesharim demonstrated through prophetic interpretation the impossibility of maintaining any kind of cultic practice in the temple in Jerusalem. The unfulfilled pro-

---

42. I wonder, furthermore, whether some of the sexuality present in the scrolls, such as in the particularly explicit form of the wisdom poem of Sir 51:13–19 (11QPsª 21:11–18), can be understood as a similar indication of female objectification and subjugation.

phetic texts and their interpretations thus become the transitional objects[43] that encourage community members to maintain a distance from Jerusalem, to keep up their posture of abandonment.[44] The pesharim keep the community self-consumed with anger in its grief at the abuse of Jerusalem by those currently in power there, or by those who have desecrated it in former times or who may return to desecrate it again. The pesharim serve the ongoing displacement of the sectarian movement.[45]

But there is a third matter. The pesharim have enabled the maintenance of the move away from the center of power and influence in Jerusalem; but the unfulfilled prophetic texts in the skilled hands of the sectarian commentators is also the transitional object that enables the move back to or at least the orientation toward Jerusalem, not in terms of destructive objectification but so that the judgment of the silent God can be located. Thus, in the pesharim there are suggestions that seem to illustrate the community's longing for a restored Jerusalem. The congregation of the poor will one day in the future take possession of the high mountain of Israel, to delight on "his holy mountain" (4QpPs^a 1–10 iii 11). More forcefully still, in 4QpIsa^d the rebuilding of Jerusalem that is described in Isa 54 seems to be used not simply to keep all that is Jerusalem's within the identity of the community, but as an indication that the community and the city have a shared and glorious future of lapis lazuli, exalted pinnacles, and stones of beryl.

For the writers of the pesharim Jerusalem is desolate. She continues to be abused. She is impure and abominable. By their rehearsal of events past, present, and yet to come, the pesharim seem to justify the transferral of all that is maternal, pure, and holy to the self-exiled community itself. By their repetition of these matters in a limited set of images and literary tropes, they reinforce and maintain the community's mental distance from Jerusalem. Yet the persistence of the melancholic position, which might lead to self-destruction, also contains

---

43. On how transitional objects function to move a subject from one psychological state to another, see the writings of D. W. Winnicott, *The Maturational Processes and the Facilitating Environment: Studies in the Theory of Emotional Development* (New York: International Universities Press, 1965); and idem, *Playing and Reality* (London: Tavistock, 1971). Winnicott is actually concerned with how such objects contribute to the process of maturation, especially in the developing of the mother–child relationship. On texts within canonical processes as transitional objects as illuminated by the Dead Sea Scrolls, see Brooke, "New Perspectives," 31–32. On Winnicott in general for the study of the Bible, see the helpful comments of Brueggemann, "Psychological Criticism," 221–23.

44. This seems to be somewhat different from how Scripture was used to encourage new members to join the community; see G. J. Brooke, "Justifying Deviance: The Place of Scripture in Converting to a Qumran Self-Understanding," in De Troyer and Lange, *Reading the Present in the Qumran Library*, 73–87.

45. Newsom writes of the self as symbolic space; that spatial definition of identity formation and maintenance is highly appropriate for the kind of displacement hinted at here. Identity moves from Jerusalem and its sanctuary to the community as secure place, sanctuary, city of refuge.

within it the seeds of hope that one day the same prophetic texts might enable the transition back to Jerusalem, a rebuilt and freshly adorned place of beauty.

3.3. The Self-Justifying Sons

I have described briefly and in an amateur fashion some of the psychodynamic melancholic aspects of the silent God and the abused mother. I turn now to the human participants implicated in the pesharim.

The continuous pesharim have much to say about their opponents. There is an almost unhealthy desire to label and shame them, whoever they may be. They are the Man of the Lie and those whom he has led astray who will perish by the sword, famine, and plague (4QpPsᵃ 1–10 i 26–27); those "led astray" (4QpHosᵃ ii 5), and those who lead "Ephraim astray" (4QpNah 3–4 ii 8); "the ruthless of the covenant" (1QpHab 2:6; 4QpPsᵃ 1–10 ii 14; iii 12; iv 1–2); "the wicked of Ephraim and Manasseh" (4QpPsᵃ 1–10 ii 18); "wicked princes" (4QpPsᵃ 1–10 iii 7); "the wicked ones" of Israel (1QpHab 5:5; 4QpPsᵃ 1–10 iii 12); "the Seekers-After-Smooth-Things" (4QpIsaᶜ 23 ii 10; 4QpNah 3–4 iii 3; iii 6–7); those "who have rejected the Torah" (4QpIsaᶜ 23 ii 14; 1QpHab 1:11; 5:11–12); and those who "abandoned God" (4QpHosᵇ frgs. 7–8, line 2). These dehumanizing stereotypes facilitate the condemnation of the community's opponents and inhibit the kind of negotiation with the other that seems to be indicated if 4QMMT is understood as addressed to those outside the movement. Perhaps by the second half of the first century B.C.E. such attempts at accommodation with those with who had different views on key cultic issues, such as purity and the marriage of priests, were no longer pertinent in the same way, and the discourse was one of implacable opposition.

However, this study is concerned more with the authors and first readers and hearers of the pesharim. How can we talk about their primary readers, those who are experiencing the silent God and who have abandoned the abused mother? They are "those who return to the Torah" (4QpPsᵃ 1–10 ii 2–3; frg. 11, line 1), "those who do the Torah" (1QpHab 7:11; 8:1; 12:4–5; 4QpPsᵃ 1–10 ii 15; ii 23), "the congregation of his chosen ones" (4QpIsaᵈ frg. 1, line 3; 4QpPsᵃ 1–10 ii 5; iii 5), "his chosen ones" (4QpNah 1–2 ii 8; 1QpHab 5:4; 9:12; 10:13; 4QpPsᵃ 1–10 iv 12), "those who do his will" (4QpPsᵃ 1–10 ii 5), "the congregation of the poor" (4QpPsᵃ 1–10 ii 10; iii 10), "the poor ones" (4QpIsaᵃ frgs. 8–10, line 7; 1QpHab 12:6), "the congregation of the community" (4QpPsᵃ 1–10 iv 19), "the men of the community" (4QpIsaᵉ frg. 9, line 3), "those who accept the appointed time of affliction … in the time of refining" (4QpPs 1–10 ii 10; ii 19; iii 3), "those who return to the wilderness" (4QpPsᵃ 1–10 iii 1), those who are "not ashamed" (4QpPsᵇ frg. 3, line 3), "the penitents of Israel" (4QpIsaᶜ 6–7 ii 16; 4QpHosᵃ i 16–17), "the sons of Zadok" (4QpIsaᶜ frg. 22, line 3), "the men of truth" (1QpHab 7:10), and "the simple ones of Judah" (1QpHab 12:4). There are a few other self-designations, but that list will suffice for a few comments on how the members of the communities of the pesharim seem to understand themselves.

Two matters are immediately striking. First, there is only very limited survival of priestly self-designations. The one instance of the "sons of Zadok" is in 4QpIsa^c, which Steudel has placed suitably early in the first half of the first century B.C.E..[46] Second, there seems to be no self-referential language of fictive kinship in what survives of the pesharim; the texts do not describe the community members as sons or brothers.[47] Although it could be that such self-designations as "sons of light" and "sons/children of Israel" were part of passages no longer extant,[48] it seems as if that dominant manner of self-description in the community rule texts has been displaced by a different set of descriptors. Why might this be?

I think that the self-descriptions used of the community members lack familial terminology for reasons that might be more complex than coincidental. To begin with, it seems as if the labels used are not simply constructs that might hide the identity of the community; indeed there are terms like "sons of Zadok" and "men of the community" that would identify those favored in these compositions, possibly even to outsiders. Rather, the lack of familial terminology may reflect something of how the relationship between the community members and its opponents is being worked through psychologically. There are two sides to the terminology that has been chosen. On the one hand, it shows that the community has turned in on itself in terms of melancholic self-abasement, poverty, penitence, and suffering in periods of affliction. On the other hand, one dominant feature of the mechanism for survival promulgated by the pesharim is the keeping of the Law, not least as the stringency in so doing can be rediscovered in the wilderness experience. Indeed, the strict observance of the Law might be considered to be yet another form of self-abasement. The only relief for this is a projection into the present that at some unknown point in the future the silent God will judge all his enemies from within the holy of holies itself. This seems to be the force of several of the interpretations but is expressed in a most climactic fashion at the end of Pesher Habakkuk: "Yahweh is in his holy temple (*hykl*)" declares Hab 2:20, "on the day of judgment God will destroy completely (*yklh*) all who serve idols" reverberates the interpretation with a mighty wordplay. The self-referential terminology of the pesharim seems to confirm in an intriguing way

---

46. Steudel, "Dating Exegetical Texts from Qumran," 47. On p. 50 Steudel has rightly noted that the pesharim "appear to reflect a late, the latest stage in the development of the terminology which was important for the community."

47. On "sons of light," see J. Vázquez Allegue, *Los hijos de la luz y los hijos de las tinieblas: El prólogo de la Regla de la Comunidad de Qumrán* (Bibliotec Midrásica 21; Estella: Verbo Divino, 2000. On the use of "brothers" see CD 6:20; 7:1–2; 1QS 5:25; 6:10.

48. In the continuous pesharim בן is preserved only three times:]*by the sons of*[(4QpIsa^a frgs. 2–6, line 5); in the quotation of Isa 19:9b–12 in 4QpIsa^c 11 ii 4; and in the phrase "sons of Zadok" (4QpIsa^c frg. 22, line 3).

the relevance of Pyper's reading of Lamentations for the better understanding of these complex commentaries.

This understanding of the self-designations in the pesharim might well have some confirmation from a reading of the Qumran data from quite another perspective. In considering the question of how Jews fitted into ancient Mediterranean society, Seth Schwartz has commented astutely on the apparent lack of concern for friendship as was common in most quarters in antiquity. Schwartz comments as follows:

> In antiquity there were small Jewish groups that attempted to enact the Torah's social vision without compromise, such as the Essenes or Dead Sea sectarians, who rejected not only patronage, friendship, and the trappings of honor but even, apparently, family and property—anything that would interfere with a life devoted to the service of God and his Torah. The Essenes and similar groups, such as the philosophical schools of Old Greece, relied on the existence in pre-destruction Judaea of unusually large numbers of well-to-do pious men from whom they could draw new adherents and new funds.[49]

In this brief reference to the Essenes or Dead Sea sectarians, Schwartz does not differentiate between the classical sources on the Essenes and the sectarian compositions among the scrolls, nor does he distinguish between the earlier and later compositions among the community texts. Nevertheless, his observation captures something of the strange character of the communities of the scrolls in the light of the rest of ancient Mediterranean society and highlights once again the dominant place of devotion to the Law in the outlook of this movement. In the more confined literary context of the pesharim alone, this distinctive perspective shows a determination to construct a view of the world in different terms, terms that might appeal to the disenfranchised in some way and whose loyalty could then be endorsed and maintained through the melancholic psychodynamics of the prophetic commentaries.

4. FUNDAMENTALISM: A COMPARATIVE CONTROL

Of course, the pesharim are not, strictly speaking, exegetical literary substitutes for the melancholic or mournful poetry of Lamentations. They seem to present a very different way of coping with the political and religious circumstances of those who composed them and those for whom they were written and to whom they were read. It is difficult to construe them straightforwardly as texts of melancholia, even though the reading strategy implied by Pyper's approach to Lamentations has possibly allowed me to bring into sharper focus some of the distinctive features of the discourse of these prophetic commentaries. Neither

---

49. S. Schwartz, *Were the Jews a Mediterranean Society? Reciprocity and Solidarity in Ancient Judaism* (Princeton: Princeton University Press, 2010), 31–32.

does it seem entirely appropriate to view them as literary constructs that are in some way part of a process of mourning for a Jerusalem that has been pillaged from within and without, violated by its own and abused by others.

Are there other ways of thinking about the psychodynamics of the sectarian exegesis of the pesharim? Here a key term might be "sectarian." What kind of sectarians were responsible for this interpretative literature? As scholarly advances are made on that front,[50] it seems appropriate at least to consider whether the mind-set of the fundamentalist as currently understood might provide a way of acting as a control on the views expressed so far in this essay—unless it is thought that fundamentalists are usually just another sort of melancholic type. With a control in operation it might then become possible to see that there are alternative ways of reading the pesharim psychologically that are also helpful toward their better understanding. This comparative control is not introduced to displace what I have already said about the silent God, the abused mother, and the self-justifying sons, but to provide some kind of balance and to show that no one psychodynamic reading is adequate in itself. After all, it is quite possible that some of the writers of the exegesis in the continuous pesharim as well as some of their hearers and readers were completely other than has been described so far.

Religious extremism of various kinds, sometimes labeled as "fundamentalism,"[51] is now a worldwide phenomenon, and those who have studied it have concluded that it is not inappropriate to study it cross-culturally and cross-

---

50. See, e.g., P. R. Davies, "Sects from Texts: On the Problems of Doing a Sociology of the Qumran Literature," in *New Directions in Qumran Studies: Proceedings of the Bristol Colloquium on the Dead Sea Scrolls, 8–10 September 2003* (ed. J. G. Campbell, W. J. Lyons, and L. K. Pietersen; LSTS 52; London: T&T Clark, 2005), 69–82; J. Jokiranta, *Social Identity and Sectarianism in the Qumran Movement* (STDJ 105; Leiden: Brill, 2012); D. J. Chalcraft, ed., *Sectarianism in Early Judaism: Sociological Advances* (BibleWorld; London: Eqinox, 2007); E. Regev, *Sectarianism in Qumran: A Cross-Cultural Perspective* (Religion and Society 45; Berlin: de Gruyter, 2007); F. García Martínez and M. Popović, eds., *Defining Identities: We, You, and the Other in the Dead Sea Scrolls: Proceedings of the Fifth Meeting of the IOQS in Groningen* (STDJ 70; Leiden: Brill, 2008). At the end of his article, "Sects from Texts," Davies wonders intriguingly what the discovery of a sect from a text might tell the modern reader about the sect's parent: "Just as Freud's psychopathology can reveal the workings of a so-called 'normal' mind, so the contours of sectarian Judaism can perhaps tell us something about the essence of Judaism itself" (p. 82).

51. J. M. Harris, "Fundamentalism: Objections from a Modern Jewish Historian," in *Fundamentalism and Gender* (ed. J. S. Hawley; Oxford: Oxford University Press, 1994), cited in M. Ruthven, *Fundamentalism: The Search for Meaning* (Oxford: Oxford University Press, 2005), 7) has problematized the use of the term: "The word fundamentalism has come to imply an orientation to the world that is anti-intellectual, bigoted, and intolerant. It is applied to those whose life-style and politics are unacceptable to modern, Western eyes and, most particularly, to those who would break down the barrier we have erected between church and state. The term fundamentalism is reserved for those who have the temerity to project their world-view onto others. Against such people we lash out with a label that immediately delegitimizes them."

religiously.[52] There are several definitions of this phenomenon in circulation and they share many features. Bruce Lawrence has described such movements as (1) comprised of secondary-level male elites; (2) utilizing a technical vocabulary or discourse; (3) professing totalistic and unquestioning allegiance to sacred Scriptures or religious authority; and (4) privileging the authority of their own leaders while subordinating democratic values and processes.[53] Alternatively put, fundamentalism is:

> the belief that there is one set of religious teachings that clearly contains the fundamental, basic, intrinsic, essential, inerrant truth about humanity and deity; that this essential truth is fundamentally opposed by forces of evil which must be vigorously fought; that this truth must be followed today according to the fundamental, unchangeable practices of the past; and that those who believe and follow these fundamental teachings have a special relationship with the deity.[54]

A significant part of several studies of fundamentalism is the view that fundamentalists tend to be defensive in a militant way. In attempting to discover why some people take up this attitude and react so vigorously, Jacques Janssen, Jan van der Lans, and Mark Dechesne suggest that the chief motivating factor is preservation of self-esteem.[55] They note further that this motivating factor is a central concern of terror management theory,[56] a theory that seeks to describe levels of defensiveness in humans on the basis of corresponding levels of death anxiety. Religion and especially fundamentalist forms of it, are coping strategies, ways of managing the fear of death. Since such existentialist fear is so widespread among humans, fundamentalisms are also an inevitable trait in the human construction of reality. Furthermore, the most significant way that the fear of death can be reduced is, not surprisingly, by focusing on something else. Janssen, van

---

52. As summarized by E. Schüssler Fiorenza, *Democratizing Biblical Studies: Toward an Emancipatory Educational Space* (Louisville: Westminster John Knox, 2009).

53. B. B. Lawrence, *Defenders of God: The Fundamentalist Revolt against the Modern Age* (Studies in Comparative Religion; Columbia: University of South Carolina Press, 1995).

54. B. Altemeyer and B. Hunsberger, "Authoritarianism, Religious Fundamentalism, Quest, and Right-Wing Authoritarianism," *International Journal for the Psychology of Religion* 2 (1992):113–33, here 118; cited by J. Janssen, J. van der Lans, and M. Dechesne, "Fundamentalism: The Possibilities and Limitations of a Social-Psychological Approach," in *Religious Identity and the Invention of Tradition: Papers Read at a NOSTER Conference in Soesterberg, January 4–6, 1999* (ed. J. W. van Henten and A. Houtepen; Studies in Theology and Religion 3; Assen: Royal Van Gorcum, 2001), 302–16, here 306.

55. Cf. the comments on self-esteem by Mitternacht, "Theissen's Integration of Psychology and New Testament Studies," 106–7. Mitternacht highlights some features of role theory, especially how self-esteem can be constructed as the individual adopts a new role, providing a way of overcoming the false antithesis between tradition and experience.

56. Janssen, van der Lans, and Dechesne, "Fundamentalism," 307.

der Lans, and Dechesne determine that terror management theory enables one to conclude that fundamentalism in itself is "a coping mechanism that makes the burdens of life bearable."[57]

One further aspect of the fundamentalist mind-set is brought out by James Barr. Barr has pointed out pertinently that "even if fundamentalists sometimes say they take the Bible literally, the facts of fundamentalist interpretation show that this is not so. What fundamentalists insist on is not that the Bible must be taken literally but that it must be so interpreted as to avoid any admission that it contains any kind of error. In order to avoid imputing error to the Bible, fundamentalists twist and turn back and forward between literal and non-literal interpretation."[58] Though that description is expressed in somewhat derogatory terms, it discloses one particular feature of how the fundamentalist works in constructing a view of the world that is rigorously consistent in how authoritative Scriptures are appropriated within such groups.

In the light of these definitions of the character of fundamentalism, what can be said of the pesharim? Are the pesharim, in general, expressions of militancy? Is their rhetorical aggressiveness a necessary diversionary tactic whereby the community can avoid its fear of death? Do the exegetical strategies visible in the prophetic commentaries consist of a mixture of literal and nonliteral interpretations so that a consistent view of the world emerges? There is not space to address these questions in detail here, but a couple of comments are in order. First, several of the definitions cited above do indeed seem to resonate with how those behind the pesharim and their readers might be envisaged, given faces. The pesharim are the products of male elites, have technical vocabulary, construct authority in a certain way, adopt a militant attitude to their opponents, offer a way of coping with anxieties induced by a particular attitude to Jerusalem and the temple, and mix literal and nonliteral interpretation in the creation of a coherent exegetical outcome. Second, there is something similar in the way that those with melancholia persist in their state of loss and the way the fundamentalist constructs an outlook that copes with existentialist angst, but the whole psychological framework might not overlap in depth.

This brief excursus into a consideration of the fundamentalist mind-set has thrown up some further perspectives that might be considered. At least it has suggested that viewing the pesharim as the representative products of a mind-set similar to that which some scholars have seen as making sense of the way the book of Lamentations has been put together is illuminating and suggestive but probably does not provide all the answers; there could well be other and better ways of applying psychodynamic approaches to these sectarian prophetic commentaries for their better understanding.

---

57. Ibid., 312.
58. J. Barr, *Fundamentalism* (London: SCM, 1978).

5. Conclusions

Pyper brings his study of Lamentations to a close with some reflections on the implications of his reading for the human self-understanding of the reader.

> Insofar as the Hebrew Bible is a source of revelation, it is a revelation of darkness as well as light, of the involvement of human—mostly, but not exclusively, male—fear, greed, insecurity and visciousness in all that speaks of the divine, and of the constant psychological process of the engendering of personifications on whom these emotions can be vented. The silent God of Lamentations, as much as the abused mother and the self-justifying son, are such personifications.[59]

In what I have tried to suggest in this essay, those responsible for the composition and transmission of the continuous pesharim in particular and some or many of their readers seem to have lost the paternity of metanarrative, the maternity of place, and the possibility of tolerance of the other as friend. The pesharim seem to reflect an attempt to provide for the restitution of much that has been lost, even if the loss is only actual in an unconscious psychological manner. That restitution comes through three overlapping devices, perhaps better understood as exegetical strategies.

First, the disjuncture with the normative story of Israel is compensated for when the voice of the silent God is heard afresh as the text in which it is embodied is rehearsed as if properly heard for the first time by the Teacher of Righteousness or his substitute. This is a quasi-prophetic activity, but it is also the wise man at work; after all, the true interpreter of dreams can both retell the dream and decode its meaning. The guarantee of the correctness of the Teacher's exegesis is found both internally in the subtlety of the exegetical devices that can be discerned in his work, but also externally in the experience of the divine presence in the community's worship.

Second, the displacement from the center of cultic activity in Jerusalem is compensated for by the eschatological aspiration for the restoration of the purity of the temple and the city of the sanctuary, an aspiration that is guaranteed by the promises of unfulfilled prophetic Scriptures. This is mirrored too in the present in the cultic activities and experiences of the worshiping community, whether at Qumran or elsewhere, when the community can think of itself as the מקדש אדם, the human anticipation of the Edenic holy of holies.[60]

Third, the self-understanding that combines a lack of priestly hierarchy and

---

59. Pyper, *Unsuitable Book*, 101.

60. See G. J. Brooke, "Miqdash Adam, Eden and the Qumran Community," in *Gemeinde ohne Tempel–Community without Temple: Zur Substituierung und Transformation des Jerusalemer Tempels und seines Kults im Alten Testament, antiken Judentum und frühen Christentum* (ed. B. Ego, A. Lange, and P. Pilhofer; WUNT 118; Tübingen: Mohr Siebeck, 1999), 285–301.

the security of fictive kinship groups with the proclamation of the need to endure suffering, persecution, and several kinds of self-abasement is compensated for by the strength of the exegesis that discloses the power of a finely balanced mind that rests secure in the revelation of the mysteries of God's servants the prophets for the community initiates, initiates whose self-understanding is also a desire to stand under the authority of the prophetic texts as they endorse the end of idolatry.

Lastly, if the psychological perspective of coping with the silent God, the abused mother, and self-justification are not an adequate profiling triad, then juxtaposition with the insights from the psychology of religion as applied to various modern groups of fundamentalists allows one to perceive that much in the interpretative activity of the sectarian compositions is not just about the construction of identity but more particularly about the preservation or reconstruction of self-esteem in a world where political turmoil and religious turmoil constantly highlight the anxiety of loss and the fear of death.

The pesharim are fascinating literary compositions, with a mind of their own.

ELEVEN

Types of Historiography
in the Qumran Scrolls

1. Introduction

The splendid two-volume *Encyclopedia of the Dead Sea Scrolls* was published in 2000.[1] Given that the library collected together in the eleven caves at and near Qumran is more or less contemporary with the production of 1 and 2 Maccabees, perhaps it might come as some surprise that there is no entry on history writing or historiography in the *Encyclopedia*, though the index refers to four places where the periodization of history is discussed, and there is one short article on the small fragment of 4Q248 known as Acts of a Greek King or now as Historical Text A. Intriguingly, the situation has changed somewhat in the last few years with the renaming of several fragmentary compositions, but the principal purpose of this short study is to present in summary form something of the variety of historiographies to be found in the approximately nine hundred manuscripts that have been recovered from the eleven caves at or near Qumran and so to make up for the lack of an entry on the topic in the *Encyclopedia*. In other words, it is not that the Qumran library is bereft of historical works—and certainly it is not lacking in various historical perspectives—but that the kind of sequential narration of events such as is found in the books of Kings and Chronicles and also in 1 and 2 Maccabees does not seem to be the way that historiography is represented in the collection.

The Index volume of Discoveries in the Judaean Desert has a section that presents a taxonomy by Armin Lange and Ulrike Mittmann-Richert of the genres of the compositions found in the Qumran library.[2] One of the sections is entitled "Historical Texts and Tales," and Lange and Mittmann-Richert conclude that "the classical Greek and modern concepts of historiography do not apply to this

---

1. L. H. Schiffman and J. C. VanderKam, eds., *Encyclopedia of the Dead Sea Scrolls* (2 vols.; New York: Oxford University Press, 2000).

2. A. Lange and U. Mittmann-Richert, "Annotated List of the Texts from the Judaean Desert Classified," in *The Texts from the Judaean Desert: Indices and an Introduction to the Discoveries in the Judaean Desert Series* (ed. E. Tov; DJD 39; Oxford: Clarendon, 2002), 115–64, here 120.

type of literature. At Qumran, only a few fragments were found that appear to recall history by mentioning historical personae and their deeds by name (e.g. 4Q332–333, 4Q468e) and are in some way comparable to Greek historiography." But rather than let the categories of either Greek or modern historiography control the agenda of the analysis of this Jewish corpus, this study attempts to lay out some of the possible types of narration, recollection, and use of the past in the corpus. Most descriptions of the scrolls from Qumran divide them into three groups: biblical, sectarian, and nonbiblical nonsectarian compositions. This division will serve us adequately in this analysis as some of the range of relevant material is described and set out and the reasons for the Qumran preference for looking at the past in ways other than in classical narrative sequences is briefly considered.

2. THE SCRIPTURES

Although in a strict sense the label "biblical" is anachronistic for the period of the scrolls,[3] it is evident that nearly every composition that is to be found in later rabbinic Bibles, as well as some others,[4] had a place in the Qumran library and so may be deemed to have had some kind of authority there. However, it is also obvious that not every biblical book carried equal weight; like most religious groups, the movement, part of which eventually settled at Qumran and was responsible for the deposits of manuscripts in the caves, in effect operated with what we can identify after the event as a kind of canon within the canon.[5] It is readily apparent that the books of Genesis, Deuteronomy, Isaiah, and the Psalms were the most widely used: more copies of these books survive than of most other books, and they are most widely referred to explicitly, alluded to implicitly, and used as models for other literary works. Thus, it is certainly the case that, at least from Gen 6 onward the primeval history and the narrative of the subsequent events leading up to the crossing of the Jordan and entry into the land were well known. It was this period to which the Qumran scriptural scholars looked back rather than the periods of the judges and monarchy.

Indeed it is now widely recognized that the books now to be found in the

---

3. See, e.g., E. Ulrich, *The Dead Sea Scrolls and the Origins of the Bible* (Studies in the Dead Sea Scrolls and Related Literature; Grand Rapids: Eerdmans, 1999), esp. 17–33.

4. Such as the book of Jubilees, the Apocryphon of Joshua, and, possibly for some or at some stage, some of the sections of the Enoch corpus. On the issue of whether Jubilees is quoted as an authority in CD 16:3–4, see D. Dimant, "Two 'Scientific' Fictions: The So-Called Book of Noah and the Alleged Quotation of Jubilees in CD 16:3–4," in *Studies in the Hebrew Bible, Qumran, and the Septuagint Presented to Eugene Ulrich* (ed. P. W. Flint, E. Tov, and J. C. VanderKam; VTSup 101; Leiden: Brill, 2006), 230–49, esp. 242–48.

5. See G. J. Brooke, "'The Canon within the Canon' at Qumran and in the New Testament," in *The Scrolls and the Scriptures: Qumran Fifty Years After* (ed. S. E. Porter and C. A. Evans; JSPSup 26; Roehampton Institute London Papers 3; Sheffield: Sheffield Academic Press, 1997), 242–66.

collection of former prophets together with the books of Chronicles are intriguingly relatively poorly represented in the Qumran collection, especially Kings and Chronicles. For the books of Kings there appear to be three manuscripts, one from each of Caves 4, 5, and 6. 4QKings contains parts of 1 Kgs 7–8;[6] 5QKings, part of 1 Kgs 1,[7] and 6QKings, portions of 1 Kgs 3; 12; 22; and 2 Kgs 5–10.[8]

For the books of Chronicles the situation is even starker.[9] One manuscript (4Q118) has been labeled as a copy of Chronicles.[10] It contains remains of two columns of writing; the contents of the second correspond to 2 Chr 28:27–29:3, but the contents of the first have no parallel in Chronicles, Kings, or what may be reconstructed as a Hebrew text based on the Greek translation of Chronicles. It is thus unlikely that 4Q118 is a straightforward copy of the books of Chronicles. Alexander Rofé has wondered whether in fact, like 4Q382 (Paraphrase of Kings), 4Q118 contains "a homiletical revision of the book of Kings that included a psalm of entreaty similar to the one attributed to Hezekiah in Isa 38:9–20."[11]

Beyond the circumstances of the accidents of preservation, what explanations might be offered for this lack of concern for Chronicles at Qumran and in its parent movement? A general answer might consider that the type of chronicling of events that is to be found in Chronicles was of little concern to these Jews. A more specific answer should consider that there was a deliberate avoidance of such historiography. "The scarcity of Chronicles at Qumran could be by chance, with several other manuscripts being lost. More likely, however, the small number of scrolls is by design, since Chronicles has a strong focus on Jerusalem and the Temple, from which the Qumran community had removed itself."[12] The reasons for such avoidance might be very complicated but, in addition to its overt empha-

---

6. See J. Trebolle Barrera, "4QKings," in *Qumran Cave 4.IX: Deuteronomy, Joshua, Judges, Kings* (ed. E. Ulrich and F. M. Cross; DJD 14; Oxford: Clarendon, 1995), 171–83. Trebolle Barrera speculates that it might be possible to suppose that the few remaining fragments come from a scroll of about 160 columns (20 metres) which contained Joshua, Judges, 1–2 Samuel, and 1–2 Kings.

7. See J. T. Milik, "I Rois," in *Les "Petites Grottes" de Qumrân: Explorations de la falaise, les grottes 2Q, 3Q, 5Q, 6Q, 7Q à 10Q, Le rouleau de cuivre* (ed. M. Baillet, J. T. Milik, and R. de Vaux; 2 vols.; DJD 3; Oxford: Clarendon, 1962), 1:171–72.

8. See M. Baillet, "Livres des Rois," in Baillet et al., *Les "Petites Grottes" de Qumrân* (DJD 3), 1: 107–12.

9. J. Trebolle Barrera ("Chronicles, First and Second Books of," in Schiffman and VanderKam, *Encyclopedia of the Dead Sea Scrolls*, 1: 129) offers a concise note on Chronicles in the Dead Sea Scrolls but with little explanation or interpretation.

10. See J. Trebolle Barrera, "4QChr," in *Qumran Cave 4.XI: Psalms to Chronicles* (ed. E. Ulrich et al.; DJD 16; Oxford: Clarendon, 2000), 295–97.

11. A. Rofé, "'No *Ephod* or *Teraphim'—oude hierateias oude dēlōn*: Hosea 3:4 in the LXX and in the Paraphrases of Chronicles and the *Damascus Document*," in *Sefer Moshe: The Moshe Weinfeld Jubilee Volume. Studies in the Bible and the Ancient Near East, Qumran, and Post-Biblical Judaism* (ed. C. Cohen, A. Hurvitz, and S. M. Paul; Winona Lake, Ind.; Eisenbrauns, 2004), 135–49, here 143 n. 22.

12. J. C. VanderKam and P. W. Flint, *The Meaning of the Dead Sea Scrolls: Their Signifi-*

sis on Jerusalem and the Temple, could include the real likelihood that works like Chronicles were being adopted and promoted by the Hasmonean priest-kings, toward whose outlook the majority of those at Qumran seem to have had considerable antagonism. More particularly, the concern in Chronicles for a chastened Davidic model of kingship might have proved an attractive model and tradition to support the Hasmonean rulers; there is nothing in the sectarian compositions at Qumran to suggest that the members of the community supported a reestablished monarchy in any form in the premessianic era. Thus, the absence of obvious manuscript copies of the books of Chronicles from the Qumran library can be understood in two ways.[13] On the one hand, the community that preserved the scrolls may well have been antipathetic to the probable Hasmonean claims to be heirs to the Davidic tradition.[14] On the other, over against Hasmonean Davidic aspirations, the community kept silent about the Davidic identification of its Messiah of Israel until the end of the first century B.C.E.

This view is endorsed by the eloquent silence of the absence of both 1 and 2 Maccabees from the collections in the Qumran caves. Historiography as a project in terms of the books of Kings or the books of Chronicles and as imitated in 1 Maccabees seems to have become a court project in the late second or early first centuries B.C.E.[15] As such, not only was such history writing seen as endorsing current rulers, but also it was in turn endorsed by them as the Hasmonean project of constructing a canon progressed.[16]

This might have left its mark also on the book of Joshua. Probably only two

---

cance for Understanding the Bible, Judaism, Jesus, and Christianity (San Francisco: HarperSanFrancisco, 2002), 118.

13. G. J. Brooke, "Between Authority and Canon: The Significance of Reworking the Bible for Understanding the Canonical Process," in *Reworking the Bible: Apocryphal and Related Texts at Qumran. Proceedings of a Joint Symposium by the Orion Center for the Study of the Dead Sea Scrolls and Associated Literature and the Hebrew University Institute for Advanced Studies Research Group on Qumran, 17–17 January, 2002* (ed. E. G. Chazon et al.; STDJ 58; Leiden: Brill, 2005), 85–104, here 88–89.

14. Cf. 1 Macc 2:57, which can be read as shifting the Davidic inheritance to the Hasmonean dynasty.See J. Goldstein, *1 Maccabees: A New Translation with Introduction and Commentary* (AB 41; New York: Doubleday, 1976), 240.

15. It is important to acknowledge that in several compositions found in the Qumran library that date to the second century B.C.E. such as the Temple Scroll, the Apocryphon of Joshua, and even the War Scroll (1QM 2:6–8:10), the influence of Chronicles is readily apparent; but in the first century that influence seems to have waned or even disappeared. For Chronicles in the Temple Scroll, see Y. Yadin, "Introduction," in idem, *The Temple Scroll* (3 vols.; Institute of Archaeology of the Hebrew University of Jerusalem; Shrine of the Book; Jerusalem: Israel Exploration Society, 1977–83), 1:82–83; Y. Thorion, "Die Sprache der Tempelrolle und die Chronikbücher," RevQ 11 (1982–84): 423–28; D. D. Swanson, "The Use of Chronicles in 11QT: Aspects of a Relationship," in *The Dead Sea Scrolls: Forty Years of Research* (ed. D. Dimant and U. Rappaport; STDJ 10; Leiden: Brill; Jerusalem: Magnes, 1992), 290–98; idem, *The Temple Scroll and the Bible: The Methodology of 11QT* (STDJ 14; Leiden: Brill, 1995).

16. For more detail on these possibilities, see G. J. Brooke, "The Books of Chronicles and

copies of the book survive from the Qumran caves[17] and 4QJosh[a] (4Q47) seems to contain an earlier form of the story of the occupation of the land than the other versions. The manuscript presents the sacrifice and reading of the Law (MT Josh 8) as preceding Josh 5, its logical place, so that the commands of Moses are obeyed as swiftly as possible. The version of the story in the MT in which the sacrifice and reading of the Law occur only after several military operations seems to have necessitated the adjustment of the command in Deut 27 so that the delay is accounted for suitably.[18] This adjustment could have taken place in the time of John Hyrcanus or shortly thereafter as a way of presenting a view of history strongly opposed to Samaritan perspectives. Thus, in these and other ways the scriptural scrolls preserved at Qumran or largely missing from the collection there disclose something of the views of Israel's history that were important to those who lived there in the closing years of the Second Temple period.

Although I have thus far highlighted the minimal presence in the predominantly first-century Qumran library of some of the historical books found in the Jewish Scriptures and have offered some explanations for this, it is important also to acknowledge that Judges and Samuel are indeed attested there as well. There are four fragmentary manuscripts of Judges.[19] There are also four copies of Samuel,[20] one of which is relatively well preserved. Parts of Nathan's oracle in 2 Sam 7 are also extensively cited in 4Q174. The suggestion here is not that these historical writings were not known and used by the sectarians at Qum-

the Scrolls from Qumran," in *Reflection and Refraction: Studies in Biblical Historiography in Honour of A. Graeme Auld* (ed. R. Rezetko et al.; VTSup 113; Leiden, Brill, 2007), 35–48.

17. See E. Ulrich, "4QJosh[a]," in Ulrich et al., *Qumran Cave 4.IX* (DJD 14), 143–52; and, in the same volume, E. Tov, "4QJosh[b]," 153–60. For the remains of possibly a third copy of Joshua from Qumran Cave 4, with parts of Josh 1–2, see J. H. Charlesworth, "X Joshua," in *Miscellaneous Texts from the Judaean Desert* (ed. J. C. VanderKam and M. Brady; DJD 38; Oxford: Clarendon, 2000), 231–39.

18. Eugene Ulrich proposes a three-stage development: an early form of the text represented by 4QJosh[a] and Josephus, a secondary Samaritan adaptation of Deut 27:4 as a specific claim, and, third, the sequence as present in the MT and the LXX ("4QJosh[a]," 146). Ulrich's view is attractive but has been questioned and challenged, not least by M. N. van der Meer, *Formation and Reformulation: The Redaction of the Book of Joshua in the Light of the Oldest Textual Witnesses* (VTSup 102; Leiden: Brill, 2004).

19. 1QJudg contains parts of Judg 6–9: D. Barthélemy, "Juges," in *Qumran Cave I* (ed. D. Barthélemy and J. T. Milik; DJD 1; Oxford, Clarendon, 1955), 62–64; see also the further identifications of fragments by É. Puech, "Les manuscrits 4QJuges[c] (=4Q50[a]) et 1QJuges (=1Q6)," in Flint et al., *Studies in the Hebrew Bible, Qumran, and the Septuagint*, 184–200. 4QJudg[a] contains parts of Judg 6: see J. Trebolle Barrera, "4QJudg[a]," in Ulrich et al., *Qumran Cave 4.IX* (DJD 14), 161–64. 4QJudg[b] contains parts of Judg 19 and 21: J. Trebolle Barrera, "4QJudg[b]," in Ulrich et al., *Qumran Cave 4.IX* (DJD 14), 165–69. 4QJudg[c] contains part of Judg 1: Puech, "Les manuscrits 4QJuges[c] (= 4Q50[a]) et 1QJuges (=1Q6)," 184–87.

20. 1QSam contains part of 1Sam 18:17–18; 2 Sam 20:6–10; 23:9–12: Barthélemy, "Juges," 64–65. For 4QSam[a-c], see F. M. Cross et al., *Qumran Cave 4.XII: 1–2 Samuel* (DJD 17; Oxford: Clarendon, 2005).

ran and in the wider movement of which they were a part. Rather, the relative paucity of these scriptural history books seems to be indicative of two things: on the one hand, the views of history embraced and endorsed at Qumran seem to have been other than those evidenced most especially in the books of Kings and the books of Chronicles and, on the other hand, in some cases, it seems as if among the reasons for alternative historiographies were theological, social, and political factors that require us to handle the extant evidence with considerable sensitivity.

3. SECTARIAN HISTORIOGRAPHY

A large amount of what is found in the Qumran library, in both the sectarian compositions and the nonscriptural nonsectarian ones, seems to be based in one way or another on earlier authoritative texts, most of which can now be found in the rabbinic Bible.[21] Nevertheless, when it comes to reflecting on and writing up the past, in the sectarian compositions historiography takes a somewhat different path and is presented not as in some way continuous with the long narrative sequences of the Jewish Scriptures but in at least three overlapping and complementary forms.

3.1. HISTORY WRITING AS EXHORTATION

In the first part of the Damascus Document, often labeled the Admonition, there is more than one type of use of history. However, most overtly, in the first two columns of CD A, there are three exhortations whose overall purpose is to encourage and sustain a particular kind of behavior based on events and figures of the past; history is recounted not for its own sake but to enhance and maintain social cohesion and identity within the movement. In the third exhortation (CD 2:14–4:12.) these past events are referred to largely in the order of the scriptural accounts: the fall of the Watchers, Noah, Abraham, the sons of Jacob, and Moses. The shortcomings of David are mentioned subsequently (CD 5:2–6). These allusions to people and events of the past are a deliberately selected reading of history in order to support a particular ideological position that has both a sense of group identity, in priests and Levites, and also an ethical imperative, to avoid the three nets of Belial to which everyone, not least Israelites, have often succumbed, both in the period before the Law was given and afterwards.

Sensitive readings of the kind of historiographical purposes present in the Damascus Document have been offered by both Albert I. Baumgarten[22]

---

21. For an attempt at describing the Qumran library in those terms, see G. J. Brooke, "The Dead Sea Scrolls," in *The Biblical World* (ed. J. Barton; 2 vols.; London: Routledge, 2002), 1:250–69.

22. A. I. Baumgarten, "The Perception of the Past in the Damascus Document," in *The Damascus Document: A Centennial of Discovery. Proceedings of the Third International Sym-*

and Maxine Grossman.[23] Baumgarten considers the historical concerns of the Damascus Document to be largely or exclusively those of a movement presenting and reflecting on its own past. He thus identifies several ways in which the composition reflects on the past by constructing identity, through the explicit description of community boundary markers (4Q266 2 i 19–20 = CD 1:16; 4Q267 lines 31–32 = CD 20:25), and the restriction on loyalties, even to one's relatives, other than to the movement. Baumgarten's attention to the community's own history is justified by the fact that one of the manuscript copies of the Damascus Document from Cave 4 (4Q266 1 a–b) contains the remnants of a preamble to the composition whose concerns seem to be some of the fundamental principles on which the movement's life is based, not least God's mighty wonders and the voice of Moses.[24] The movement does not seem concerned to link itself with the ideology of Israel in the times of the kings or in the early part of the postexilic period; rather, it traces its identity first to the formative moments of Israel itself. Thus, it is important to recognize that the historiographical priority within the concern to construct the movement's identity is Moses and the pre-Mosaic period, not subsequent circumstances. The mention of David in CD 5 is a negative exception that proves the rule.

Grossman's reading of the Damascus Document is a bold attempt to suggest how its various parts could have been read by different audiences. For her the identity issues surround the themes of priesthood and exile through which the composition can be read as asserting the role of the community as the true remnant of Israel, indeed as Israel itself. The authors or editors of the composition are perceived as reading history as a matter of transgression against God, often repeated, rather than as a series of events that demand multiple interpretations in their own right. Thus, the Damascus Document limits its attention to any past event that does not fit the theme. Grossman's presentation of multiple readers does not inhibit the conclusion that the past is handled highly selectively and largely for exhortatory purposes. This ideological and thematic approach to past events explains why it is difficult to construct the actual history of the movement from the text, as is evident by the number of scholarly arguments about how that might be done.[25]

---

posium of the Orion Center for the Study of the Dead Sea Scrolls and Associated Literature, 4–8 February, 1998 (ed. J. M. Baumgarten, E. G. Chazon, and A. Pinnick; STDJ 34; Leiden, Brill, 2000), 1–15.

23. M. L. Grossman, Reading for History in the Damascus Document: A Methodological Study (STDJ 45; Leiden: Brill, 2002).

24. The fragment has some parallels also in 4Q267; for the text see J. M. Baumgarten, ed., Qumran Cave 4.XII: The Damascus Document (4Q266–273) (DJD 18; Oxford: Clarendon, 1996), 32.

25. As is pointed out helpfully by C. Hempel, The Damascus Texts (CQS 1; Sheffield: Sheffield Academic Press, 2000), 54–70.

3.2. Prophesied History

Most modern attempts at writing a history of the Qumran community have relied heavily on the so-called pesharim, the biblical commentaries, for their information.[26] A minority of scholars have argued that except for a few generalities this is largely inappropriate:[27] the pesharim are not an overt form of history writing, are not outlines of past events, recent or otherwise. As the varieties of even the consensus view of the history of the Qumran community and its predecessors attest, little can be securely known about the circumstances of the historical origins and development of the movement from the pesharim. More fruitful for historical reconstruction might be such compositions such as MMT,[28] when read carefully with social as well as historical questions in mind.

But despite their reluctance to tell us about the origins and development of the Essene movement, the pesharim may indeed be considered to be a type of historiography. Together with various prophetic texts proper, there is a considerable group of supposedly unfulfilled scriptural blessings, curses, oracles, and promises, many of which are cited explicitly and given some form of interpretation, commonly as pesher. What is taking place historiographically in these interpretative compositions? The Pesher Habakkuk (1QpHab 6:12–7:8) declares that the prophets did not understand what was revealed to them, thinking it commonly to be about the events of their own times and God's purposes for them. But, for the Qumran commentators, the real meaning of the oracles of old is now made plain by the contemporary interpreter, the validity of whose interpretation is discernible in his more than adequate use of a variety of hermeneutical methods as keys to unlocking the present meaning of past utterances. The events of the past referred to in the words of the prophets may still convey some typological significance, as the reuse of much of their phraseology in the pesher proper suggests, but the primary referent of such oracles is present circumstances. In addition to the so-called continuous pesharim, which are running commentaries on Isaiah and some of the Twelve, there are sections in compositions such as the Damascus

---

26. See, e.g., H. Stegemann, *Die Enstehung der Qumrangemeinde* (Bonn: Rheinische Friedrich-Wilhelms-Universität, 1971). The most recent attempt to assert that the primary historical importance of the pesharim is for the construction of the history of the community is that by J. H. Charlesworth, *The Pesharim and Qumran History: Chaos or Consensus?* (Grand Rapids: Eerdmans, 2002).

27. E.g., G. J. Brooke, "The Pesharim and the Origin of the Dead Sea Scrolls," in *Methods of Investigation of the Dead Sea Scrolls and the Khirbet Qumran Site: Present Realities and Future Prospects* (ed. M. O. Wise et al.; Annals of the New York Academy of Sciences 722; New York: New York Academy of Sciences, 1994), 339–54.

28. See, e.g., F. García Martínez, "4QMMT in a Qumran Context," and H. Eshel, "4QMMT and the History of the Hasmonean Period," in *Reading 4QMMT: New Perspectives on Law and History* (ed. J. Kampen and M. Bernstein; SBLSymS 2; Atlanta: Scholars Press, 1996), 15–27 and 53–65, respectively.

Document that can also be included in this category, such as the interpretation of Amos 9:11 and Num 24:17 in CD 7:16–21.

Pesher is largely about writing an analysis from prophetic tradition about present circumstances; unfulfilled past revelation is interpreted atomistically to address and describe the present.[29] The past is looked to for the present, not past events but past unfulfilled prophecies. Since most history writing is concerned to inform the present by consideration of the past, the pesharim can justifiably be seen as a form of historiography.

3.3. PERIODIZED HISTORY

In the sectarian compositions, periodized history seems to take two forms. First, there are those compositions in which the scheme of history seems to be based principally in the presentation of the whole of world history. The concern of the author is usually to place himself at the appropriate moment on a time line derived from such a schematization. Much of this approach is taken over from what is presented in the historical schemes of apocalyptic literature, such as the Apocalypse of Weeks and the schemes of world empires of Daniel, or the jubilee schemes of the quasi-apocalyptic book of Jubilees. In the Qumran sectarian literature, we have already the possible reading of the Damascus Document in this way, as the Teacher is described as arising after 410 years, exercising a ministry of unstated length that is followed by a period of forty more years before the end: this can be reconstructed into a schematic pattern of 490 years from the time of the exile until the end, a grand jubilee period of ten sets of jubilee years. In all these cases, the pattern seems to be all-important with key events taking place at significant points in the cycle in the scheme, rather than necessarily at times fixed in some objective fashion.

Two further sectarian compositions come readily to mind as overtly schematic in this way. In Ages of Creation (4Q180),[30] history is divided into a sequence of periods based on the divine ordering of affairs: "before he created them, he set up their activities." It seems as if each period has ten generations, and special attention is given at the start to the twenty generations from Adam to Abraham. However, it is not just the periodization that is important; certain events are named, such as the sin of the angels, the change of Abram's name, the visit of the three angels, and the destruction of Sodom and Gomorrah, while other events are omitted. Thus, there is more to the composition than schematization alone, though the schematization predominates. In 11QMelchizedek, which J. T. Milik

---

29. Put well by J. Jokiranta, "Pesharim: A Mirror of Self-Understanding," in *Reading the Present in the Qumran Library: The Perception of the Contemporary by Means of Scriptural Interpretations* (ed. K. De Troyer and A. Lange; SBLSymS 30; Atlanta: Society of Biblical Literature, 2005), 23–34.

30. The most thorough analysis of this composition is that by D. Dimant, "The 'Pesher on the Periods' (4Q180) and 4Q181," *IOS* 9 (1979): 77–102.

attempted to describe as a further copy of the Ages of Creation,[31] there is reference to a jubilee scheme: "And this thing will occur in the first week of the Jubilee
that follows the nine Jubilees. And the Day of Atonement is the end of the tenth
Jubilee, when all the Sons of Light and the men of the lot of Melchizedek will be
atoned for."[32] It seems as if there are ten jubilee periods (or weeks), after which
there is an eleventh period of eschatological fulfillment. This pattern seems to
echo that of the Apocalypse of Weeks (1 En. 93:3–10; 91:1–17) and to be echoed in
turn in the schematic pattern of eleven sevens in the Lukan genealogy.[33] History
can be summed up in ten units, with the beginning or end of the eleventh as a
new start.

A second kind of periodization is concerned not so much with the whole of
world history but rather with how sequences of events can be patterned against
the round represented in the annual calendar or set of annual calendars, which
produce particular cyclical patternings of human affairs. There are very few references by name to actual historical figures from the time of the scrolls, so when
they are mentioned, they demand comment. Thus, in the scheme of things it
seems that the events surrounding the actual historical figures of Salome Alexandra and Aemelius Scaurus are juxtaposed not with Jewish or Roman history writ
large but with calendrical matters inasmuch as these are reflected in the cycles
of priestly courses. It is intriguing to note that, whereas for a generation scholars have known of these historical references apparently as part of texts listing
priestly courses, the fragments containing these historical allusions have recently
been relabeled and are now presented as part of Historical Text C (4Q331), Historical Text D (4Q332), and Historical Text E (4Q333).[34] This reclassification
seems to reflect an assumption that mention of actual historical figures makes
a composition into some kind of work of history. But that does not seem to be a
strong reason for determining genre. Given the calendrical character of the lists
of priestly courses that form the framework of the content of the fragments in all
three manuscripts, it seems better to suppose that here periodization drives the
presentation and the mention of particular historical events and circumstances
provides these lists of priestly courses and their times of service with an annalistic component.

31. J. T. Milik, "Milkî-sedeq et Milkî-reša' dans les anciens écrits juifs et chrétiens," *JJS*
23 (1972): 95–114.

32. See F. García Martínez, E. J. C. Tigchelaar, and A. S. van der Woude, eds., *Qumran
Cave 11.II: 11Q2–18, 11Q20–31* (DJD 23; Oxford, Clarendon, 1998), 221–41.

33. See R. J. Bauckham, *Jude and the Relatives of Jesus in the Early Church* (Edinburgh:
T. & T. Clark, 1990), 315–73.

34. J. A. Fitzmyer, "4QHistorical Text C, 4QHistorical Text D and 4QHistorical Text E,"
in *Qumran Cave 4.XXVI: Cryptic Texts* (ed. S. J. Pfann); and *Miscellanea, Part 1* (ed. P. S.
Alexander, in consultation with J. C. VanderKam and M. Brady; DJD 36; Oxford: Clarendon,
2000), 275–89.

Part of another composition, Commentary on Genesis A,[35] might best belong in this category too. The work seems to be drawn from a variety of sources, but the opening sections, which rework parts of the primeval history, do so by fitting its events to certain significant calendrical moments. Thus, the flood is narrated so as to last for exactly one year of 364 days, and the key events during that year scrupulously avoid happening on the Sabbath. Abram's arrival in the land is also related in the context of suitable chronological calculations.[36]

There seems to be only very little on offer in the sectarian scrolls that might allow us to determine whether the periodization of history should be viewed principally in linear terms from beginning to end, perhaps a utopian end, or more in restorative terms in which ultimately the goal of history is the reclamation of Eden.[37] The slender role given to Gen 1–3, particularly Adam and Eden,[38] in any sectarian text may suggest that schematization is largely linear in intent, but the cyclical nature of the priestly courses and of the calendar in general might suggest rather that the Qumran view of the periodization of history was a combination of both linear and cyclical approaches. Whatever the case, the belief seems to have been that God had ordered all things before creation and all things were coming round shortly to the end.[39] It was this sense of the order of time that was

---

35. G. J. Brooke, "4QCommentary on Genesis A," in *Qumran Cave 4.XVII: Parabiblical Texts, Part 3* (ed. G. J. Brooke et al., in consultation with J. C. VanderKam; DJD 22; Oxford: Clarendon, 1996), 185–207.

36. These calendrical and chronological calculations have led Moshe Bernstein to argue that the principal feature of the exegesis represented in 4Q252 is attention to problems in the plain meaning of the text: Bernstein, "4Q252: From Re-Written Bible to Biblical Commentary," *JJS* 45 (1994): 1–27; idem, "4Q252: Method and Context, Genre and Sources," *JQR* 85 (1994–95): 61–79.

37. On the possibilities of both perspectives, at least in the case of messianism, see the insightful comments reflecting the work of Gershom Scholem of L. H. Schiffman, *The Eschatological Community of the Dead Sea Scrolls: A Study of the Rule of the Congregation* (SBLMS 38; Atlanta: Scholars Press, 1989), 1–10.

38. A point observed, e.g., by M. E. Stone, "The Axis of History at Qumran," in *Pseudepigraphic Perspectives: The Apocrypha and Pseudepigrapha in Light of the Dead Sea Scrolls. Proceedings of the International Symposium of the Orion Center for the Study of the Dead Sea Scrolls and Associated Literature, 12–14 January 1997* (ed. E. G. Chazon and M. E. Stone; STDJ 31; Leiden: Brill, 1999), 133–49. Stone proposes that the axis of history for the Qumran sectarian lay in the interplay between Enochic and Noachic traditions, largely as these were connected with explaining the origins of evil. What little evidence there is for Eden in the sectarian and other scrolls is summed up neatly by E. J. C. Tigchelaar, "Eden and Paradise: The Garden Motif in Some Early Jewish Texts (1 Enoch and Other Texts Found at Qumran)," in *Paradise Interpreted: Representations of Biblical Paradise in Judaism and Christianity* (ed. G. P. Luttikhuizen; TBN 2; Leiden: Brill, 1999), 37–62.

39. The perspective of the periods of history explicitly underlies the view of T. S. Beall, "History and Eschatology at Qumran: Messiah," in *Judaism in Late Antiquity, Part 5, The Judaism of Qumran: A Systemic Reading of the Dead Sea Scrolls* (ed. A. J. Avery-Peck, J. Neusner,

the dominant concern of the sectarians, not the sequential narration of long lists of events from the past.

Where does this variety of history writing, or uses of past events and people, with its ambivalence toward the history books that were later to become canonical, come from? It is clear that much of what seems distinctive in the sectarian scrolls has its forebears in earlier Jewish traditions, and many of those are still preserved for us in the Qumran library. We turn briefly to consider something of the range of nonsectarian historiographical options found in the caves.

4. Nonsectarian Historiography

As for the nonbiblical nonsectarian compositions found in the Qumran caves, historiography may be considered to take several forms. Because all these manuscripts are preserved in the Qumran library, it may be taken that in some form or other they retained some kind of significance for those who collected and preserved them. Thus, to a greater or lesser extent, these forms of historiography need to be put together with those that appear to be more explicitly sectarian so as to give a more comprehensive picture of the principal types of historiography that were current at Qumran in the first century B.C.E.

4.1. The Historical Novel

The book of Tobit has been found in both Hebrew and Aramaic in Qumran Cave 4.[40] It is a nonsectarian novel some of whose features may indeed have appealed to readers at Qumran, such as its interest in acts of piety, preserving Jewish identity apart from the gentiles, and the practice of some kind of exorcistic healing. The plot and subplot are given a quasi-historical setting in the reign of Shalmaneser, king of the Assyrians,[41] perhaps because the tale genuinely reflected the lives of some pious Jewish family, but more probably because the author realized that

---

and B. D. Chilton; Handbook of Oriental Studies, Section 1, The Near and Middle East 57; Leiden: Brill, 2001), 125–46, esp. 126–27.

40. For text and comments, see J. A. Fitzmyer, *The Dead Sea Scrolls and Christian Origins* (Studies in the Dead Sea Scrolls and Related Literature; Grand Rapids: Eerdmans, 2000), esp. 131–235. See also I. Fröhlich, "Tobit against the Background of the Dead Sea Scrolls," in *The Book of Tobit: Text, Tradition, Theology. Papers of the First International Conference on the Deuterocanonical Books, Pápa, Hungary, 20–21 May, 2004* (ed. G. G. Xeravits and J. Zsengellér; JSJSup 98; Leiden: Brill, 2005), 55–70. On some of the possible historical readings of Tobit, see S. Goldman, "Tobit and the Jewish Literary Tradition," in *Studies in the Book of Tobit: A Multidisciplinary Approach* (ed. M. Bredin; LSTS 55; London: T&T Clark, 2006), 90–98, esp. 96–98, where Zionist historicist reading is described.

41. On the historical details in the book of Tobit see A. R. Millard, "Judith, Tobit, Ahiqar and History" in *New Heaven and New Earth: Prophecy and the Millennium. Essays in Honour of Anthony Gelston* (ed. P. J. Harland and C. T. R. Hayward; VTSupp 77; Leiden: Brill, 1999), 195–203.

a historical setting could ground the verisimilitude of the tale and therefore make it more effective for didactic purposes.[42]

The so-called Proto-Esther manuscripts may fall into the same category. These seem to contain some version of a story of a Jew in the court of the Persian king Darius, possibly Darius I. Though not as close to the book of Esther as Milik originally tried to argue,[43] the quasi-historical setting again provides verisimilitude to the narrative. The earlier (4Q242–246)[44] and later written forms of the Daniel court tales show that this genre of historical novel persisted in Judaism right through the Second Temple period. In all these instances history, or more properly historiographical contextualization, is not present to assist in the understanding of the past or to show its significance for the author's or audience's present, but it is used to serve an ideological purpose in the narrative.

4.2. REWRITTEN SCRIPTURAL TEXTS

Although for a variety of reasons there is apparently not much interest among those who collected the Qumran library together in the kind of history writing preserved in the books of Kings and Chronicles, scriptural sources are nevertheless used for a variety of historiographical purposes in nonsectarian or presectarian compositions. These purposes become clear in some of the several kinds of rewritten scriptural compositions that have survived at Qumran. Most obviously the rewritten forms of the Pentateuch include sections that cover both the halakhic and narrative issues posed by the various forms of the pentateuchal books. The tendency among rewritten compositions such as the Rewritten Pentateuch manuscripts (4Q365–367)[45] is to harmonize the sources, so that the narratives are made consistent and therefore all the more credible, both as history and as revelation. One wonders what kind of polemical situation was provoking this rewriting activity in the mid-Second Temple period, but it is not difficult to suppose that there were some who were questioning the authority of some or all of the pentateuchal traditions on the basis of inconsistencies.

There were also more specialist kinds of rewriting activity taking place.

---

42. See Lange and Mittmann-Richert, "Annotated List of the Texts," 120. They list Tobit in the category of "Historical Texts and Tales."

43. J. T. Milik, "Les modèles araméens du livre d'Esther dans la Grotte 4 de Qumrân," *RevQ* 15 (1991–92): 321–99; see also S. White Crawford, "Has Esther Been Found at Qumran? 4QProto-Esther and the Esther Corpus," *RevQ* 17 (1996): 307–25.

44. See J. J. Collins and P. W. Flint, "Pseudo-Daniel," in Brooke et al., *Qumran Cave 4.XVII* (DJD 22), 95–164; and, in the same volume, É. Puech, "Apocryphe de Daniel," 165–84. See also Lange and Mittmann-Richert, "Annotated List of the Texts," 120; they list 4Q242 with Tobit as belonging in the group "Historical Texts and Tales," of which the "historical texts were concerned with theological and moral interpretations of historical events and with the aetiological foundation of cultic traditions."

45. See E. Tov and S. White, "Reworked Pentateuch," in *Qumran Cave 4.VIII: Parabiblical Texts, Part 1* (ed. J. C. VanderKam; DJD 13; Oxford: Clarendon, 1994), 187–351.

Pride of place has to be given in the second quarter of the second century B.C.E. to the book of Jubilees, a rewritten form of Genesis and parts of Exodus in which events are fitted to a particular schematic chronology of the history of the world, which is divided into jubilee periods with the exodus taking place in A.M. 2401, exactly 49 jubilee periods from creation. Michel Testuz suggested that the author is proposing that a new era in world history begins with the giving of the Law on Sinai.[46] Such schematization is of a piece with the kind of halakhic position that the text also proclaims, in which the leading figures of the pre-Mosaic period anticipate the giving of the Law in the way they behave.

Together with such a work can be placed the rewritten lives of the prophets in such compositions as the Apocryphon of Jeremiah and Pseudo-Ezekiel, as well as the reworked forms of the Samuel and Elijah-Elisha cycles in such compositions as the Visions of Samuel (4Q160), the Apocryphon of Samuel-Kings (6Q9), the Fragment mentioning Elisha (4Q481a), and the Paraphrase of Kings (4Q382).[47] Characteristic of these compositions is the historicization of narrative elements in the prophetic materials: biographical "facts" and other details are supplied.

4.3. PERIODIZED HISTORY

The book of Jubilees has already been described briefly, but schematic history is presented also in a number of other compositions. Most significantly, the Enochic Apocalypse of Weeks[48] and the use of Jeremiah's seventy years as seventy weeks (70 x 7 years = 490 years) in Dan 9 are examples of the use of periods based on the number seven that were current in some circles of Judaism in the second half of the Second Temple period. A similar historical schema is present in the Apocryphon of Jeremiah. In her survey of how historical sequences assist in the ordering of the fragments of the various manuscripts, Devorah Dimant notes that 4Q390 frg. 1, line 2 has the Israelites delivered into the hands of the priests for seventy years; that 4Q390 frg. 1, lines 7–8 depict a turn for the worse in "the seventh jubilee of the devastation of the land"; and that 4Q387 2 ii 3–4 refers to "the completion of ten jubilees of years."[49] The events of Jeremiah's ministry appear to be fitted into a historical schema well beyond anything offered in any of the scriptural versions of Jeremiah; all the other events described are subservient to this ideological view of history. As mentioned above, the periodized

---

46. M. Testuz, *Les idées religieuses du livre de Jubilés* (Geneva: E. Droz, 1960).

47. For information on all these texts and others that are similar, see G. J. Brooke, "Parabiblical Prophetic Narratives," in *The Dead Sea Scrolls after Fifty Years: A Comprehensive Assessment* (ed. P. W. Flint and J. C. VanderKam; 2 vols.; Leiden: Brill, 1998), 271–301.

48. Perhaps with some boldness, the single fragment assigned to 4Q247 is thought to be a pesher-like commentary on the Apocalypse of Weeks: M. Broshi, "4QPesher on the Apocalypse of Weeks," in Pfann et al., *Qumran Cave 4.XXVI* (DJD 36), 187–91.

49. D. Dimant, ed., *Qumran Cave 4.XXI: Parabiblical Texts, Part 4: Pseudo-Prophetic Texts* (DJD 30; Oxford: Clarendon, 2001), 96–99.

historical perspective of the Damascus Document can be construed along similar lines and several other sectarian compositions seem to share the same or a similar schema.

4.4. HISTORICAL ACTS

In the *Encyclopedia of the Dead Sea Scrolls* one text alone is designated as a historical work of some sort, the so-called Acts of a Greek King. In subsequent contributions to the series of the official publications of the scrolls, Discoveries in the Judaean Desert, a handful of compositions have been renamed and described as historical works.

Historical Text A (formerly Acts of a Greek King) is now described by its editors as "a genuine historical composition which is part of an apocalyptic work."[50] The text in the single remaining fragment shows some affinities with Dan 11 and mentions a number of events that can more or less certainly be linked with Antiochus IV, especially his activities in Egypt before the Maccabean revolt, including the capture of Jerusalem and the looting of the temple. The editors suggest that the author of the text might have seen the desecration of the temple as a kind of historical turning point, after which a new era would begin, but the text is too limited to be certain. Perhaps it was composed in 168 B.C.E. after Antiochus's second invasion of Egypt and so provides an example of a historical work in which the author sees himself at a pivotal moment.

Three very fragmentary manuscripts are labeled Historical Text C, Historical Text D, and Historical Text E because they contain the names of actual historical personages in them. These manuscripts may be nonsectarian, but I have already discussed them briefly under the sectarian categories I have constructed in the previous section, since they seem to overlap with the sectarian priestly concerns of the Mishmarot texts. In addition, because the names are from the first century B.C.E. it seems most likely that the manuscripts are sectarian. The Historical Text C (4Q331)[51] is so called because Yohanan (probably John Hyrcanus I) and Salome Alexandra are explicitly mentioned in it. Ten very small fragments are assigned to the manuscript, which is now entirely distinguished from the calendrical Mishmarot texts with which it had been associated for several years. Little can be said about the historiographical significance of this composition beyond that, in the light of the Mishmarot texts[52] and the hints of the names of priestly course in some fragments, it is likely that the mention of historical personages is entirely secondary to the overall concern in the fragments for the rotation of the priestly courses. To label this text historical is probably inappropriate, but

---

50. M. Broshi and E. Eshel, "4Q Historical Text A," in Pfann et al., *Qumran Cave 4.XXVI* (DJD 36), 192–200, here 192.

51. J. A. Fitzmyer, "4QHistorical Text C, 4QHistorical Text D, and 4QHistorical Text E," in Pfann et al., *Qumran Cave 4.XXVI* (DJD 36), 275–89.

52. 4Q320, 4Q321, 4Q321a, 4Q323, 4Q324, 4Q325, 4Q328, 4Q329, 4Q329a.

further study is clearly required. Likewise, the three small fragments assigned to Historical Text D (4Q332) also contain references to historical persons in association with the particular priestly courses that were officiating in Jerusalem at the time of the events mentioned. Once again it is difficult to ascertain the historiographical significance of the composition. Historical Text E (4Q333) is like Historical Text D. The two small fragments assigned to this manuscript mention the Roman proquaestor of Syria in 65–61 B.C.E., Aemelius Scaurus, in the context of a sequence of priestly courses.

Historical Text F (4Q468e) is extant in one small fragment which appears to contain the end of a column of writing.[53] The last line mentions a certain Potlais, who is identified by the editor with Ptollas mentioned by Josephus in *Ant.* 17.219, a friend of the tetrarch Archelaus. The identification is made probable through mention of the slaughter of a crowd; Archelaus was indeed responsible for such a slaughter shortly after the death of Herod the Great. However, the name Ptollas is sufficiently common, at least outside Palestine, for there to be some doubt about the identification. Historical Text G (4Q468f)[54] consists of one small fragment which mentions "the sons of Gilead" and "Edom," but the editor rightly comments that "the content, genre, author, and date" of the text cannot be determined.

Little emerges from this brief survey; it seems that if a proper name is preserved on a fragment, then the editorial decision has been taken to label the composition "historical," even if there is some evidence that the name may be part of some other kind of composition. Little can be gleaned from these fragments about historiography in the period, whether sectarian or nonsectarian, apart from the fact that the very paucity of the material seems to indicate that those who put together and preserved the Qumran library were not inclined to collect or compose the kinds of writings that modern interpreters would label as "history" writing of some sort. The presectarian materials that the sectarians preserved are not lengthy or detailed narratives of events, either from a political or military angle, as are found in other contexts in antiquity.

4.5. Liturgical History

Some psalms (such as Pss 105–106) and other poetic compositions refer to historical events, often largely in the sequence of the inherited traditions. In a liturgical context, as in exhortatory or admonitory literary and social contexts, this kind of rehearsal of history commonly has to do with providing social identity to a group of worshipers. With regard to some liturgical compositions, a similar kind of historicization can be observed as with some of the rewritten prophetic texts.

---

53. M. Broshi, "4QHistorical Text F," in Pfann et al., *Qumran Cave 4.XXVI* (DJD 36), 406–11.

54. A. Lange, "4QHistorical Text G," in Pfann et al., *Qumran Cave 4.XXVI* (DJD 36), 412–13.

This has long been known from the development of the superscriptions in the Psalms, which increasingly identify them with particular moments in David's life. Similar shifts, however, can be observed in the noncanonical psalms found at Qumran, in which superscriptions play a significant role in associating a particular poem with a particular historical figure.[55] This historical specification reveals that Jewish editors in the Second Temple period were concerned, as opportunity arose, to flesh out some of the characters of the past, displaying them not least as full participants in the human drama whose psychological needs such liturgical poetry often attempts to meet. Those who read or pray such poems are enabled to cope with their own circumstances through identifying with the similar issues as supposedly faced by leading figures of the past.

4.6. Listed History

Past events and people are also represented in lists. These can take several forms. In the Qumran collection three varying kinds of examples can be cited. To begin with, the work of Ben Sira is preserved in the Qumran caves. Ben Sira's list of events in 16:7–10 and his sequence of great personages from the past assembled in his catalogue in praise of famous men (44:1–50:24) are lists more or less in sequence according to biblical chronologies.

In addition, there are genealogical types of lists, such as the very poorly preserved 4Q338,[56] an opisthograph that may have contained a list of the patriarchs.[57] The so-called Prayer of Enosh (4Q369),[58] better understood as part of a composition concerning Israel,[59] contains a genealogy in 1 i 9–10 from Kenan to Enoch based on Gen 5:3–32, but its overall historiographical purpose is not entirely clear. 4Q479 is the very fragmentary and poorly preserved Text Mentioning Descendants of David; what survives does not seem to list them, though David himself is mentioned.[60] Then there is 4Q339, the so-called List of False Prophets, an Aramaic text, and probably therefore nonsectarian, that lists seven or eight false prophets from Balaam onward.[61] Other lists of proper names could

---

55. See, e.g., some of the compositions in 4Q380 and 4Q381: E. M. Schuller, "Non-Canonical Psalms," in *Qumran Cave 4.VI: Poetical and Liturgical Texts, Part 1* (ed. E. Eshel et al.; DJD 11; Oxford: Clarendon, 1998), 75–172.

56. See E. Tov, "4QGenealogical List?" in Pfann et al., *Qumran Cave 4.XXVI* (DJD 36), 290.

57. J. T. Milik, *The Books of Enoch: Aramaic Fragments of Qumrân Cave 4* (Oxford: Clarendon, 1976), 139.

58. H. Attridge and J. Strugnell, "Prayer of Enosh," in *Qumran Cave 4.VIII* (ed. VanderKam; DJD 13), 353–62, see n. 44.

59. See J. Kugel, "4Q369 'Prayer of Enosh' and Ancient Biblical Interpretation," *DSD* 5 (1998): 119–48.

60. E. Larson and L. H. Schiffman, "4QText Mentioning Descendants of David," in Brooke et al., *Qumran Cave 4.XVII* (DJD 22), 297–99.

61. M. Broshi and A. Yardeni, "4QList of False Prophets," in *Qumran Cave 4.XIV: Parabiblical Texts, Part 2* (ed. M. Broshi, in consultation with J. C. VanderKam; DJD 19; Oxford:

well have been scribal exercises of one sort or another: 4QExercitum Calumni C contains a list of names in a writing exercise and is of no historiographical significance.[62]

Third, there are schematized lists or historical reviews whose purpose is not altogether clear. For example, Pseudo-Daniel (4Q243–244)[63] provides a list of events from the patriarchs to the exile as well as some references to events in the Hellenistic era, together with some closing section on the circumstances of the eschatological era. Lists of this kind are close to the presentations of schematized history reviewed above briefly under "Periodized History."

5. Conclusion

The wide range of compositions considered in this short study under the over-arching heading of historiography makes it all the more remarkable that the *Encyclopedia of the Dead Sea Scrolls* has no article dedicated to the topic of history and history writing in the scrolls. However, the lack of such an article might also speak eloquently of how historiography and the Dead Sea Scrolls should be handled, not as a topic in the foreground but as a matter of background. Clearly, the Qumran sectarians and the movement from which they originated had a range of manuscript materials available to them with historical information in various forms. But for the people who preserved these manuscripts the task was not one of preserving or creating long sequential narratives of the past, whether from a political or military perspective, as other earlier and contemporary Jewish historians were concerned with. For the Qumran sectarians, the past was of little or no value in itself; rather, it could be plundered to give the community a better sense of its own identity and to provide meaning to the present by assisting in identifying more precisely God's plans, and more precisely just when God would be bringing the present world order to an end. Theological and eschatological concerns predominate, probably with no small dose of anti-Hellenism. In reality, it has ever been so with most history writing or uses of history—it has been undertaken to illuminate the author's present.

Clarendon, 1995), 77–79. At the end the editors prefer to read "[Hananiah son of Az]ur, [a prophet from Gib]eon" (cf. Jer 28), but E. Qimron and A. Rofé have independently proposed reading the last line as "[Yohanan son of Sim]eon," a reference to John Hyrcanus I (cf. *J.W.* 1.68–69; *Ant.* 13.300): E. Qimron, "On the Interpretation of the List of False Prophets," *Tarbiz* 63 (1994): 273–75; A. Rofé, "The List of False Prophets from Qumran: Two Riddles and Their Solutions," *Ha'aretz,* April 13, 1994, B11.

62. For the edition of this text, see J. Naveh, "4QExercitum Calami C," in Pfann et al., *Qumran Cave 4.XXVI* (DJD 36), 291–93. For more perspectives on this writing exercise, see also G. J. Brooke, "4Q341: An Exercise for Spelling and for Spells?" in *Writing and Ancient Near Eastern Society: Papers in Honour of Alan R. Millard* (ed. P. Bienkowski, C. B. Mee, and E. A. Slater. LHBOTS 426; London: T & T Clark International, 2005), 271–82; P. R. Callaway, "Some Thoughts on Writing Exercise (4Q341)," *Qumran Chronicle* 13/2–4 (2006): 147–51.

63. See Collins and Flint, "Pseudo-Daniel," 140–45.

TWELVE

WHAT MAKES A TEXT HISTORICAL?
ASSUMPTIONS BEHIND THE CLASSIFICATION
OF SOME DEAD SEA SCROLLS

1. INTRODUCTION

A series of fragmentary manuscripts from Qumran's Cave 4 has been designated with the label "Historical Text," sometimes so it seems for want of anything better. But what caused the scholars assigned those compositions to label them in that way? The purpose of this paper in honor of Lester L. Grabbe, one of the leading historians of the Second Temple period, is to explore and expose some of the assumptions behind the classification of some Dead Sea Scrolls as "Historical Texts." This paper is concerned more with genre than with the usefulness of these particular very fragmentary manuscripts for the construction of late Second Temple history.

2. THE MANUSCRIPTS

The label "Historical Text" has been given to the following seven fragmentary manuscripts.

4Q248	Historical Text A
4Q578	Historical Text B
4Q331	papHistorical Text C
4Q332	Historical Text D
4Q333	Historical Text E
4Q468e	Historical Text F
4Q468f	Historical Text G

The use of capital/upper case letters to designate each manuscript indicates that they are all considered to be separate compositions without any overlap with one another. A few words on the content of each set of fragments will be in order.

2.1. 4Q248 Historical Text A[1]

A single fragment with parts of ten lines of writing, penned in an early Herodian formal hand, has been assigned to 4Q248. Before the publication of its principal edition it had been labeled "Acts of a Greek King" or "Pseudo-History," but the principal editors suggest that it "is a genuine historical composition which is part of an apocalyptic work."[2] Line 2 contains mention of Egypt and Greece, line 4 talks of a siege, line 6 describes someone coming to Egypt to sell its land, line 7 mentions the Temple City, line 8 talks of the overthrow of other nations and a return to Egypt, and the content of lines 9 and 10 seems to describe what will happen after the disempowerment of the "holy people," perhaps a return of the children of Israel. Magen Broshi and Esther Eshel suggest that it is most likely that it is Antiochus IV Epiphanes who lies behind the descriptions in the fragment.[3] Daniel R. Schwartz has agreed but offered an alternative interpretation of the details, giving priority to some of the features of 2 Maccabees and reading 4Q248 against that information.[4] Preferring to retain 1 Maccabees as the principal comparative source, Hanan Eshel has also agreed with both the general and the detailed identifications of the principal editors and has elaborated upon them; for him 4Q248 is a remnant of an apocalyptic work.[5]

While the overall identification of the allusions in 4Q248 with the activities of Antiochus IV is very plausible, the fragmentary character of the data leaves many questions incapable of resolution. Whatever the case, it does seem secure to assert that the tenor of the contents of the fragment changes in lines 9–10: "and when the shattering of the power of the ho[ly] people [comes to an end]/ [then shall] all these things [be fulfilled.] The children of[Israel] shall repent [."[6] The phraseology in lines 9–10a is restored by the editors from Dan 12:7. The descriptions of events in those two lines as in the future means that what is represented in the fragment as whole is not a straightforward recitation of events from the past. Indeed, Broshi and E. Eshel have recognized this clearly and start their commentary on the fragment with the astute comment that "4Q248 is a remnant

---

1. M. Broshi and H. Eshel, "4QHistorical Text A," in *Qumran Cave 4.XXVI: Cryptic Texts and Miscellanea, Part 1* (ed. S. J. Pfann et al.; DJD 36; Oxford: Clarendon, 2000), 192–200.

2. Ibid., 192.

3. M. Broshi and E. Eshel, "The Greek King Is Antiochus IV (4QHistorical Text = 4Q248)," *JJS* 48 (1997): 120–29.

4. D. R. Schwartz, *2 Maccabees* (Commentaries on Early Jewish Literature; Berlin: de Gruyter, 2008); idem, "Antiochus IV Epiphanes in Jerusalem," in *Historical Perspectives: From the Hasmoneans to Bar Kokhba in Light of the Dead Sea Scrolls. Proceedings of the Fourth International Symposium of the Orion Center for the Study of the Dead Sea Scrolls and Associated Literature, 27–31 January, 1999* (ed. D. Goodblatt, A. Pinnick, and D. R. Schwartz; STDJ 37; Leiden: Brill, 2001), 45–56.

5. H. Eshel, *The Dead Sea Scrolls and the Hasmonean State* (Studies in the Dead Sea Scrolls and Related Literature; Grand Rapids: Eerdmans, 2008), 14–18.

6. Broshi and E. Eshel, "4QHistorical Text A," 197.

of a larger composition, which resembles Daniel 11."[7] 4Q248 lines 9–10 represent the shift from events described under the guise of *vaticinium ex eventu* to predictive prophecy. It is well known that in Dan 11, vv. 21–39 correspond to what can be reconstructed from other sources about the times of Antiochus IV, but 11:40–45 are predictive of events that never took place. It has even been argued that the author of the War Rule knew that Dan 11:40–45 were unfulfilled and deliberately used those verses at the start of the composition.[8] Broshi and E. Eshel have proposed that the first five lines of 4Q248 are "virtually a pastiche of these Danielic verses" (i.e., Dan 11:21–39).[9] Just as the move in Dan 11 from known history to unfulfilled prediction has enabled scholars to date the book of Daniel after 165 B.C.E., so the similar shift in 4Q248 encourages the principal editors to date its composition to shortly after Antiochus's second invasion of Egypt in 168 B.C.E. On that basis they conclude that "the last editor of the book of Daniel took the phrase found in Dan 12:7 from 4QHistorical Text A."[10]

While many scholars have discerned all kinds of historical details lying behind large sections of the book of Daniel, few nowadays would assert that its overall genre was history, in either an ancient or a modern sense. Whatever the case may be concerning the identification of events in the first few lines of the extant fragment of 4Q248, the overall text does indeed seem to belong closely to the kind of writing exemplified in Dan 11–12. It seems to be an apocalyptic text of some kind. If the fragment's principal editors are correct, it might even be a source for the phraseology of Dan 12:7.

All this implies that 4Q248 should be understood, directly or indirectly, as apocalyptic source material for the book of Daniel. In terms of its literary associations it is closest to other compositions that now survive in the Qumran collection and that seem to lie behind the book of Daniel. These include 4Q242 (Prayer of Nabonidus), 4Q243–4Q245 (Pseudo-Daniel), and 4Q246 (Apocryphon of Daniel). In the *Preliminary Concordance*, 4Q248 was designated as Pseudo-History.[11] One wonders whether the fact that it is in Hebrew rather than Aramaic has caused it to lose its close association with the other Danielic traditions and to become more overtly "historical." In terms of its survival and inclusion in the Qumran collection, it is further evidence for the ongoing influence of the book of Daniel and its literary forebears in the ideological background of the Qumran community and its parent movement. That influence has to be expressed with nuance, since the apocalyptic worldview of Daniel was combined with several

---

7. Ibid.

8. D. Flusser, *Judaism of the Second Temple Period*, vol. 1, *Qumran and Apocalypticism* (Grand Rapids: Eerdmans; Jerusalem: Magnes, 2007), 140–58 (Hebrew original, 1980).

9. Broshi and E. Eshel, "4QHistorical Text A," 199.

10. Ibid.

11. R. E. Brown, J. A. Fitzmyer, W. G. Oxtoby, and J. Teixidor (arranged by H.-P. Richter), *A Preliminary Concordance to the Hebrew and Aramaic Fragments from Qumrân Caves II–X* (5 vols.; Göttingen: Printed Privately, 1988).

other matters, not least Deuteronomistic covenantal theology.[12] Overall, rather than assigning 4Q248 the somewhat ambiguous designation "Historical Text," it would be better labeled as an apocalypse associated with Daniel literature.

2.2. 4Q578 Historical Text B[13]

Jean Starcky had put together several fragments on the same museum plate with the inventory number 320. Émile Puech, with considerable skill, has distinguished the fragments from one another and provided more or less satisfactory identifications for them. One fragment of four lines, with remnants of a final *nun* in a fifth written supralinearly, contains the name *ptlmys* (פתלמיס) once in full, and twice partially. The fragment contains little else apart from a possible reading of *bnw* (בנו) "his son," in line 3. Puech affirms that the understanding of the complete example of the name in line 2 must remain ambiguous: it could be the name of a Ptolemy or the place-name Ptolemais given to Acre in 261 B.C.E. by Ptolemy II.

Puech appropriately considers three options for the suitable generic classification of the fragment.[14] In the first place, he is inclined to rule out that the fragment with its repetition of the proper name three times is a scribal exercise, because in his opinion it is unlikely that a scribal exercise would contain a supralinear correction or addition. Second, he wonders whether the fragment could have contained a list of a genealogical kind. The possible reading of *bnw* (בנו), "his son," in line 3 might encourage this understanding. But Puech's preference is to suggest that the fragment belongs to a document "de type historique."

From dating 4Q578 paleographically to the second half of the second century B.C.E., Puech excludes from consideration references to Ptolemais or to any Ptolemy after about 130 B.C.E. Although all his comments are offered with qualification and great caution, Puech looks to the middle of the second century to offer a plausible explanation for the references in this small fragment.[15]

> Parmi les événements qui ont pu et dû intéresser au premier plan les membres de la Communauté du vivant de la première generation qumranienne et touchant aux premières décennies de la fondation, de 152 à 130 environ, on doit envisager ceux qui so sont produits sous le Prêtre Impie Jonathan (voir 4Q523) et sous Simon son frère. L'on sait par ailleurs l'animosité dont ils furent l'objet de la part du mouvement essénien.

---

12. See J. J. Collins, "The Apocalyptic Worldview of Daniel," in *Enoch and Qumran Origins: New Light on a Forgotten Connection* (ed. G. Boccaccini; Grand Rapids: Eerdmans, 2005), 59–66.

13. É. Puech, "4QComposition historique B," in *Qumrân Grotte 4.XVIII: Textes hébreux (4Q521–4Q528, 4Q576–4Q579)* (ed. É. Puech; DJD 25; Oxford: Clarendon, 1998), 205–8.

14. Ibid., 207–8.

15. Ibid., 207.

Puech goes through various events as represented in 1 Macc 10–13 in which either Ptolemais or a Ptolemy is mentioned. If the final supralinear *nun* might belong to Jonathan (or even to Simon, Tryphon, Beth-Shan, or Sidon), then there are multiple circumstances in the third quarter of the second century B.C.E. that might be reflected in 4Q578. For Puech, attention to those historical circumstances is most likely, given the probable importance of such events for the beginning of the "Essene community."

Puech's task is difficult, but the range and content of his comments disclose his assumptions and predispositions with regard to the consensus about the historical background of the origins of the sectarian movement reflected in the sectarian scrolls. For Puech, as for many others, that movement is both Essene and based at Qumran from the middle of the second century B.C.E. While both elements may require some nuance, namely, that Essenism was a diverse phenomenon from the outset and that Qumran was possibly not occupied until a generation later, the historical reconstruction offers a context for making some kind of sense of the few words extant in the small fragment of 4Q578 and as such also provide a generic tag.

However, although there are a few references to actual historical figures and events in some of the sectarian compositions found in the Qumran library, the absence from that library of what can be clearly labeled as history in Jewish or Hellenistic terms must suggest that more caution is required before history in any strictly defined contemporary form is found in the collection. Too little survives of 4Q578 to award it a generic label: "Historical Text" may be entirely misleading.

2.3. 4Q331 papHistorical Text C[16]

Ten small fragments, in Hasmonean script, are assigned to this manuscript. Joseph Fitzmyer, its principal editor, has noted how its designation has changed over the years: Józef T. Milik associated the manuscript with the Mishmarot texts (4Q320, 4Q321, etc.)[17]; Stephen Reed catalogued it first as "papEssene chronicle[a]"[18] and then as "papHistorical Work[a]."[19] Fitzmyer has noted that the title given to 4Q331–4Q333 is derived from the catalogue list originally published by Emanuel Tov where the three manuscripts are labeled "Historical Work," as in Reed's 1993

---

16. J. A. Fitzmyer, "4QpapHistorical Text C," in Pfann et al., *Qumran Cave 4.XXVI* (DJD 36), 275–80.

17. J. T. Milik, "Le travail d'édition des manuscrits du Désert de Juda," in *Volume de Congrès: Strasbourg 1956* (VTSup 4. Leiden: Brill, 1957), 25.

18. S. A. Reed, *Dead Sea Scrolls Inventory Project: List of Documents, Photographs and Museum Plates* (Fasc. 10; Claremont, Calif.: Ancient Biblical Manuscript Center, 1992), 28.

19. S. A. Reed, *The Dead Sea Scrolls on Microfiche: Inventory List of Photographs* (ed. M. J. Lundberg; Leiden: Brill and IDC, 1993), 78; S. A. Reed, *The Dead Sea Scrolls Catalogue: Documents, Photographs and Museum Inventory Numbers* (ed. and rev. M. J. Lundberg with the collaboration of M. B. Phelps; SBLRBS 32; Atlanta: Scholars Press, 1994), 98.

list.[20] That designation was used again by Tov and Stephen Pfann in the catalogues accompanying the Dead Sea Scroll microfiches.[21] In the principal edition, the title is adjusted to "Historical Text." Fitzmyer has also pointed out that the decision by Shemaryahu Talmon to distinguish 4Q331–4Q333 from the Mishmarot texts proper because they do not mention the priestly courses in the same way caused their separate publication.[22] One suspects that it was this distinction that provoked the renaming of the three fragmentary manuscripts as "chronicle" or as "Historical Text." Such a suspicion is confirmed by the way these fragments are referred to by Jonathan Ben-Dov and Stéphane Saulnier as "historical texts with mishmarot notations," and the conclusion offered that these historical texts should be separated from the calendrical texts on both material and contextual grounds.[23] Although the fragmentary character of 4Q331–4Q333 prevents one from being certain that there was a single, coherent, "annalistic calendar" in several copies,[24] nevertheless it would seem that the alignment of events and people with priestly courses, as part of a dating system, must indicate the priority being given to the courses in presenting the people and events schematically, rather than that such information about the priestly courses is offered in an arbitrary way in a composition that otherwise deserves the generic label "history": "These compositions are characterized by using the priestly rosters as a calendrical element in order to indicate when certain historical events happened."[25]

Indeed, Fitzmyer has declared straightforwardly that "'Historical Text'" is used as a title for these fragments because they mention names of rulers in the Hasmonean dynasty associated with events in ancient Judea, for example, Hyrcanus and Salome Alexandra.[26] On that basis Fitzmyer juxtaposes the manuscript with 4Q448 (4QApocryphal Psalm and Prayer), which mentions a king Jonathan, though 4Q448 has never been entitled a "Historical Text." From these statements it is clear on what grounds this highly fragmentary manuscript has been entitled

---

20. Fitzmyer, "4QpapHistorical Text C," 275; E. Tov, "The Unpublished Qumran Texts from Qumran Caves 4 and 11," *BA* 55 (1992): 99.

21. E. Tov and S. J. Pfann, *The Dead Sea Scrolls on Microfiche: Companion Volume* (Leiden: Brill and IDC, 1993), 40; E. Tov and S. J. Pfann, *The Dead Sea Scrolls on Microfiche: Companion Volume* (2nd rev. ed.; Leiden: Brill and IDC, 1995), 40.

22. S. Talmon and J. Ben-Dov, "A. Calendrical Documents and Mishmarot," in *Qumran Cave 4.XVI: Calendrical Texts* (ed. S. Talmon, J. Ben-Dov, and U. Glessmer; DJD 21; Oxford: Clarendon, 2001), 12–13.

23. J. Ben-Dov and S. Saulnier, "Qumran Calendars: A Survey of Scholarship 1980–2007," *Currents in Biblical Research* 7 (2008): 133.

24. M. O. Wise, *Thunder in Gemini and Other Essays on the History, Language and Literature of Second Temple Palestine* (JSPSup 15; Sheffield: JSOT Press, 1994), 221.

25. F. García Martínez, "The History of the Qumran Community in the Light of Recently Available Texts," in *Qumran between the Old and New Testaments* (ed. F. H. Cryer and T. L. Thompson; JSOTSup 290; Copenhagen International Seminar 6. Sheffield: Sheffield Academic Press, 1998), 201.

26. Fitzmyer, "4QpapHistorical Text C," 275.

"Historical," but one can still inquire whether that is adequate justification for such a generic classification.

In the most substantial fragment, two proper names are preserved, Yoḥanan and Shelamzion (Salome). Fitzmyer takes the first to be a reference to John Hyrcanus I and the second to refer to Salome Alexandra. Kenneth Atkinson agrees,[27] while H. Eshel is uncertain about the identification of Yoḥanan.[28] In addition, in the same fragment the term "priest" is preserved. Little is legible in the other papyrus fragments associated with this manuscript, though in frg. 5 it is highly likely that [Yeḥez]kel is to be restored. This is the name of one of the priestly courses (1 Chr 24:16). Which way around should the text be read? As a list of historical figures who happen to be juxtaposed with some mention of priests and their courses or as a list of priestly courses whose rota of duty is used as the device to chronicle some key people and events? Atkinson supports Wise and insists that the mention of the priestly courses means that this fragmentary manuscript should "be viewed as calendrical works that likely belonged to one or more Mishmarot documents."[29] But the truth of the matter is more honestly expressed by H. Eshel: they "mention the priestly courses and some historical events. These scrolls are extremely fragmentary and it is impossible to ascertain their precise intent or purpose";[30] later he sides with those who see in 4Q331 some kind of annal, designating all three fragmentary sets of remains as Annalistic Texts.[31]

In the contribution on "Shelamzion Alexandra" to the *Encyclopedia of the Dead Sea Scrolls*, Tal Ilan describes how the references to her are to be found in Cave 4 Calendrical Document C[a] (4Q322) and C[e] (4Q324b),[32] but this is clearly a double error, confusing the Mishmarot designation of the *Preliminary Concordance* with the designation Calendrical Document and then assigning the wrong Cave 4 manuscript numbers in the light of that misdesignation.[33] Given all the lists of manuscripts that had been published well before the appearance of the *Encyclopedia*, it is surprising that this was not corrected. What it indicates, however, is the reluctance of scholars like Ilan to move the fragmentary occurrences of historical names into compositions for which their presence becomes constitutive.

It is well known that priests produce lists. While agreeing with H. Eshel's caution, stated above, it is most likely that 4Q331 is indeed some kind of annal, even an annalistic calendar, as Michael Wise proposed. To say more is difficult,

27. K. Atkinson, "Representations of History in 4Q331 (4QpapHistorical Text C), 4Q332 (4QHistorical Text D), 4Q333 (4QHistorical Text E), and 4Q468e (4QHistorical Text F): An Annalistic Calendar Documenting Portentous Events?" *DSD* 14 (2007): 132–33.

28. H. Eshel, *Dead Sea Scrolls and the Hasmonean State*, 137.

29. Atkinson, "Representations of History," 128.

30. H. Eshel, *Dead Sea Scrolls and the Hasmonean State*, 136.

31. Ibid., 142.

32. T. Ilan, "Shelamzion Alexandra," in *Encyclopedia of the Dead Sea Scrolls* (ed. L. H. Schiffman and J. C. VanderKam; 2 vols.; New York: Oxford University Press, 2000), 2:873.

33. Brown et al., *Preliminary Concordance*.

though building on the suggestions of Wise and others, Atkinson has proposed that 4Q331, 4Q332, 4Q333, and 4Q468e are all copies of "portentous calendars" written to commemorate the downfall of their Hasmonean adversaries.[34]

In this discussion of genre it is necessary to discern what might be put simplistically as a difference between primary and secondary data. The designation of 4Q331 as "Historical" seems most likely based on the presence of two names that can be reasonably securely identified with actual figures of the late second of early first centuries B.C.E. This approach is to align a text like that contained on 4Q331 with a coin, seal, or some other artefact that might contain the name of a historical personage. Such artefacts are usually contemporary with those named, even if they survive after their demise. But for those who analyze texts and attempt to give them names according to generic categories, "Historical" is a genre label that defines secondary data, namely, how particular authors have constructed one or more figures or events, usually of the past, for their own purposes, purposes that can fall within a broad range, though based on a modern appreciation of the function of historiography in the ancient and classical worlds, of which Jewish historiography was a part.

The debate about the suitable designation of a composition such as 4Q331 should not be determined solely by its references to known historical figures. The debate should concern whether what can be discerned in 4Q331 as a literary whole seems to reflect some kind of historiographical genre. In other words, from a maximalist perspective, the genre issue is whether annals or annalistic calendars are some kind of history writing, in a full sense. Wise has argued strongly, using Cicero, that these kinds of chronicles are the kinds of written materials that "precede history."[35] From a minimalist perspective, the lack of enough information for the modern reader to be certain about the genre of 4Q331 at least leaves the designation of the composition as historical without adequate warrant.

2.4. 4Q332 HISTORICAL TEXT D[36]

The story of the naming of 4Q332 is very similar to that of 4Q331.[37] Tov's 1992 list seems to have been pivotal in causing Reed to adjust his designation. The three small fragments assigned to this manuscript are inscribed in an early Herodian hand. In frg. 1, line 2, and in frg. 3, line 3, in contexts outlining various dates, mention is made of Jedaiah, a common priestly name but here one of the priestly courses (1 Chr 24:7). Just possibly there is a reference to either *gwlyym* or *kty'ym* in line 4; Fitzmyer marginally prefers the latter, a preference that also informs his restoration in frg. 3, line 2: [ש הרג הכת]יאים הרג ש] ("the leader of the

---

34. Atkinson, "Representations of History," 125.

35. Wise, *Thunder in Gemini*, 221.

36. J. A. Fitzmyer, "4QHistorical Text D," in Pfann et al., *Qumran Cave 4.XXVI* (DJD 36), 281–86.

37. Ibid., 281.

Kitt]im killed S["].[38] In frg. 2, lines 2–3 contain various dating formulae, which the author seems concerned to align with one another. In the other extant phrases there are mentions of Arabs (probably in line 1), Salome Alexandra (line 4) and a rebellious Hyrcanus (line 6), whom Fitzmyer, following Wise, identifies with Hyrcanus II.[39]

As with 4Q331, the composition seems to be written from a priestly calendrical perspective, a perspective that does not have any identifiable sectarian elements. It is difficult to explain the juxtaposition of historical figures and events with the priestly courses on any other ground. It is hard not to agree with Wise that 4Q332 "was a calendrical work incorporating references to selected historical events."[40] Furthermore the description of Hyrcanus as involved in rebelling encourages the view that the priestly author supported Aristobulus in the civil strife of the 60s B.C.E., so that whatever people and events are being aligned with the run of things in the temple are not presented in an entirely neutral fashion—which goes against the impression that "the preserved fragments offer no value judgments concerning the events mentioned."[41] As to conclusions about the genre of 4Q332, no more can be stated than has already been said in relation to 4Q331.

2.5. 4Q333 Historical Text E[42]

As with the naming of 4Q331 and 4Q332, the same story applies to 4Q333. To 4Q333 are assigned two small fragments of skin that contain writing in a "semiformal Herodian hand."[43] Fragment 1 contains the small remains of the end of eight lines, in four of which there seems to be reference to the priestly courses, as in 4Q331 and 4Q332, but this time with reference to Jahezkel (1 Chr 24:16) and Gamul (1 Chr 24:17); in lines 4 and 7 the phrase *hrg 'mlyws* (הרג אמליוס; "Aemilius killed") is extant twice. In frg. 2 all that survives reads *'yš yhwdy* (איש יהודי; "a Jewish man"). It is widely agreed that the historical reference is to the massacre of one or more people by M. Aemilius Scaurus, quaestor under Pompey. From 65–61 B.C.E. he was the proquaestor of Syria and was put in charge of Syria and Judea by Pompey. Though Josephus does not explicitly link Scaurus with the aftermath of the fall of Jerusalem in 63 B.C.E., Scaurus seems to have become embroiled in the civil strife between Aristobulus and Hyrcanus, the details of

---

38. Ibid., 283.

39. Ibid., 285; Wise, *Thunder in Gemini*, 210–11.

40. M. O. Wise, "Dating the Teacher of Righteousness and the *Floruit* of His Movement," *JBL* 122 (2003): 72.

41. García Martínez, "History of the Qumran Community in the Light of Recently Available Texts," 201.

42. J. A. Fitzmyer, "4QHistorical Text E," in Pfann et al., *Qumran Cave 4.XXVI* (DJD 36), 287–89.

43. Ibid.

which have been much discussed.[44] Important for our purposes is that once again events are recounted in relation to the service of the priestly courses, implying that these fragments are part of a composition like that to be found in 4Q331 and 4Q332. Of 4Q333 Atkinson concludes that it "should also be viewed as part of a Mishmarot composition similar to 4QMishmarot D in which the author chose to document and commemorate events, including the use of double dates, with reference to the priestly courses."[45] 4Q331, 4Q332, and 4Q333 may all contain historical information, but they are all annalistic texts. The same comments on genre as have been made for 4Q331 and 4Q332 apply to 4Q333.

2.6. 4Q468E HISTORICAL TEXT F[46]

To 4Q468e is assigned a single small fragment in a mixed semi-cursive script with parts of three lines extant, in only two of which are there legible words. Line 2 reads: ה[רוג את רוב הגבר]ים ("ki]lling the multitude of me[n"); line 3 reads: פותלאיס והנפש אשר[. The interpretation of the line is disputed. In a preliminary publication Broshi proposed that the Hebrew should be translated as "]Potlais and the people that [".[47] He understood the proper name as a Hellenized form of the Hebrew Putiel (cf. Exod. 6:25) and he proposed that the Potlais mentioned in the text could be the same figure as the Ptollas of Josephus's *Ant.* 17.219, a courtier and friend of the tetrarch Archelaus. He further wondered whether the fragment alluded to the massacre of protesters in the temple perpetrated by Archelaus in 4 B.C.E. That preliminary study provoked three responses, by William Horbury, Schwartz, and John Strugnell, all of whom suggested that the name should be read as Peitholaus and the text understood as a reference to the activities of a Jewish general of that name active in the middle of the first century B.C.E.[48] Peitholaus first supported the Romans in punishing the rebels behind Aristobulus, then he changed sides, ending up himself being executed by the Romans (Josephus, *War* 1.162–163, 172, 180; *Ant.* 14.84–85, 93–95, 120). In the principal edition, Broshi seems to have been unable to take account of these suggestions and

---

44. E.g., Wise, *Thunder in Gemini*, 211–18; D. R. Schwartz, "Aemilius Scaurus, Marcus," in *Encyclopedia of the Dead Sea Scrolls* (ed. L. H. Schiffman and J. C. VanderKam; 2 vols.; New York: Oxford University Press, 2000), 1:9–10; Atkinson, "Representations of History," 138–42; H. Eshel, *Dead Sea Scrolls and the Hasmonean State*, 138–42.

45. Atkinson, "Representations of History," 128–29.

46. M. Broshi, "4QHistorical Text F," in *Qumran Cave 4.XXVI: Cryptic Texts and Miscellanea, Part 1* (ed. S. J. Pfann et al.; DJD 36; Oxford: Clarendon, 2000), 406–11.

47. M. Broshi, "Ptolas and the Archelaus Massacre (4Q468g = Histroical Text B)," *JJS* 49 (1998): 341–45.

48. W. Horbury, "The Proper Name in 4Q468g: Peitholaus?" *JJS* 50 (1999): 310–11; D. R. Schwartz, "4Q468g: Ptollas?" *JJS* 50 (1999): 308–9; and J. Strugnell, "The Historical Background to 4Q468g [=4QHistorical Text B]," *RevQ* 19/73 (1999): 137–38.

repeated his earlier identification.[49] Several scholars have supported Horbury, Schwartz, and Strugnell.[50]

Whatever the identification of the figure concerned, Broshi has offered some helpful and detailed thoughts on the genre of 4Q468e, by comparing it with the other known texts that contain proper names of historical figures.[51] On the basis of the few words that survive, he has declared boldly that "4Q468e is certainly not a history book, in the style of the Maccabees. It is unlikely that the Qumran 'libraries' would have included such a work among their books which were exclusively of a religious nature. It may seem that the fragment belongs to the genre of calendars recording disastrous days, which can be called 'portentous calendars.'"[52] Atkinson has agreed with this generic label: "portentous calendar."[53] Eshel has preferred to align 4Q468e with 4Q331–4Q333 as all copies of the same Annalistic Text. Although 4Q468e seems to deal with disastrous events, Broshi is inclined to associate the composition with Megillat Ta'anit, a calendrical list of positive historical events from the Hasmonean and Roman periods in month order from Nisan to Adar, events whose commemoration was not to be linked to public fasting. In her detailed treatment of that composition, Vered Noam has concluded not unsuitably that the text "does not belong to the genre of historical writing," whatever she might mean by the generic term.[54] If the comparison with 4Q331–4Q333 and 4Q468e is worth anything, the same would seem to be the case: they are not historical writing but probably some kind of calendrical or annalistic compositions. There is no corroborative evidence to identify it as part of a pesher, as Strugnell wondered.[55]

2.7. 4Q468f Historical Text G[56]

In current lists of manuscripts from the Qumran caves, the last to be assigned a title with "Historical" in it is 4Q468f. This consists of one fragment with the ends of six lines preserved, probably from the bottom of a column. In the *Preliminary Concordance* this fragment is labeled as "pshist A," "Pseudo-Historical Text A";[57] in Tov's list it is not differentiated but is described as part of an "Apocryphon."[58]

---

49. Broshi, "4QHistorical Text F," 406–11.

50. E.g., Wise, "Dating the Teacher of Righteousness," 79–80; Atkinson, "Representations of History,"143; H. Eshel, *Dead Sea Scrolls and the Hasmonean State*, 142–44.

51. Broshi, "4QHistorical Text F," 408–9.

52. Ibid., 409.

53. Atkinson, "Representations of History," 148.

54. V. Noam, *Megillat Ta'anit: Versions, Interpretation, History with a Critical Edition* (Jerusalem: Yad Ben Zvi, 2003), 340.

55. Strugnell, "Historical Background to 4Q468g," 137.

56. A. Lange, "4Q468f. 4QHistorical Text G," in Pfann et al., *Qumran Cave 4.XXVI* (DJD 36), 412–13.

57. Brown et al., *Preliminary Concordance*, 2.562.

58. Tov, "Unpublished Qumran Texts," 102.

The extant phrases of the fragment include "the sons of Gilead," "the land," "Edom" (or "Adam"), and "seven." Lange takes forward the original designation of the fragment and suggests on the basis of such content that "4Q468f preserves the remnants of a historical text."[59] Such a suggestion is surely no more than a shot in the dark.

Apart from the numeral "seven," the collocation of the vocabulary in this fragment is best aligned either with Ps 60:9–11 (repeated in Ps 108:9–11) or with Amos 1:3–8 (Gilead in the first oracle; Edom in the second) and 11–13 (Edom in the fourth oracle; Gilead in the fifth). It is with poetry and prophetic oracles that the text is most likely to find generic resonance, not historical writing of any kind. This is borne out by the fact that of the two other occurrences of Gilead in the nonbiblical scrolls found in the Qumran caves, one is in the poorly preserved 4Q171, frg. 13, which contains an interpretation of either Ps 60:8–9 or Ps 108:8–9 (the other is in the representation of Deut 2:36 in 4Q364 24a–c, line 12, which is akin to a scriptural citation). Here again, the occurrence of a proper name has caused a modern scholar to make a generic suggestion that is highly unlikely. Proper names, whether of places or people, can be used in almost any genre. What is all the more surprising is that Lange in his principal edition of 4Q468f has made no reference to the other uses of Gilead in the nonscriptural scrolls.

As for reading *'dm* (אדם) as "Edom" rather than "Adam" or "man," while the context might suggest this, all the other certain occurrences of Edom in the non-scriptural scrolls are written plene as *'dwm* (אדום) making it possible that there is a reference to Adam here. If so, then the other occurrences of Adam in the nonscriptural scrolls from the Qumran collection would indicate that a nonhistorical context would be preferable for understanding 4Q468f. In fact, it is worth noting that, of the few certain occurrences of Adam, one is in 4Q171 (1+3–4 iii 2), in the same composition where Gilead is interpreted in some way. Again, Lange makes no reference to this possible collocation.

Overall, it would seem that "Historical Text" is a thoroughly inappropriate and misleading designation for this small fragment. Two place-names have prompted a generic label that says more about the assumptions of the editors than about the text, and the move from pseudo-history to "historical" reveals much.

3. Historiography in the Qumran Manuscripts

3.1. Types of Historiography in the Dead Sea Scrolls

The problematic nature of the use of "Historical Text" as a genre label for these few small fragments can be brought into focus even more clearly. A first task is to

---

59. Lange, "4Q468f. 4QHistorical Text G," 412.

outline and describe the various types of historiography that do actually occur in slightly more extensive forms amongst the scrolls.

It is intriguing to note that of all the scriptural books that are preserved in the Qumran collection, apart from 1–2 Samuel, the historical books proper, Joshua, Judges, 1–2 Kings, 1–2 Chronicles, Ezra–Nehemiah, are the least well represented. What has survived of the books of Samuel might indicate that few grand conclusions should be drawn from this paucity of evidence, not least since it could be partly the result of accident. Nevertheless, the quotation of and allusion to these historical works in the sectarian literature are also rather limited. For example, for the Damascus Document Jonathan G. Campbell notes nothing from those works that make up the so-called Deuteronomistic History and only a handful of references to Ezra 9; Neh 7; 9; and 10; and 2 Chr 36.[60] All those works were evidently known, but they do not form a significant part of the ideology of the sectarian movement the remnants of whose manuscript collection were found in the eleven caves. There may be a variety of reasons for this, among which might be the Hasmonean interest in some of those works, particularly Chronicles, for their own ideological purposes.[61]

As in their Scriptures, so in the Qumran library there are many compositions with elements that might be defined as historical or historiographical, but "not a single one of the thousands of Qumran fragments detached from hundreds of manuscripts can be classified as historical."[62] In the *Encyclopedia of the Dead Sea Scrolls* there is no article on history writing or historiography. Nobody would deny that there is some historical data to be gleaned from both the sectarian and nonsectarian compositions found in the Qumran caves, but the general consensus is that there are no remains in the caves that merit the generic label "History" in either the classical or modern senses. The historiography to be found in the scrolls is rich and varied:[63] references to Israel's past, often with a view to its use in the construction of sectarian identity, occur in many genres such as exhortations, hymns, and legal texts. In the pesharim, the unfulfilled past revelation is interpreted atomistically to address and describe the present, usually in a veiled and ambiguous way. In several genres history is presented in a periodized form: Ages of Creation offers such divine ordering in one way; 11QMelchizedek

---

60. J. G. Campbell, *The Use of Scripture in the Damascus Document 1–8, 19–20* (BZAW 228; Berlin: de Gruyter, 1995), 179–82.

61. G. J. Brooke, "The Books of Chronicles and the Scrolls from Qumran," in *Reflection and Refraction: Studies in Biblical Historiography in Honour of A. Graeme Auld* (ed. R. Rezetko, T. H. Lim, W. B. Aucker; VTSup 113; Leiden: Brill, 2007), 35–48.

62. G. Vermes, "The Essenes and History," *JJS* 32 (1981): 18–31. Repr. in idem, *Jesus and the World of Judaism* (London: SCM, 1983), 126–39; repr. in idem, *Scrolls, Scriptures and Early Christianity* (LSTS 56; London: T&T Clark, 2005), 29.

63. G. J. Brooke, "Types of Historiography in the Qumran Scrolls," in *Ancient and Modern Scriptural Historiography/L'historiographie biblique, ancienne et moderne* (ed. G. J. Brooke and T. Römer; BETL 207; Leuven: Peeters, 2007), 211–30.

refers to it in another; and Jubilees writes it into the tradition in yet another way. In those compositions there is the implication that things are reaching a climax of some sort. In addition, there are various lists: genealogies of various kinds, lists of false prophets, annalistic texts. Historiography in the Qumran collection is of a sort other than works such as 1 Maccabees or the military and political histories of Greco-Roman writers, including Josephus.

3.2. "Historical" because They May Be of Use to Modern Historians

It seems as if several, if not all, of the seven fragmentary compositions considered briefly above have been labeled as "historical" because they are considered to be possibly of use to modern historians. There has been much debate, especially in relation to the so-called history of Israel, about what constitutes responsible history writing. Among the elements of responsibility are the careful and sensitive handling of source materials, which in the first place should be understood, so far as is possible, in their own terms, whether they are part of someone's Bible or materials such as the writings of Josephus.[64] As Rolf Rendtorff has stressed for the Old Testament, "Der Text selbst ist mehr und vor allem etwas anderes als eine Quelle historischer Informationen."[65]

Lester Grabbe has written much of a pragmatic nature about how in particular the history of the Second Temple period can be written. "But when all is said and done, most historians have a positivistic goal: they are trying to get at the question of 'what actually happened' and do not regard that as an absurd goal. They are trying to reconstruct a particular historical entity, whether of the recent or remote past. For most historians, this is what 'doing history' is about."[66] This definition of the task of the historian allows us to see that for the most part those fragments from the Qumran caves that have been labeled as "historical" have been given their designation largely because they are seen to be useful to the historian or the historical interests of the Qumran scholar. The fragmentary compositions are not being taken seriously on their own terms.

It is from that historian's perspective, the desire to describe "what actually happened," that several scholars have used these texts. For example, Wise lists in chronological order the thirty-one items from all the compositions that mention a recognizable place, person, or process from the high priesthood of Onias III in 174 B.C.E. (4Q245 frg. 1, line 9) to the plunder of Jerusalem in 37 B.C.E. (1QpHab

---

64. L. L. Grabbe, "Hat die Bibel doch Recht? A Review of T. L. Thompson's *The Bible in History*," *Scandinavian Journal of the Old Testament* 14 (2000): 120–28.

65. R. Rendtorff, "Wie sieht Israel seine Geschichte?" in *Rethinking the Foundations: Historiography in the Ancient World and in the Bible. Essays in Honour of John Van Seters* (ed. S. L. McKenzie, T. Römer, and H. H. Schmid; BZAW 294; Berlin: de Gruyter, 2000), 206.

66. L. L. Grabbe, "Are Historians of Ancient Palestine Fellow Creatures–or Different Animals?" in *Can a 'History of Israel' Be Written?* (ed. L. L. Grabbe; JSOTSup, 245; European Seminar in Historical Methodology, 1. Sheffield: Sheffield Academic Press, 1997), 19–20.

9:4–7).[67] Some of Wise's identifications may be challenged, but a range of compositions of various genres and none are referred to. Or again, Geza Vermes, who has had a very long-standing interest in the history of the Qumran community and of Jewish history in the three centuries before the fall of the temple, has offered a survey of all the proper names in the compositions found in the Qumran caves to show that the parameters of the construction of a history of the Qumran community fall within the second and first centuries B.C.E.[68] Yet again, Atkinson has listed all the nonbiblical proper names in the Qumran texts to argue somewhat arbitrarily that "the formative years of the Qumran community should be situated approximately from 76 B.C.E. to ca. 51 B.C.E.."[69] In most detail, H. Eshel has considered all the historical allusions in the sectarian and nonsectarian compositions found in the Qumran caves.[70]

From this perspective, the compositions from the Qumran caves that have been labeled as "historical" fall into three categories. In the first place, there are some compositions, like 4Q248 and 4Q321–4Q333, whose content may genuinely assist with the better understanding of the history of the period. Though there is still a large amount of creative imagination that is required from the scholar, it is possible to use such texts to contribute to a better sketch of various historical circumstances. In a second subgroup can be put fragments, like 4Q578, that may well contain the name of a historical person or place but which remain highly ambiguous. The use of such material for historical reconstruction depends on its juxtaposition with other source materials; it is those other materials that permit the modern reader to resolve some of the ambiguity present in the data. 4Q578 is an example of this kind of ambiguous fragment; having dated it paleographically, Puech resolves its ambiguity by setting it alongside the broader context of Essenism in the second century B.C.E. That contextual juxtaposition may itself be open to challenge, but it is a possible though subjective framework offered by one interpreter. In a third group are those compositions in which there may well be a proper name of a place or person, but that name or place cannot be given a historical context with any certainty at all. 4Q468f is an example of such a fragment. Its own internal juxtaposition of the ambiguous *'dm* (אדם) with Gilead encourages a particular, though far from certain interpretation as Edom; beyond that the best comparative texts are in the Psalms and the prophets. This fragment does not contain historical information and is of no direct use to the historian, though it may indicate what poetic or prophetic traditions remained of concern to those who penned the fragment, or who copied or owned it.

---

67. Wise, "Dating the Teacher of Righteousness," 81.

68. E.g., G. Vermes, "Le cadre historique des manuscrits de la mer Morte," *Recherches de Science Religieuse* 41 (1953): 5–29

69. Atkinson, "Representations of History," 145–47.

70. Eshel, *Dead Sea Scrolls and the Hasmonean State.*

3.3. Not "Historical" because They Are Akin to Ancient Historiography

When one looks briefly at the Jewish literature of the late Second Temple period that has been considered under the label of historiography, compositions from the Qumran library, whether sectarian or not, are largely absent. For example, the revised Schürer,[71] for literature composed in Hebrew or Aramaic, has listed under "Historiography" 1 Maccabees, the history of John Hyrcanus, and the work of Josephus, though it is also suggested that there are four types of Jewish historical documents in this period: genealogies, Megillat Ta'anit, pesharim, and *m. Aboth* 1.[72] For literature composed in Greek the same compendium avoids the label "historiography" and speaks sweepingly of "prose literature about the past," some of which might more closely resemble some forms of Greco-Roman historiography than others.[73] Developing and summarizing earlier work,[74] under the title of "Jewish Historiography," Harold Attridge included fragmentary Greco-Jewish historians, the Maccabean histories, Philo, and Josephus.[75] In George W. E. Nickelsburg's 2005 survey of *Jewish Literature between the Bible and the Mishnah* the system of classification is both historical and literary, but there is not even an entry for "history" or "historiography" in the extensive index.[76]

Since so much in the Qumran literary collection is related in one way or another to scriptural and other authoritative materials, it is not surprising that the problems that scholars have addressed for several generations in relation to the historical purposes of scriptural texts should persist in the literature from the Qumran caves. In considering the views of Elias Bickerman and Arnaldo Momigliano on why most of late Second Temple and early rabbinic Judaism is ahistorical, Vermes has concluded that "Qumran historiography ... constitutes a transitional phase from a prophetic presentation of events to a quasi-prophetic exegesis of biblical texts in the form of the Dead Sea *pesher* literature. For those 'historians,' the true meaning of the occurrences of their time was to be sought

---

71. E. Schürer, *The History of the Jewish People in the Age of Jesus Christ (175 B.C.–A.D. 135)* (rev. and ed. G. Vermes, F. Millar, and M. Goodman; 3 vols. in 4 parts; Edinburgh: T&T Clark, 1973–87), 3.1:180–86.

72. Ibid., 186.

73. Ibid., 505–58: Demetrius, Eupolemus, 2 Maccabees, Joseph and Aseneth, Testament of Job, etc.

74. H. Attridge, "Historiography" and "Josephus," in *Jewish Writings of the Second Temple Period: Apocrypha, Pseudepigrapha, Qumran Sectarian Writings, Philo, Josephus* (ed. M. Stone; Compendia Rerum Iudaicarum ad Novum Testamentum 2/II. Assen: Van Gorcum; Philadelphia: Fortress, 1984), 157–232.

75. H. Attridge, "Jewish Historiography," in *Early Judaism and Its Modern Interpreters* (ed. R. A. Kraft and G. W. E. Nickelsburg; The Bible and Its Modern Interpreters 2; Philadelphia: Fortress; Atlanta: Scholars Press, 1986), 311–43.

76. G. W. E. Nickelsburg, *Jewish Literature between the Bible and the Mishnah: A Historical and Literary Introduction* (2nd ed; Minneapolis: Fortress, 2005).

in the mysterious significance, revealed by God to the Teacher of Righteousness, of divinely inspired predictions uttered in the past."[77]

In addition, it is clear that many significant studies on ancient history writing or on the historiography of antiquity have had as their primary focus Greco-Roman sources that have had their own distinctive cultural agenda, whether as histories proper or as biographies. Several scholars of the Hebrew Bible have taken these Greco-Roman historians seriously, particularly in a new wave of discussion over the last thirty years or more; scholars of Josephus have also occupied themselves with suitable comparative texts; and New Testament scholars have also been interested in the same classical writers in their attempts at defining the Gospels and Acts.

In the opening of his work, Herodotus has provided what has become a standard definition of history writing:

> I, Herodotus of Halicarnassus, am here setting forth my history, that time may not draw the color from what man has brought into being, nor those great and wonderful deeds, manifested by both Greeks and barbarians, fail of their report, and, together with all this, the reason why they fought one another.[78]

Lucian (second century C.E.) has also played a significant part in generic definition through his treatise *How to Write History*. Willem C. van Unnik summarized Lucian's work in a list of ten "standard rules" for the writing of "hellenistic historiography," which may be summarized as follows: (1) noble subject, (2) public benefit, (3) lack of bias/partisanship, (4) fitting beginning and end, (5) collection of material, (6) selection and variety, (7) disposition and order, (8) vividness of narration, (9) topographical details, and (10) speeches suitable to speaker and occasion.[79] Although there may be some considerable irony in Lucian's presentation,[80] a "noble subject," in Greek and Roman antiquity, "was one that allowed the historian to deal with the public lives and vicissitudes of states and peoples on the grand scale," and history was largely political history, especially the description of war.[81]

Though the Qumran community and the wider movement of which it was

---

77. Vermes, "Essenes and History," 29.

78. D. Grene, *Herodotus: The History* (Chicago: University of Chicago Press, 1987), 33.

79. W. C. van Unnik, "Luke's Second Book and the Rule of Hellenistic Historiography," in *Les Actes des Apôtres: Traditions, rédaction, théologie* (ed. J. Kremer; BETL 48. Leuven: University Press, 1979), 37–60.

80. L. C. A. Alexander, "Marathon or Jericho? Reading Acts in Dialogue with Biblical and Greek Historiography," in *Auguries: The Jubilee Volume of the Sheffield Department of Biblical Studies* (ed. D. J. A. Clines and S. D. Moore; JSOTSup 269. Sheffield: Sheffield Academic Press, 1998), 92–125. Repr. in *Ancient and Modern Scriptural Historiography/L'historiographie biblique, ancienne et moderne* (ed. G. J. Brooke and T. Römer; BETL 207; Leuven: Peeters, 2007), 283–310.

81. Alexander, "Marathon or Jericho?" 289.

a part may have been interested in the construction of a quasi-historical rhetorical polemic against their enemies, it was not concerned with the writing of history that might emulate the ideals of Herodotus or accord with the prescriptions of Lucian.[82] As has been noted above, its concerns are largely exegetical and chronistically schematic: they are theological and eschatological concerns, rather than concerns that are expressed in the causal explanations of the narratives of political and military history.

4. Conclusion

In considering the seven fragmentary manuscripts that have been labeled as "Historical Text," this brief analysis has attempted to discover why such a label was thought appropriate in each case and to expose some of the assumptions behind such generic description. It can be recognized fairly easily that any use of the label "Historical Text" that might imply that these fragments contained parts of histories akin to other Jewish or non-Jewish histories of the period is indeed unwarranted. The modern yearning to know what happened in Judea in the two or three centuries before the Roman destruction of the temple in 70 c.e. must not lead to a distortion of the data or an emasculation of the evidence. Fortunately there are sound and reliable historians like Lester Grabbe to guide us all in the suitable historical reading of the remains.

---

82. K. Atkinson, "Anti-Roman Polemics in the Dead Sea Scrolls and Related Literature: Their Later Use in John's Apocalypse," *Qumran Chronicle* 12 (2004): 109–22.

THIRTEEN

THE SCROLLS FROM QUMRAN
AND OLD TESTAMENT THEOLOGY

1. INTRODUCTION

The purpose of this chapter is to show how the Qumran scrolls, through their very existence and because of their contents, both highlight the problems that beset anyone who tries to engage in the task of Old Testament theology and offer some clues as to how that task might be approached.[1] The scrolls created a great stir when they first came to light. In addition to what could become known concerning the history of late Second Temple period Palestinian Judaism, for Old Testament scholars excitement lay especially in what might be learned of the history of the biblical text; for New Testament scholars interest lay particularly in what might be discovered about Jewish eschatology, especially messianism, in a period approximately contemporary with Jesus himself.[2] Among other mat-

---

1. An earlier form of this chapter was published in a volume to honor Rolf Knierim, from whom I learned both skills in attention to detail and also many other methodological insights. The term Qumran in the title and throughout refers simply to the place where the various manuscripts were found; in this chapter, I define when necessary which texts may reflect the ideology of the community that was resident there or the wider movement of which it was a part.

2. For the history of the biblical text, see especially the summary collection of essays in F. M. Cross and S. Talmon, eds., *Qumran and the History of the Biblical Text* (Cambridge, Mass.: Harvard University Press, 1975); for a recent survey on the matter, see R. S. Hendel, "Assessing the Text-Critical Theories of the Hebrew Bible after Qumran," in *The Oxford Handbook of the Dead Sea Scrolls* (ed. T. H. Lim and J. J. Collins; Oxford: Oxford University Press, 2010), 281–302. For the scrolls and the New Testament, the following early collections have stood the test of time: K. Stendahl, ed., *The Scrolls and the New Testament* (London: SCM Press, 1958); M. Black, ed., *The Scrolls and Christianity: Historical and Theological Significance* (Theological Collections 11; London: SPCK, 1969); J. Murphy-O'Connor, ed., *Paul and Qumran: Studies in New Testament Exegesis* (London: Chapman, 1968; reissued as *Paul and the Dead Sea Scrolls* with a new foreword by J. H. Charlesworth, New York: Crossroad, 1990); J. H. Charlesworth, ed., *John and Qumran* (London: Chapman, 1972; reissued as *John and the Dead Sea Scrolls* with a new foreword, New York: Crossroad, 1990). The need for new work on the scrolls and the New Testament has been highlighted by F. García Martínez in his review of the reissue of the last two volumes in *JSJ* 22 (1991): 125–26. See also J. A. Fitzmyer, *The Dead Sea Scrolls*

ters, the slow progress up to 1991 in publishing all the scrolls resulted in scholars engaged in biblical studies concluding frustratingly that there was little or nothing new that could be learned from the scrolls that had not already been covered in a mass of learned studies.[3] All that was deemed necessary was a cursory nod in the direction of the scrolls and the summary findings of the first generation of investigators; then one was free to return to some narrower specialist biblical concern.[4] Biblical theologians have been particularly prone to this attitude to the scrolls, because of the natural assumption that the primary, even sole, object of their discourses was the canon; all other literary works could be deemed secondary. But the evidence of the scrolls will not go away and should be taken into account in the questioning and honing of the task of Old Testament theologians. In any case, since 1991, when access to unpublished manuscripts was permitted,[5] the situation has changed: the scrolls have now all been edited in principal editions and they are due to come back into the limelight as a full range of approaches to them is undertaken. This chapter is a brief attempt to express why and how they should influence the task of Old Testament theology.

Within the discipline of Old Testament theology there has long been a tension between two approaches.[6] On the one hand are those who have attempted

and Christian Origins (Studies in the Dead Sea Scrolls and Related Literature; Grand Rapids: Eerdmans, 2000); G. J. Brooke, *The Dead Sea Scrolls and the New Testament: Essays in Mutual Illumination* (London: SPCK; Minneapolis: Fortress, 2005); and J. Frey, "Critical Issues in the Investigation of the Scrolls and the New Testament," in Lim and Collins, *Oxford Handbook of the Dead Sea Scrolls,* 517–45.

3. J. Strugnell argued that there was plenty of new research to be done on what was available when he wrote ("The Qumran Scrolls: A Report on Work in Progress," in *Jewish Civilization in the Hellenistic-Roman Period* [ed. S. Talmon; JSPSup 10; Sheffield: JSOT Press, 1991], 105–6); however, the lack of progress in publishing the whole corpus certainly inhibited some nonspecialist scholars .

4. This nod toward the scrolls is visible, for example, in the way the endpapers of some of the Hermeneia series of commentaries contain photographs of a relevant Qumran manuscript, but the commentary remains focused on the MT.

5. The history of the debate about the process of publication of the scrolls and the scholarly pressure applied can be found in many places: see, e.g., G. J. Brooke, P. R. Davies, and P. R. Callaway, *The Complete World of the Dead Sea Scrolls* (London: Thames and Hudson, 2002; rev. ed. 2011), 22–35; J. C. VanderKam and P. W. Flint, *The Meaning of the Dead Sea Scrolls: Their Significance for Understanding the Bible, Judaism, Jesus, and Christianity* (San Francisco: HarperSanFrancisco, 2002), 381–403; W. W. Fields, *The Dead Sea Scrolls: A Short History* (Leiden: Brill, 2006); H. Shanks, *Freeing the Dead Sea Scrolls and Other Adventures of an Archaeology Outsider* (London: Continuum, 2010), 125–60; G. Vermes, *The Story of the Scrolls* (London: Penguin Books, 2010), 3–92; J. C. VanderKam, *The Dead Sea Scrolls Today* (2nd ed.; Grand Rapids: Eerdmans, 2010), 227–41.

6. Rolf Knierim himself has described something of this tension from his own perspective in "Cosmos and History in Israel's Theology," *HBT* 3 (1981): 59–62, and in "The Task of Old Testament Theology," *HBT* 6 (1984): 25–57. Part of the vast literature includes R. E. Clements, *A Century of Old Testament Study* (Guildford: Lutterworth, 1976), 118–40; H. G. Revent-

to make some sense of the whole Old Testament, even the whole Christian Bible, on the basis of acknowledging the status of the collection as canon[7] and then proceeding to locate its central motif, its ideological kernel, the common denominator shared by its various parts.[8] On the other hand are those who, while acknowledging that the extent of the canon gives them their material, have attempted to pay somewhat closer attention to the findings of historical-critical research and so have organized their systematization of the Old Testament around a historical reconstruction that the texts themselves may imply. This historical approach naturally tends to be more permissive of the pluralism and variety within the Old Testament itself. More recently some have attempted to find a third way, almost combining the canonical and historical approaches, by paying attention both to the traditions that make up any particular Old Testament book (its prehistory and composition) and its effect on and subsequent treatment within the believing communities that accorded it some status. The very existence of the Dead Sea Scrolls, but the scrolls from Qumran in particular, sheds light in several ways on all these approaches within the so-called discipline of Old Testament theology.

2. The Existence of the Scrolls and
Old Testament Theology: Canon and Text

To begin with, the Qumran scrolls highlight dramatically the problem of the definition of the canon. Many modern writers point to the end of the first century c.e. for the delimitation of the Jewish canon (Hebrew Bible),[9] but since Old Testament theology has largely been the preserve of Protestant (especially German)

---

low, *Problems of Old Testament Theology in the Twentieth Century* (London: SCM, 1985); J. H. Hayes and F. C. Prussner, *Old Testament Theology: Its History and Development* (London: SCM, 1985); W. Brueggemann, *Theology of the Old Testament: Testimony, Dispute, Advocacy* (Minneapolis: Fortress, 1997); R. Rendtorff, *The Canonical Hebrew Bible: A Theology of the Old Testament* (Tools for Biblical Study 7; Leiden: Deo, 2006); J. W. Rogerson, *A Theology of the Old Testament: Cultural Memory, Communication and Being Human* (London: SPCK, 2009); B. C. Ollenburger, "Theology, OT," *NIDB* 5:560–64.

7. On the problems of the various meanings of the term "canon," see, e.g., J. Barr, *Scripture: Canon, Authority, Criticism* (Oxford: Clarendon, 1983), 49–126. On the implications of the scrolls for issues of canon, see, e.g., E. C. Ulrich, *The Dead Sea Scrolls and the Origins of the Bible* (Studies in the Dead Sea Scrolls and Related Literature; Grand Rapids: Eerdmans, 1999), 51–78; E. M. Schuller, "The Dead Sea Scrolls and Canon and Canonization," in *Kanon in Konstruktion und Dekonstruktion: Kanonisierungsprozesse religiöser Texte von der Antike bis zur Gegenwart. Ein Handbuch* (ed. E.-M. Becker and S. Scholz; Berlin: de Gruyter, 2012), 293–314.

8. What this unitive approach to the Bible owes to the influence of Karl Barth is helpfully and summarily described, e.g., by J. Rogerson, "The Old Testament," in *The Study and Use of the Bible* (ed. J. Rogerson, C. Rowland, and B. Lindars; History of Christian Theology 2; Basingstoke: Marshall, Morgan & Scott, 1989), 139–42.

9. A putative Council of Jamnia cannot be held responsible for anything; see, e.g., D. E. Aune, "On the Origins of the 'Council of Javneh' Myth," *JBL* 110 (1991): 491–93. However, it is still the case that the earliest enumerations of the biblical books are from the first few dec-

scholars over the last two hundred years, the actual working assumption has generally been that it is the Hebrew canon as established within Protestantism since the Reformation that is the subject matter ripe for theological systematization. Before the scrolls were discovered, it was obvious that this was a pragmatic but problematic definition, for it effectively excluded a mass of material held variously in authoritative, even possibly canonical, esteem by the early churches and by not a few contemporary Christians. But the working assumption concerning the extent of the canon was based on another; namely, that the Protestant Old Testament contained not simply all the Hebrew Scriptures that had survived but all that had existed in the early Second Temple period and before. Though manifestly historically false, this assumption about the precanonical antiquity of the canon seemed to be confirmed by the attitudes of late Second Temple period authors such as Ben Sira. Furthermore, it seemed as if text critics could confirm the antiquity of the Hebrew texts, and thus their status, through their ability to isolate the causes of variants and errors in the manuscript and versional evidence: for example, all major variants in the LXX were considered to be the responsibility of the Greek translators and did not witness to a plurality of Hebrew texts. On such bases the Old Testament canon in its Hebrew text form as acknowledged at the time of the Reformation could be understood as both singularly representative and coherent.

The problem of the definition of the canon, which the existence of the scrolls highlights, is precisely in the area of the relationship of the precanonical authoritative texts to the contents of the canon itself. In relation to the extent of the canon, the existence of actual manuscripts from the mid-Second Temple period discloses something of the breadth of literature available in Palestine for the literate elite. The matter of the canon is thus not a straightforward matter of inclusivity but a reflection of a determined policy of exclusivity, exercised by some dominant group.[10] The large number of pseudepigrapha demonstrates how some authors or groups went about trying to establish their writings as authoritative. The problem is posed even in the New Testament, where there is evidence that some early Jewish Christians assigned authoritative status to texts such as Enoch (Jude 14–15).[11] If it is clearly acknowledged that the definition of the extent of the

---

ades after the fall of the temple; see Josephus, *Ag.Ap.* 1.37–42 (22 books), and 4 Ezra 14:45 (24 books).

10. As argued, e.g., by M. Smith, *Palestinian Parties and Politics That Shaped the Old Testament* (2nd ed; London: SCM, 1987), 1–10.

11. See R. J. Bauckham, "James, 1 and 2 Peter, Jude," in *It Is Written: Scripture Citing Scripture. Essays in Honour of Barnabas Lindars SSF* (ed. D. A. Carson and H. G. M. Williamson; Cambridge: Cambridge University Press, 1988), 303-6; idem, *Jude and the Relatives of Jesus in the Early Church* (Edinburgh: T&T Clark, 1990), 137–39, 210–17; G. J. Brooke, "Torah, Rewritten Torah and the Letter of Jude," in *Torah in the New Testament: Papers Delivered at the Manchester–Lausanne Seminar of June 2008* (ed. M. Tait and P. S. Oakes; LNTS 401; London: T&T Clark International, 2009), 180–93. The extant parts of 1 Enoch in 4QEn^c 1 i 15–17 show

canon is a particular feature of domineering forms of both Judaism and Christianity, especially from the period immediately following the fall of the Second Temple, then the use of such definitions today for forming a systematic appreciation of the texts in relation to the thinking of ancient Israel is at worst arbitrary, at best little more than an intriguing attempt at discovering what might have been in the minds of some of those involved in delimiting the canon with a view to making that relevant in some way for today's reader.

Those who would wish to discover what may be the central or controlling motif of the biblical material may play down the problem of identifying the criteria (and their sociopolitical significance) lying behind the definition of the canon through asserting that it is the center, about which there was widespread agreement over an extended period, which can justifiably form the base material for any theological systematization. This center is located within the threefold categorization of texts known from the second century B.C.E. onward. In this respect, appeal can be made to the prologue of Ben Sira, which speaks three times of the law, the prophets, and the other books, or to a text like Luke 24:44, which mentions the law of Moses, the prophets, and the psalms, to show that over a period of three hundred years or more, the very period that begins the epoch of Jewish and Christian self-definitions, there was a widespread understanding of what categories of texts were authoritative.[12] Although we know of groups who operated on a more restricted canon, the manuscripts from Qumran suggest that for one or more groups the number of texts with authority exceeded the later delimitations. The delimitation of the canon is a matter of excluding as well as of including various writings. The fluidity in the number of authoritative texts for various Jewish groups in the Second Temple period shows how historically determined is the canon adopted by Old Testament theologians.

It needs to be made clear that it is not just a question of insisting that the whole breadth of Jewish literature should be taken into account in defining how modern theological statements about canonical texts should be given historical nuance. Rather, in the precanonical period various Jewish groups had varying collections of authoritative texts and through the status accorded these writings the use and form of the books that were later to become canonical for the rabbis

---

that the quotation in Jude is an exegetically adjusted text; the book of Enoch thus had living authority.

12. The dominant late Second Temple categorization of authoritative Scriptures was as "the Law and the Prophets": see, e.g., J. Barton, *Oracles of God: Perceptions of Ancient Prophecy in Israel after the Exile* (2nd ed.; London: Darton Longman & Todd, 2007). However, it is probably best to understand the prologue in Ben Sira by his grandson as referring to three categories of text. 4 Ezra 14:45 notes that, in addition to the twenty-four scriptural books, there are seventy books written last for the wise among the people. The debate about whether 4QMMT refers to two, three, or even more authoritative categories continues: see T. H. Lim, "Authoritative Scriptures and the Dead Sea Scrolls," in Lim and Collins, *Oxford Handbook of the Dead Sea Scrolls*, 303–22.

were variously influenced. From an angle other than the text-critical it is thus clear that the writings that are later to be included in the canon are passed on in particular contexts of scribal activity that sometimes lead to their significant modification. It is impossible as yet to identify any uniform perspective as the hallmark of the scribal traditors of the biblical texts found in the Qumran caves, but analysis of each manuscript in turn discloses something of the viewpoint of its copyist(s).

The overall theological outlook of the group to be linked with the Qumran site (say, in the first century B.C.E.) might be measured by the number of manuscript copies to have survived there of any particular work and by the references in any texts to other texts deemed authoritative.[13] Alongside the large number of copies of Deuteronomy, Isaiah, and the Psalms can be put the similarly substantial numbers for copies of works like Jubilees, Enoch, the Rule of the Community, and even MMT.[14] Furthermore, though an argument from silence, the absence or near absence of certain texts later included in the canon needs to be noted: Esther, Ezra-Nehemiah, 1 and 2 Chronicles.[15] In addition, some texts that are generally agreed to be closely associated with the ideology of the community at Qumran speak of other writings in a way that assigns them some authority: the references to the "Book of the Divisions of Times into Their Jubilees and Weeks" in CD 16:3–4[16] and to a saying of Levi introduced in a standard and suitably authoritative way in CD 4:15–16,[17] the possible allusion to a second law in 4Q177

---

13. See the analysis of the number of biblical manuscripts in J. C. VanderKam, *The Dead Sea Scrolls and the Bible* (Grand Rapids: Eerdmans, 2012), 2–4. H. Stegemann concluded that the relative paucity of copies of the Temple Scroll in the Qumran caves suggests that that composition was only of antiquarian interest there ("The Literary Composition of the Temple Scroll and Its Status at Qumran," in *Temple Scroll Studies: Papers Presented at the International Symposium on the Temple Scroll, Manchester, December 1987* (ed. G. J. Brooke; JSPSup 7; Sheffield: JSOT Press, 1989), 143.

14. There may be seventeen copies of Jubilees, eleven manuscripts containing various sections of the Enoch literature, thirteen copies of the Rule of the Community, and seven copies of MMT.

15. On the very limited interest in Ezra-Nehemiah and Chronicles among those responsible for putting manuscripts in the Qumran caves, see the intriguing suggestions of G. Garbini, *History and Ideology in Ancient Israel* (London: SCM, 1988), 209 n. 60; G. J. Brooke, "The Books of Chronicles and the Scrolls from Qumran," in *Reflection and Refraction: Studies in Biblical Historiography in Honour of A. Graeme Auld* (ed. R. Rezetko, T. H. Lim, W. B. Aucker; VTSup 113; Leiden: Brill, 2007), 35–48.

16. Identified with the book of Jubilees by most scholars, e.g., C. Rabin, *The Zadokite Documents* (Oxford: Clarendon Press, 1958), 75; but see also the comments by D. Dimant, "Two 'Scientific Fictions: The So-called Book of Noah and the Alleged Quotation of Jubilees in CD 16:3–4," in *Studies in the Hebrew Bible, Qumran, and the Septuagint Presented to Eugene Ulrich* (ed. P. W. Flint, E. Tov, and J. C. VanderKam; VTSup 101; Leiden: Brill, 2006), 230–49.

17. On the identification of the quotation, see J. C. Greenfield, "The Words of Levi Son of Jacob in Damascus Document IV,15–19," *RevQ* 13 (1988): 319–22.

frgs. 1–4, lines 13–14,[18] and the mentions of a Book of Hagu/Hagi (CD 10:6; 13:2; 14:7–8; 1QSa 1:7).[19] Furthermore, in 11QPs[a] so-called apocryphal psalms are juxtaposed with psalms now present in the canonical Psalter.[20]

The scrolls found at Qumran show that it is not just the extent of the canon that is problematic but also the form of its text. Though we may be able to see that in Palestine in the late Second Temple period there was a gradual shift in some circles (even evident in some of the Qumran scriptural manuscripts) toward standardizing the form of the text along the lines of what became the dominant Hebrew text-type in the Tannaitic period and thereafter, there is a widespread pluriformity of text-types among the so-called biblical texts, so much so that it may be preferable in several instances to talk of individual texts rather than of types.[21] When many of these manuscripts were as yet unpublished with even preliminary analysis, and because the precise form of the text has not been a subject upon which Jewish and Christian writers of the classical period dwelled when discussing the canonical status of biblical books, Old Testament theologians cannot be held entirely to blame for not taking all this more obviously into account. However, now that all has been published for several years, such theologians should acknowledge that their stance in giving priority to the Protestant ordering of the MT and its particular text-type is merely pragmatic and should not be the sole basis for uniform theological approaches to the various books.

For the texts that are close to the core of any collection of authoritative materials for Palestinian Jews of the late Second Temple period, the Qumran scrolls have made it easy for scholars to draw attention to the existence of multiple Hebrew editions. Eugene Ulrich has elegantly summarized something of the significance of double editions of various biblical books: for Exodus the text of 4QpaleoExod[m] is a secondary edition compared with the MT and LXX; for 1 Samuel the Qumran Samuel manuscripts let us see that, whereas in 1 Sam 1–2 the MT may be the earlier form and the *Vorlage* of the LXX a secondary edition, in 1 Sam 17–18 it is the other way round; for Jeremiah the scrolls support the conclusion that the LXX displays an earlier edition of the entire book and the MT an expanded second edition; and for Dan 4–6 the MT and the Old Greek exhibit

---

18. This second law was identified with the Temple Scroll by Y. Yadin, *The Temple Scroll: The Hidden Law of the Dead Sea Sect* (London: Weidenfeld & Nicolson, 1985), 226–28.

19. Though this might be an apocryphal work, it might be no more than a euphemism for the Torah, as is maintained by L. H. Schiffman, *The Eschatological Community of the Dead Sea Scrolls: A Study of the Rule of the Congregation* (SBLMS 38; Atlanta: Scholars Press, 1989), 15.

20. See J. A. Sanders, *The Dead Sea Psalms Scroll* (Ithaca, N.Y.: Cornell University Press, 1967), 10–14. The significant point made first by Sanders is that in all the various psalms in this scroll the tetragrammaton is written consistently in paleo-Hebrew, and so all the psalms may have the same status.

21. A point made most explicitly in his earlier research by E. Tov, "Hebrew Biblical Manuscripts from the Judaean Desert: Their Contribution to Textual Criticism," *JJS* 39 (1988): 28–32; reprinted in a slightly revised form in Talmon, *Jewish Civilization in the Hellenistic-Roman Period*, 126–32.

two different editions of chs. 4–6, both apparently being secondary.[22] The proper acknowledgment of such information radically relativizes the status of any text. In most cases a pure or original (or "inspired") form slips beyond the grasp of the theologian or historian. It becomes natural to insist that theological analysis must be based on the final form of the text as we have it,[23] but then the question remains concerning whose theological perspective is being investigated on the basis of such a final form; it is rarely that of ancient Israel.

Although all this undermines the understanding of the value of the biblical text (an MT ordered by Protestants) for those modern interpreters who consider it from an idealistic (or conservative) standpoint, for others it suggests much more realistically that texts can never be viewed in a vacuum apart from the communities whose members composed them and the communities that subsequently copied and preserved them for a wide variety of reasons. And so it must be acknowledged that the literary remains from the hundreds of years between the exodus and the fall of the first temple are a very slender basis for establishing the religion(s) of Israel in that period and its (their) central theological insights. Here the evidence from Qumran is a very valuable historical control, for we have the literary remains of a community or communities that can be suitably dated and assessed; in that community or the movement of which it was a part, which undoubtedly was literate in a nonexemplary fashion, there is a very great variety of opinion, so much so that only recently have scholars begun to attempt to clarify and classify it.

Some might say that this is to overstate the case, but an example of the kind of problem for theological assessment of the Old Testament can be found in 4QGenExod[a] for Gen 22:14. The relevant fragment of the manuscript reads '] l[h]ym yr'h 'šr y'[mr. Since the combination of letters yr'h 'šr y'mr occurs only in Gen 22:14 in the whole MT, the identification of the biblical passage is not seriously in doubt. However, as James Davila has pointed out,[24] all the ancient witnesses attest YHWH for the 'lhym of 4QGenExod[a]. Although several scholars have detected a difficulty with YHWH in Gen 22:14, without textual support all emendations, however plausible and ingenious, have looked like scholarly tampering with the text. 4QGenExod[a] now provides textual support for all those who have reckoned that the whole pericope should be construed as consistently Elohistic (whatever that might imply). Some large and significant issues remain to be sorted out: the original reading, the place of composition of the pericope, the theological ethos of the original composer, the date of the change, and the relationship between Gen 22:1–19 (in some form) and 2 Chr 3:1. For those want-

---

22. Ulrich, *Dead Sea Scrolls and the Origins of the Bible*, 99–120.

23. Working with the final form of the text is one of the fundamental principles of the "Forms of the Old Testament Literature" project co-edited by Rolf Knierim and Gene M. Tucker; but the question now remains, Which final form?

24. J. R. Davila, "The Name of God at Moriah: An Unpublished Fragment from 4QGen-Exod[a]," *JBL* 110 (1991): 577–82.

ing to work theologically only with the final form of the text as in the MT, the problems can be glossed over, but for anyone with a historical perspective, the final MT form can no longer be understood adequately, even correctly, without some clear justification of its particular reading in this place for the divine epithet and all that goes with it.

A further intriguing example is visible in 11QpaleoLev frg. 1, lines 1–2, a place in the manuscript where there seems to have been deliberate scribal alteration to the text involving an assimilation with another passage in Leviticus. There are many instances of assimilation in manuscripts,[25] but few where the process can be clearly seen to be deliberate. That such was the case in 11QpaleoLev frg. 1, lines 1–2 is apparent because the scribe has actually marked off the passage he has included (indicated here by braces).[26] His text of Lev 18:27 now reads: "for all of] these abominations they did [{they did these things and I abhorred them and I have said t]o you, You shall inherit[ ]their l[a]nd} the men of the land who were befo[re you and it became de]filed, the land." In this way the two passages on sexual defilement (Lev 18:6–25 and 20:10–22) are inextricably linked and, if more of the manuscript had survived, we might have found other harmonistic assimilations in the presentation of the text of Lev 18.[27] Again, those who are concerned to make theology out of the MT alone will find no difficulty in rejecting the parenthetical reading of 11QpaleoLev 1, but they may well end up providing a theologically harmonized interpretation of the passages on sexual immorality, just as the scribe of 11QpaleoLev has done. Those whose concern is more historically oriented will see in the scribal handling of Lev 18:27 an appealing example of how one traditor in his particular situation was attempting to show something of the significance of the text as he passed it on. This scribal adjustment is not an error but a deliberate updating and improvement of the text. There are many other examples of this taking place, all of which show how in precanonical times a text could remain authoritative and relevant in successive generations, not as a static object of veneration but as part of a lively scribal interpretative tradition.

This brief description of a few matters from the Qumran literary evidence shows that the extent of the canon and the form of its text need to be taken into account by those who engage in the task of Old Testament theology. More precisely, the existence of the scrolls declares that the task of Old Testament theology, if it is to be connected in any way with historical realities, can only ever be done in relation to particular communities. The scrolls provide an opportunity and a challenge to those theologians who remain concerned to ground their

---

25. See, e.g., E. Tov, "The Nature and Background of Harmonizations in Biblical Manuscripts," *JSOT* 31 (1985): 3–29.

26. The text of this section of 11QpaleoLev can be found in D. N. Freedman and K. A. Mathews, *The Paleo-Hebrew Leviticus Scroll (11QpaleoLev)* (Winona Lake, Ind.: Eisenbrauns, 1985), 36 (plate 3, p. 103).

27. As in 11QT[a] 66:11–17.

theological analysis in historical-critical exegesis and the socioreligious setting and function of texts.

3. The Contents of the Scrolls and Old Testament Theology: Cultic Integration

Turning from the questions that the existence of the scrolls pose for the theologian of the Old Testament to honing the theologian's task on the basis of their content, it is important to preface any remarks with a word of caution concerning the nature of the manuscripts from the eleven caves at Qumran as a collection. Among the scrolls it is easy enough to identify what, somewhat anachronistically, we might call "biblical" texts. While some may contain readings reflecting a particular viewpoint, it is impossible to locate anything in the variants that could fairly be labeled narrowly or distinctively sectarian.[28] A second group of texts are those that seem to use certain technical terms more or less consistently and which may be held to represent the viewpoint of the community or communities that produced them and passed them on. Among these texts would be placed those that use the term *yaḥad* in a particular way.[29] The third group of texts, that is, the rest, is more difficult to assess. The question remains whether, together with the second group, these other nonbiblical texts reflect a coherent perspective, whether some of them have been preserved in the caves for purely antiquarian purposes, or whether they actually form a more heterogeneous collection, perhaps from Jerusalem, of the spread of literature available in late Second Temple period Palestine.

Given the conclusion that it is necessary for theological analysis to be done in relation to particular communities, it is appropriate to focus a few comments about what the Old Testament theologian might attempt to describe by addressing some matters that arise primarily out of the texts that are most closely associated with those who were resident at Qumran or associated with the movement of which that community was a part. Since it is theology with which we are concerned, it is appropriate to begin with the understanding of God. There has been considerable interest in the dualisms implied in some texts: these involve angelology (angel of darkness/angel of truth), society (sons of light/men of the lot of Belial), and ethics (spirit of truth/spirit of falsehood). But there is no corresponding theological ontological dualism. In fact, the very same pericope that con-

---

28. There is no evidence, e.g., in 4QpaleoExod^m for the distinctive Samaritan reading in the Exodus Decalogue pericope.

29. Some scholars, such as S. Talmon ("Between the Bible and the Mishna," in idem, *The World of Qumran from Within: Collected Studies* [Jerusalem: Magnes, 1989], 16–19) have identified the community that resided at Qumran with the Yaḥad, partly to dissociate them from the Essenes, but matters might not be quite so simple. See A. Schofield, *From Qumran to the Yaḥad: A New Paradigm of Textual Development for* The Community Rule (STDJ 77; Leiden: Brill, 2009).

tains the most dualistic expressions is prefaced with an insistence on the singular origin of all things from God: "from the God of knowledge comes all that is and shall be.… The laws of (*mšpty*) all things are in his hand."[30]

Yet, despite this clear monotheistic assertion, the angelology of some texts suggests that both in thought and in experience there was a need for some form of qualification. The Songs of the Sabbath Sacrifice, which may or may not be a narrowly sectarian text, contain numerous designations for heavenly beings.[31] Of particular note are the uses of *'ēlîm* ("gods") and *'ĕlôhîm* ("gods"), often in various combinations, such as *'ēley 'ôr* ("gods of light") and *'ĕlôhēy ḥayyim* ("living gods").[32] Particularly frequent in the Sabbath Songs is the designation *'ēley da'at* ("gods of knowledge"), which may be a counterpart to the overarching epithet of God as *'el haddē'ôt* ("God of knowledge"; 1QS 3:15). This correspondence gives the impression that for the traditors of these texts it was clear that the highly significant epithets for angels in Pss 29:1 and 89:7 (*bny 'lhym*; "sons of God/ heavenly beings") and Dan 11:36 (*'l 'lym*; "God of gods") demonstrated that it was through the angelic beings that God could be experienced as active. Several uses of *'lwhym* ("God/gods") in the Sabbath Songs are ambiguous but in expressions such as *kwl 'lwhym* ("all gods/divine beings") there is some unequivocal evidence for the use of *'lwhym* of angels, as also in the use of Ps 82:1 in 11QMelch 2:10 of Melchizedek. What God desired, the angels carried out; when the angelic Melchizedek acts as judge, he does so as God's agent.

This developed angelology is commonly supposed to protect the transcendence of God,[33] sometimes a protectiveness that is read as Israel's near loss of the sense of the divine altogether. But that is to tell only half the story. Alongside the

---

30. 1QS 3:15–4:26. See W. H. Brownlee, "The Ineffable Name of God," *BASOR* 226 (1977): 39–46. 1QS 3:15–18 and 4:18–26 beautifully sum up how Israel's God is concerned with cosmos and history, and qualitatively with righteousness, matters that Knierim sees as programmatic for the suitable theological reading of Old Testament texts. See Knierim, "Cosmos and History," 63–73; and idem, "Task of Old Testament Theology," 42–43.

31. C. A. Newsom began by concluding cautiously that "the scroll of the Sabbath Shirot is a product of the Qumran community" (*Songs of the Sabbath Sacrifice: A Critical Edition* [HSS 27; Atlanta: Scholars Press, 1985], 4) but more recently has written that "the various pieces of evidence are probably best interpreted as pointing toward a non-Qumran origin for the *Sabbath Songs*" (C. A. Newsom, J. H. Charlesworth with B. A. Strawn and H. W. L. Rietz, "Angelic Liturgy: Songs of the Sabbath Sacrifice [4Q400–4Q407, 11Q17, Mas1k]," in *The Dead Sea Scrolls: Hebrew, Aramaic, and Greek Texts with English Translations*, vol. 4B, *Angelic Liturgy: Songs of the Sabbath Sacrifice* [Princeton Theological Seminary Dead Sea Scrolls Project 4B; Tübingen: Mohr Siebeck; Louisville: Westminster John Knox, 1999], 4).

32. *'ĕlôhēy ḥayyim* seems to be reflected in the particular designation for God that Josephus ascribes to the Essenes: "At the beginning and at the end they bless God as the giver of life (χορηγὸν τῆς ζωῆς)" (*War* 2.131).

33. See, e.g., the classic statement on angelology made by W. Eichrodt, *Theology of the Old Testament* (2 vols.; OTL; London: SCM, 1967), 2:200: "it served in the first place to illustrate the exaltedness of Yahweh."

transcendent origin of all things needs to be put the life and raison d'être of the believing communities. A text such as the Songs of the Sabbath Sacrifice shows that when the community is aligned suitably with the purposes of God, particularly as those are expressed in the Torah as correctly understood and practiced, then in its worship it will be aligned with or even participating in the worship of the angels whose primary function is the praise of God.[34] This is the case even though the group asserting this may well not be active in any way in the dominant location of God's presence, the temple. In fact, the community may have considered itself to be an anticipation of the place of God's worship which God himself would one day create;[35] this would be like a return to Eden.[36]

This sense of the presence of the reality of God in the worship of the community, especially the Sabbath worship,[37] has important implications for the debate within the discipline of Old Testament theology concerning whether creation or history should be seen as the dominant ideological perspective controlling the literary materials, both in themselves and in their analysis.[38] The functional definition of God that features so prominently in 1QS 3:15, "from the God of knowledge comes all that is and will be," contains both elements. God is the creator of all things, not just as the prime mover but as one who remains responsible for all that will be. The community's view of the future, essentially its eschatology, is an expectation both of a future defeat of Belial and all those of his lot and one that expects that such a victory will restore all things to their original purposes, which were visible in Eden and will be made manifest in the heavenly temple, which is to be built precisely according to the divine blueprint.

The assessment of these juxtaposed motifs, of cosmos and eschatology, of creation and history, has been present in recent decades both in the debate about the proper focus of Old Testament theology and in scholarly considerations of apocalyptic. The rediscovery of cosmology in apocalyptic has been in large measure the result of a careful analysis of the various subgenres that make up the texts that might be grouped together under the overarching umbrella of "descriptions of visions or auditions framed in a narrative." The two principal

---

34. Newsom, *Songs of the Sabbath Sacrifice*, 23–38.

35. As is the most likely interpretation of the phrase *mqdš 'dm* in 4Q174: see G. J. Brooke, *Exegesis at Qumran: 4QFlorilegium in Its Jewish Context* (JSOTSup 29; Sheffield: JSOT Press, 1985), 184–87; D. Dimant, "4QFlorilegium and the Idea of the Community as Temple," in *Hellenica et Judaica: Hommage à Valentin Nikiprowetzky* (ed. A. Caquot, M. Hadas-Lebel and J. Riaud; Collection de la Revue des études juives 3; Leuven: Peeters, 1986), 176–80, 188–89.

36. M. O. Wise thinks that this return will take place in two stages, the first human-made, the second divinely created; for him *mqdš 'dm*, "the temple of Adam," in 4Q174 corresponds to the first stage ("4QFlorilegium and the Temple of Adam," *RevQ* 15 [1991–92]: 103–32).

37. This particular keeping of the Sabbath through worship is a strong feature of the sectarian compositions found in the Qumran caves and is the clearest way that law and cult are woven together, that cyclic cosmic time and history are combined, in the self-understanding of the movement; see Knierim, "Cosmos and History," 80–85.

38. See ibid., 59–74.

subcategories have now been recognized as cosmological and eschatological.[39] Though some apocalypses proper may stress one or the other, they are commonly represented together. Thus, for all that Enoch has visions of the heavens and is thus introduced to the makeup of the cosmos, he is also shown how judgment and justice are being and will be worked out. Though the Qumran community is falsely labeled apocalyptic, the combination of interwoven cosmological and eschatological perspectives is very important in the self-definition of its members and the wider movement of which they were a part.

The self-definition of the community does not rest in its being persecuted by the Jerusalem hierarchy. The date and extent of such persecution are very debatable in any case. Rather, the community's self-definition seems to depend on its determination to order its life to provide for worship according to its understanding of the purposes of God discernible in the ordering of nature which have been engraved in a statute for ever (khwq hrwt l'd; 1QS 10:6). The hymnic material at the end of 1QS makes it clear that the following of the appointed times as reflected in the seasons of the years is the underlying assumption behind all that has been said earlier in the Rule of the Community about joining the community and living out one's life as a member of it. It is the determination to accept the calendar of 364 days as most clearly reflecting how God has made himself known in the order of nature that affects everything else in the community's organization and practice of the Law. This calendar is not based, as is commonly assumed, solely on the sun; it is not a straightforward solar calendar. Rather, it is based in the first place in the unit of seven days, the week, which is the period of the ordering of creation (hence six is significant) and a day of rest (Sabbath). The annual calendar is organized as fifty-two weeks of seven days. The pericope on David's compositions in 11QPs^a 27:3–11 makes this clear: David wrote "songs to sing before the altar over the whole burnt perpetual offering every day, for all the days of the year, 364; and for offerings of the Sabbaths, 52 songs."[40]

Furthermore, this fifty-two week calendar paid very close attention to the moon's phases. The Mishmarot texts emphasize this plainly.[41] Though there are many details yet to be interpreted correctly, it seems likely that the twenty-four priestly courses of 1 Chr 24:7–18 were assigned in rotation so that in a six-year cycle they would return to their original positions.[42] There is no attempt to turn the twenty-four courses into twenty-six so that the whole system might fit

---

39. E.g., J. J. Collins labels these two basic generic categories "the 'historical' apocalypses" and "otherworldly journeys" (*Daniel: With an Introduction to Apocalyptic Literature* [FOTL 20; Grand Rapids: Eerdmans, 1984], 6–19).

40. Sanders, *Dead Sea Psalms Scroll*, 87.

41. See S. Talmon and J. Ben-Dov, "Calendrical Documents and Mishmarot," in *Qumran Cave 4.XVI: Calendrical Texts* (ed. S. Talmon, J. Ben-Dov, and U. Glessmer; DJD 21; Oxford: Clarendon, 2001), 1–166.

42. Knierim's comments on creation as cyclic cosmic time are significant in this respect too: "Cosmos and History," 80–85.

together more readily. Rather, perhaps because twelve (and its multiples) was also a significant number for the community as for others,[43] a system was devised that allowed for twenty-four courses to service fifty-two weeks, a system whose benefits prevented any one course from claiming any particular preeminence as the one always on duty at a particular festival. It is possible that here there is a good example of an authoritative priestly text not being altered because it could be seen to fit the overall chronometric perspective of the community.

The effect of following the 364-day calendar is that the Sabbath never coincides with the principal days of any festival nor with the first day of any month. At one stroke all the problems over which prescriptions take precedence when there is a clash with the Sabbath, which beset some forms of Judaism, are avoided. The natural order engraved in statute has not been revealed in order to show conflict with some other law. God's purposes, when appreciated aright, are consistent in themselves. The scribal attitude that is reflected in the process of the harmonization of legal materials is the precise counterpart to these assumptions concerning the coherence and consistency of what can be known about God from the Torah and the natural order of creation.

An effect of allocating the priestly courses in rotation is that, according to the calendric information at the end of 4QS^c the total calendar rotates every six jubilee periods (294 years).[44] The practice of the annual cycle very quickly leads to chronometric calculations beyond the weekly and annual unit. The hymnic section at the end of 1QS makes this clear: "the seasons of years to their weeks and at the beginning of their weeks to the season of release (*drwr*)," Beyond the week of years it is the jubilee cycle that dominates the periodization of history. This plays a part in how the history of the past was viewed and recounted. Above all such jubilee periodization is visible in the book of Jubilees itself, but it is also apparent, for example, in the so-called Psalms of Joshua.[45]

Just as the past is understood in jubilee cycles, so is the future. 6Q12 talks of what will happen "after the jubilees." Above all, in 11QMelch at the end of the tenth jubilee period there is atonement for all the sons of light and the men of the lot of Melchizedek; this is the Day of Atonement at which Melchizedek seems to preside, certainly as the agent of God's judgment, probably also as a heavenly high priest who can "proclaim to them liberty, forgiving them the wrongdoings of all their iniquities" (11QMelch 2:6). For all that some of the details are unclear, it remains plain that the climax of the tenth jubilee on the Day of Atonement involves the celebratory release that is based in the right ordering of worship. Cosmology and eschatology come together.

---

43. See J. M. Baumgarten, "The Duodecmal Courts at Qumran, the Apocalypse, and the Sanhedrin," *JBL* 95 (1976): 59–78; reprinted in idem, *Studies in Qumran Law* (SJLA 24; Leiden: Brill, 1977), 145–71.

44. See Talmon and Ben-Dov, "Calendrical Documents and Mishmarot," 1–36.

45. Newsom, "'Psalms of Joshua' from Qumran Cave 4," 56–73; see esp. 4Q379 frg. 12, line 5 on the jubilee reckoning for the entry into Canaan.

This cosmological and eschatological self-understanding is expressed predominantly and practically in the application of the Torah in worship. The Qumran handling of the tradition falls precisely within the tension of the matrix that historians of the late Second Temple period have often represented in terms of the temple and the law.[46] This arena of cultic practice also becomes a focus for defining the different groups of humanity. Just as the eschatological battles will be led by priests and those who are set in battle order are as pure as those admitted to the temple precincts, so the eschatological sanctuary will not be polluted by any unqualified people. Thus, in 1QM 7:4–6 one reads that "no man who is lame, or blind, or crippled or afflicted with a lasting bodily blemish or smitten with a bodily impurity, none of these shall march out to war with them," and "no man shall go down with them on the day of battle who is impure because of his fount, for the holy angels shall be with their hosts." In a corresponding manner in 4Q174 1:3–4 one reads of the exclusion of the Ammonite, the Moabite, the bastard, the stranger, and the proselyte from the future sanctuary. The reasons for the exclusion are very similar in both cases. In 1QM it is because the "holy angels shall be with their hosts"; in 4Q174 because "his holy ones are there." The justification in part for the strict application of Deut 23 to the eschatological activities of the community rests in the presence of angels.

The community's attitude to the will of God as disclosed in the natural ordering of things in weeks and years is the basis for their own closer self-definition in relation to the rest of Israel, including renegade members of the early community. The opening pages of the Damascus Document make it clear in a repetitive fashion that the community of that text, perhaps a predecessor of the Qumran community, differentiated itself from others who were considered to have transgressed the covenant and violated the precept (*ḥwq*; CD 1:20; 2:6).[47] In the third introductory exhortation the reader is told that the Watchers fell because they did not keep the commandments (*mṣwt*; CD 2:18) of God; and the rest of Israel has sadly also been led astray. These general categorizations are not given specific justification until the end of this third introductory exhortation. The first time the reader is given specific criteria of differentiation regarding the content of the commandments (*mṣwt*; CD 3:12) the hidden things are involved, namely, "His holy Sabbaths and his glorious feasts, the testimonies of his righteousness, and the ways of his truth and the desires of his will which a man must do in order to live" (CD 3:14–16).[48] The three nets of Belial, which will undoubtedly ensnare the

---

46. As classically presented, e.g., by J. Maier, *Zwischen den Testamenten: Geschichte und Religion in der Zeit des zweiten Tempels* (Neue Echter Bibel, Ergänzungsband zum Alten Testament 3; Würzburg: Echter, 1990), 212–35.

47. In a way not dissimilar to its usage in CD, Knierim ("Cosmos and History," 87) says of *ḥwq* that "when used in connection with the creation and existence of the world [it] comes close to being the Hebrew word itself for world-order."

48. It is noteworthy that the reading of the traditions according to CD is not unlike that of K. Koch, "Wort und Einheit des Schöpfergottes in Memphis und Jerusalem," *ZTK* 62 (1965):

rest of Israel, because they are three kinds of righteousness in disguise, are fornication, riches, and the profanation of the temple. Again the natural order and the moral order correspond to the right ordering of the cult, the way of worship.[49]

According to the Damascus Document this differentiation between the community and the rest of Israel is a matter well in the past with ongoing significance. According to 1QpHab 11:2–8 this differentiation is a matter of the more recent history of the community: the Wicked Priest has pursued the Teacher of Righteousness on the Day of Atonement. According to a text like 4Q174, this differentiation will be the hallmark of the community in the future. Since some kind of observance of the Sabbath, though not necessarily liturgical worship on that day, was common to all Jews in the late Second Temple period, the basis of this differentiation in the Sabbath is not in itself sectarian, even though the practice of the Sabbath by the communities of D and S may have been distinctive.

In making sense of the worldview of the people of the communities reflected in textssuch as the Rule of the Community (S) and the Damascus Document (D), it is important to note the broader bases on which their outlook was built. The significance of these communities and their texts cannot be dismissed through labeling them as narrowly sectarian. Rather, they present a significant reading of earlier traditions, as significant in their own ways as the approximately contemporary readings of those same traditions by the communities whose literary deposit is the New Testament.

This study has tried to show in a very brief compass that the theological outlook of the S and D communities was based on attitudes to tradition and the created order that were mindful of the consistency of God in himself and in his activity in the world. The ordering of the cosmos in weeks, months, years, weeks of years, and jubilee periods provides for a periodization of history that allows one to see who in the past lived their lives according to God's precepts and who in the present is not being led astray, and to estimate when those who keep to the correct application of the commandments will be vindicated. The historical, especially eschatological outlook of the communities depends on their knowledge of the God who creates and sustains the cosmos.

The cognitive dissonance that may result from their having a minority perspective in late Second Temple period Judaism, and unfulfilled expectations, is accommodated through the sense of the proximity of the creator God through his angelic agents. Since the principal function of angels is to praise God, so the lifestyle of the members of the community is dominated not by the living out

---

251–93; quoted approvingly by Knierim, "Cosmos and History," 71–72. Perhaps it is not too much to say that a careful reading of some of these early Jewish texts can provide suitable insight into how the earlier traditions may best be handled theologically.

49. This is akin to what Knierim ("Cosmos and History," 81) has argued for on the basis of Gen 1 in another context: "the cosmic order itself reflects the ongoing presence of creation. It remains loyal to its origin. This ongoing presence of creation is, therefore, an ultimate presence."

of divine action in the world, even though they consider themselves to be the elect, but by Torah-based worship in which the histories of the world, Israel, and the community are integrated under the dominant perspective of the divinely ordered cosmos. All is oriented toward God as universal creator and based in a wider field of thought than ever came to be the contents of the canon.

4. Conclusion

The lessons here for the practice of Old Testament theology are manifold. There should be nothing controversial about stating that if Old Testament theology is to claim any historical validity, then the texts that form its basis cannot be studied apart from particular sociopolitical and religious contexts. Sound exegesis, the basis of sound theological extrapolation, will always try to take account of such contexts. The theological bases of the worldviews of the individuals and groups belonging to those contexts cannot be definitively derived solely from the canonical texts; even the theological principles of those who determined the final extent of the canon cannot be derived solely from those texts. More obviously, the validity of any community's theological worldview cannot be verified from the texts alone. In addition, in respect to the later canonical books, the preservation of a wide range of earlier textual forms of those books provides some clues as to the motivation of various scribes in reflecting the overall coherence of how the created order is reflected in the Torah; the authority of the traditions lay in the very fact that they needed to be reworked, interpreted, and updated, not in the veneration of any particular form of the text as providing the hermeneutical key for giving meaning to present experience.

In the scrolls from Qumran, especially those that can be most readily associated with the viewpoint of the community there, we have a glimpse of the religious perspectives of a particular Jewish group that was attempting to make sense of the world and to give meaning to its experience in light of some basic theological assumptions. Before the temple was destroyed and before the extent of the canon was delimited, this group had already put into practice a lifestyle based on received lively traditions, a lifestyle that tried to integrate Torah and cult, creation and history, cosmology and eschatology. In the light of that attempt, Old Testament theologians might find guidelines for their task of describing in a historically coherent and honest fashion the relationship between God and the world, especially as that may be summed up in the prayer and praise of a believing community of any period, and as that is represented in various ways in the various editions of the books that now come to make up various canons.

Bibliography

Abegg, Martin, Peter Flint, and Eugene Ulrich. *The Dead Sea Scrolls Bible: The Oldest Known Bible Translated for the First Time into English.* San Francisco: HarperSanFrancisco, 1999.

Alexander, Loveday C. A. "Marathon or Jericho? Reading Acts in Dialogue with Biblical and Greek Historiography." Pages 92–125 in *Auguries: The Jubilee Volume of the Sheffield Department of Biblical Studies.* Edited by David J. A. Clines and Stephen D. Moore. Journal for the Study of the Old Testament: Supplement Series 269. Sheffield: Sheffield Academic Press, 1998. Repr., pages 283–310 in *Ancient and Modern Scriptural Historiography/L'historiographie biblique, ancienne et moderne.* Edited by George J. Brooke and Thomas Römer. Bibliotheca ephemeridum theologicarum lovaniensium 207. Leuven: Peeters, 2007.

Alexander, Philip S. "The Bible in Qumran and Early Judaism." Pages 35–62 in *Text in Context: Essays by Members of the Society for Old Testament Study.* Edited by A. D. H. Mayes. Oxford: Clarendon, 2000.

———. "Insider/Outsider Labelling and the Struggle for Power in Early Judaism." Pages 83–100 in *Religion, Language, and Power.* Edited by Nile Green and Mary Searle-Chatterjee. Routledge Studies in Religion 10. New York: Routledge, 2008.

———. "Literacy among Jews in Second Temple Palestine: Reflections on the Evidence from Qumran." Pages 3–24 in *Hamlet on a Hill: Semitic and Greek Studies Presented to Professor T. Muraoka on the Occasion of His Sixty-Fifth Birthday.* Edited by M. F. J. Baasten and W. Th. van Peursen. Orientalia Lovaniensia Analecta 118. Leuven: Peeters. 2003.

———. "Midrash." Pages 452–59 in *A Dictionary of Biblical Interpretation.* Edited by R. J. Coggins and J. L. Houlden; London: SCM, 1990.

———. "Retelling the Old Testament." Pages 99–121 in *It Is Written: Scripture Citing Scripture. Essays in Honour of Barnabas Lindars, SSF.* Edited by D. A. Carson and H. G. M. Williamson. Cambridge: Cambridge University Press, 1987.

Alexander, Philip S., and G. Vermes. *Qumran Cave 4.XIX: Serekh Ha-Yaḥad and Two Related Texts.* Discoveries in the Judaean Desert 26. Oxford: Clarendon, 1998.

Alkier, Stefan, and Richard B. Hays, eds. *Die Bibel im Dialog der Schriften: Konzepte intertextueller Bibellektüre.* Neutestamentliche Entwürfe zur Theologie

10. Tübingen: Francke, 2005. English: Richard B. Hays, Stefan Alkier, and Leroy A. Huizenga, eds. *Reading the Bible Intertextually*. Waco: Baylor University Press, 2009.

Allegro, John Marco. *The Dead Sea Scrolls and the Christian Myth*. Newton Abbot: Westbridge Books, 1979.

———. "Further Messianic References in Qumran Literature." *Journal of Biblical Literature* 75 (1956): 174–87.

Allison, Dale C. *Constructing Jesus: Memory, Imagination, and History*. Grand Rapids: Baker Academic, 2010.

Altemeyer, B., and B. Hunsberger. "Authoritarianism, Religious Fundamentalism, Quest, and Right-Wing Authoritarianism." *International Journal for the Psychology of Religion* 2 (1992): 113–33.

Anderson, G. W., ed. *Tradition and Interpretation: Essays by Members of the Society for Old Testament Study*. Oxford: Clarendon, 1979.

Ap-Thomas, D. R. *A Primer of Old Testament Text Criticism*. 2nd ed. Facet Books 14. Philadelphia: Fortress, 1966.

Assmann, Jan. "Collective Memory and Cultural Identity." *New German Critique* 65 (1995): 125–33.

———. *Moses the Egyptian: The Memory of Egypt in Western Monotheism*. Cambridge, Mass.: Harvard University Press, 1997.

———. *Religion and Cultural Memory: Ten Studies*. Cultural Memory in the Present. Stanford: Stanford University Press, 2006. German original: *Religion und kulturelles Gedächtnis*. Munich: Beck, 2000.

Atkins, Peter. *Memory and Liturgy: The Place of Memory in the Composition and Practice of Liturgy*. Aldershot: Ashgate, 2004.

Atkinson, Kenneth. "Anti-Roman Polemics in the Dead Sea Scrolls and Related Literature: Their Later Use in John's Apocalypse." *Qumran Chronicle* 12 (2004): 109–22.

———. "Representations of History in 4Q331 (4QpapHistorical Text C), 4Q332 (4QHistorical Text D), 4Q333 (4QHistorical Text E), and 4Q468e (4QHistorical Text F): An Annalistic Calendar Documenting Portentous Events?" *Dead Sea Discoveries* 14 (2007): 125–51.

Attridge, Harold W. "Historiography" and "Josephus." Pages 157–232 in *Jewish Writings of the Second Temple Period: Apocrypha, Pseudepigrapha, Qumran Sectarian Writings, Philo, Josephus*. Edited by Michael E. Stone. Compendia Rerum Iudaicarum ad Novum Testamentum 2/II. Assen: Van Gorcum; Philadelphia: Fortress, 1984.

———. "Jewish Historiography." Pages 311–43 in *Early Judaism and Its Modern Interpreters*. Edited by Robert A. Kraft and George W. E. Nickelsburg. Bible and Its Modern Interpreters 2. Philadelphia: Fortress; Atlanta: Scholars Press, 1986.

Attridge, Harold W., and John Strugnell. "Prayer of Enosh." Pages 353–62 in *Qumran Cave 4.VIII: Parabiblical Texts, Part 1*. Edited by James C. VanderKam. Discoveries in the Judaean Desert 13. Oxford: Clarendon, 1994.

Aune, David E. "On the Origins of the 'Council of Javneh' Myth." *Journal of Biblical Literature* 110 (1991): 491–93.

Baasten, M. F. J. "Nominal Clauses Containing a Personal Pronoun in Qumran Hebrew." Pages 1–16 in *The Hebrew of the Dead Sea Scrolls and Ben Sira: Proceedings of a Symposium Held at Leiden University, 11–14 December 1995.* Edited by T. Muraoka and J. F. Elwolde. Studies on the Texts of the Desert of Judah 26. Leiden: Brill, 1997.

Baillet, Maurice. "Livres des Rois." Pages 107–12 in vol. 1 of *Les "Petites Grottes" de Qumrân: Explorations de la falaise, les grottes 2Q, 3Q, 5Q, 6Q, 7Q à 10Q, Le rouleau de cuivre.* Edited by M. Baillet, J. T. Milik, and R. de Vaux. 2 vols. Discoveries in the Judaean Desert 3. Oxford: Clarendon, 1962.

Barr, James. *Fundamentalism.* London: SCM, 1978.

———. *Scripture: Canon, Authority, Criticism.* Oxford: Clarendon, 1983.

Barstad, H. "Prophecy at Qumran?" Pages 104–20 in *In the Last Days: On Jewish and Christian Apocalyptic and Its Period.* Edited by Knud Jeppesen, Kirsten Nielsen, and Bent Rosendal. Aarhus: Aarhus University Press, 1994.

Barthélemy, Dominique. *Les devanciers d'Aquila.* Supplements to Vetus Testamentum 10. Leiden: Brill, 1963.

———. "Juges." Pages 62–65 in *Qumran Cave I.* Edited by Dominique Barthélemy and Józef T. Milik. Discoveries in the Judaean Desert 1. Oxford, Clarendon, 1955.

Barton, John. *Oracles of God: Perceptions of Ancient Prophecy in Israel after the Exile.* 2nd ed. London: Darton, Longman & Todd, 2007.

Barton, Stephen C., Loren T. Stuckenbruck, and Benjamin G. Wold, eds. *Memory in the Bible and Antiquity: The Fifth Durham–Tübingen Research Symposium (Durham, September 2004).* Wissenschaftliche Untersuchungen zum Neuen Testament 212. Tübingen: Mohr Siebeck, 2007.

Bauckham, Richard J. "James, 1 and 2 Peter, Jude." Pages 303–17 in *It Is Written: Scripture Citing Scripture. Essays in Honour of Barnabas Lindars SSF.* Edited by D. A. Carson and H. G. M. Williamson. Cambridge: Cambridge University Press, 1988.

———. *Jude and the Relatives of Jesus in the Early Church.* Edinburgh: T&T Clark, 1990.

Baumgarten, Albert I. *The Flourishing of Jewish Sects in the Maccabean Era: An Interpretation.* Supplements to the Journal for the Study of Judaism 55. Leiden: Brill, 1997.

———. "The Perception of the Past in the Damascus Document." Pages 1–15 in *The Damascus Document: A Centennial of Discovery. Proceedings of the Third International Symposium of the Orion Center for the Study of the Dead Sea Scrolls and Associated Literature, 4–8 February, 1998.* Edited by Joseph M. Baumgarten, Esther G. Chazon, and Avital Pinnick. Studies on the Texts of the Desert of Judah 34. Leiden, Brill, 2000.

Baumgarten, Joseph M. "The Duodecimal Courts at Qumran, the Apocalypse, and the Sanhedrin." *Journal of Biblical Literature* 95 (1976): 59–78. Repr., pages 145–71 in *Studies in Qumran Law*. Studies in Judaism in Late Antiquity 24. Leiden: Brill, 1977.

——, ed. *Qumran Cave 4.XII: The Damascus Document (4Q266–273)*. Discoveries in the Judaean Desert 18. Oxford: Clarendon, 1996.

Bautch, Kelley Coblentz. *A Study of Geography of 1 Enoch 17–19: 'No One Has Seen What I Have Seen.'* Supplements to the Journal for the Study of Judaism 81. Leiden: Brill, 2003.

Beall, T. S. "History and Eschatology at Qumran: Messiah." Pages 125–46 in *Judaism in Late Antiquity*. Part 5, *The Judaism of Qumran: A Systemic Reading of the Dead Sea Scrolls*. Edited by Alan J. Avery-Peck, Jacob Neusner, and Bruce D. Chilton. Handbook of Oriental Studies, Section 1, The Near and Middle East 57. Leiden: Brill, 2001.

Beebee, Thomas O. *The Ideology of Genre: A Comparative Study of Generic Instability*. University Park: Pennsylvania State University Press, 1994.

Ben-Dov, Jonathan, and Stéphane Saulnier. "Qumran Calendars: A Survey of Scholarship 1980–2007." *Currents in Biblical Research* 7 (2008): 131–79.

Bengtsson, Håkan. "What's in a Name? A Study of Sobriquets in the Pesharim." Ph.D. diss., Uppsala, 2000.

Berger, Peter L. *The Heretical Imperative: Contemporary Possibilities of Religious Affirmation*. Garden City, N.Y.: Doubleday, 1979.

Bernstein, Moshe J. "*4Q159* Fragment 5 and the 'Desert Theology' of the Qumran Sect." Pages 43–56 in *Emanuel: Studies in Hebrew Bible, Septuagint and Dead Sea Scrolls in Honor of Emanuel Tov*. Edited by Shalom M. Paul et al. Supplements to Vetus Testamentum 94. Leiden: Brill, 2003.

——. "4Q252: From Re-Written Bible to Biblical Commentary." *Journal of Jewish Studies* 45 (1994): 1–27.

——. "4Q252: Method and Context, Genre and Sources." *Jewish Quarterly Review* 85 (1994–95): 61–79.

——. "The Contribution of the Qumran Discoveries to the History of Early Jewish Biblical Interpretation." Pages 215–38 in *The Idea of Biblical Interpretation: Essays in Honor of James L. Kugel*. Edited by Hindy Najman and Judith H. Newman. Supplements to the Journal for the Study of Judaism 83. Leiden: Brill, 2004.

——. "Divine Titles and Epithets and the Sources of the *Genesis Apocryphon*." *Journal of Biblical Literature* 128 (2009): 291–310.

——. "The Genre(s) of the Genesis Apocryphon." Pages 317–43 in *Aramaica Qumranica: Proceedings of the Conference on the Aramaic Texts from Qumran in Aix-en-Provence, 30 June–2 July 2008*. Edited by Katell Berthelot and Daniel Stökl Ben Ezra. Studies on the Texts of the Desert of Judah 94. Leiden: Brill, 2010.

——. "'Rewritten Bible': A Generic Category Which Has Outlived Its Usefulness?" *Textus* 22 (2005): 169–96.

Berrin, Shani L. *The Pesher Nahum Scroll from Qumran: An Exegetical Study of 4Q169*. Studies on the Texts of the Desert of Judah 53. Leiden: Brill, 2004.

———. "Qumran Pesharim." Pages 110–33 in *Biblical Interpretation at Qumran*. Edited by Matthias Henze. Studies in the Dead Sea Scrolls and Related Literature. Grand Rapids: Eerdmans, 2005.

Betz, Otto. *Offenbarung und Schriftforschung in der Qumransekte*. Wissenschaftlicht Untersuchungen zum Neuen Testament 6. Tübingen: Mohr Siebeck, 1960.

Black, Matthew, ed. *The Scrolls and Christianity: Historical and Theological Significance*. Theological Collections 11. London: SPCK, 1969.

Bockmuehl, Markus. "The Dead Sea Scrolls and the Origins of Biblical Commentary." Pages 3–29 in *Text, Thought and Practice in Qumran and Early Christianity: Proceedings of the Ninth International Symposium of the Orion Center for the Study of the Dead Sea Scrolls and Associated Literature, Jointly Sponsored by the Hebrew University Center for the Study of Christianity, 11–13 January, 2004*. Edited by Ruth A. Clements and Daniel R. Schwartz. Studies on the Texts of the Desert of Judah 84. Leiden: Brill, 2009.

———. *Seeing the Word: Refocusing New Testament Study*. Studies in Theological Interpretation. Grand Rapids: Baker Academic, 2006.

Boyarin, Daniel. "Issues for Further Discussion: A Response." *Semeia* 69–70 (1995): 293–97.

Branham, Joan. "Hedging the Holy at Qumran: Walls as Symbolic Devices." Pages 117–31 in *Qumran, the Site of the Dead Sea Scrolls: Archaeological Interpretations and Debates. Proceedings of a Conference Held at Brown University, November 17–19, 2002*. Edited by Katharina Galor, Jean-Baptiste Humbert, and Jürgen Zangenberg. Studies on the Texts of the Desert of Judah 57. Leiden: Brill, 2006.

Brenner, Athalya, and Frank H. Polak, eds. *Performing Memory in Biblical Narrative and Beyond*. Bible in the Modern World 25. Amsterdam Studies in the Bible and Religion 3. Sheffield: Sheffield Phoenix, 2009.

Brooke, George J. "4Q158: Reworked Pentateuchᵃ or 4QReworked Pentateuch A?" *Dead Sea Discoveries* 8 (2001): 219–41.

———. "4Q252 and the 153 Fish of John 21:11." Pages 253–65 in *Antikes Judentum und Frühes Christentum: Festschrift für Hartmut Stegemann zum 65. Geburtstag*. Edited by Bernd Kollmann, Wolfgang Reinbold, and Annette Steudel. Beihefte zur Zeitschrift für die neutestamentliche Wissenschaft 97. Berlin: de Gruyter, 1999.

———. "4Q341: An Exercise for Spelling and for Spells?" Pages 271–82 in *Writing and Ancient Near Eastern Society: Papers in Honour of Alan R. Millard*. Edited by Piotr Bienkowski, Christopher B. Mee, and Elizabeth A. Slater. Library of Hebrew Bible/Old Testament Studies 426. London: T&T Clark International, 2005.

———. "4QCommentary on Genesis A." Pages 185–207 in *Qumran Cave 4.XVII: Parabiblical Texts, Part 3*. Edited by George J. Brooke et al., in consultation with James C. VanderKam. Discoveries in the Judaean Desert 22. Oxford: Clarendon, 1996.

————. "Between Authority and Canon: The Significance of Reworking the Bible for Understanding the Canonical Process." Pages 85–104 in *Reworking the Bible: Apocryphal and Related Texts at Qumran. Proceedings of a Joint Symposium by the Orion Center for the Study of the Dead Sea Scrolls and Associated Literature and the Hebrew University Institute for Advanced Studies Research Group on Qumran, 15–17 January, 2002.* Edited by Esther G. Chazon, Devorah Dimant, and Ruth A. Clements. Studies on the Texts of the Desert of Judah 58. Leiden: Brill, 2005.

————. "The Biblical Texts in the Qumran Commentaries: Scribal Errors or Exegetical Variants?" Pages 85–100 in *Early Jewish and Christian Exegesis: Studies in Memory of William Hugh Brownlee.* Edited by Craig A. Evans and William F. Stinespring. Society of Biblical Literature Homage Series 10. Atlanta: Scholars Press, 1987.

————. "The Books of Chronicles and the Scrolls from Qumran." Pages 35–48 in *Reflection and Refraction: Studies in Biblical Historiography in Honour of A. Graeme Auld.* Edited by Robert Rezetko, Timothy H. Lim, and W. Brian Aucker. Supplements to Vetus Testamentum 113. Leiden: Brill, 2007.

————. "'Canon' in the Light of the Qumran Scrolls." Pages 81–98 in *The Canon of Scripture in Jewish and Christian Tradition/Le canon des Écritures dans les traditions juive et chrétienne.* Edited by Philip S. Alexander and Jean-Daniel Kaestli. Publications de l'Institut romand des sciences bibliques 4. Lausanne: Éditions du Zèbre, 2007.

————. "'The Canon within the Canon' at Qumran and in the New Testament." Pages 242–66 in *The Scrolls and the Scriptures: Qumran Fifty Years After.* Edited by Stanley E. Porter and Craig A. Evans. Journal for the Study of the Pseudepigrapha: Supplement Series 26. Roehampton Institute London Papers 3. Sheffield: Sheffield Academic Press, 1997.

————. "The Dead Sea Scrolls." Pages 253–65 in vol. 1 of *The Biblical World.* Edited by John Barton. 2 vols. London: Routledge, 2002.

————. *The Dead Sea Scrolls and the New Testament: Essays in Mutual Illumination.* London: SPCK; Minneapolis: Fortress, 2005.

————. "The Deuteronomic Character of 4Q252." Pages 121–35 in *Pursuing the Text: Studies in Honor of Ben Zion Wacholder on the Occasion of His Seventieth Birthday.* Edited by John C. Reeves and John Kampen. Journal for the Study of the Old Testament: Supplement Series 184. Sheffield: Sheffield Academic Press, 1994.

————. "*E pluribus unum*: Textual Variety and Definitive Interpretation in the Qumran Scrolls." Pages 107–19 in *The Dead Sea Scrolls in Their Historical Context.* Edited by Timothy H. Lim et al. Edinburgh: T&T Clark, 2000.

————. *Exegesis at Qumran: 4QFlorilegium in Its Jewish Context.* Journal for the Study of the Old Testament: Supplement Series 29. Sheffield: JSOT Press, 1985. Repr., Atlanta: Society of Biblical Literature, 2006.

————. "From 'Assembly of Supreme Holiness for Aaron' to 'Sanctuary of Adam':

The Laicization of Temple Ideology in the Qumran Scrolls and Its Wider Implications." *Journal for Semitics* 8/2 (1996): 119–45.

———. "From Bible to Midrash: Approaches to Biblical Interpretation in the Dead Sea Scrolls by Modern Interpreters." Pages 1–19 in *Northern Lights on the Dead Sea Scrolls: Proceedings of the Nordic Qumran Network 2003–2006.* Edited by Anders Klostergaard Petersen et al. Studies on the Texts of the Desert of Judah 80. Leiden: Brill, 2009.

———. "Genesis Commentaries (4Q252–254)." Pages 667–68 in *The Eerdmans Dictionary of Early Judaism.* Edited by John J. Collins and Daniel C. Harlow. Grand Rapids: Eerdmans, 2010.

———. "Hypertextuality and the 'Parabiblical' Dead Sea Scrolls." Pages 43–64 in *In the Second Degree: Paratextual Literature in Ancient Near Eastern and Ancient Mediterranean Culture and Its Reflections in Medieval Literature.* Edited by Philip S. Alexander, Armin Lange, and Renate J. Pillinger. Leiden: Brill, 2010.

———. "Isaiah 40:3 and the Wilderness Community." Pages 117–32 in *New Qumran Texts and Studies: Proceedings of the First Meeting of the International Organization for Qumran Studies, Paris 1992.* Edited by George J. Brooke with the assistance of Florentino García Martínez. Studies on the Texts of the Desert of Judah 15. Leiden: Brill, 1994.

———. "Joseph, Aseneth, and Lévi-Strauss." Pages 185–200 in *Narrativity in Biblical and Related Texts/La narrativité dans la Bible et les textes apparentés.* Edited by George J. Brooke and Jean-Daniel Kaestli. Bibliotheca ephemeridum theologicarum lovaniensium 149. Leuven: Leuven University Press, 2000.

———. "Justifying Deviance: The Place of Scripture in Converting to a Qumran Self-Understanding." Pages 73–87 in *Reading the Present in the Qumran Library: The Perception of the Contemporary by Means of Scriptural Interpretation.* Edited by Kristin De Troyer and Armin Lange. Society of Biblical Literature Symposium Series 30. Atlanta: Society of Biblical Literature, 2005.

———. "Miqdash Adam, Eden and the Qumran Community." Pages 285–301 in *Gemeinde ohne Tempel—Community without Temple: Zur Substituierung und Transformation des Jerusalemer Tempels und seines Kults im Alten Testament, antiken Judentum und frühen Christentum.* Edited by Beate Ego et al. Wissenschaftliche Untersuchungen zum Neuen Testament 118. Tübingen: Mohr Siebeck, 1999.

———. "Moving Mountains: From Sinai to Jerusalem." Pages 73–89 in *The Significance of Sinai: Traditions about Divine Revelation in Judaism and Christianity.* Edited by George J. Brooke, Hindy Najman, and Loren T. Stuckenbruck. Themes in Biblical Narrative 12. Leiden: Brill, 2008.

———. "New Perspectives on the Bible and Its Interpretation in the Dead Sea Scrolls." Pages 19–37 in *The Dynamics of Language and Exegesis at Qumran.* Edited by Devorah Dimant and Reinhard G. Kratz. Forschungen zum Alten Testament 2/35. Tübingen: Mohr Siebeck, 2009.

———. "Parabiblical Prophetic Narratives." Pages 271–301 in vol. 1 of *The Dead Sea Scrolls after Fifty Years: A Comprehensive Assessment.* Edited by Peter W. Flint and James C. VanderKam. 2 vols. Leiden: Brill, 1998.

———. "The Pesharim and the Origin of the Dead Sea Scrolls." Pages 339–54 in *Methods of Investigation of the Dead Sea Scrolls and the Khirbet Qumran Site: Present Realities and Future Prospects.* Edited by Michael O. Wise et al. Annals of the New York Academy of Sciences 722. New York: New York Academy of Sciences, 1994.

———. "Prophecy and Prophets in the Dead Sea Scrolls: Looking Backwards and Forwards." Pages 151–65 in *Prophets, Prophecy and Prophetic Texts in the Second Temple Period.* Edited by Michael H. Floyd and Robert D. Haak. Library of Hebrew Bible/Old Testament Studies 427. London: T&T Clark, 2006.

———. "Qumran Pesher: Towards the Redefinition of a Genre." *Revue de Qumrân* 10/40 (1981): 483–503.

———. "Reading the Plain Meaning of Scripture in the Dead Sea Scrolls." Pages 67–90 in *Jewish Ways of Reading the Bible.* Edited by George J. Brooke. Journal of Semitic Studies Supplement 11. Oxford: Oxford University Press, 2000.

———. Review of Emanuel Tov, *Textual Criticism of the Hebrew Bible. Journal of Semitic Studies* 48 (2003): 421.

———. "Rewritten Bible." Pages 777–81 in vol. 2 of *Encyclopedia of the Dead Sea Scrolls.* Edited by Lawrence H. Schiffman and James C. VanderKam. 2 vols. New York: Oxford University Press, 2000.

———. "The Rewritten Law, Prophets and Psalms: Issues for Understanding the Text of the Bible." Pages 31–40 in *The Bible as Book: The Hebrew Bible and the Judaean Desert Discoveries.* Edited by Edward D. Herbert and Emanuel Tov. London: British Library; New Castle, Del.: Oak Knoll; Grand Haven: Scriptorium Center for Christian Antiquities, 2002.

———. "Shared Intertextual Interpretations in the Dead Sea Scrolls and the New Testament." Pages 35–57 in *Biblical Perspectives: Early Use and Interpretation of the Bible in Light of the Dead Sea Scrolls: Proceedings of the First International Symposium of the Orion Center for the Study of the Dead Sea Scrolls and Associated Literature, 12–14 May 1996.* Edited by Michael E. Stone and Esther G. Chazon. Studies on the Texts of the Desert of Judah 28. Leiden: Brill, 1998.

———. "Some Comments on 4Q252 and the Text of Genesis." *Textus* 19 (1998): 1–25.

———. "The Structure of 1QHᵃ XII 5–XIII 4 and the Meaning of Resurrection." Pages 15–33 in *From 4QMMT to Resurrection: Mélanges qumraniens en hommage à Émile Puech.* Edited by Florentino García Martínez et al. Studies on the Texts of the Desert of Judah 61. Leiden: Brill, 2006.

———. "The Temple Scroll and the Archaeology of Qumran, ʿAin Feshkha and Masada." *Revue de Qumrân* 13 (1988): 225–37.

———. "Torah, Rewritten Torah and the Letter of Jude." Pages 180–93 in *Torah in the New Testament: Papers Delivered at the Manchester–Lausanne Seminar of June 2008*. Edited by Michael Tait and Peter S. Oakes. Library of New Testament Studies 401. London: T&T Clark International, 2009.

———. "The Twelve Minor Prophets and the Dead Sea Scrolls." Pages 19–43 in *Congress Volume: Leiden 2004*. Edited by André Lemaire. Supplements to Vetus Testamentum 109. Leiden: Brill, 2006.

———. "Types of Historiography in the Qumran Scrolls." Pages 211–30 in *Ancient and Modern Scriptural Historiography/L'historiographie biblique, ancienne et moderne*. Edited by George J. Brooke and Thomas Römer. Bibliotheca ephemeridum theologicarum lovaniensium 207. Leuven: Peeters, 2007.

———. "Was the Teacher of Righteousness Considered to Be a Prophet?" Pages 77–97 in *Prophecy after the Prophets? The Contribution of the Dead Sea Scrolls to the Understanding of Biblical and Extra-Biblical Prophecy*. Edited by Kristin De Troyer and Armin Lange, with Lucas L. Schulte. Contributions to Biblical Exegesis and Theology 52. Leuven: Peeters, 2009.

Brooke, George J., Philip R. Davies, and Phillip R. Callaway. *The Complete World of the Dead Sea Scrolls*. London: Thames & Hudson, 2002.

Brooke, George J., and Barnabas Lindars, eds. *Septuagint, Scrolls and Cognate Writings: Papers Presented to the International Symposium on the Septuagint and Its Relations to the Dead Sea Scrolls and Other Writings (Manchester, 1990)*. Society of Biblical Literature Septuagint and Cognate Studies 33. Atlanta: Scholars Press, 1992.

Broshi, M. "4QHistorical Text F." Pages 406–11 in *Qumran Cave 4.XXVI: Cryptic Texts; Miscellanea, Part 1*. Edited by Stephen J. Pfann et al. Discoveries in the Judaean Desert 36. Oxford: Clarendon, 2000.

———. "4QPesher on the Apocalypse of Weeks." Pages 187–91 in *Qumran Cave 4.XXVI: Cryptic Texts; Miscellanea, Part 1*. Edited by Stephen J. Pfann et al. Discoveries in the Judaean Desert 36. Oxford: Clarendon, 2000.

———. "Ptolas and the Archelaus Massacre (4Q468g = Histroical Text B)." *Journal of Jewish Studies* 49 (1998): 341–45.

Broshi, Magen, and Esther Eshel. "4QHistorical Text A." Pages 192–200 in *Qumran Cave 4.XXVI: Cryptic Texts and Miscellanea, Part 1*. Edited by Stephen J. Pfann et al. Discoveries in the Judaean Desert 36. Oxford: Clarendon, 2000.

———. "The Greek King Is Antiochus IV (4QHistorical Text = 4Q248)." *Journal of Jewish Studies* 48 (1997): 120–29.

Broshi, Magen, and Ada Yardeni. "4QList of False Prophets." Pages 77–79 in *Qumran Cave 4.XIV: Parabiblical Texts, Part 2*. Edited by Magen Broshi, in consultation with James C. VanderKam. Discoveries in the Judaean Desert 19. Oxford: Clarendon, 1995.

Brown, Raymond E., Joseph A. Fitzmyer, W. G. Oxtoby, and J. Teixidor (arranged by Hans-Peter Richter). *A Preliminary Concordance to the Hebrew and Aramaic Fragments from Qumrân Caves II–X*. Göttingen: Printed Privately, 1988.

Brownlee, William H. "The Ineffable Name of God." *Bulletin of the American Schools of Oriental Research* 226 (1977): 39–46.

———. *The Midrash Pesher of Habakkuk: Text, Translation, Exposition with an Introduction.* Society of Biblical Literature Monograph Series 24. Missoula, Mont.: Scholars Press, 1979.

Bruce, F. F. *Biblical Exegesis in the Qumran Texts.* Grand Rapids: Eerdmans, 1956.

Brueggemann, Walter. "Psychological Criticism: Exploring the Self in the Text." Pages 213–32 in *Method Matters: Essays on the Interpretation of the Hebrew Bible in Honor of David L. Petersen.* Edited by Joel M. LeMon and Kent H. Richards. Society of Biblical Literature Resources for Biblical Study 56. Atlanta: Society of Biblical Literature, 2009.

———. *Theology of the Old Testament: Testimony, Dispute, Advocacy.* Minneapolis: Fortress, 1997.

Callaway, P. R. "Some Thoughts on Writing Exercise (4Q341)." *Qumran Chronicle* 13/2–4 (2006): 147–51.

Campbell, Jonathan G. *The Use of Scripture in the Damascus Document 1–8, 19–20.* Beihefte zur Zeitschrift für die alttestamentliche Wissenschaft 228. Berlin: de Gruyter, 1995.

Capper, B. J. "The Palestinian Cultural Context of the Earliest Christian Community of Goods." Pages 323–56 in *The Book of Acts in Its Palestinian Setting.* Edited by Richard J. Bauckham. The Book of Acts in Its First Century Setting 4. Grand Rapids: Eerdmans, 1995.

Certeau, Michel de. *The Practice of Everyday Life.* Translated by Steven Rendall. Berkeley: University of California Press, 1984.

Chalcraft, David J., ed. *Sectarianism in Early Judaism: Sociological Advances.* BibleWorld. London: Eqinox, 2007.

Charlesworth, James H., ed. *John and Qumran.* London: Chapman, 1972. Reissued as *John and the Dead Sea Scrolls* with a new foreword, New York: Crossroad, 1990.

———. *The Pesharim and Qumran History: Chaos or Consensus?* Grand Rapids: Eerdmans, 2002.

———. "X Joshua." Pages 231–39 in *Miscellaneous Texts from the Judaean Desert.* Edited by James C. VanderKam and Monica Brady. Discoveries in the Judaean Desert 38. Oxford: Clarendon, 2000.

Charlesworth, J. H., F. M. Cross, et al., eds. *The Dead Sea Scrolls: Hebrew, Aramaic, and Greek Texts with English Translations.* Vol. 4B, *Angelic Liturgy: Songs of the Sabbath Sacrifice.* Princeton Theological Seminary Dead Sea Scrolls Project. Tübingen: Mohr Siebeck; Louisville: Westminster John Knox, 1999.

Clements, Ronald E. *A Century of Old Testament Study.* Guildford: Lutterworth, 1976.

Colie, Rosalie L. *The Resources of Kind: Genre-Theory in the Renaissance.* Una's Lectures. Berkeley: University of California Press, 1973.

Collins, John J. "The Apocalyptic Worldview of Daniel." Pages 59–66 in *Enoch and Qumran Origins: New Light on a Forgotten Connection*. Edited by Gabriele Boccaccini. Grand Rapids: Eerdmans, 2005.

———. *Daniel: With an Introduction to Apocalyptic Literature*. Forms of the Old Testament Literature 20. Grand Rapids: Eerdmans, 1984.

———. "Tradition and Innovation in the Dead Sea Scrolls." Pages 1–23 in *The Dead Sea Scrolls: Transmission of Traditions and Production of Texts*. Edited by Sarianna Metso, Hindy Najman, and Eileen M. Schuller. Studies on the Texts of the Desert of Judah 92. Leiden: Brill, 2010.

———. "The Yaḥad and 'The Qumran Community.'" Pages 81–96 in *Biblical Traditions in Transmission: Essays in Honour of Michael A. Knibb*. Edited by Charlotte Hempel and Judith M. Lieu. Supplements to the Journal for the Study of Judaism 111. Leiden: Brill, 2006.

Collins, John J., and Peter W. Flint. "Pseudo-Daniel." Pages 95–164 in *Qumran Cave 4.XVII: Parabiblical Texts, Part 3*. Edited by George J. Brooke et al., in consultation with James C. VanderKam. Discoveries in the Judaean Desert 22. Oxford: Clarendon, 1996.

Collins, M. A. *The Use of Sobriquets in the Qumran Dead Sea Scrolls*. Library of Second Temple Studies 67. London: T&T Clark, 2009.

Cook, E. M. "What Was Qumran? A Ritual Purification Centre." *Biblical Archaeology Review* 22/6 (1996): 39–75.

Cook, J. "Semiotics." Pages 454–56 in vol. 2 of *Dictionary of Biblical Interpretation*. Edited by John H. Hayes. Nashville: Abingdon, 1999.

Crawford, Sidnie White. "Has Esther Been Found at Qumran? 4QProto-Esther and the Esther Corpus." *Revue de Qumrân* 17 (1996): 307–25.

———. *Rewriting Scripture in Second Temple Times*. Studies in the Dead Sea Scrolls and Related Literature. Grand Rapids: Eerdmans, 2008.

Cross, Frank Moore, et al. *Qumran Cave 4.XII: 1–2 Samuel*. Discoveries in the Judaean Desert 17. Oxford: Clarendon, 2005.

Cross, Frank Moore, and Shemaryahu Talmon, eds., *Qumran and the History of the Biblical Text*. Cambridge, Mass.: Harvard University Press, 1975.

Davies, P. R. "History and Hagiography." Pages 87–105 in *Behind the Essenes: History and Ideology in the Dead Sea Scrolls*. Brown Judaic Studies 94. Atlanta: Scholars Press, 1987.

———. *Scribes and Schools: The Canonization of the Hebrew Scriptures*. Library of Ancient Israel. Louisville: Westminster John Knox, 1998.

———. "Sects from Texts: On the Problems of Doing a Sociology of the Qumran Literature." Pages 69–82 in *New Directions in Qumran Studies: Proceedings of the Bristol Colloquium on the Dead Sea Scrolls, 8–10 September 2003*. Edited by Jonathan G. Campbell, William J. Lyons, and Lloyd K. Pietersen. Library of Second Temple Studies 52. London: T&T Clark, 2005.

———. "Space and Sects in the Qumran Scrolls." Pages in 81–98 in *"Imagining" Biblical Worlds: Studies in Spatial, Social and Historical Constructs in Honor of James W. Flanagan*. Edited by David M. Gunn and Paula M. McNutt. Journal for the Study of the Old Testament: Supplement Series 359. London: Sheffield Academic Press, 2002.

———. "What History Can We Get from the Scrolls, and How?" Pages 31–46 in *The Dead Sea Scrolls: Texts and Context*. Edited by Charlotte Hempel. Studies on the Texts of the Desert of Judah 90. Leiden: Brill, 2010.

Davila, James R. "7. 4QGenᵍ." Pages 57–60 in *Qumran Cave 4.VII: Genesis to Numbers*. Edited by E. Ulrich et al. Discoveries in the Judaean Desert 12. Oxford: Clarendon, 1994.

———. "The Name of God at Moriah: An Unpublished Fragment from 4QGenExodᵃ." *Journal of Biblical Literature* 110 (1991): 577–82.

———. "New Qumran Readings for Genesis One." Pages 3–11 in *Of Scribes and Scrolls: Studies on the Hebrew Bible, Intertestamental Judaism, and Christian Origins Presented to John Strugnell on the Occasion of his Sixtieth Birthday*. Edited by Harold W. Attridge, John J. Collins, and Thomas H. Tobin. College Theology Society Resources in Religion 5. Lanham, Md.: University Press of America, 1990.

Davis, Michael Thomas, and Brent A. Strawn, eds. *Qumran Studies: New Approaches, New Questions*. Grand Rapids: Eerdmans, 2007.

Dempster, S. G. "Torah, Torah, Torah: The Emergence of the Tripartite Canon." Pages 87–127 in *Exploring the Origins of the Bible: Canon Formation in Historical, Literary, and Theological Perspective*. Edited by Craig A. Evans and Emanuel Tov. Grand Rapids: Baker Academic, 2008.

Derrida, Jacques. "The Law of Genre." *Glyph: Johns Hopkins Textual Studies* 7 (1980): 172–97.; Repr., *Critical Inquiry* 7 (1980): 55–81.

Dimant, Devorah. "1 Enoch 6–11: A Fragment of a Parabiblical Work." *Journal of Jewish Studies* 53 (2002): 223–37.

———. "4QFlorilegium and the Idea of the Community as Temple." Pages 165–89 in *Hellenica et Judaica: Hommage à Valentin Nikiprowetzky*. Edited by A. Caquot, M. Hadas-Lebel and J. Riaud. Collection de la Revue des études juives 3. Leuven: Peeters, 1986.

———. "Non pas l'exil au desert mais l'exil spirituel: L'interprétation d'Isaïe 40,3 dans la *Règle de la Communauté*." Pages 17–36 in *Qoumrân et le judaïsme du tournant de notre ère: Actes de la Table Ronde, Collège de France, 16 Novembre 2004*. Edited by André Lemaire and Simon C. Mimouni. Collection de la Revue des études juives 40. Paris: Peeters, 2006.

———. "Not Exile in the Desert but Exile in the Spirit: The Pesher of Isa. 40:3 in the *Rule of the Community*." *Meghillot: Studies in the Dead Sea Scrolls* 2 (2004): 21–36.

———. "The 'Pesher on the Periods' (4Q180) and 4Q181." *Israel Oriental Studies* 9 (1979): 77–102.

———, ed. *Qumran Cave 4.XXI: Parabiblical Texts, Part 4: Pseudo-Prophetic Texts*. Discoveries in the Judaean Desert 30. Oxford: Clarendon, 2001.

———. "The Qumran Manuscripts: Contents and Significance." Pages 23–58 in *Time to Prepare the Way in the Wilderness: Papers on the Qumran Scrolls by Fellows of the Institute for Advanced Studies of the Hebrew University, Jerusalem, 1989–1990*. Edited by Devorah Dimant and Lawrence H. Schiffman. Studies on the Texts of the Desert of Judah 16. Leiden: Brill, 1995.

———. "Sectarian and Non-Sectarian Texts from Qumran: The Pertinence and Usage of a Taxonomy." *Revue de Qumrân* 24/93 (2009): 7–18.

———. "Two 'Scientific' Fictions: The So-Called Book of Noah and the Alleged Quotation of Jubilees in CD 16:3–4." Pages 230–49 in *Studies in the Hebrew Bible, Qumran, and the Septuagint Presented to Eugene Ulrich*. Edited by Peter W. Flint, Emanuel Tov, and James C. VanderKam. Supplements to Vetus Testamentum 101. Leiden: Brill, 2006.

Docherty, Susan E. *The Use of the Old Testament in Hebrews: A Case Study in Early Jewish Bible Interpretation*. Wissenschaftliche Untersuchungen zum Neuen Testament 2/260. Tübingen: Mohr Siebeck, 2009.

Doering, Lutz. "Excerpted Texts in Second Temple Judaism: A Survey of the Evidence." Pages 1–38 in *Selecta colligere II: Beiträge zur Technik des Sammelung und Kompilierung griechischer Texte von der Antiker bis zum Humanismus*. Edited by R. M. Piccione and M. Perkams. Hellenica 18. Alessandria: Editioni dell'Orso, 2005.

Duff, David, ed. *Modern Genre Theory*. London: Pearson Education, 2000.

Dunn, James D. G. "Jesus in Oral Memory: The Initial Stages of the Jesus Tradition." *Society of Biblical Literature Seminar Papers* 39 (2000): 287–326.

———. *Jesus Remembered*. Christianity in the Making 1. Grand Rapids: Eerdmans, 2003.

Eichrodt, Walther. *Theology of the Old Testament*. 2 vols. Old Testament Library. London: SCM, 1961–67.

Ellens, J. Harold, and Wayne G. Rollins, eds. *Psychology and the Bible: A New Way to Read the Scriptures*. 4 vols. Praeger Perspectives. Psychology, Religion, and Spirituality. Westport, Conn.: Praeger, 2004.

Elliger, Karl. *Studien zum Habakuk-Kommentar vom Toten Meer*. Beiträge zur historischen Theologie 15. Tübingen: J. C. B. Mohr, 1953.

Ellis, E. Earle. "Midrash Pesher in Pauline Hermeneutics." *New Testament Studies* 2 (1955–56): 127–33. Repr., pages 173–81 in *Prophecy and Hermeneutics in Early Christianity: New Testament Essays*. Wissenschaftliche Untersuchungen zum Neuen Testament 18. Tübingen: Mohr Siebeck, 1978.

Erll, Astrid, and Ansgar Nünning, eds. *A Companion to Cultural Memory Studies*. Berlin: de Gruyter, 2010.

Eshel, Hanan. "4QMMT and the History of the Hasmonean Period." Pages 53–65 in *Reading 4QMMT: New Perspectives on Law and History*. Edited by John Kampen and Moshe Bernstein. Society of Biblical Literature Symposium Series 2. Atlanta: Scholars Press, 1996.

———. *The Dead Sea Scrolls and the Hasmonean State*. Studies in the Dead Sea Scrolls and Related Literature. Grand Rapids: Eerdmans, 2008.

Eyerman, Ron. "The Past in the Present: Culture and the Transmission of Memory." *Acta Sociologica* 47/2 (2004): 159–69.

Falk, Daniel K. *The Parabiblical Texts: Strategies for Extending the Scriptures in the Dead Sea Scrolls*. Library of Second Temple Studies 63. Companion to the Qumran Scrolls 8. London: T&T Clark, 2007.

Fernández Marcos, Natalio. "The Genuine Text of Judges." Pages 33–45 in Sôfer Mahîr: *Essays in Honour of Adrian Schenker Offered by Editors of* Biblia Hebraica Quinta. Edited by Yohanan A. P. Goldman, Arie van der Kooij, and Richard D. Weis. Supplements to Vetus Testamentum 110. Leiden: Brill, 2006.

———. "The Hebrew and Greek Text of Judges." Pages 1–16 in *The Earliest Text of the Hebrew Bible: The Relationship between the Masoretic Text and the Hebrew Base of the Septuagint Reconsidered*. Edited by Adrian Schenker. Society of Biblical Literature Septuagint and Cognate Studies 52. Atlanta: Society of Biblical Literature, 2003.

Fields, Weston W. *The Dead Sea Scrolls: A Short History*. Leiden: Brill, 2006.

Finkel, Asher. "The Pesher of Dreams and Scriptures." *Revue de Qumrân* 4 (1963–64): 357–70.

Fishelov, David. *Metaphors of Genre: The Role of Analogies in Genre Theory*. University Park: Pennsylvania State University Press, 1993.

Fitzmyer, Joseph A. "4QHistorical Text C, 4QHistorical Text D and 4QHistorical Text E." Pages 275–89 in *Qumran Cave 4.XXVI: Cryptic Texts; Miscellanea, Part 1*. Edited by Stephen J. Pfann et al. Discoveries in the Judaean Desert 36. Oxford: Clarendon, 2000.

———. *The Dead Sea Scrolls and Christian Origins*. Studies in the Dead Sea Scrolls and Related Literature. Grand Rapids: Eerdmans, 2000.

———. *The Genesis Apocryphon of Qumran Cave 1 (1Q20): A Commentary*. 3rd ed. Biblica et orientalia 18B. Rome: Pontifical Biblical Institute, 2004.

Flint, Peter W. *The Dead Sea Psalms Scrolls and the Book of Psalms*. Studies on the Texts of the Desert of Judah 17. Leiden: Brill, 1997.

Flusser, David. *Judaism of the Second Temple Period*. Vol. 1, *Qumran and Apocalypticism*. Grand Rapids: Eerdmans; Jerusalem: Magnes, 2007.

Foucault, Michel. *Power Knowledge: Selected Interviews and Other Writings 1972–77*. New York Pantheon, 1980.

Fowler, Alastair. *Kinds of Literature: An Introduction to the Theory of Genres and Modes*. Oxford: Clarendon, 1982.

Fraade, Steven D. "Hagu, Book of." Page 327 in vol. 1 of *Encyclopedia of the Dead Sea Scrolls*. Edited by Lawrence H. Schiffman and James C. VanderKam. 2 vols. New York: Oxford University Press, 2000.

Franklin, Cynthia G. *Writing Women's Communities: The Politics and Poetics of Contemporary Multi-Genre Anthologies*. Madison: University of Wisconsin Press, 1997.

Freedman, D. N., and K. A. Mathews. *The Paleo-Hebrew Leviticus Scroll (11Qpa-leoLev)*. Winona Lake, Ind.: Eisenbrauns, 1985.

Frey, Jörg. "Critical Issues in the Investigation of the Scrolls and the New Testament." Pages 517–45 in *The Oxford Handbook of the Dead Sea Scrolls*. Edited by Timothy H. Lim and John J. Collins. Oxford: Oxford University Press, 2010.

Fröhlich, Ida. "Tobit against the Background of the Dead Sea Scrolls." Pages 55–70 in *The Book of Tobit: Text, Tradition, Theology. Papers of the First International Conference on the Deuterocanonical Books, Pápa, Hungary, 20–21 May, 2004*. Edited by Géza G. Xeravits and József Zsengellér. Supplements to the Journal for the Study of Judaism 98. Leiden: Brill, 2005.

Frow, John. *Genre*. New Critical Idiom. London: Routledge, 2006.

———. "Intertextuality and Ontology." Pages 45–55 in *Intertextuality: Theories and Practices*. Edited by Michael Worton and Judith Still. Manchester: Manchester University Press, 1990.

Garbini, Giovanni. *History and Ideology in Ancient Israel*. London: SCM, 1988.

García Martínez, Florentino. "4QMMT in a Qumran Context." Pages 15–27 in *Reading 4QMMT: New Perspectives on Law and History*. Edited by John Kampen and Moshe Bernstein. Society of Biblical Literature Symposium Series 2. Atlanta: Scholars Press, 1996.

———, ed. *The Dead Sea Scrolls Translated: The Qumran Texts in English*. 2nd ed. Leiden: Brill, 1996.

———. "The History of the Qumran Community in the Light of Recently Available Texts." Pages 194–216 in *Qumran between the Old and New Testaments*. Edited by Frederick H. Cryer and Thomas L. Thompson. Journal for the Study of the Old Testament: Supplement Series 290. Copenhagen International Seminar 6. Sheffield: Sheffield Academic Press, 1998.

García Martínez, Florentino, and Mladen Popović, eds. *Defining Identities: We, You, and the Other in the Dead Sea Scrolls: Proceedings of the Fifth Meeting of the IOQS in Groningen*. Studies on the Texts of the Desert of Judah 70. Leiden: Brill, 2008.

García Martínez, Florentino, and Eibert J. C. Tigchelaar, eds. *The Dead Sea Scrolls Study Edition*. 2 vols. Leiden: Brill, 1997.

García Martínez, Florentino, Eibert J. C. Tigchelaar, and A. S. van der Woude, eds. *Qumran Cave 11.II: 11Q2–18, 11Q20–31*. Discoveries in the Judaean Desert 23. Oxford, Clarendon, 1998.

Gedi, Noa, and Yigal Elam. "Collective Memory—What Is It?" *History and Memory* 8 (1996): 30–50.

Genette, Gérard. *L'Œuvre de l'art: immanence et transcendance*. Paris: Éditions du Seuil, 1994.

Gerhart, Mary. *Genre Choices, Gender Questions*. Oklahoma Project for Discourse and Theory 9. Norman: University of Oklahoma Press, 1992.

Gertner, M. "Terms of Scriptural Interpretation: A Study in Hebrew Semantics." *BSOAS* 25 (1962): 1–27.

Gibson, Roy K., and Christina Shuttleworth Kraus, eds., *The Classical Commentary: Histories, Practices, Theory*. Mnemosyne Supplements 232. Leiden: Brill, 2002.

Goldman, Shalom. "Tobit and the Jewish Literary Tradition." Pages 90–98 in *Studies in the Book of Tobit: A Multidisciplinary Approach*. Edited by Mark Bredin. Library of Second Temple Studies 55. London: T&T Clark, 2006.

Goldstein, Jonathan. *1 Maccabees: A New Translation with Introduction and Commentary*. Anchor Bible 41. New York: Doubleday, 1976.

Goode, Erich. *Deviant Behavior: An Interactionist Approach*. Englewood Cliffs, N.J.: Prentice-Hall, 1978.

Grabbe, Lester L. "Are Historians of Ancient Palestine Fellow Creatures—or Different Animals?" Pages 19–36 in *Can a 'History of Israel' Be Written?* Edited by Lester L. Grabbe. Journal for the Study of the Old Testament: Supplement Series 245. European Seminar in Historical Methodology 1. Sheffield: Sheffield Academic Press, 1997.

———. "Hat die Bibel doch Recht? A Review of T. L. Thompson's *The Bible in History*." *Scandinavian Journal of the Old Testament* 14 (2000): 117–39.

Graham, S. L."Intertextual Trekking: Visiting the Iniquity of the Fathers upon 'The Next Generation.'" *Semeia* 69–70 (1995): 195–219.

Greenfield, Jonas C. "The Words of Levi Son of Jacob in Damascus Document IV,15–19." *Revue de Qumrân* 13 (1988): 319–22.

Grene, David. *Herodotus: The History*. Chicago: University of Chicago Press, 1987.

Griel, Arthur, and David Rudy. "Social Cocoons: Encapsulation and Identity Transformation Organizations." *Sociological Inquiry* 54 (1984): 260–78.

Grossman, Maxine L. *Reading for History in the Damascus Document: A Methodological Study*. Studies on the Texts of the Desert of Judah 45. Leiden: Brill, 2002.

———, ed. *Rediscovering the Dead Sea Scrolls: An Assessment of Old and New Approaches and Methods*. Grand Rapids: Eerdmans, 2010.

Gruber, M. I. "Biblical Interpretation in Rabbinic Literature: Historical and Philological Aspects." Pages 217–34 in *The Encyclopedia of Judaism*. Vol. 1, *A–E*. Edited by Jacob Neusner, Alan J. Avery-Peck, and William Scott Green. Leiden: Brill, 2005.

Gruenwald, I. "Jewish and Christian Messianism: The Psychoanalytic Approach of Heinz Kohut," Pages 247–75 in *From Freud to Kohut*, vol. 1 of *Psychology and the Bible: A New Way to Read the Scriptures*. Edited by J. Harold Ellens and Wayne G. Rollins. Praeger Perspectives. Psychology, Religion, and Spirituality. Westport, Conn.: Praeger, 2004.

Halbwachs, Maurice. *On Collective Memory*. Edited, translated, and with an Introduction by Lewis A. Coser. Heritage of Sociology. Chicago: University of Chicago Press, 1992. French originals, 1941 and 1952.

Handelman, Susan A. *The Slayers of Moses: The Emergence of Rabbinic Interpretation in Modern Literary Theory*. SUNY Series on Modern Jewish Literature and Culture. Albany: State University of New York Press, 1982.

Harris, J. M. "Fundamentalism: Objections from a Modern Jewish Historian." Pages 137–73 in *Fundamentalism and Gender*. Edited by John Stratton Hawley. Oxford: Oxford University Press, 1994.

Hayes, John H., and Frederick C. Prussner. *Old Testament Theology: Its History and Development*. London: SCM, 1985.

Hays, Richard B. *Echoes of Scripture in the Letters of Paul*. New Haven: Yale University Press, 1989.

Heger, Paul. "The Development of Qumran Law: Nistarot, Niglot and the Issue of 'Contemporization.'" *Revue de Qumrân* 23 (2007–8): 167–206.

Hempel, Charlotte. *The Damascus Texts*. Companion to the Qumran Scrolls 1. Sheffield: Sheffield Academic Press, 2000.

Hendel, Ronald S. "Assessing the Text-Critical Theories of the Hebrew Bible after Qumran." Pages 281–302 in *The Oxford Handbook of the Dead Sea Scrolls*. Edited by Timothy H. Lim and John J. Collins. Oxford: Oxford University Press, 2010.

———. *The Text of Genesis 1–11: Textual Studies and Critical Edition*. New York: Oxford University Press, 1998.

———. "The Text of the Torah after Qumran." Pages 8–11 in *The Dead Sea Scrolls Fifty Years after Their Discovery: Proceedings of the Jerusalem Congress, July 20–25, 1997*. Edited by Lawrence H. Schiffman, Emanuel Tov, and James C. VanderKam. Jerusalem: Israel Exploration Society and Shrine of the Book, 2000.

Hess, Richard S. "The Dead Sea Scrolls and Higher Criticism of the Hebrew Bible: The Case of 4QJudgᵃ." Pages 122–28 in *The Scrolls and the Scriptures: Qumran Fifty Years After*. Edited by Stanley E. Porter and Craig A. Evans; Journal for the Study of the Pseudepigrapha: Supplement Series 26. Sheffield: Sheffield Academic Press, 1997.

Hezser, Catherine. *Jewish Literacy in Roman Palestine*. Texts and Studies in Ancient Judaism 81. Tübingen: Mohr Siebeck, 2001.

Hirsch, Eric D. *Validity in Interpretation*. New Haven: Yale University Press, 1967.

Hirschfeld, Y. "A Community of Hermits above Ein Gedi" (in Hebrew). *Cathedra* 96 (2000): 7–40.

Hobsbawm, Eric, and Terence Ranger, eds. *The Invention of Tradition*. Past and Present Publications. Cambridge: Cambridge University Press, 1983.

Holm-Nielsen, Svend. *Hodayot: Psalms from Qumran*. Acta theologica danica 2. Aarhus: Universitetsforlaget, 1960.

Horbury, W. "The Proper Name in 4Q468g: Peitholaus?" *Journal of Jewish Studies* 50 (1999): 310–11.

Horgan, Maurya P. "Pesharim." Pages 1–193 in *The Dead Sea Scrolls: Hebrew, Aramaic, and Greek Texts with English Translations*. Vol. 6B, *Pesharim, Other Commentaries, and Related Documents*. Edited by James H. Charlesworth et al. Princeton Theological Seminary Dead Sea Scrolls Project 6B. Tübingen: Mohr Siebeck; Louisville: Westminster John Knox, 2002.

―――. *Pesharim: Qumran Interpretations of Biblical Books*. Catholic Biblical Quarterly Monograph Series 8. Washington, D.C.: Catholic Biblical Association of America, 1979.

Housman, A. E. "The Application of Thought to Textual Criticism." *Proceedings of the Classical Association* 18 (1922): 67–84.

Hughes, Julie A. *Scriptural Allusions and Exegesis in the Hodayot*. Studies on the Texts of the Desert of Judah 59. Leiden: Brill, 2006.

Humbert, Jean-Baptiste. "L'espace sacré à Qumrân: propositions pour l'archéologie." *Revue biblique* 101 (1994): 161–214.

Ilan, Tal. "Shelamzion Alexandra." Pages 872–74 in vol. 2 of *Encyclopedia of the Dead Sea Scrolls*. Edited by Lawrence H. Schiffman and James C. VanderKam. 2 vols. New York: Oxford University Press, 2000.

Inge, John. *A Christian Theology of Place*. Explorations in Practical, Pastoral and Empirical Theology. Aldershot: Ashgate, 2003.

Jackson, Bernard S. *Studies in the Semiotics of Biblical Law*. Journal for the Study of the Old Testament: Supplement Series 314. Sheffield: Sheffield Academic Press, 2000.

Janssen, Jacques, Jan van der Lans, and Mark Dechesne. "Fundamentalism: The Possibilities and Limitations of a Social-Psychological Approach." Pages 302–16 in *Religious Identity and the Invention of Tradition: Papers Read at a NOSTER Conference in Soesterberg, January 4–6, 1999*. Edited by Jan Willem van Henten and Anton Houtepen. Studies in Theology and Religion 3. Assen: Royal Van Gorcum, 2001.

Jassen, Alex P. *Mediating the Divine: Prophecy and Revelation in the Dead Sea Scrolls and Second Temple Judaism*. Studies on the Texts of the Desert of Judah 68. Leiden: Brill, 2007.

Jokiranta, Jutta. *Social Identity and Sectarianism in the Qumran Movement*. Studies on the Texts of the Desert of Judah 105. Leiden: Brill, 2012.

―――. "Pesharim: A Mirror of Self-Understanding." Pages 23–34 in *Reading the Present in the Qumran Library: The Perception of the Contemporary by Means of Scriptural Interpretations*. Edited by Kristin De Troyer and Armin Lange. Society of Biblical Literature Symposium Series 30. Atlanta: Society of Biblical Literature, 2005.

―――. "Social Identity Approach: Identity-Constructing Elements in the Psalms Pesher." Pages 85–109 in *Defining Identities: We, You, and the Other in the Dead Sea Scrolls: Proceedings of the Fifth Meeting of the IOQS in Groningen*. Edited by Florentino García Martínez and Mladen Popović. Studies on the Texts of the Desert of Judah 70. Leiden: Brill, 2007.

―――. "Social Scientific Approaches to the Dead Sea Scrolls." Pages 246–63 in *Rediscovering the Dead Sea Scrolls: An Assessment of Old and New Approaches and Methods*. Edited by Maxine L. Grossman. Grand Rapids: Eerdmans, 2010.

———. "Sociological Approaches to Qumran Sectarianism." Pages 200–231 in *The Oxford Handbook of the Dead Sea Scrolls*. Edited by Timothy H. Lim and John J. Collins. Oxford: Oxford University Press, 2010.

Joyce, P. "Lamentations and the Grief Process: A Psychological Reading." *Biblical Interpretation* 1 (1993): 304–20.

Katriel, Tamar. "Sites of Memory: Discourses of the Past in Israeli Pioneering Settlement Museums." Pages 99–135 in *Cultural Memory and the Construction of Identity*. Edited by Dan Ben-Amos and Liliane Weissberg. Detroit: Wayne State University Press, 1999.

Kelber, Werner H., and Samuel Byrskog, eds. *Jesus in Memory: Traditions in Oral and Scribal Perspectives*. Waco: Baylor University Press, 2009.

Kille, D. A. "Psychology and Biblical Studies." Pages 684–85 in vol. 4 of *The New Interpreter's Dictionary of the Bible*. Edited by Katharine Doob Sakenfeld et al. Nashville: Abingdon, 2009.

Kister, Menahem. "Biblical Phrases and Hidden Biblical Interpretations and Pesharim." Pages 27–39 in *The Dead Sea Scrolls: Forty Years of Research*. Edited by Devorah Dimant and Uriel Rappaport. Studies on the Texts of the Desert of Judah 10. Leiden: Brill; Jerusalem: Magnes Press and Yad Izhak Ben-Zvi, 1992.

Knibb, M. A. "1 Enoch." Pages 184–319 in *The Apocryphal Old Testament*. Edited by Hedley F. D. Sparks. Oxford: Clarendon, 1984.

———. *Het Boek Henoch: Het eerste of het Ethiopische boek van Henoch*. Deventer: Hermes, 1983.

———. "The Book of Daniel in Its Context." Pages 16–35 in vol. 1 of *The Book of Daniel: Composition and Reception*. Edited by John J. Collins and Peter W. Flint. 2 vols. Supplements to Vetus Testamentum 82. Formation and Interpretation of Old Testament Literature 2. Leiden: Brill, 2001.

———. "The Book of Enoch in the Light of the Qumran Wisdom Literature." Pages 193–210 in *Wisdom and Apocalypticism in the Dead Sea Scrolls and in the Biblical Tradition*. Edited by Florentino García Martínez. Bibliotheca ephemeridum theologicarum lovaniensium 168. Leuven: Peeters, 2003.

———. "Commentary on 2 Esdras." Pages 76–307 in *The First and Second Books of Esdras*. Edited by R. J. Coggins and M. A. Knibb. Cambridge Bible Commentary. Cambridge: Cambridge University Press, 1979.

———. "The Date of the Parables of Enoch: A Critical Review." *New Testament Studies* 25 (1979): 345–59.

———. "Eschatology and Messianism in the Dead Sea Scrolls." Pages 379–402 in vol. 2 of *The Dead Sea Scrolls after Fifty Years: A Comprehensive Assessment*. Edited by Peter W. Flint and James C. VanderKam. 2 vols. Leiden: Brill, 1999.

———. "The Ethiopic Book of Enoch." Pages 26–55 in *Outside the Old Testament*. Edited by Marinus de Jonge. Cambridge: Cambridge University Press, 1985.

———. *The Ethiopic Book of Enoch: A New Edition in the Light of the Aramaic Dead Sea Fragments*. In consultation with Edward Ullendorff. Oxford: Clarendon, 1978.

——. "Exile in the Damascus Document." *Journal for the Study of the Old Testament* 25 (1983): 99–117.

——. "The Exile in the Literature of the Intertestamental Period." *Heythrop Journal* 17 (1976): 253–72.

——. "Interpreting the Book of Enoch: Reflections on a Recently Published Commentary." *Journal for the Study of Judaism* 33 (2002): 437–50.

——. "Jubilees and the Origins of the Qumran Community." An Inaugural Lecture in the Department of Biblical Studies. King's College, London, 1989.

——. "Messianism in the Pseudepigrapha in the Light of the Scrolls." *Dead Sea Discoveries* 2 (1995): 165–84.

——. "A New Edition of the Ethiopic Enoch in the Light of the Aramaic Dead Sea Fragments." Ph.D. diss., School of Oriental and African Studies, London, 1974.

——. "A Note on 4Q372 and 4Q390." Pages 164–77 in *The Scriptures and the Scrolls: Studies in Honour of A. S. van der Woude on the Occasion of His 65th Birthday.* Edited by F. García Martínez, A. Hilhorst, and C. J. Labuschagne. Supplements to Vetus Testamentum 49. Leiden: Brill, 1992.

——. "Prophecy and the Emergence of the Jewish Apocalypses." Pages 155–80 in *Israel's Prophetic Tradition: Essays in Honour of Peter R. Ackroyd.* Edited by Richard Coggins, Anthony Phillips, and M. A. Knibb. Cambridge: Cambridge University Press, 1982.

——. *The Qumran Community.* Cambridge Commentaries on Writings of the Jewish and Christian World 200 BC to AD 200, 2. Cambridge: Cambridge University Press, 1987.

——. "The Teacher of Righteousness–A Messianic Title?" Pages 51–65 in *A Tribute to Géza Vermès: Essays on Jewish and Christian Literature and History.* Edited by Philip R. Davies and Richard T. White. Journal for the Study of the Old Testament: Supplement Series 100. Sheffield: JSOT Press, 1990.

——. *Translating the Bible: The Ethiopic Version of the Old Testament.* The Schweich Lectures of the British Academy 1995. Oxford: Oxford University Press for the British Academy, 1999.

——. "The Translation of 1 Enoch 70.1: Some Methodological Issues." Pages 340–54 in *Biblical Hebrew, Biblical Texts: Essays in Memory of Michael P. Weitzman.* Edited by Ada Rapoport-Albert and Gillian Greenberg. Journal for the Study of the Old Testament: Supplement Series 333. The Hebrew Bible and Its Versions 2. Sheffield: Sheffield Academic Press, 2001.

——. "The Use of Scripture in 1 Enoch 17–19." Pages 165–78 in *Jerusalem, Alexandria, Rome: Studies in Ancient Cultural Interaction in Honour of A. Hilhorst.* Edited by Florentino García Martínez and Gerard P. Luttikhuizen. Supplements to the Journal for the Study of Judaism 82. Leiden: Brill, 2003.

——. "Which Parts of 1 Enoch Were Known to Jubilees? A Note on the Interpretation of Jubilees 4.16–25." Pages 254–62 in *Reading from Right to Left: Essays on the Hebrew Bible in Honour of David J.A. Clines.* Edited by J. Cheryl Exum and H. G. M. Williamson. Journal for the Study of the Old Testament: Supplement Series 373. London: Sheffield Academic Press, 2003.

———. "'You are indeed wiser than Daniel': Reflections on the Character of the Book of Daniel." Pages 399–411 in *The Book of Daniel in the Light of New Findings*. Edited by A. S. van der Woude. Bibliotheca ephemeridum theologicarum lovaniensium 106. Leuven: Peeters, 1993.

Knierim, Rolf. "Cosmos and History in Israel's Theology." *Horizons in Biblical Theology* 3 (1981): 59–123.

———. "The Task of Old Testament Theology." *Horizons in Biblical Theology* 6 (1984): 25–57.

Koch, Klaus. "Wort und Einheit des Schöpfergottes in Memphis und Jerusalem." *Zeitschrift für Theologie und Kirche* 62 (1965): 251–93.

Kooij, Arie van der. "Textual Criticism of the Hebrew Bible: Its Aim and Method." Pages 729–39 in *Emanuel: Studies in Hebrew Bible, Septuagint, and Dead Sea Scrolls in Honor of Emanuel Tov*. Edited by Shalom M. Paul, Robert A. Kraft, Lawrence H. Schiffman, and Weston W. Fields with Eva Ben-David. Supplements to Vetus Testamentum 94. Leiden: Brill, 2003.

———. "The Textual Criticism of the Hebrew Bible before and after the Qumran Discoveries." Pages 167–77 in *The Bible as Book: The Hebrew Bible and the Judaean Desert Discoveries*. Edited by Edward D. Herbert and Emanuel Tov. London: British Library; New Castle, Del.: Oak Knoll; Grand Haven: Scriptorium Center for Christian Antiquities, 2002.

Korpel, Marjo C. A., and Josef M Oesch, eds. *Delimitation Criticism: A New Tool for Biblical Scholarship*. Pericope 1. Assen: Van Gorcum, 2000.

Koskenniemi, E., and P. Lindqvist. "Rewritten Bible, Rewritten Stories: Methodological Aspects." Pages 11–39 in *Rewritten Bible Reconsidered: Proceedings of the Conference in Karkku, Finland, August 24–26, 2006*. Edited by Antti Laato and Jacques van Ruiten. Studies in Rewritten Bible 1. Turku: Åbo Akademi University; Winona Lake, Ind.: Eisenbrauns, 2008.

Kratz, Reinhard G. "Eyes and Spectacles: Wellhausen's Method of Higher Criticism." *Journal of Theological Studies* 60 (2009): 381–402.

Kristeva. Julia. *La révolution du langage poétique: L'avant-garde à la fin du XIXe siècle, Lautréamont et Mallarmé*. Paris: Éditions du Seuil, 1976.

Kugel, James L. "4Q369 'Prayer of Enosh' and Ancient Biblical Interpretation." *Dead Sea Discoveries* 5 (1998): 119–48.

Laato, Antti, and Jacques van Ruiten, eds. *Rewritten Bible Reconsidered: Proceedings of the Conference in Karkku, Finland, August 24–26, 2006*. Studies in Rewritten Bible 1. Turku: Åbo Akademi University; Winona Lake, Ind.: Eisenbrauns, 2008.

Lacoste, Jean-Yves. *Expérience et absolu: Questions disputées sur l'humanité de l'homme*. Epiméthée. Paris: Presses universitaires de France, 1994.

Lange, Armin. "4QHistorical Text G." Pages 412–13 in *Qumran Cave 4.XXVI: Cryptic Texts; Miscellanea, Part 1*. Edited by Stephen J. Pfann et al. Discoveries in the Judaean Desert 36. Oxford: Clarendon, 2000.

———. "The Determination of Fate by the Oracle of Lot in the Dead Sea Scrolls, the Hebrew Bible and Ancient Mesopotamian Literature." Pages 39–48 in

Sapiential, Liturgical and Poetical Texts from Qumran: Proceedings of the Third Meeting of the International Organization for Qumran Studies, Oslo 1998. Published in Memory of Maurice Baillet. Studies on the Texts of the Desert of Judah 35. Leiden: Brill, 2000.

———. "From Literature to Scripture: The Unity and Plurality of the Hebrew Scriptures in Light of the Qumran Library." Pages 51–107 in *One Scripture or Many? Canon from Biblical, Theological, and Philosophical Perspectives.* Edited by Christine Helmer and Christof Landmesser. Oxford: Oxford University Press, 2004.

———. *Handbuch der Textfunde vom Toten Meer.* Band 1, *Die Handschriften biblischer Bücher von Qumran und den anderen Fundorten.* Tübingen: Mohr Siebeck, 2009.

———. "In the Second Degree: Ancient Jewish Paratextual Literature in the Context of Graeco-Roman and Ancient Near Eastern Literature. Pages 3–40 in *In the Second Degree: Paratextual Literature in Ancient Near Eastern and Ancient Mediterranean Culture and Its Reflections in Medieval Literature.* Edited by Philip S. Alexander, Armin Lange, and Renate J. Pillinger. Leiden: Brill, 2010.

———. "The Status of the Biblical Texts in the Qumran Corpus and the Canonical Process." Pages 21–30 in *The Bible as Book: The Hebrew Bible and the Judaean Desert Discoveries.* Edited by Edward D. Herbert and Emanuel Tov. London: British Library; New Castle, Del.: Oak Knoll; Grand Haven: Scriptorium Center for Christian Antiquities, 2002.

Lange, Armin, Ulrich Dahmen, and Hermann Lichtenberger, eds. *Die Textfunde vom Toten Meer und der Text der Hebräischen Bibel.* Neukirchen-Vluyn: Neukirchener Verlag, 2000.

Lange, Armin, and Ulrike Mittmann-Richert. "Annotated List of the Texts from the Judaean Desert Classified." Pages 115–64 in *The Texts from the Judaean Desert: Indices and an Introduction to the Discoveries in the Judaean Desert Series.* Edited by Emanuel Tov. Discoveries in the Judaean Desert 39. Oxford: Clarendon, 2002.

Larson, E., and L. H. Schiffman. "4QText Mentioning Descendants of David." Pages 297–99 in *Qumran Cave 4.XVII: Parabiblical Texts, Part 3.* Edited by George J. Brooke et al., in consultation with James C. VanderKam. Discoveries in the Judaean Desert 22. Oxford: Clarendon, 1996.

Lawrence, Bruce B. *Defenders of God: The Fundamentalist Revolt against the Modern Age.* Studies in Comparative Religion. Columbia: University of South Carolina Press, 1995.

Le Donne, Anthony. *The Historiographical Jesus: Memory, Typology, and the Son of David.* Waco: Baylor University Press, 2009.

Lefebvre, Henri. *The Production of Space.* Translated by Donald Nicholson-Smith. Oxford: Basil Blackwell, 1991.

Lemmelijn, Bénédicte. "The So-Called 'Major Expansions' in SamP, 4Qpaleo-Exod^m and 4QExod^j of Ex 7:14–11:10: On the Edge between Textual Criticism and Literary Criticism." Pages 429–39 in *X Congress of the International Organization for Septuagint and Cognate Studies: Oslo, 1998*. Edited by Bernard A. Taylor. Society of Biblical Literature Septuagint and Cognate Studies 51. Atlanta: Society of Biblical Literature, 2001.

———. "What Are We Looking for in Doing Old Testament Text-Critical Research?" *Journal of Northwest Semitic Languages* 23 (1997): 69–80.

Lewis, Charlton T., and Charles Short. *A Latin Dictionary*. Oxford: Clarendon, 1962.

Licht, Jacob. *The Thanksgiving Scroll: A Scroll from the Wilderness of Judaea, Text, Introduction, Commentary and Glossary*. (In Hebrew). Jerusalem: Bialik Institute, 1957.

Lied, Liv Ingeborg. "Another Look at the Land of Damascus: The Spaces of the *Damascus Document* in the Light of Edward W. Soja's Thirdspace Approach." Pages 101–25 in *New Directions in Qumran Studies: Proceedings of the Bristol Colloquium on the Dead Sea Scrolls, 8–10 September 2003* Edited by Jonathan G. Campbell, William John Lyons, and Lloyd K. Pietersen. Library of Second Temple Studies 52. London: T&T Clark International, 2005.

Lim, Timothy H. "Authoritative Scriptures and the Dead Sea Scrolls." Pages 303–22 in *The Oxford Handbook of the Dead Sea Scrolls*. Edited by Timothy H. Lim and John J. Collins. Oxford: Oxford University Press, 2010.

———. "Midrash Pesher in the Pauline Letters." Pages 280–92 in *The Scrolls and the Scriptures: Qumran Fifty Years After*. Edited Stanley E. Porter and Craig A. Evans. Journal for the Study of the Pseudepigrapha: Supplement Series 26. Roehampton Institute London Papers 3. Sheffield: Sheffield Academic Press, 1997.

Lim, Timothy H., and John J. Collins, eds. *The Oxford Handbook of the Dead Sea Scrolls*. Oxford: Oxford University Press, 2010.

Linafelt, Tod. "Surviving Lamentations." *Horizons in Biblical Theology* 17 (1995): 45–61.

———. *Surviving Lamentations: Catastrophe, Lament, and Protest in the Afterlife of a Biblical Book*. Chicago: University of Chicago Press, 2000.

Lofland, John, and Rodney Stark. "Becoming a World-Saver: A Theory of Conversion to a Deviant Perspective." *American Sociological Review* 30 (1965): 862–75.

Maas, Paul. *Textual Criticism*. Translated by Barbara Flower. Oxford: Clarendon, 1958.

Machiela, Daniel A. *The Dead Sea Genesis Apocryphon: A New Text and Translation with Introduction and Special Treatment of Columns 13–17*. Studies on the Texts of the Desert of Judah 79. Leiden: Brill, 2009.

Macksey, Richard. "Foreword." Pages xi–xxii in *Paratexts: Thresholds of Interpretation*. Edited by Gérard Genette. Translated by Jane E. Lewin. Literature, Culture, Theory 20. Cambridge: Cambridge University Press, 1997.

Magness, Jodi. *The Archaeology of Qumran and the Dead Sea Scrolls*. Studies in the Dead Sea Scrolls and Related Literature. Grand Rapids: Eerdmans, 2002.

————. "Communal Meals and Sacred Space at Qumran." Pages 15–28 in *Shaping Community: The Art and Archaeology of Monasticism. Papers from a Symposium Held at the Frederick R. Weisman Museum, University of Minnesota, March 10–12, 2000*. Edited by Sheila McNally. BAR International Series 941. Oxford: Archaeopress, 2001. Repr., pages 81–112 in *Debating Qumran: Collected Essays on Its Archaeology*. Interdisciplinary Studies in Ancient Culture and Religion 4. Leuven: Peeters, 2004.

Maier, Johann. "Early Jewish Biblical Interpretation in the Qumran Literature." Pages 108–29 in *Hebrew Bible/Old Testament: The History of Its Interpretation*. Vol. 1, *From the Beginnings to the Middle Ages (Until 1300)*. Edited by Magne Sæbø. Göttingen: Vandenhoeck & Ruprecht, 1996.

————. *Die Qumran Essener: Die Texte vom Toten Meer I*. Uni-Taschenbücher 224. Munich: Reinhardt, 1995.

————. *Zwischen den Testamenten: Geschichte und Religion in der Zeit des zweiten Tempels*. Neue Echter Bibel, Ergänzungsband zum Alten Testament 3. Würzburg: Echter, 1990.

Mandel, Paul. "The Origins of Midrash in the Second Temple Period." Pages 9–34 in *Current Trends in the Study of Midrash*. Edited by Carol Bakhos. Supplements to the Journal for the Study of Judaism 106. Leiden: Brill, 2006.

Marguerat, Daniel, and Adrian Curtis, eds. *Intertextualités: La Bible en échos*. Le monde de la Bible 40. Geneva: Labor et Fides, 2000.

Matza, David. *Becoming Deviant*. Englewood Cliffs, N.J.: Prentice-Hall, 1969.

McKane, William. *A Critical and Exegetical Commentary on Jeremiah*. 2 vols. International Critical Commentary. Edinburgh: T&T Clark, 1986–96.

McLay, R. Timothy. *The Use of the Septuagint in New Testament Research*. Grand Rapids: Eerdmans, 2003.

Meer, Michaël N. van der. *Formation and Reformulation: The Redaction of the Book of Joshua in the Light of the Oldest Textual Witnesses*. Supplements to Vetus Testamentum 102. Leiden: Brill, 2004.

Mendels, Doron. *Memory in Jewish, Pagan and Christian Societies of the Graeco-Roman World: Fragmented Memory–Comprehensive Memory–Collective Memory*. Library of Second Temple Studies 45. London: T&T Clark International, 2004.

Metso, Sarianna. "Whom Does the Term Yaḥad Identify?" Pages 213–35 in *Biblical Traditions in Transmission: Essays in Honour of Michael A. Knibb*. Edited by Charlotte Hempel and Judith M. Lieu. Supplements to the Journal for the Study of Judaism 111. Leiden: Brill, 2006. Repr., pages 63–84 in *Defining Identities: We, You, and the Other in the Dead Sea Scrolls: Proceedings of the Fifth Meeting of the IOQS in Groningen*. Edited by Florentino García Martínez and Mladen Popović. Studies on the Texts of the Desert of Judah 70. Leiden: Brill, 2008.

Milgrom, Jacob, and Lidija Novakovic. "Catena A (4Q177 = 4QCatª)." Pages 286–303 in *The Dead Sea Scrolls: Hebrew, Aramaic, and Greek Texts with*

English Translations. Vol. 6B, *Pesharim, Other Commentaries, and Related Documents*. Edited by James H. Charlesworth et al. Princeton Theological Seminary Dead Sea Scrolls Project 6B. Tübingen: Mohr Siebeck; Louisville: Westminster John Knox, 2002.

Milik, Józef T. "I Rois." Pages 171–72 in *Les "Petites Grottes" de Qumrân: Explorations de la falaise, les grottes 2Q, 3Q, 5Q, 6Q, 7Q à 10Q, Le rouleau de cuivre*. Edited by M. Baillet, J. T. Milik, and R. de Vaux. 2 vols. Discoveries in the Judaean Desert 3. Oxford: Clarendon, 1962.

———. "Milkî-sedeq et Milkî-reša' dans les anciens écrits juifs et chrétiens." *Journal of Jewish Studies* 23 (1972): 95–114.

———. "Les modèles araméens du livre d'Esther dans la Grotte 4 de Qumrân." *Revue de Qumrân* 15 (1991–92): 321–99.

———. *Qumran Cave I*. Discoveries in the Judaean Desert 1. Oxford: Clarendon, 1955.

———. *Ten Years of Discovery in the Wilderness of Judaea*. Studies in Biblical Theology 26. London: SCM, 1959.

———. "Le travail d'édition des manuscrits du Désert de Juda." Pages 17–26 in *Volume du Congrès: Strasbourg 1956*. Supplements to Vetus Testamentum 4. Leiden: Brill, 1957.

Milik, Józef T., with the collaboration of Matthew Black. *The Books of Enoch: Aramiac Fragments of Qumrân Cave 4*. Oxford: Clarendon Press, 1976.

Millard, Alan R. "Judith, Tobit, Ahiqar and History." Pages 195–203 in *New Heaven and New Earth: Prophecy and the Millennium. Essays in Honour of Anthony Gelston*. Edited by P. J. Harland and C. T. R. Hayward. Supplements to Vetus Testamentum 77. Leiden: Brill, 1999.

———. *Reading and Writing in the Time of Jesus*. Biblical Seminar 69. Sheffield: Sheffield Academic Press, 2000.

Mitternacht, D. "Theissen's Integration of Psychology and New Testament Studies: Learning Theory, Psychodynamics, and Cognitive Psychology." Pages 101–17 in *From Freud to Kohut*, vol. 1 of *Psychology and the Bible: A New Way to Read the Scriptures*. Edited by J. Harold Ellens and Wayne G. Rollins. Praeger Perspectives. Psychology, Religion, and Spirituality. Westport, Conn.: Praeger, 2004.

Murphy-O'Connor, Jerome, ed., *Paul and Qumran: Studies in New Testament Exegesis*. London: Chapman, 1968. Reissued as *Paul and the Dead Sea Scrolls* with a new foreword by James H. Charlesworth. New York: Crossroad, 1990.

Najman, Hindy. *Seconding Sinai: The Development of Mosaic Discourse in Second Temple Judaism*. Supplements to the Journal for the Study of Judaism 77. Leiden: Brill, 2003.

———. "Towards a Study of the Uses of the Concept of Wilderness in Ancient Judaism." *Dead Sea Discoveries* 13 (2006): 99–113.

Naveh, J. "341. 4QExercitium Calami C." Pages 291–93 in *Qumran Cave 4.XXVI: Cryptic Texts; Miscellanea, Part 1*. Edited by Stephen J. Pfann et al. Discoveries in the Judaean Desert 36. Oxford: Clarendon, 2000.

Newsom, Carol A. "The 'Psalms of Joshua' from Qumran Cave 4." *Journal of Jewish Studies* 39 (1988): 56–73.

———. *The Self as Symbolic Space: Constructing Identity and Community at Qumran*. Studies on the Texts of the Desert of Judah 52. Leiden: Brill, 2004.

———. *Songs of the Sabbath Sacrifice: A Critical Edition*. Harvard Semitic Studies 27. Atlanta: Scholars Press, 1985.

Newsom, Carol A., J. H. Charlesworth with B. A. Strawn and H. W. L. Rietz. "Angelic Liturgy: Songs of the Sabbath Sacrifice [4Q400–4Q407, 11Q17, Mas1k]," in *The Dead Sea Scrolls: Hebrew, Aramaic, and Greek Texts with English Translations*. Vol. 4B, *Angelic Liturgy: Songs of the Sabbath Sacrifice*. Princeton Theological Seminary Dead Sea Scrolls Project 4B. Tübingen: Mohr Siebeck; Louisville: Westminster John Knox, 1999.

Nickelsburg, George W. E. *Jewish Literature between the Bible and the Mishnah: A Historical and Literary Introduction*. 2nd ed. Minneapolis: Fortress, 2005.

Nissinen, Martti. "*Pesharim* as Divination: Qumran Exegesis, Omen Interpretation and Literary Prophecy." Pages 43–60 in *Prophecy after the Prophets? The Contribution of the Dead Sea Scrolls to the Understanding of Biblical and Extra-Biblical Prophecy*. Edited by Kristin De Troyer and Armin Lange, with Lucas L. Schulte. Contributions to Biblical Exegesis and Theology 52. Leuven: Peeters, 2009.

Noam, Vered. *Megillat Ta'anit: Versions, Interpretation History with a Critical Edition*. Jerusalem: Yad Ben Zvi, 2003.

O'Connor, M. "Discourse Linguistics and the Study of the Hebrew Bible." Pages 17–42 in *Congress Volume: Basel 2001*. Edited by André Lemaire. Supplements to Vetus Testamentum 92. Leiden: Brill, 2002.

O'Donnell, J. J. Review of Glenn W. Most, ed., *Commentaries—Kommentare* (Aporemata: Kritische Studien zur Philologiegeschichte 4; Göttingen: Vandenhoeck & Ruprecht, 1999). *Bryn Mawr Classical Review* 19 (2000): 468.

Øklund, Jorunn. "The Language of Gates and Entering: On Sacred Space in the Temple Scroll." Pages 149–65 in *New Directions in Qumran Studies: Proceedings of the Bristol Colloquium on the Dead Sea Scrolls, 8-10 September 2003*. Edited by Jonathan G. Campbell, William J. Lyons, and Lloyd K. Pietersen. Library of Second Temple Studies 52. London: T&T Clark International, 2005.

Olick, J. K., and J. Robbins. "Social Memory Studies: From 'Collective Memory' to the Historical Sociology of Mnemonic Practices." *Annual Review of Sociology* 24 (1998): 105–40.

Ollenburger, Ben C. "Theology, OT." Pages 560–64 in vol. 5 of *The New Interpreter's Dictionary of the Bible*. Edited by Katharine Doob Sakenfeld et al. Nashville: Abingdon, 2009.

Oppenheim, A. Leo. *The Interpretation of Dreams in the Ancient Near East: With a Translation of an Assyrian Dream Book*. Transactions of the American Philosophical Society 46/3. Philadelphia: American Philosophical Society, 1956.

Orlinsky, H. M. "Studies in the St. Mark's Isaiah Scroll IV." *JQR* 43 (1952–53): 329–40.

Perloff, Marjorie, ed. *Postmodern Genres*. Oklahoma Project for Discourse and Theory 5. Norman: University of Oklahoma Press, 1989.

Petersen, Anders Klostergaard. "Rewritten Bible as a Borderline Phenomenon—Genre, Textual Strategy, or Canonical Anachronism?" Pages 285–306 in *Flores Florentino: Dead Sea Scrolls and Other Early Jewish Studies in Honour of Florentino García Martínez*. Edited by Anthony Hilhorst, Émile Puech, and Eibert J. C. Tigchelaar. Supplements to the Journal for the Study of Judaism 122. Leiden: Brill, 2007.

Pfann, Stephen J. "A Table in the Wilderness: Pantries and Tables, Pure Food and Sacred Space." Pages 159–78 in *Qumran, the Site of the Dead Sea Scrolls: Archaeological Interpretations and Debates. Proceedings of a Conference Held at Brown University, November 17–19, 2002*. Edited by Katharina Galor, Jean-Baptiste Humbert, and Jürgen Zangenberg. Studies on the Texts of the Desert of Judah 57. Leiden: Brill, 2006.

Pietersen, Lloyd K. "Teaching, Tradition and Thaumaturgy: A Sociological Examination of the Polemic of the Pastorals." Ph.D. diss., University of Sheffield, 2000.

Postgate, J. P. "Textual Criticism." Pages 708–15 in vol. 14 of *Encyclopaedia Britannica*. London: Encyclopedia Brittanica, 1929.

Puech, Émile. "4QComposition historique B." Pages 205–8 in *Qumrân Grotte 4.XVIII: Textes hébreux (4Q521–4Q528, 4Q576–4Q579)*. Edited by Émile Puech. Discoveries in the Judaean Desert 25. Oxford: Clarendon, 1998.

———. "Apocryphe de Daniel." Pages 185–84 in *Qumran Cave 4.XVII: Parabiblical Texts, Part 3*. Edited by George J. Brooke et al., in consultation with James C. VanderKam. Discoveries in the Judaean Desert 22. Oxford: Clarendon, 1996.

———. *La croyance des Esséniens en la vie future: Immortalité, resurrection, vie éternelle? Histoire d'une croyance dans le Judaïsme ancien*. Études bibliques 22. Paris: J. Gabalda, 1993.

———. "Les manuscrits 4QJuges^c (= 4Q50^a) et 1QJuges (= 1Q6)." Pages 184–200 in *Studies in the Hebrew Bible, Qumran, and the Septuagint Presented to Eugene Ulrich*. Edited by Peter W. Flint, Emanuel Tov, and James C. VanderKam. Supplements to Vetus Testamentum 101. Leiden: Brill, 2006.

———. *Qumrân Grotte 4.XXII: Textes araméens, première partie 4Q529-549*. Discoveries in the Judaean Desert 31. Oxford: Clarendon, 2001.

Pyper, Hugh S. *An Unsuitable Book: The Bible as Scandalous Text*. Bible in the Modern World 7. Sheffield: Sheffield Phoenix, 2005.

Qimron, Elisha. *The Hebrew of the Dead Sea Scrolls*. Harvard Semitic Studies 29. Atlanta: Scholars Press, 1986.

———. "On the Interpretation of the List of False Prophets." *Tarbiz* 63 (1994): 273–75.

Rabin, Chaim. *The Zadokite Documents*. 2nd rev. ed. Oxford: Clarendon, 1958.

Rabinowitz, I. "*Pêsher/Pittârôn:* Its Biblical Meaning and Its Significance in Qumran Literature." *Revue de Qumrân* 8/30 (1973): 219–32.

Rambo, Lewis R. *Understanding Religious Conversion.* New Haven: Yale University Press, 1993.

Reed, Stephen A. *The Dead Sea Scrolls Catalogue: Documents, Photographs and Museum Inventory Numbers.* Edited and revised by Marilyn J. Lundberg with the collaboration of Michael B. Phelps. Society of Biblical Literature Resources for Biblical Study 32. Atlanta: Scholars Press, 1994.

———. *Dead Sea Scrolls Inventory Project: List of Documents, Photographs and Museum Plates.* Fascicle 10. Claremont, Calif.: Ancient Biblical Manuscript Center, 1992.

———. *The Dead Sea Scrolls on Microfiche: Inventory List of Photographs.* Edited by Marilyn J. Lundberg. Leiden: Brill and IDC, 1993.

Regev, Eyal. *Sectarianism in Qumran: A Cross-Cultural Perspective.* Religion and Society 45. Berlin: de Gruyter, 2007.

Rendtorff, Rolf. *The Canonical Hebrew Bible: A Theology of the Old Testament.* Tools for Biblical Study 7. Leiden: Deo, 2006.

———. "Wie sieht Israel seine Geschichte?" Pages 197–206 in *Rethinking the Foundations: Historiography in the Ancient World and in the Bible. Essays in Honour of John Van Seters.* Edited by Steven L. McKenzie, Thomas Römer, and Hans Heinrich Schmid. Beihefte zur Zeitschrift für die alttestamentliche Wissenschaft 294. Berlin: de Gruyter, 2000.

Reumann, John. "Introduction." Pages 1–12 in *A Primer of Old Testament Text Criticism.* Edited by D. R. Ap-Thomas. London: Epworth, 1947.

Reventlow, Henning Graf. *History of Biblical Interpretation.* Vol. 1, *From the Old Testament to Origen.* Society of Biblical Literature Resources for Biblical Study 50. Atlanta: Society of Biblical Literature, 2009.

———. *Problems of Old Testament Theology in the Twentieth Century.* London: SCM, 1985.

Robinson, H. W., ed. *Record and Revelation: Essays on the Old Testament by Members of the Society for Old Testament Study.* Oxford: Clarendon, 1938.

Rofé, Alexander. "The Biblical Text in Light of Historico-Literary Criticism: The Reproach of the Prophet-Man in Judg 6:7–10 and 4QJudgᵃ" (in Hebrew). Pages 33–44 in *On the Border Line: Textual Meets Literary Criticism.* Edited by Ziporah Talshir and Daliyah Amara. Beer-Sheva 18. Beersheva: Ben-Gurion University of the Negev Press, 2005.

———. "Historico-Literary Aspects of the Qumran Biblical Scrolls." Pages 30–39 in *The Dead Sea Scrolls Fifty Years after Their Discovery: Proceedings of the Jerusalem Congress, July 20–25, 1997.* Edited by Lawrence H. Schiffman, Emanuel Tov, and James C. VanderKam. Jerusalem: Israel Exploration Society and Shrine of the Book, 2000.

———. "The List of False Prophets from Qumran: Two Riddles and Their Solutions." *Ha'aretz,* April 13, 1994, B11.

———. "'No *Ephod* or *Teraphim*'—*oude hierateias oude dēlōn*: Hosea 3:4 in the LXX and in the Paraphrases of Chronicles and the *Damascus Document.*" Pages 135–49 in *Sefer Moshe: The Moshe Weinfeld Jubilee Volume. Studies in the Bible and the Ancient Near East, Qumran, and Post-Biblical Judaism.* Edited by Chaim Cohen, Avi Hurvitz, and Shalom M. Paul. Winona Lake, Ind.: Eisenbrauns, 2004.

Rogerson, John W. "The Old Testament." Pages 139–42 in *The Study and Use of the Bible.* Edited by John Rogerson, Christopher Rowland, and Barnabas Lindars. History of Christian Theology 2. Basingstoke: Marshall, Morgan & Scott, 1989.

———. *A Theology of the Old Testament: Cultural Memory, Communication and Being Human.* London: SPCK, 2009.

Ruthven, Malise. *Fundamentalism: The Search for Meaning.* Oxford: Oxford University Press, 2005.

Ruzer, Serge. "The New Covenant, the Reinterpretation of Scripture and Collective Messiahship." Pages 215–37 in *Mapping the New Testament: Early Christian Writings as a Witness for Jewish Biblical Exegesis.* Jewish and Christian Perspectives 13. Leiden: Brill, 2007.

———. "Who Was Unhappy with the Davidic Messiah?" Pages 101–29 in *Mapping the New Testament: Early Christian Writings as a Witness for Jewish Biblical Exegesis.* Jewish and Christian Perspectives 13. Leiden: Brill, 2007.

Said, Edward W. *The World, the Text, and the Critic.* 1983. Repr., London: Vintage, 1991.

Sanders, E. P. "The Dead Sea Sect and Other Jews: Commonalities, Overlaps and Differences." Pages 7–43 in *The Dead Sea Scrolls in Their Historical Context.* Edited by Timothy H. Lim et al. Edinburgh: T&T Clark, 2000.

Sanders, J. A. *The Dead Sea Psalms Scroll.* Ithaca, N.Y.: Cornell University Press, 1967.

Sanderson, Judith E. *An Exodus Scroll from Qumran: 4QpaleoExod^m and the Samaritan Tradition.* Harvard Semitic Studies 30. Atlanta: Scholars Press, 1986.

Saukkonen, J. "The Story behind the Text: Scriptural Interpretation in 4Q252." Ph.D. diss., University of Helsinki, 2005.

Schams, Christine. *Jewish Scribes in the Second-Temple Period.* Journal for the Study of the Old Testament: Supplement Series 291. Sheffield: Sheffield Academic Press, 1998.

Schiffman, Lawrence H. *The Eschatological Community of the Dead Sea Scrolls: A Study of the Rule of the Congregation.* Society of Biblical Literature Monograph Series 38. Atlanta: Scholars Press, 1989.

———. *The Halakhah at Qumran.* Studies in Judaism in Late Antiquity 16. Leiden: Brill, 1975.

———. *Sectarian Law in the Dead Sea Scrolls: Courts, Testimony, and the Penal Code.* Brown Judaic Studies 33. Chico, Calif.: Scholars Press, 1983.

Schiffman, Lawrence H., and James C. VanderKam, eds. *Encyclopedia of the Dead Sea Scrolls.* 2 vols. New York: Oxford University Press, 2000.

Schmid, Konrad. *The Old Testament: A Literary History.* Minneapolis: Fortress, 2012. German original, *Literaturgeschichte des Alten Testaments.* Darmstadt: Wissenschaftliche Buchgesellschaft, 2008.

Schofield, Alison. *From Qumran to the* Yaḥad: *A New Paradigm of Textual Development for* The Community Rule. Studies on the Texts of the Desert of Judah 77. Leiden: Brill, 2009.

Schuller, Eileen M. "The Dead Sea Scrolls and Canon and Canonization." Pages 293–314 in *Kanon in Konstruktion und Dekonstruktion: Kanonisierungsprozesse religiöser Texte von der Antike bis zur Gegenwart. Ein Handbuch.* Edited by Eve-Marie Becker and Stefan Scholz. Berlin: de Gruyter, 2012.

———. "Non-Canonical Psalms." Pages 75–172 in *Qumran Cave 4.VI: Poetical and Liturgical Texts, Part 1.* Edited by Esther Eshel, in consultation with James C. VanderKam and Monica Brady. Discoveries in the Judaean Desert 11. Oxford: Clarendon, 1998.

Schürer, Emil. *The History of the Jewish People in the Age of Jesus Christ (175 B.C.– A.D. 135).* Revised and edited by Geza Vermes, Fergus Millar, and Martin Goodman. 3 vols. in 4 parts. Edinburgh: T&T Clark, 1973–87.

Schüssler Fiorenza, Elisabeth. *Democratizing Biblical Studies: Toward an Emancipatory Educational Space.* Louisville: Westminster John Knox, 2009.

Schwartz, Daniel R. *2 Maccabees.* Commentaries on Early Jewish Literature. Berlin: de Gruyter, 2008.

———. "4Q468g: Ptollas?" *Journal of Jewish Studies* 50 (1999): 308–9.

———. "Aemilius Scaurus, Marcus." Pages 9–10 in vol. 1 of *Encyclopedia of the Dead Sea Scrolls.* Edited by Lawrence H. Schiffman and James C. VanderKam. 2 vols. New York: Oxford University Press, 2000.

———. "Antiochus IV Epiphanes in Jerusalem." Pages 45–56 in *Historical Perspectives: From the Hasmoneans to Bar Kokhba in Light of the Dead Sea Scrolls. Proceedings of the Fourth International Symposium of the Orion Center for the Study of the Dead Sea Scrolls and Associated Literature, 27–31 January, 1999.* Edited by David Goodblatt, Avital Pinnick, and Daniel R. Schwartz. Studies on the Texts of the Desert of Judah 37. Leiden: Brill, 2001.

Schwartz, Seth. *Were the Jews a Mediterranean Society? Reciprocity and Solidarity in Ancient Judaism.* Princeton: Princeton University Press, 2010.

Segal, M. "Between Bible and Rewritten Bible." Pages 10–28 in *Biblical Interpretation at Qumran.* Edited by Matthias Henze. Studies in the Dead Sea Scrolls and Related Literature. Grand Rapids: Eerdmans, 2005.

Seidman, N. "Burning the Book of Lamentations." Pages 278–88 in *Out of the Garden: Women Writers on the Bible.* Edited by Christina Büchmann and Celina Spiegel. New York: Fawcett Columbine, 1994.

Shanks, Hershel. *Freeing the Dead Sea Scrolls and Other Adventures of an Archaeology Outsider.* London: Continuum, 2010.

Sheldrake, Philip. *Spaces for the Sacred: Place, Memory, and Identity*. London: SCM, 2001.

Skehan, P. W., E. Ulrich, and J. E. Sanderson, eds. *Qumran Cave 4.IV: Palaeo-Hebrew and Greek Biblical Manuscripts*. Discoveries in the Judaean Desert 9. Oxford: Clarendon, 1992.

Slomovic, E. "Toward an Understanding of the Exegesis in the Dead Sea Scrolls." *Revue de Qumrân* 7 (1969–71): 3–15.

Smith, Mark S. *Palestinian Parties and Politics That Shaped the Old Testament*. 2nd ed. London: SCM, 1987.

———. "Remembering God: Collective Memory in Israelite Religion." *Catholic Biblical Quarterly* 64 (2002): 631–51.

Soja, Edward. *Thirdspace: Journeys to Los Angeles and Other Real-and-Imagined Places*. Cambridge, Mass.: Blackwell, 1996.

Sollamo, R. "Panegyric on Redaction Criticism." Pages 684–96 in *Houses Full of All Good Things: Essays in Memory of Timo Veijola*. Edited by Juha Pakkala and Martti Nissinen. Publications of the Finnish Exegetical Society 95. Helsinki: Finnish Exegetical Society, 2008.

Sontag, Susan. *Representing the Pain of Others*. New York: Farrar, Straus & Giroux, 2003.

Steck, Odil Hannes. *Die erste Jesajarolle von Qumran (1QIsa)*. Vol. 1, *Schreibweise als Leseanteilung für ein Prophetenbuch*. Stuttgarter Bibelstudien 173. Stuttgart: Katholisches Bibelwerk, 1998.

Stegemann, Hartmut. *Die Enstehung der Qumrangemeinde*. Inaugural-Dissertation, Bonn, 1971.

———. *The Library of Qumran: On the Essenes, Qumran, John the Baptist, and Jesus*. Grand Rapids: Eerdmans, 1998.

———. "The Literary Composition of the Temple Scroll and Its Status at Qumran." Pages 123–48 in *Temple Scroll Studies: Papers Presented at the International Symposium on the Temple Scroll, Manchester, December 1987*. Edited by George J. Brooke. Journal for the Study of the Pseudepigrapha: Supplement Series 7. Sheffield: JSOT Press, 1989.

———. "The Qumran Essenes: Local Members of the Main Jewish Union in Late Second Temple Times." Pages 83–166 in *The Madrid Qumran Congress: Proceedings of the International Congress on the Dead Sea Scrolls, Madrid 18–21 March, 1991*. Edited by Julio Trebolle Barrera and Luis Vegas Montaner. Studies on the Texts of the Desert of Judah 11. Leiden: Brill, 1992.

Stendahl, Krister, ed., *The Scrolls and the New Testament*. London: SCM, 1958.

Steudel, Annette. "Dating Exegetical Texts from Qumran." Pages 39–53 in *The Dynamics of Language and Exegesis at Qumran*. Edited by Devorah Dimant and Reinhard G. Kratz. Forschungen zum Alten Testament 2/35. Tübingen: Mohr Siebeck, 2009.

———. "Eschatological Interpretation of Scripture in 4Q177 (4QCatena^a)." *Revue de Qumrân* 14/55 (1989–90): 473–81.

————. *Der Midrasch zur Eschatologie aus der Qumrangemeinde (4QMidrEschat^{a.b})*: *Materielle Rekonstruktion, Textbestand, Gattung und traditionsgeschichtliche Einordnung des durch 4Q174 ("Florilegium") und 4Q177 ("Catena A") repräsentierten Werkes aus den Qumranfunden.* Studies on the Texts of the Desert of Judah 13. Leiden: Brill, 1994.

Stone, Michael E. "The Axis of History at Qumran." Pages 133–49 in *Pseudepigraphic Perspectives: The Apocrypha and Pseudepigrapha in Light of the Dead Sea Scrolls. Proceedings of the International Symposium of the Orion Center for the Study of the Dead Sea Scrolls and Associated Literature, 12–14 January 1997.* Edited by Esther G. Chazon and Michael E. Stone. Studies on the Texts of the Desert of Judah 31. Leiden: Brill, 1999.

Strugnell, John. "The Historical Background to 4Q468g [=4QHistorical Text B]." *Revue de Qumrân* 19/73 (1999): 137–38.

————. "Notes en marge du volume V des «Discoveries in the Judaean Desert of Jordan»." *Revue de Qumrân* 7 (1969–70): 163–276.

————. "The Qumran Scrolls: A Report on Work in Progress." Pages 94–106 in *Jewish Civilization in the Hellenistic-Roman Period.* Edited by Shemaryahu Talmon. Journal for the Study of the Pseudepigrapha: Supplement Series 10. Sheffield: JSOT Press, 1991.

Stuckenbruck, Loren T. "The Legacy of the Teacher of Righteousness in the Dead Sea Scrolls." Pages 23–49 in *New Perspectives on Old Texts: Proceedings of the Tenth International Symposium of the Orion Center for the Study of the Dead Sea Scrolls and Associated Literature, 9–11 January, 2005.* Edited by Esther G. Chazon, Betsy Halpern-Amaru, and Ruth A. Clements. Studies on the Texts of the Desert of Judah 88. Leiden: Brill, 2010.

————. "The Teacher of Righteousness Remembered: From Fragmentary Sources to Collective Memory in the Dead Sea Scrolls." Pages 75–94 in *Memory in the Bible and Antiquity: The Fifth Durham–Tübingen Research Symposium (Durham, September 2004).* Edited by Stephen C. Barton, Loren T. Stuckenbruck, and Benjamin G. Wold. Wissenschaftliche Untersuchungen zum Neuen Testament 212. Tübingen: Mohr Siebeck, 2007.

Swanson, Dwight D. "How Scriptural Is Re-Written Bible?" *Revue de Qumrân* 21/83 (2004): 407–27.

————. *The Temple Scroll and the Bible: The Methodology of 11QT.* Studies on the Texts of the Desert of Judah 14. Leiden: Brill, 1995.

————. "The Use of Chronicles in 11QT: Aspects of a Relationship." Pages 290–98 in *The Dead Sea Scrolls: Forty Years of Research.* Edited by Devorah Dimant and Uriel Rappaport. Studies on the Texts of the Desert of Judah 10. Leiden: Brill; Jerusalem: Magnes, 1992.

Sweeney, Marvin A. "Form Criticism: The Question of the Endangered Matriarchs in Genesis." Pages 17–38 in *Method Matters: Essays on the Interpretation of the Hebrew Bible in Honor of David L. Petersen.* Edited by Joel M. LeMon and Kent H. Richards. Society of Biblical Literature Resources for Biblical Study 56. Atlanta: Society of Biblical Literature, 2009.

Syreeni, Kari. "Coping with the Death of Jesus: The Gospels and the Theory of Grief Work." Pages 63–86 in *From Gospel to Gnostics,* vol. 3 of *Psychology and the Bible: A New Way to Read the Scriptures.* Edited by J. Harold Ellens and Wayne G. Rollins. Praeger Perspectives. Psychology, Religion, and Spirituality. Westport, Conn.: Praeger, 2004.

Talmon, Shemaryahu. "Between the Bible and the Mishna." Pages 11–52 in idem, *The World of Qumran from Within: Collected Studies.* Jerusalem: Magnes, 1989.

———. "The 'Desert' Motif in the Bible and in Qumran Literature." Pages 31–63 in *Biblical Motifs: Origins and Transformations.* Edited by Alexander Altmann. Philip W. Lown Institute of Advanced Judaic Studies, Brandeis University, Studies and Texts 3. Cambridge, Mass.: Harvard University Press, 1966.

———. "The Old Testament Text." Pages 159–99 in *The Cambridge History of the Bible.* Vol. 1, *From the Beginnings to Jerome.* Edited by P. R. Ackroyd and C. F. Evans. Cambridge: Cambridge University Press, 1970.

———. "The Transmission History of the Text of the Hebrew Bible in the Light of Biblical Manuscripts from Qumran and Other Sites in the Judean Desert." Pages 40–50 in *The Dead Sea Scrolls Fifty Years after their Discovery: Proceedings of the Jerusalem Congress, July 20–25, 1997.* Edited by Lawrence H. Schiffman, Emanuel Tov, and James C. VanderKam. Jerusalem: Israel Exploration Society and Shrine of the Book, 2000.

Talmon, Shemaryahu, and Jonathan Ben-Dov, "A. Calendrical Documents and Mishmarot." Pages 1–166 in *Qumran Cave 4.XVI: Calendrical Texts.* Edited by Shemaryahu Talmon, Jonathan Ben-Dov, and U. Glessmer. Discoveries in the Judaean Desert 21. Oxford: Clarendon, 2001.

Testuz, Michel. *Les idées religieuses du livre de Jubilés.* Geneva: E. Droz, 1960.

Thorion, Y. "Die Sprache der Tempelrolle und die Chronikbücher." *Revue de Qumrân* 11 (1982–84): 423–28.

Tigchelaar, Eibert J. C. "Eden and Paradise: The Garden Motif in Some Early Jewish Texts (1 Enoch and Other Texts Found at Qumran)." Pages 37–62 in *Paradise Interpreted: Representations of Biblical Paradise in Judaism and Christianity.* Edited by Gerard P. Luttikhuizen. Themes in Biblical Narrative 2. Leiden: Brill, 1999.

Todorov, Tzvetan. *The Fantastic: A Structural Approach to a Literary Genre.* Translated by Richard Howard. Ithaca, N.Y.: Cornell University Press, 1975.

Tov, Emanuel. "4QGenealogical List?" Page 290 in *Qumran Cave 4.XXVI: Cryptic Texts; Miscellanea, Part 1.* Edited by Stephen J. Pfann et al. Discoveries in the Judaean Desert 36. Oxford: Clarendon, 2000.

———. "4QJosh^b." Pages 153–60 in *Qumran Cave 4.IX: Deuteronomy, Joshua, Judges, Kings.* Edited by Eugene C. Ulrich, Frank Moore Cross, et al. Discoveries in the Judaean Desert 14. Oxford: Clarendon, 1995.

———. "Biblical Texts as Reworked in Some Qumran Manuscripts with Special Attention to 4QRP and 4QParaGen-Exod." Pages 111–34 in *The Commu-*

nity of the Renewed Covenant: The Notre Dame Symposium on the Dead Sea Scrolls. Edited by Eugene Ulrich and James C. VanderKam. Christianity and Judaism in Antiquity Series 10. Notre Dame, Ind.: University of Notre Dame Press, 1994.

———. "Foreword." Pages ix–x in *Qumran Cave 4.VIII: Parabiblical Texts, Part 1.* Edited by James C. VanderKam. Discoveries in the Judaean Desert 13. Oxford: Clarendon, 1994.

———. "Further Evidence for the Existence of a Qumran Scribal School." Pages 199–216 in *The Dead Sea Scrolls Fifty Years after Their Discovery: Proceedings of the Jerusalem Congress, July 20–25, 1997.* Edited by Lawrence H. Schiffman, Emanuel Tov, and James C. VanderKam. Jerusalem: Israel Exploration Society and Shrine of the Book, 2000.

———. *The Greek Minor Prophets Scroll from Naḥal Ḥever (8ḤevXIIgr) (The Seiyâl Collection I).* Discoveries in the Judaean Desert 8. Oxford: Clarendon Press, 1990.

———. "Hebrew Biblical Manuscripts from the Judaean Desert: Their Contribution to Textual Criticism." *Journal of Jewish Studies* 39 (1988): 5–37. Repr., pages 126–32 in *Jewish Civilization in the Hellenistic-Roman Period.* Edited by Shemaryahu Talmon. Journal for the Study of the Pseudepigrapha: Supplement Series 10. Sheffield: JSOT Press, 1991.

———. "Jeremiah." Pages 145–207 in *Qumran Cave 4.X: The Prophets.* Edited by Eugene Ulrich et al. Discoveries in the Judaean Desert 15. Oxford: Clarendon, 1997.

———. "The Nature and Background of Harmonizations in Biblical Manuscripts." *Journal for the Study of the Old Testament* 31 (1985): 3–29.

———. *Scribal Practices and Approaches Reflected in the Texts Found in the Judean Desert.* Studies on the Texts of the Desert of Judah 54. Leiden: Brill, 2004.

———, ed. *The Texts from the Judaean Desert: Indices and an Introduction to the Discoveries in the Judaean Desert Series.* Discoveries in the Judaean Desert 39. Oxford, Clarendon, 2002.

———. "Textual Criticism (OT)." Pages 393–412 in vol. 6 of *The Anchor Bible Dictionary.* Edited by David Noel Freedman. 6 vols. New York: Doubleday, 1992.

———. *Textual Criticism of the Hebrew Bible.* 2nd ed. Assen: Van Gorcum; Minneapolis: Fortress, 2001. 3rd rev. and expanded ed. Minneapolis: Fortress, 2012.

———. "The Textual Status of 4Q364–367 (4QPP)." Pages 43–82 in *The Madrid Qumran Congress: Proceedings of the International Congress on the Dead Sea Scrolls, Madrid, 18–21 March 1991.* Edited by Julio Trebolle Barrera and Luis Vegas Montaner. Studies on the Texts of the Desert of Judah 11. Leiden: Brill, 1992.

———. "The Unpublished Qumran Texts from Qumran Caves 4 and 11." *Biblical Archaeologist* 55 (1992): 94–104.

Tov, Emanuel, and Stephen J. Pfann. *The Dead Sea Scrolls on Microfiche: Companion Volume*. Leiden: Brill and IDC, 1993. 2nd rev. ed. Leiden: Brill and IDC, 1995.

Tov, Emanuel, and Sidnie White, "Reworked Pentateuch." Pages 187–351 in *Qumran Cave 4.VIII: Parabiblical Texts, Part 1*. Edited by James C. VanderKam. Discoveries in the Judaean Desert 13. Oxford: Clarendon, 1994.

Trebolle Barrera, Julio. "4QChr." Pages 295–97 in *Qumran Cave 4.XI: Psalms to Chronicles*. Edited by Eugene Ulrich et al. Discoveries in the Judaean Desert 16. Oxford: Clarendon, 2000.

———. "4QJudgᵃ." Pages 161–64 in *Qumran Cave 4.IX: Deuteronomy, Joshua, Judges, Kings*. Edited by Eugene Ulrich and Frank Moore Cross. Discoveries in the Judaean Desert 14. Oxford: Clarendon, 1995.

———. "4QJudgᵇ." Pages 165–69 in *Qumran Cave 4.IX: Deuteronomy, Joshua, Judges, Kings*. Edited by Eugene Ulrich and Frank Moore Cross. Discoveries in the Judaean Desert 14. Oxford: Clarendon, 1995.

———. "4QKings." Pages 171–83 in *Qumran Cave 4.IX: Deuteronomy, Joshua, Judges, Kings*. Edited by Eugene Ulrich and Frank Moore Cross. Discoveries in the Judaean Desert 14. Oxford: Clarendon, 1995.

———. "Chronicles, First and Second Books of." Page 129 in vol. 1 of *Encyclopedia of the Dead Sea Scrolls*. Edited by Lawrence H. Schiffman and James C. VanderKam. 2 vols. New York: Oxford University Press, 2000.

Tzoref, Shani, and Mark Laughlin. "Theme and Genre in 4Q177 and Its Scriptural Selections." Pages 169–89 in *The Mermaid and the Partridge: Essays from the Copenhagen Conference on Revising Texts from Cave Four*. Edited by Jesper Høgenhaven and George J. Brooke. Studies on the Texts of the Desert of Judah 96. Leiden: Brill, 2011.

Ullman, C. "Cognitive and Emotional Antecedents of Religious Conversion." *Journal of Personality and Social Psychology* 43 (1982): 183–92.

Ulrich, Eugene C. "4QJoshᵃ," in *Qumran Cave 4.IX: Deuteronomy, Joshua, Judges, Kings*. Edited by Eugene C. Ulrich and Frank Moore Cross. Discoveries in the Judaean Desert 14. Oxford: Clarendon, 1995.

———. "4QJoshuaᵃ and Joshua's First Altar in the Promised Land." Pages 89–104 in *New Qumran Texts and Studies: Proceedings of the First Meeting of the International Organization for Qumran Studies, Paris 1992*. Edited by George J. Brooke with Florentino García Martínez. Studies on the Texts of the Desert of Judah 15. Leiden: Brill, 1994.

———. "The Absence of 'Sectarian Variants' in the Jewish Scriptural Scrolls Found at Qumran." Pages 179–95 in *The Bible as Book: The Hebrew Bible and the Judaean Desert Discoveries*. Edited by Edward D. Herbert and Emanuel Tov. London: British Library; New Castle, Del.: Oak Knoll; Grand Haven: Scriptorium Center for Christian Antiquities, 2002.

———. "The Bible in the Making: The Scriptures Found at Qumran." Pages 51–66 in *The Bible at Qumran: Text, Shape, and Interpretation*. Edited by Peter W.

Flint. Studies in the Dead Sea Scrolls and Related Literature. Grand Rapids: Eerdmans, 2001.

———. The Biblical Qumran Scrolls: Transcriptions and Textual Variants. Supplements to Vetus Testamentum 134. Leiden: Brill, 2010.

———. The Dead Sea Scrolls and the Origins of the Bible. Studies in the Dead Sea Scrolls and Related Literature. Grand Rapids: Eerdmans, 1999.

———. "Deuteronomistically Inspired Scribal Insertions into the Developing Biblical Texts: 4QJudg[a] and 4QJer[a]." Pages 489–506 in Houses Full of All Good Things: Essays in Memory of Timo Veijola. Edited by Juha Pakkala and Martti Nissinen. Publications of the Finnish Exegetical Society 95. Helsinki: Finnish Exegetical Society; Göttingen: Vandenhoeck & Ruprecht, 2008.

———. "The Developmental Composition of the Book of Isaiah: Light from 1QIsa[a] on Additions in the MT." Dead Sea Discoveries 8 (2001): 288–305.

———. "From Literature to Scripture: The Growth of a Text's Authoritativeness." Dead Sea Discoveries 10 (2003): 3–25.

———. "A Greek Paraphrase of Exodus on Papyrus from Qumran Cave 4." Pages 287–98 in Studien zur Septuaginta—Robert Hanhart zu Ehren: Aus Anlaß seines 65. Geburtstages. Edited by Detlef Fraenkel et al. Mitteilungen des Septuaginta-Unternehmens 20. Göttingen: Vandenhoeck & Ruprecht, 1990.

———. "Impressions and Intuition: Sense Division in Ancient Manuscripts of Isaiah." Pages 279–307 in Unit Delimitation in Biblical Hebrew and Northwest Semitic Literature. Edited by Marjo C. A. Korpel and Josef M. Oesch. Pericope 4. Assen: Van Gorcum, 2003.

———. "The Text of the Hebrew Scriptures at the Time of Hillel and Jesus." Pages 85–108 in Congress Volume: Basel 2001. Edited by André Lemaire. Supplements to Vetus Testamentum 92. Leiden: Brill, 2002.

Unnik, W. C. van. "Luke's Second Book and the Rule of Hellenistic Historiography." Pages 37–60 in Les Actes des Apôtres: Traditions, rédaction, théologie. Edited by J. Kremer. Bibliotheca ephemeridum theologicarum lovaniensium 48. Leuven: University Press, 1979.

VanderKam, James C. The Dead Sea Scrolls and the Bible. Grand Rapids: Eerdmans, 2012.

———. The Dead Sea Scrolls Today. 2nd ed. Grand Rapids: Eerdmans, 2010.

———. Enoch and the Growth of an Apocalytpic Tradition. Catholic Biblical Quarterly Monograph Series 16. Washington, D.C.: Catholic Biblical Association of America, 1984.

———. "Sinai Revisited." Pages 44–60 in Biblical Interpretation at Qumran. Edited by Matthias Henze. Studies in the Dead Sea Scrolls and Related Literature. Grand Rapids: Eerdmans, 2005.

VanderKam, James C., and Peter W. Flint. The Meaning of the Dead Sea Scrolls: Their Significance for Understanding the Bible, Judaism, Jesus, and Christianity. San Francisco: HarperSanFrancisco, 2002.

Vázquez Allegue, Jaime. Los hijos de la luz y los hijos de las tinieblas: El prólogo *de la Regla de la Comunidad de Qumrán.* Biblioteca Midrásica 21. Estella: Verbo Divino, 2000.

———. "Memoria colectiva e identidad de grupo en Qumrán." Pages 89–104 in *Flores Florentino: Dead Sea Scrolls and Other Early Jewish Studies in Honour of Florentino García Martínez.* Edited by Anthony Hilhorst, Émile Puech, and Eibert J. C. Tigchelaar. Supplements to the Journal for the Study of Judaism 122. Leiden: Brill, 2007.

Vermes, Geza. "Le cadre historique des manuscrits de la mer Morte." *Recherches de Science Religieuse* 41 (1953): 5–29.

———. *The Complete Dead Sea Scrolls in English.* London: Penguin, 1998. 5th rev. ed.; London: Penguin, 2004.

———. "The Essenes and History." *Journal of Jewish Studies* 32 (1981): 18–31. Repr., pages 126–39 in idem, *Jesus and the World of Judaism.* London: SCM, 1983. Repr., pages 18–30 in idem, *Scrolls, Scriptures and Early Christianity.* Library of Second Temple Studies 56. London: T&T Clark International, 2005.

———. "Lebanon—The Historical Development of an Exegetical Tradition." Pages 26–39 in idem, *Scripture and Tradition in Judaism: Haggadic Studies.* 2nd ed. Studia post-biblica 4. Leiden: Brill, 1983.

———. *Scripture and Tradition in Judaism: Haggadic Studies.* 2nd ed. Studia post-biblica 4. Leiden: Brill, 1973. 1st ed. 1961.

———. *The Story of the Scrolls: The Miraculous Discovery and True Significance of the Dead Sea Scrolls.* London: Penguin Books, 2010.

Waltke, Bruce K. "Samaritan Pentateuch." Pages 932–40 in vol. 5 of *The Anchor Bible Dictionary.* Edited by David Noel Freedman. 6 vols. New York: Doubleday, 1992.

Weis, P. R. "The Date of the Habakkuk Scroll." *Jewish Quarterly Review* 41 (1950): 125–54.

Weissberg, Liliane. "Introduction." Pages 7–26 in *Cultural Memory and the Construction of Identity.* Edited by Dan Ben-Amos and Liliane Weissberg. Detroit: Wayne State University Press, 1999.

Weissenrieder, Annette, and Robert B. Coote, eds. *The Interface of Orality and Writing: Speaking, Seeing, Writing in the Shaping of New Genres.* Wissenschaftliche Untersuchungen zum Neuen Testament 260. Tübingen: Mohr Siebeck, 2010.

Wilson, Andrew M., and Lawrence M. Wills. "Literary Sources of the Temple Scroll." *Harvard Theological Review* 75 (1982): 275–88.

Winnicott, D. W. *The Maturational Processes and the Facilitating Environment: Studies in the Theory of Emotional Development.* New York: International Universities Press, 1965.

———. *Playing and Reality.* London: Tavistock, 1971.

Wise, Michael O. "4QFlorilegium and the Temple of Adam." *Revue de Qumrân* 15 (1991–92): 103–32.

———. "Dating the Teacher of Righteousness and the *Floruit* of His Movement." *Journal of Biblical Literature* 122 (2003): 53–87.

———. *Thunder in Gemini and Other Essays on the History, Language and Literature of Second Temple Palestine*. Journal for the Study of the Pseudepigrapha: Supplement Series 15. Sheffield: JSOT Press, 1994.

Wise, Michael O., Martin G. Abegg, and Edward M. Cook. *The Dead Sea Scrolls: A New Translation*. San Francisco: HarperSanFrancisco, 1996.

Wold, Benjamin G. "Memory in the Dead Sea Scrolls: Exodus, Creation and Cosmos." Pages 47–74 in *Memory in the Bible and Antiquity: The Fifth Durham–Tübingen Research Symposium (Durham, September 2004)*. Edited by Stephen C. Barton, Loren T. Stuckenbruck, and Benjamin G. Wold. Wissenschaftliche Untersuchungen zum Neuen Testament 212. Tübingen: Mohr Siebeck, 2007.

Yadin, Yigael. *The Temple Scroll*. 3 vols. Institute of Archaeology of the Hebrew University of Jerusalem. Shrine of the Book. Jerusalem: Israel Exploration Society, 1977–83.

———. *The Temple Scroll: The Hidden Law of the Dead Sea Sect*. London: Weidenfeld & Nicolson, 1985.

Zahn, Molly M. "The Problem of Characterizing the Reworked Pentateuch Manuscripts: Bible, Rewritten Bible, or None of the Above?" *Dead Sea Discoveries* 15 (2008): 315–39.

———. *Rethinking Rewritten Scripture: Composition and Exegesis in the 4QReworked Pentateuch Manuscripts*. Studies on the Texts of the Desert of Judah 95. Leiden: Brill, 2011.

———. "Rewritten Scripture." Pages 323–36 in *The Oxford Handbook of the Dead Sea Scrolls*. Edited by Timothy H. Lim and John J. Collins. Oxford: Oxford University Press, 2010.

Index of Ancient Sources

Index of Modern Authors

CPSIA information can be obtained at www.ICGtesting.com
Printed in the USA
BVOW08s2025041013

332779BV00003B/4/P